W9-AET-953

DATE DUE

Return Material Promptly

PA076778

3

18.00

IMPEACHMENT:

THE

CONSTITUTIONAL

PROBLEMS

Raoul Berger

Harvard University Press
Cambridge, Massachusetts
London, England

TO MY DEAR FRIENDS
AT HARVARD

Library of Congress Catalog Number 73-75055
ISBN 0-674-44478-7 (paper)

ACKNOWLEDGMENTS

This study was pursued in the incomparable library of Harvard Law School, greatly facilitated by the quarters furnished to me by the Faculty, and in no little part inspired by admission to what is surely one of the goodliest intellectual Round Tables extant.

To members of the Faculty who have generously taken time to read one or the other portions of the manuscript and to give me the benefit of their views I am additionally indebted: Jerome A. Cohen, Verne Countryman, John P. Dawson, Paul A. Freund, Albert Sachs, David L. Shapiro and Samuel E. Thorne. I should be remiss did I not express special appreciation to Morton J. Horwitz, who has always found time to debate some knotty point, and to Stanley N. Katz of the University of Chicago who, during a sojourn at Harvard, called my attention to early American sources which I might have overlooked. To him, too, I owe more than the formal acknowledgment one makes to an editor. My thanks are also due to Morton Keller of Brandeis University.

All sins of commission and omission are, of course, my own. If I have persisted in "error" it was not for want of searching criticism but because one must have the fortitude to adhere to hard-won conclusions which are not shaken by criticism, however high its source.

Quotations from *The Court and the Country*, Perez Zagorin (Copyright © 1969 by Perez Zagorin), are reprinted by permission of Atheneum Publishers. Special thanks are due to the publishers mentioned in the bibliography for lightening the labors of scholarship by permitting quotation without further ado.

Thanks are also due to the editors of the *University of Southern California Law Review* and the *Yale Law Journal* for permission to reprint Chapters II and IV, which appeared therein, respectively.

AUTHOR'S NOTE

Spelling and capitalization in all quotations have been conformed to present-day American usage.

CONTENTS

ABBREVIATIONS

Adams	Adams, John, *Works* (Boston, 1850)
1 *Ann. Cong.*	*Annals of Congress,* vol. 1, 1789, 2d ed. (Washington, D.C., Gales & Seaton, 1834; print bearing running-head "History of Congress")
Bacon	Bacon, Matthew, *A New Abridgment of the Laws of England* (London, 1768)
Bailyn	Bailyn, Bernard, *Ideological Origins of the American Revolution* (Cambridge, Mass., 1967)
Berger, *Congress v. Court*	Berger, Raoul, *Congress v. The Supreme Court* (Cambridge, Mass., 1969)
Berger, Executive Privilege	———— "Executive Privilege v. Congressional Inquiry," 12 *UCLA L. Rev.* 1044, 1288 (1965)
Blackstone	Blackstone, Sir William, *Commentaries on the Laws of England* (Oxford, 1765–1769)
Borkin	Borkin, Joseph, *The Corrupt Judge* (New York, 1962)
Brock	Brock, W. R., *An American Crisis: Congress and Reconstruction* (London, 1963)
Campbell, *Chancellors*	Campbell, Lord John, *Lives of the Chancellors* (London, 1848–1850)
Campbell, *Justices*	Campbell, Lord John, *Lives of the Chief Justices* (New York, 1874)
Chafee	Chafee, Zechariah, Jr. *Three Human Rights in the Constitution* (Lawrence, Kan. 1956)
Chandler I	Chandler v. Judicial Council of the Tenth Circuit, 382 U.S. 1003 (1966)
Chandler II	Chandler v. Judicial Council of the Tenth Circuit, 398 U.S. 74 (1970)
Coke, *Institutes*	Coke, Sir Edwards, *Institutes of the Laws of England* (London, 1628–1645)

Cong. Globe (C.G.) 40.II.134	*Congressional Globe,* 40th Cong. 2d Sess., p. 134 (other volumes and pages will be similarly cited)
Dewitt	Dewitt, David M., *The Impeachment and Trial of Andrew Johnson* (New York, 1903)
Elliot	Elliot, Jonathan, *Debates in the Several State Conventions on the Adoption of the Federal Constitution* (Washington, D.C., 1936)
E.R.	English Reports
Farrand	Farrand, Max, *The Records of the Federal Convention of 1787* (New Haven, Conn., 1911)
Federalist	*The Federalist* (New York, 1937)
Hallam	Hallam, Henry, *Constitutional History of England* (London, 1884)
Hatsell	Hatsell, John, *Precedents of Proceedings in the House of Commons* (London, 1796)
Hawkins	Hawkins, William, *History of Pleas of the Crown* (London, 1716)
Hill	Hill, Christopher, *The Century of Revolution* (New York, 1961)
Holdsworth	Holdsworth, Sir William, *A History of English Law* (London, 1903–1938)
Howell	*Howell's State Trials* (London, 1809–1826)
Jefferson, *Manual*	Jefferson, Thomas, *Manual of Parliamentary Practice* (1801)
L.Q.R.	*Law Quarterly Review*
Lomask	Lomask, Milton, *Andrew Johnson: President on Trial* (New York, 1960)
McKitrick	McKitrick, Eric, *Andrew Johnson and Reconstruction* (Chicago, 1960)
Malone	Malone, Dumas, *Jefferson and His Times* (Boston, 1948–1970)
Morison	Morison, Samuel Eliot, *Oxford History of the American People* (New York, 1965)
Otis	Otis, Merrill, *A Proposed Tribunal: Is it Constitutional?* 7 Kan. City. L. Rev. 3 (1938)
Plucknett, *Concise History*	Plucknett, Theodore, *Concise History of the Common Law* (Boston, 1956)

Poore Poore, Ben P., *Federal and State Constitutions, Colonial Charters* (Washington, D.C., 1877)

Rawle Rawle, William, *A View of the Constitution* (Philadelphia, 1829)

Roberts Roberts, Clayton, *The Growth of Responsible Government in Stuart England* (Cambridge, 1966)

Rushworth Rushworth, John, *Historical Collections* (London, 1721)

Russell Russell, Conrad, "The Theory of Treason in the Trial of Strafford," 80 *Eng. Hist. Rev.* 30 (1965)

Shartel Shartel, Burke, "Federal Judges: Appointment, Supervision and Removal—Some Possibilities under the Constitution," 28 *Mich. L. Rev.* 870 (1930)

Simpson Simpson, Alexander, *A Treatise on Federal Impeachment* (Philadelphia, 1916)

Stephen Stephen, Sir J. F., *History of Criminal Law* (London, 1883)

Story Story, Joseph, *Commentaries on the Constitution of the United States* (Boston, 1905)

Trevelyan Trevelyan, G. M., *Illustrated History of England* (London, 1956)

Trial *The Trial of Andrew Johnson*, Congressional Globe, 40th Cong. 2d Sess. Supp. (1868)

Tucker Tucker, St. George, ed., *Blackstone's Commentaries* (Philadelphia, 1803)

Warren Warren, Charles, *The Supreme Court in United States History* (Boston, 1922)

Wharton Wharton, Francis, *State Trials of the United States* (Philadelphia, 1849)

Wilson Wilson, James, *Works* (Cambridge, Mass., 1967)

Wooddeson Wooddeson, Richard, *Laws of England* (Dublin, 1792)

Zagorin Zagorin, Perez, *The Court and the Country* (New York, 1969)

PREFACE

When Chapter II of this book, "High Crimes and Misdemeanors," was submitted as a separate article to the editors of the *Southern California Law Review* in midsummer of 1970, Watergate and the subsequent possibility that President Nixon might be impeached were buried in the future. Through a remarkable conjunction of events, publication of the book in 1973 coincided with the emergence of impeachment as a distinct possibility, and that chapter suddenly ceased to be merely of antiquarian interest and became highly "relevant." What was originally written for scholars and jurists thus became of interest to a wider public; and it now seems desirable to summarize Chapter II in simpler fashion so that what otherwise might seem like an impenetrable historical thicket will be more widely understood.

HIGH CRIMES AND MISDEMEANORS

The Constitution provides for impeachment for "Treason, Bribery, or *other* high Crimes and Misdemeanors." "High crimes and misdemeanors," the historical sources show, meant both "high crimes and *high* misdemeanors." The key word is "high," and to lose sight of this and consider that the reference is to "crimes and misdemeanors" is to indulge in the kind of thinking which would identify a shoe-tree with a tree. They are entirely different.

In English law, from which our impeachment is borrowed, "high crimes and misdemeanors" were offenses against the state, like treason or bribery, triable by Parliament under the law of Parliament. When

"high crimes and misdemeanors" was first employed
there was in fact no such crime as a "misdemeanor."
"Crimes and misdemeanors," on the other hand, are
offenses against the individual, like murder and assault,
triable by courts under the general criminal law. In
England impeachment was criminal in nature because
removal from office and criminal punishment were
united in one proceeding, so that a man could lose his
office and his head at one blow.

The Framers made a sharp departure from the English practice—they divorced impeachment and removal
from indictment and criminal trial. Political passions
no longer could sweep an officer to the gallows. The
sole consequence of a separate trial for impeachment
by the Senate was to be removal from office and disqualification, plainly not criminal penalties. If the offense also constituted a crime, the offender could be
tried criminally before a court. The meaning of this
separation is highlighted by the Bill of Rights. If impeachment be regarded as criminal in nature, then an
impeachment would preclude indictment, or indictment
would preclude impeachment, because the Fifth Amendment forbids that a person shall be "subject for the
same offense to be twice put in jeopardy." And since
the Sixth Amendment provides for trial by jury "in *all*
criminal prosecutions," a conclusion that impeachment
is criminal might require trial by jury rather than the
Senate. Thus avoidance of such constitutional doubts
counsels an interpretation that impeachment is civil in
essence, not criminal.

True it is that the Constitution employs criminal
terminology in the impeachment provisions, but that
derives from the English wedding of criminal and impeachment proceedings. It was convenient for the
Framers to use familiar terms in order to identify both
the criminal and civil offenses which proceeded from
the very same act. In everyday terms, an assault and
battery can give rise both to a criminal proceeding and
to a suit for damages; and no one would maintain that
because the words "assault and battery" are used to
describe the acts upon which the suit for damages is
based that the suit is in consequence criminal in nature.

Even, therefore, were impeachment to proceed on facts which also constituted an indictable crime, the impeachment proceeding, being civil, would not require proof "beyond a reasonable doubt."

Finally, the Founders were well aware of the meaning of "high crimes and misdemeanors"; repeatedly they referred to the familiar English categories—"subversion of the Constitution" (usurpation of power), "abuse of power," "betrayal of trust," "neglect of duty," and the like. To insist, as defense counsel habitually do, that an indictable crime is required for impeachment would, as Justice Joseph Story stated 140 years ago, enable impeachable offenders to escape scot-free and render the impeachment provisions "a complete nullity." For federal law contains only such crimes as Congress enacts by statute; and in the 185 years since the adoption of the Constitution, Congress has never seen fit to make "usurpation of power," "abuse of power," and the like indictable offenses, reflecting a continuing judgment by the impeachment tribunals that indictable crimes are not a prerequisite to impeachment, as four convictions by the Senate for nonindictable offenses confirm.

Since publication of the book, a much mooted claim has been that impeachment must precede indictment, and that claim is examined in the Epilogue. There too I shall dissect a lengthy memorandum submitted by President Nixon's chief defense counsel, Mr. James St. Clair, to the House Judiciary Committee and broadcast to the nation, wherein Mr. St. Clair invokes history for the proposition that impeachment requires an indictable crime as its basis. It may be worthy of note that my demonstration to the contrary in Chapter II has been accepted by eminent scholars: Professors Thomas Emerson, Willard Hurst, Nathaniel Nathanson, Telford Taylor, and Dean Robert Kramer.

Acknowledgment is made to the editors of the *Yale Law Journal* for permission to reprint the materials set forth in the Epilogue.

Raoul Berger
June 12, 1974

INTRODUCTION

Impeachment, with us largely a means for the ouster of corrupt judges,[1] was for the English "the chief institution for the preservation of the government." [2] By means of impeachment Parliament, after a long and bitter struggle, made ministers chosen by the King accountable to it rather than the Crown, replacing absolutist pretensions by parliamentary supremacy.[3] Impeachment began in the late fourteenth century when the Commons undertook to prosecute before the Lords the most powerful offenders and the highest officers of the Crown.[4] With the immense accretion of royal power during the Tudor period, however, parliamentary fires were damped and impeachment fell into disuse. Now the King turned to Parliament to legitimate his sanguinary dismissals and reprisals by a bill of attainder, a legislative condemnation to death without a trial.[5] The follies of James I led Parliament once

---

1. Joseph Borkin, *The Corrupt Judge* (New York, 1962).
2. Said by the House of Commons in 1679, quoted 1 Sir W. S. Holdsworth, *A History of English Law* 383 (London, 3d ed. 1922). See Edmund Burke at infra, Conclusion, text accompanying n. 3.
3. Recounted in Zechariah Chafee, *Three Human Rights in the Constitution* 98–140 (Lawrence, Kan., 1956); 1 Holdsworth 380–384 (3d ed. 1922); Clayton Roberts, *The Growth of Responsible Government in Stuart England* (Cambridge, 1966).
4. 4 John Hatsell, *Precedents of Proceedings in the House of Commons* 63 (London, 1796); infra, Chapter II, text accompanying nn. 22–26. In a pioneer study of impeachment, Hatsell explains that the Commons filed complaints with the Lords "against persons of the highest rank and favor with the Crown . . . whose elevated situation placed them above the reach of complaint from private individuals, who, if they failed in obtaining redress, might afterwards become the objects of resentment of those, whose tyrannical oppression they had presumed to call in question." Ibid. Holdsworth states that the House of Lords was "essentially a court for great men and great causes." 1 Holdsworth 380 (3d ed. 1922). See also M. V. Clarke, "The Origin of Impeachment," in *Oxford Essays in Medieval History* 165–166, 173 (Oxford, 1934); Roberts 7. These facts were noted by an early American commentator on the Constitution, William Rawle, *A View of the Constitution* 210 (Philadelphia, 2d ed. 1829).
5. Infra, Chapter I, text accompanying nn. 99–102.

1

more to flex its muscles and to revive impeachment after a lapse of about 160 years, in order to bring corrupt and oppressive ministers to heel.[6] Direct attack on the King being unthinkable save by the path that led Charles I to the block, Parliament indulged in the fiction that the King could do no wrong but was misled by his ministers.[7]

Where the object of Jacobean impeachments had been the reformation of abuses and "not the venting of private spleen or party hatreds,"[8] where the impeachment of the Earl of Strafford (1642) had been designed to break the back of Charles I's absolutist aspirations,[9] the moving force after the Restoration came to be party intrigue in a factional struggle for power.[10] From an "appeal to the nation against wicked ministers,"[11] impeachment was transformed into a clumsy instrument for striking at unpopular royal policies;[12] and it was then supplanted by an Address of Parliament to the King asking for removal of a minister. This came to be regarded as a vote of censure and no confidence,[13] and thus by degrees ministerial accountability to the Parliament was achieved.[14] Thereafter impeachment again fell into relative disuse, though the spectacular, long-drawn impeachment of Warren Has-

---

6. "From 1459 to 1621, a period of 162 years, no impeachment appears to have taken place," 1 Sir J. F. Stephen, *History of Criminal Law* 158 (London, 1883). "It was not till Parliament reasserted itself under James I and Charles I that it became natural or perhaps possible to use impeachment for the punishment of ministers considered corrupt or oppressive." Ibid. See Roberts 23–28. James' ill-considered attempts to promote the interests of Catholicism fanned the flames. Chafee 11.

7. The "difficulties of attacking the King made Parliament throw the chief blame on his outstanding advisers." Chafee 103. Blackstone states: "For as a king cannot misuse his power, without the advice of evil counsellors, and the assistance of wicked ministers, these men may be examined and punished." 1 Sir William Blackstone, *Commentaries on the Laws of England* 244 (Oxford, 1765–1769). Impeachment, states Roberts 435, "transformed the legal maxim that the King can do no wrong into the political principle that he could not assume responsibility for the unpopular and unsuccessful actions of his ministers." For impeachments grounded on giving pernicious "advice," see infra, Chapter II, text accompanying n. 91.

8. Roberts 32.

9. G. M. Trevelyan, *Illustrated History of England* 403–404 (London, 1956).

10. Roberts 182.

11. Ibid. 220.

12. Ibid. 218.

13. Ibid. 244, 267, 360.

14. See supra, n. 3; J. H. Dougherty, "Inherent Limitations upon Impeachment," 23 *Yale L. J.* 60, 69 (1913).

tings, spearheaded by that paladin of American liberty, Edmund Burke, was under way while the Federal Convention sat in Philadelphia.[15]

Thoughout the heyday of impeachments relatively few judges had been impeached, and these not so much for corruption as for lending themselves to hated royal policies, as when Robert Berkley and John Finch labored on behalf of Charles's "Ship-Money Tax" to circumvent the need of coming to Parliament for money.[16] Even the fall of Lord Chancellor Francis Bacon, ostensibly for corruption, was more, we are told, because he was a "sycophantic minister." [17] And the several Chief Justices and Justices were impeached, not because there was no other way of removing them —for judicial appointments were generally at the royal pleasure [18] and easily terminable, witness James's abrupt dismissal of Coke— [19] but because they had served their royal master too well, and presumably enjoyed his protection.

Once initiated to topple giants—Strafford, Clarendon, Hastings—impeachment has sunk in this country to the ouster of dreary little judges for squalid misconduct.[20] Our preoccupation with judicial impeachment tends to obscure the grand design of the Framers, to whom impeachment of judges was decidedly periph-

---

15. There were the impeachments of Lord Chancellor Macclesfield, 16 *Howell's State Trials* (Cobbett's Collection) 767 (1725) (London, 1809); Lord Lovat, 18 Howell 529 (1746); Warren Hastings (1787–1795). For abstract of charges in the Hastings impeachment, see Alexander Simpson, *A Treatise on Federal Impeachment* 167–188 (Philadelphia, 1916). The disuse of impeachment testifies not so much to the abandonment of an outmoded instrument of government as to the flexible good sense and incorruptibility of English administration. The parallel removal by Address, become statute for the removal of judges in 1700 (infra, Chapter IV, text accompanying n. 131), has found employment against a judge only once in the intervening centuries. H. R. W. Wade, *Administrative Law* 281 (Oxford, 2d ed. 1967). For an English evaluation in 1791 of the place of impeachment in the future, see infra, Chapter II, n. 214.
16. Impeachment of Justices Robert Berkley and John Finch for high treason and other great misdemeanors, 3 Howell 1283; charges abstracted in Simpson 105–109. Despite the charges of subversion of fundamental law and the like, their real sin was to exert pressure in favor of the "Ship-Money Tax." 2 Henry Hallam, *Constitutional History of England* 15–24 (London, 1884); 1 T. B. Macaulay, *Critical and Historical Essays* 448–450 (London, 1890); Evan Haynes, *Selection and Tenure of Judges* 60 (1944). See also infra, Chapter I, n. 111; Chapter II, nn. 175, 176.
17. Roberts 27.
18. Charles H. McIlwain, "The Tenure of English Judges," 7 *Am. Pol. Sci. Rev.* 217, 218 (1913); 7 Edward Foss, *The Judges of England* 4 (London, 1857); 6 Holdsworth 503–510 (1924).
19. 5 Holdsworth 430–440 (2d ed. 1937).
20. Borkin, passim.

eral. The Framers were steeped in English history; [21] the shades of despotic kings and conniving ministers marched before them. [22] Notwithstanding the predominant fear of oppression at the hands of Congress (in no little part the product of state legislative excess during the 1776–1787 period), [23] and the consciousness that the Executive powers were on the whole rather limited, [24] there was yet a nagging concern (noted by Madison with respect to the earlier period [25]) that the Executive might be transformed into a monarchy. [26] The problem of cabinet "accountability" to Parliament was not really relevant under our tripartite system of government, in which members of the Cabinet are responsible to the President alone. [27] It was not developments in parliamentary government during the eighteenth century upon which the eyes of the Framers were fixed, but rather on the seventeenth century, [28] the great period when Parliament struggled to curb ministers who were the tools of royal oppression. Familiarity with absolutist Stuart claims [29] raised the specter of

---

21. H. T. Colbourn, *The Lamp of Experience* 19, 25, 156, 183, 185 (Chapel Hill, N.C., 1965); Bernard Bailyn, *Ideological Origins of the American Revolution* (Cambridge, Mass., 1967). See also infra, John Adams, at Chapter IV, text accompanying n. 95; n. 97; n. 4; Chapter VII, text accompanying nn. 17–20; James Wilson, 2 Jonathan Elliot, *Debates in the Several State Conventions on the Adoption of the Federal Constitution* (Washington, D.C., 2d ed. 1836), 449, 470, 487.
Senator Maclay derided some of the "high ideas of English jurisprudence" in the First Congress. William Maclay, *Sketches of Debates in the First Senate of the United States, 1789–91,* 102 (Harrisburg, Pa., 1880).
22. Infra, n. 29; Chapter II, n. 215; Chapter IV, n. 97.
23. Raoul Berger, *Congress v. The Supreme Court* 8–14, 82, 126–127, 132, 182 (Cambridge, Mass., 1969).
24. Raoul Berger, "Executive Privilege v. Congressional Inquiry," 12 *U.C.L.A. L. Rev.* 1044, 1071–1076 (1965).
25. "The founders of our republics," i.e., the States, said Madison, "seem never for a moment to have turned their eyes from the danger to liberty from the overgrown and all-grasping prerogative of an hereditary magistrate . . . They seem never to have recollected the danger from legislative usurpations." *The Federalist,* No. 48 at p. 322 (New York, 1937). By the time of the Convention, disenchantment with excesses of State legislatures had set in (Berger, *Congress v. Court* 10–11), but as late as 1791 James Wilson still felt it necessary to admonish the American people that it was time to regard executive and judiciary equally with the legislature as representatives of the people. 1 James Wilson, *Works* 293 (R. G. McCloskey ed., Cambridge, Mass., 1967).
26. Infra, Chapter II, n. 216.
27. Infra, Chapter II, n. 207.
28. For the impact of seventeenth-century revolutionary thought on the Colonists, see Bernard Bailyn, *Ideological Origins of the American Revolution* (Cambridge, Mass., 1967). Cf. Julius Goebel, Jr., "Constitutional History and Constitutional Law," 38 *Colum. L. Rev.* 555, 563 (1938).
29. Bailyn 29n refers to the "universally despised apologists of Stuart authoritarianism." See infra, Chapter II, n. 215.

a President swollen with power and grown tyrannical; and fear of presidential abuses prevailed over frequent objections that impeachment threatened his independence.[30] So the Framers confided to Congress the power, if need be, to remove the President, to tear down his arbitrary ministers and "favorites." [31] This was but another reflection of colonial partiality to the legislative branch, which, as James Wilson noted, sprang from the fact that the Assemblies were their own, whereas Governors and Judges had been saddled on the Colonists by the King or his minions.[32] And it was yet another cog in the system of checks and balances, an exception to the separation of powers,[33] albeit a narrowly channeled exception.[34] Fear of Executive usurpation emphatically did not prompt the Framers to throw the President and his ministers to the wolves.

The constitutional grant of power to impeach raises important questions. Is it limited to criminal offenses? Is it unlimited? Does it exclude other means of removal? Does it comprehend insanity, incapacity, or nonofficial misconduct? Are members of Congress exempt from impeachment? These and still other questions have yet to receive satisfactory resolution.[35] Bald assertion, proceeding from assumptions that are at war with the intention of the Framers, has too often substituted for analysis. Resort to the historical sources and close analysis of the several textual provisions may throw fresh light on the problems. To grasp the place of impeachment in the constitutional scheme, and its

30. 2 Max Farrand, *The Records of the Federal Convention of 1787*, 64–69 (New Haven, Conn., 1911); cf. infra, Chapter II, nn. 167–171; text accompanying nn. 213–225.
31. Infra, Chapter IV, text accompanying nn. 85–88; Chapter II, n. 228; for royal "favorites" see infra, Chapter II, n. 95.
32. Infra, Chapter II, n. 222; cf. statement of Justice Brandeis, infra, Chapter II, n. 225.
33. Infra, Chapter IV, text accompanying n. 88.
34. Infra, Chapter II, text accompanying nn. 157–172.
35. Kurland states with respect to removal of judges that "there is more literature than learning." Philip Kurland, "The Constitution and the Tenure of Federal Judges: Some Notes from History," 36 *U. Chi. L. Rev.* 665, 688 (1969). Stolz refers to the opposing views of Burke Shartel and Judge Merrill Otis as "some distinguished though partisan scholarship of about thirty years ago." Preble Stolz, "Disciplining Federal Judges: Is Impeachment Hopeless?" 57 *Calif. L. Rev.* 659, 660 (1969).

potential role for the future, we need better to understand the use to which it was put in the past. For it was with the historical past in mind that the Founders wrought.[36]

---

36. For the Founders, "history was the most obvious source of information, for they knew that they must 'judge of the future' by the past." Gordon Wood, *The Creation of the American Republic 1776–1787*, 6–7 (Chapel Hill, N.C., 1969). See infra, Chapter I, n. 107; Chapter IV, n. 4.

Chapter I

THE PARLIAMENTARY POWER TO DECLARE RETROSPECTIVE TREASONS

The heroic age in the struggle for parliamentary supremacy was the seventeenth century,[1] when Englishmen struck out against Stuart pretensions [2] and when Parliament claimed anew the power to declare ministerial acts treasonable retrospectively. Bloody as that power appears today, it played a mighty role in the achievement of English liberty. It was the treason trials that crowded the impeachment stage and that familiarized the Founders with the high political purposes served by impeachment. And though the Framers replaced the bloody sanctions for treason with removal alone, though they defined treason tightly and forever limited the power of Congress to broaden its scope, retroactively or otherwise, the lessons of those trials were not lost on them.

The treason trials were filled with incessant debate whether a retroactive declaration of treason was lawless by virtue of the great treason statute, 25 Edw. III; [3] and if we are properly to evaluate the conduct of Parliament it is necessary to examine that act and its history closely. For such evaluation some understanding of the role and powers of the medieval Parliament is essential, and if that may tax the patience of the gentle reader, it will by contrast make the subsequent chapters less

---

1. Between 1621 "and 1725 there were fifty cases of impeachments brought to trial. Since. that date there have been only four." 1 Sir William S. Holdsworth, *A History of English Law* 382 (3d ed. 1922).
2. Infra, text accompanying nn. 108–115.
3. 1 Statutes at Large 244 (1350) (William Hawkins ed., London, 1735).

7

formidable. The preamble of the treason statute recites, "Whereas divers opinions have been before this time in what case treason shall be laid, and in what not; the King, at the request of the Lords and of the Commons, hath made a declaration in the manner as hereafter followeth."

There ensues an enumeration of specific treasonable acts, for example, levying war against, or encompassing the death of, the King, or adhering to his enemies; which is followed by a proviso, often referred to as the *salvo,*

And because that many other like cases of treason may happen in time to come, which a man cannot think nor declare at this present time, it is accorded, that if any other case, supposed treason, which is not above specified, doth happen before any Justices, the Justices shall tarry without any going to judgment of the treason, till the cause be shewed and declared before the King and his Parliament, whether it ought to be judged treason or other felony.

The effect of the *salvo* was debated again and again in the seventeenth century; opponents of the impeachments argued that the *salvo* limited the power of Parliament, raising a great constitutional issue. For Sir Matthew Hale nothing less than an act of Parliament in which the Commons joined with the Lords was required to settle a doubtful case.[4] And varying views have been expressed by Lord Campbell and by Stephen, Holdsworth, and McIlwain. It remains a teasing problem.

Let us begin, as for the most part seventeenth-century exegetes did not, with the setting of the statute in the fourteenth century, the mischief the draftsmen were asked to cure, painstaking study of the language they employed, reference to prior parliamentary practice, and Parliament's own conduct in the ensuing half-century.

---

4. 1 Sir Matthew Hale, *History of Pleas of the Crown* 259 (Philadelphia, 1st Amer. ed. 1847).

The *salvo* reference to what "doth happen before any Justices" suggests that the Act was aimed at proceedings which originated in the courts; and some antecedent history indicates that the courts had in fact been the source of the mischief. Tanner tells us that the vagueness of the offense led the Commons to complain of the arbitrary decisions of the courts, and "in 1351 they presented a petition praying 'that whereas the King's Justices in various counties adjudge persons indicted before them to be traitors for sundry matters not known to the Commons to be treason, it would please the King by his Council and the great wise men of the law to declare what are treasons in this present Parliament.' On this petition was founded the Statute of Treasons of 1352." [5] The omission to mention treason proceedings which originated in Parliament is the more significant because there had been such proceedings involving great personages—the Earl of Lancaster (1322), Roger Mortimer, Earl of March (1330) [6]—not long before the statute was enacted. The statutory focus on cases that "happen before any Justices" was therefore not fortuitous. The judges who drafted the statute [7] responded to the petition of the Commons by enumerating and describing treasons confided to the Justices for decision, and by instructing them to consult Parliament in doubtful cases.[8] In this they followed a familiar pattern.

The work of the early Parliament, as is well known,

---

5. J. R. Tanner, *Tudor Constitutional Documents 1485–1603*, p. 375 (Cambridge, 1922). See also J. G. Bellamy, *The Law of Treason in the Later Middle Ages* 86 (Cambridge, 1970). Blackstone also adverts to the "great latitude left in the breast of the judges, to determine what was treason, or not so: whereby the creatures of tyrannical Princes had opportunity to create abundance of constructive treasons." 4 Sir William Blackstone, *Commentaries on the Law of England* 75 (Oxford, 1765–1769). For citations to judicial "constructive treasons" in 1305–1349, see 3 Holdsworth 290–291 (3d ed. 1923).

6. 1 Howell 39, 51. Although these employed "articles of impeachment," the modern form of impeachment, i.e., a charge by the Commons tried by the Lords, came later, circa 1386. M. V. Clarke, "The Origin of Impeachment," in *Oxford Essays in Medieval History* 165, 183 (Oxford, 1934); cf. 4 Hatsell 62–63.

7. H. G. Richardson & G. O. Sayles, "The Early Statutes," 50 *L.Q.R.* 201, 540, 545 (1934); Theodore Plucknett, *Concise History of the Common Law* 322 (Boston, 5th ed. 1956); Bellamy, supra, n. 5 at 86.

8. The framers of 25 Edw. III "attempted to guard against the creation of fresh treasons by judicial interpretation by a clause which required that the statute should be interpreted not by the Judges, but by Parliament." 3 Holdsworth 291 (3d ed. 1923).

was in great part what we would call "judicial," [9] the judging of particular cases. Some fifty-five years prior to 25 Edw. III, in 1295, Fleta had stated that before the King in his Parliament "doubts are determined regarding judgments, new remedies are devised for wrongs newly brought to light, and . . . justice dispensed to every one according to his deserts." [10] There had been cases "that had proved too hard or too novel for the judges in the separate courts"; [11] and in such cases, the King in Parliament might by a ruling or instruction "resolve the doubt or disagreement, and get the court concerned moving again." [12] *Staunton v. Staunton* (1340) is illustrative. Plucknett states that a difficult question was posed in the Common Pleas and was decided by Parliament on a petition by one of the parties. Parliament then ordered the court to proceed. Common Pleas found an objection to the parliamentary procedure, and again a petition brought the matter before the King and his Council in Parliament who read the record and agreed that the demandant should recover; judgment was then given in the Common Pleas.[13] Reflecting the same practice, a 1340 statute "decreed that in any case which to the judges seemed so difficult that it could not properly be determined without the assent of parliament the tenor of the process was to be brought into the next parliamentary session and a judgment made which the justices were to pronounce in their court." [14] Bellamy considers that the draftsmen of the 1352 Act "probably borrowed the

---

9. Extracts from relevant scholarly works bearing on our problem have been collected by Gerald P. Bodet, *Early English Parliaments, High Courts, Royal Councils or Representative Assemblies* (Boston, 1968), among them F. W. Maitland, ed., *Memoranda de Parliamento* (Rolls Series, 1893) in Bodet at 15, 17; Sir J. G. Edwards, *Historians and the Medieval English Parliament* (Glasgow, 1960) in Bodet at 38. See also C. H. McIlwain, *High Court of Parliament and Its Supremacy* 25, 109 (Hamden, Conn. 1962); H. G. Richardson & G. O. Sayles, "Parliament and Great Councils in Medieval England," 77 *L. Q. R.* 213, 407, 414 (1961); G. R. Elton, *The Tudor Constitution* 228–229 (Cambridge, 1960).
10. Quoted in Bodet, supra, n. 9 at ix; Richardson & Sayles, supra, n. 9 at 230, 407.
11. McIlwain, *High Court* supra, n. 9 at 25. An ordinance of 1311 states that Parliament must be held once a year for hearing pleas, including those "whereon the Justices are of divers opinions." Ibid. 113.
12. Edwards, in Bodet, supra, n. 9 at 39.
13. Theodore Plucknett, *Statutes and Their Interpretation in the First Half of the Fourteenth Century* 23–24 (Cambridge, 1922).
14. Bellamy, supra, n. 5 at 88.

procedure, although they seem to have intended that the Justices should give the judgment and not parliament." [15]

The terms of the Treason Statute [16] buttress Bellamy's view. The text does not call upon the Justices to turn a doubtful case over to Parliament and to relinquish it altogether. Rather it directs the Justices to "tarry without going to judgment, till [Parliament "declare"] whether it ought to be judged Treason or other Felony." This declaration by Parliament is differentiated from "whether" the cause "ought to be judged," and inferably the entry of "judgment" pursuant to the declaration is to be by the Justices, who had merely been instructed to "tarry without going to judgment till," and only until, that declaration issued.

However that may be, it seems quite clear that neither the antecedent circumstances—a complaint by the Commons against the overwide construction by the Justices—nor the language of the statute suggest a need or an intention to limit the power of Parliament in any way whatever. Instead, as Professor Rezneck justly concluded, the Act "was intended as a check upon the lower courts, to which the practice of making constructive treasons was forbidden. The power to interpret the existing [non-defined] law was reserved instead to a higher Court, the High Court of Parliament. The clause did not create or invest parliament with a new right; it merely stated what was the current practice . . . the reflection of a familiar usage." [17] Why indeed should the King and his High Court of Parliament now confer upon themselves a familiar power

15. Ibid. Holdsworth states that Parliament would "either settle the case or give instructions to the court below as to how it should be settled." 1 Holdsworth 368, 378n (3d ed. 1922). See also infra, text accompanying n. 68.

16. In approaching the ancient statute we may be emboldened by the words of Lord Chancellor Erskine, then defending Horne Tooke, "a STATUTE is ever present to speak for itself, in all courts and in all ages." 25 Howell 1, 268 (1794).

17. Samuel Rezneck, "The Early History of the Parliamentary Declaration of Treason," 42 Eng. Hist. Rev. 497, 513 (1927). My concurrence with Rezneck that the salvo did not purport to confer a new right on Parliament (see also Blackstone, infra, text accompanying n. 85) constrains me to dissent from Bellamy's statement that "Parliamentary attainder . . . owed much to the great statute of treason of 1352 wherein the means had been provided for the declaration of doubtful crimes in Parliament." Bellamy, supra, n. 5 at 204.

which they had exercised over the years? The Lords, as will shortly appear, declared their power to be "by ancient custom of Parliament," that is, inherent and therefore independent of statute.

It is one of the oddities of history that the known cases of treason which came to Parliament in the fifty years that followed 25 Edw. III, with perhaps one exception, were not "doubtful cases" referred by the Justices; "they originated in parliament itself." [18] There is not the slightest indication in those cases that Parliament felt itself restricted in any way by the *salvo,* let alone by the treasons enumerated in the Act, as some were much later to argue. The one case which originated before the Justices was that of John Imperiall (1380), a Genoese ambassador who was murdered in London while carrying a royal safe-conduct. The offender was indicted for "high treason," but the Judges, "it being out of the statute 25 Edw. III, could not proceed." [19] Parliament was summoned to deal with the case; it "declared" that "such a crime amounted to treason;" and "the last act was made by the Justices." [20] It is plain that the treason so "declared" by Parliament fell outside the enumerated treasons of 25 Edw. III.

A more striking illustration is furnished by the Appeals (private criminal accusations) filed by certain Lords in the House of Lords against the Earl of Suffolk

18. Rezneck, supra, n. 17 at 508.
19. The quotation is from the argument of Oliver St. John in the Strafford impeachment, who went on to say, "This is in the Parliament Roll. 3 R. 2, n. 18, and Hilary Term 3 R. 2, rot. 31, in the King's Bench." 3 Howell 1511. In his argument in defense of Strafford, Sir Richard Lane had anticipated St. John: "according to this reservation [*salvo*], in the 8th of R. 2d, one who was charged before the King's Bench was afterwards referred to the parliament; and there, though the fact was not contained in the body of the statute, yet because of the proviso afore-mentioned it was adjudged treason." And, he continued, "In the 11th of the same king, the duke of Ireland, and Nevil archbishop of York, were impeached of high treason . . . and notwithstanding the Statute, were convicted thereof by the *salvo.*" 3 Howell 1475. The latter case is discussed infra, sub nom. Earl of Suffolk, text accompanying nn. 21–22. The Imperiale or Imperiall case is discussed in 3 Edward Coke, *Institutes of the Laws of England* 8 (1628–1645), and more fully by Rezneck, supra, n. 17 at 502. The power of Parliament, withheld from the judges, to declare fresh treasons, was noticed in 1397 by the Justices, for whom Thyrning spoke. Quoted Rezneck, supra, at 505. Holdsworth considers that "The case of John Imperiall (1380) was decided under this clause." 3 Holdsworth 291 n. 6 (3d ed. 1923).
20. Rezneck, supra, n. 17 at 502.

(Michael de la Pole) and others in 1386.[21] As was earlier noted, the main categories of 25 Edw. III were encompassing the death of the King, levying war against him, or adhering to his enemies. In contrast, the Appeals for "high treason" were based on charges that the accused had taken advantage of the tender age of the King, imposed false views upon him, kept him in obedience to themselves (Art. 1); that they made him swear that he "would live and die with them" (Art. 2); that they caused him to make a gift of the whole realm of Ireland and advised him that by that grant Robert de Vere had been made King of Ireland (Arts. 5 and 11), and that one of the accused, Sir Nicholas Brambre, had executed certain debtors "without due process" (Art. 12). All these were held "high treason," and none can be fitted into any category specified in 25 Edw. III.

This was no oversight. During the interval that the Lords were examining the Articles

the Justices, Serjeants, and other sages of the law, both of the realm and law civil, were charged by the king to give their faithful advice to the lords of the parliament how they ought to proceed in the abovesaid Appeal. Then the said Justices, Serjeants, and sages of both laws having taken these matters into their deliberation, answered the said lords of parliament, that they had seen and well understood the tenor of the said Appeal, and affirmed that it was not made nor brought according as the one law or other required. Upon which the said lords of parliament, having taken deliberation and advice, it was by the assent of the king with their common accord declared, That in so high a crime as is laid in this Appeal, and which touches the person of the king and the estates of this realm, and is perpetrated by persons who are peers thereof . . . the cause cannot be tried elsewhere but in parliament, *nor by any other law or court, except that of parliament;* and

---

21. 1 Howell 89. The date given in Howell is 1388, but the correct date is 1386. S. B. Chrimes, "Richard II's Questions to the Judges," 1387, 72 *L. Q. R.* 365, 370 (1956). Initially the Commons had impeached the accused of high crimes and misdemeanors, 1 Howell 91; certain Lords then brought an Appeal of high treason, ibid. 101–110, which furnished the basis of the judgment, ibid. 112.

that it belongs to the lords of parliament, and to their free
choice and liberty, by ancient custom of parliament, to
be judges in such cases ... and thus it shall be done in
this case by award of parliament ... since the process or
order used in inferior courts is only as they are intrusted
with the execution of the ancient laws and customs of the
realm, and ordinances and establishments of parliament:
and it was the judgment of the lords of parliament, by
assent of the King, that this Appeal was well and duly
brought ... according to the *laws and course of parliament,* and by which they will award and judge it.[22]

Thus, despite judicial advice that the charges of treason were not made "according" to the law "of the
realm," the Lords insisted that the case was triable only
by the "course of Parliament" as distinguished from the
"ordinances and establishments of parliament," that is,
the statutes,[23] which bound the "inferior courts." Expressed not long after 25 Edw. III, this is an authoritative assertion of parliamentary power to adjudge
treason, untrammeled by statute. So too, when a complaint of misconduct which fell outside the statutory
treason categories was made against Sir Thomas Talbot
in 1394, the King and Lords were asked "to declare
the nature, penalty, and judgement appropriate" to
the offense, and they declared it to be high treason.[24]

---

22. 1 Howell 113 (emphasis added). In the wake of the Suffolk impeachment, the Justices, who had earlier been charged by the King to advise
the Lords how to proceed, answered a set of questions put to them by
Richard II and stated that no impeachment could be carried out without
the King's will, and that the participants in the impeachment were traitors.
Chrimes, supra, n. 21 at 379–380. As Professor Chrimes notes, the issue
whether the judges were coerced is a matter of controversy. Chrimes at
365–368. Moreover the Commons speedily impeached the Justices, and
they were convicted and exiled by the Lords. 1 Howell 119–120; Chrimes
387. The unfortunate John Blake, who had drafted the questions at the
King's command, was impeached and convicted, hanged, drawn, and
quartered, 1 Howell 120; Chrimes 385; testimony, parenthetically, that the
Lords did not consider themselves bound by the 25 Edw. III definitions.
   Chrimes deduces from the fact that the Commons petitioned the King
in 1357 for "leave to bring in certain impeachments" that impeachment
was dependent upon his consent. Chrimes 380–381. But the fact that it
had been employed to bring down the very judges who had advised Richard
that the impeachers were dependent on his will seems to lend the later
petition an air of mechanical obeisance. Certainly future Parliaments did
not consider that impeachment depended upon royal consent.
   23. "A statute was something established, an ordinance was something
ordained, and during our period the words were used interchangeably."
Plucknett, supra, n. 13 at 33. See also Richardson & Sayles, supra, n. 7 at
202, 556.
   24. Discussed in Rezneck, supra, n. 17 at 503.

These declarations were not so far removed from the enactment of 25 Edw. III as to be without significance as contemporary constructions by the highest judicial tribunal; and in my judgment they confirm that the statute left the powers of Parliament untouched.

In sum, the petition of the Commons in 1351 sought relief from the "constructive treason" interpretations of the Justices, and 25 Edw. III did no more than respond to that petition. In referring doubtful cases to the King and his Parliament the statute followed earlier practice, and it nowise purported to limit Parliament for the future, if indeed it could do so.[25] Neither the terms nor the history of the statute indicate that it was to have any application to cases originating in Parliament itself.[26] And the conduct of the Lords in several cases in the next fifty years shows that they considered their powers to be utterly unaffected by the statute.

SEVENTEENTH-CENTURY INTERPRETATIONS

What seems so plain when viewed in the frame of the fourteenth-century materials becomes quite muddied as the turbulent political currents of the seventeenth century pour into the stream.[27] A number of strange interpretations then emerge, having at least one thing in common—they take little account of the fourteenth-century materials or of the difficulties of bending the text to the desired interpretation. In the *Clarendon* proceedings, for example, the Lords asked the Justices for their opinion respecting charges of high treason lodged by the Earl of Bristol;[28] the unanimous reply by Chief Justice Forster was that when the

---

25. See infra, text accompanying n. 85; and n. 92.
26. Yet the learned Serjeant Maynard, the first editor of the Year Books, arguing during the impeachment of Chief Justice Scroggs for the power of Parliament to declare a retroactive treason, stated that by 25 Edw. III "the judgment of treason, in doubtful cases, is expressly reserved to Parliament," 8 Howell 202, apparently oblivious to the fact that that statute did not purport to govern any cases but those arising before the Justices.
27. I question whether "The most illuminating period in the history of the clause is undoubtedly the seventeenth century, when it gave rise to a controversy of considerable proportions." Rezneck, supra, n. 17 at 498. There was more heat than light.
28. 6 Howell 312–314.

case is presented "in a judicial way before the House of Peers only . . . no treasons could be declared nor adjudged, but as were expressly within the letter of the 25 E. 3." [29] Read literally this would confine the "judicial way" of the Lords to the enumerated treasons and read the *salvo* out of the statute. Coleman stated the case somewhat more modestly: treason could not be "declared . . . unless there be resemblance to some other like case." [30] A treason charge, said Goodrick, must come "within the words of the statute." [31]

Let us pass over the casual assumption by Forster, Coleman, and Goodrick that the *salvo* governed cases originating in Parliament, and consider its effect on the power of Parliament in cases referred by the Justices. The pertinent language is "because that many other like cases of treason . . . which a man cannot think of declare at this present time, it is accorded, that if any other case, supposed treason, which is not above specified, doth happen before any Justices . . ." Coke thought this was designed to deprive the Justices of the power to decide the "like" cases "as they do in other cases by equal and like reason," that is, by analogy.[32] But this does not compel the conclusion that the *salvo* was meant to limit the power of *Parliament* to the decision of "like" cases. The *salvo* should be understood rather in the broad terms later employed by Serjeant Maynard: "What treason is, no man can define, nor describe. In that statute it is not; but treasons are enumerated . . . If such an offence, as men cannot define, should happen, the judges are to acquaint the parliament with it." [33] Even in the desperate struggle for the life of Strafford in 1640 his counsel, Sir Richard Lane, conceded, as Stephen correctly states, that under

---

29. Ibid. 312, 316. Sir Heneage Finch urged that treason ought to be confined to one who had "literally offended" 25 Edw. III. ibid. 328.
30. 6 Howell 344.
31. Ibid. 343.
32. George Leak's Case, 12 Co. 15, 17, 77 E. R. 1297, 1299 (1608). Does this mean that if "any other case . . . supposed treason, which is not above specified," did not "resemble" the enumerated categories, the Justices were required to dismiss the case rather than refer it to Parliament? That is a possible construction but not a necessary or even a practical one. It may be doubted that the Justices would have felt constrained to dismiss and forego the reference.
33. 8 Howell 202; Scroggs proceedings.

the "*salvo,* while it was in force, Parliament acting judicially . . . could declare new treasons." [34]

Sir Matthew Hale, writing some thirty-five years later, had his own interpretation of the *salvo.* Apparently he considered that the parliamentary power to enter judgment in "particular cases" originating in Parliament was untouched, that such declarations were not "pursuant to the statute," that action under the statute required a "bill declaratively" in which *both* Houses participated. He took no account of the earlier practice of referring doubtful cases to Parliament for judgment; nor did he explain how an act designed to limit the "constructive treasons" of the Justices can be construed anywise to limit the power of Parliament, nor why Parliament should by statute surrender its power of judgment respecting cases referred by the Justices yet preserve its power to adjudge fresh treasons in "original" cases. And he posits a participation of the Commons in the enactment of statutes that is far from clear in 1352. His words have engendered controversy and call for careful analysis: "the authoritative decision of these *casus omissi* is reserved to the king and his parliament, *viz.* the king and both his houses of parliament; and the most regular and ordinary way is to do it by a bill declaratively . . ." [35]

Holdsworth read Hale to refer to "legislative power," [36] whereas McIlwain concluded that for Hale "a valid judgment as well as a valid statute required the action of both houses." [37] Although Hale limited action under the *salvo* to legislative enactments, he recognized that Parliament had declared treason in an "original" case, the *Talbot* case,[38] and that another

---

34. 2 Stephen 253n. Lord Chancellor Campbell's interpretation of Lane's argument as insistence "to demonstration" that the Parliament could act under the *salvo* only in its "legislative capacity" was properly rejected by Stephen. Ibid. For Lane's view see supra, n. 19. It was because Lane recognized that Parliament's judicial function was preserved by the *salvo* that he turned to the repeals.

35. 1 Hale, supra, n. 4 at 259.

36. 1 Holdsworth 378 (3d ed. 1922).

37. McIlwain, *High Court,* supra, n. 9 at 248.

38. 1 Hale, supra, n. 4 at 259. He also says of the Northumberland and Talbot decisions, "tho they be decisions and judgments of great weight, yet they are not authoritative declarations to serve this act of 25 E. 3, but it must be by the king and both houses of parliament." Ibid. 260. These cases are discussed by Rezneck, supra, n. 17 at 503–505.

"original" case, the *Suffolk* case, contained "divers articles, which surely were not treason within the statute of 25 E. 3. yet had judgment of high treason given against them by the lords in parliament:" He did not deny the power but explained that "this was no declaration of parliament pursuant to the statute of 25 E. 3 because the king and commons did not consent *per modum legis declarativae,* for the judgment was only by the lords." It was "but a particular judgment in a particular case, which was not conclusive, when the like case came before judges." [39] Hale's "not conclusive" deduction is confirmed by the terms of the statute, for the jurisdiction of the Justices was limited to the enumerated cases. If nonspecified cases arose before them, they were required to "tarry" for a declaration by Parliament. Since no exception was made for a case that might be governed by a prior "declaration" of Parliament, such a declaration could not relieve them of the duty to refer the fresh case. Consequently that declaration was "not conclusive" for the Justices; [39a] they could not in a fresh case enter final judgment in reliance upon the prior "declaration." In sum, for Hale the *salvo* eliminated the parliamentary power to render judgment in referred cases; it left that power untouched in cases that originated in Parliament; and the *salvo* required enactment of a statute to settle a referred case, a conclusion, as will appear, that may be doubted on still other grounds.

In the *Clarendon* proceedings (1667), Solicitor General, Sir Heneage Finch, attempted to dispose of the "judicial" power by asking what seemed to him the unanswerable question: "Would our ancestors leave what was to be resolved treason to the Lords, and themselves have no share in it?" [40] He cannot have sought participation in the *judicial* declaration by the Lords, because in a conference during the self-same proceedings between committees of the Lords and Commons, the Commons were told that the Lords

---

39. 1 Hale, supra, n. 4 at 264.
39a. Cf. 4 Hatsell 220n. Indeed, Parliament "warned the courts against applying the recent cases as precedent." Quoted Rezneck, supra, n. 17 at 510n.
40. 6 Howell 348; Clarendon proceedings.

"must be tender of their own judicial proceedings," and they in turn assured the Lords, "It is true they ought [to] be jealous that we should intrench on their power; but the Commons were so far from that, that they thought the judicial power better lodged with them than in the Commons themselves." [41] Judicial declarations admittedly did not require participation by the Commons; Finch's argument was therefore that the *salvo* confined Parliament to legislative declarations by both Houses because the Commons would never have surrendered the right to participate in such declarations. Both Hale and Finch were indulging in the sort of seventeenth-century historical thinking which sought to root in the past powers that the Commons only later achieved or desired.[42]

Although no less a scholar than Holdsworth apparently viewed the *salvo* phrase "before the King and his parliament" as posing the question "how far the Commons had a right to share in judicial powers of Parliament," a matter he thought not clear at this time,[43] the learning respecting the role of the Commons in the mid-fourteenth century discloses with considerable certainty that the Commons did not participate in the judicial function of the King and his Parliament and in all probability had no share, beyond the lodging of petitions with the King and his Parliament, in the enactment of statutes. Inasmuch as the view that the *salvo* confined Parliament to "legislative" declarations of fresh treasons was frequently reiterated in the seventeenth-century debates, it will be useful briefly to survey the Commons' role at the time 25 Edw. III was enacted, if only to show that the meaning of the *salvo* does not turn on participation by the Commons in declarations, judicial or legislative, thereunder.

To begin with the "judicial" function, when the King holds "his court in his council in his parliaments" to

---

41. Ibid. 360. Shortly afterward, in the Danby proceedings, the Lords advised the Commons that "this court . . . is, and ever must be, tender in the matters relating to their judicature." 11 Howell 801. And see infra, n. 86.

42. J. G. A. Pocock, *The Ancient Constitution and Feudal Law* 47 (Cambridge, 1957). See also Rezneck, supra, n. 17 at 498.

43. 1 Holdsworth 377-378 (3d ed. 1922).

dispense justice and determine doubts regarding judgment, said Fleta in 1295, "there are present prelates, earls, barons, magnates and other learned men." [44] As Richardson and Sayles remark, "Of any further elements he said nothing." [45] At this time, the reign of Edward I, there was but one assembly, in which "there were also present, humbly in the background, the representative knights and burghers," said Trevelyan, "not likely to speak unless they were first spoken to in such a presence." [46] In 1305 these representatives "stood unobtrusively in the background, petitioning the crown for justice and then retiring while king and council . . . discussed the great affairs of state." [47] The knights and burgesses had "no inherent right to participate in this judicial work"; [48] and before long they disqualified themselves from serving as judges by assuming first the role of complainant and then of prosecutor.[49] In 1368 the Commons complained of Sir John Lee, steward of the royal household. The "charges were examined before the King [and] Lords . . . he was sentenced presumably by the Lords." [50] On the complaint of the

---

44. Quoted, Bodet, supra, n. 9 at ix; Richardson & Sayles, supra, n. 9 at 230.
45. Richardson & Sayles, supra, n. 9 at 219.
46. G. M. Trevelyan, *Illustrated History of England* 194 (London, 1956).
47. Bodet, supra, n. 9 at ix, paraphrasing Maitland, Introduction, *Memoranda de Parliamento* 1305; Plucknett, *Concise History* 323. And see Desire Pasquet, *Essays on the Origin of the House of Commons* (Cambridge, 1925), in Bodet, supra, at 49. Jolliffe states, "In presenting themselves before the official council of Edward I, or before the Magnum Concilium of Edward II and Edward III, the commons appear as an external subordinate body, and, though they find unity for themselves in joining to present common petitions, there is never any tendency for them to become merged in the magnate Council." J. E. A. Jolliffe, *The Constitutional History of Medieval England* 374–375 (London, 2d ed. 1947).
48. C. R. Lovell, *English Constitutional and Legal History* 167 (Oxford, 1962); cf. Jolliffe, supra, n. 47 at 374. Charges of high treason against the Bishop of Hereford in 1323 were "examined before the king and lords." 1 Howell 39. In the trial of Roger de Mortimer in Parliament (1330), the King "charges you, Earls and Barons, the Peers of his Realm . . . that you do right and lawful judgment to the said Roger . . . Wherefore the said Earls, Barons and Peers, as Judges of Parliament awarded and adjudged." In the same Parliament the King charged them to give judgment against Simon de Bereford, Knight, who had aided Mortimer, and, though the "Peers, as judges of Parliament" did give judgment, they disclaimed for the future a duty to render judgment "on others than Peers." 3 Zechariah Chafee, *Documents on Fundamental Human Rights* 646–649 (Cambridge, Mass., 1952).
49. The obverse with respect to Lords was noted by Richardson & Sayles, supra, n. 9 at 228: "Judges, however, cannot at the same time be petitioners, and petitions of general import fell to be presented by the representatives of the commons."
50. Clarke, supra, n. 6 at 77–78. For early Parliamentary trials of "great offenders" see 1 Holdsworth 378 (3d ed. 1922).

Commons against Lord Latimer in 1376, judgment was given "by the Prelates and Lords in full Parliament." [51] So too, when the Earl of Suffolk was impeached by the Commons in 1386 for "high crimes and misdemeanors" and fled, certain Lords brought criminal Appeals for "high treason." The Lords alone sat in judgment. [52] And the Lords (with the King) again declared treason in 1394 in the *Talbot* case. [53] Even when the Commons were greatly grown in stature (1667), they yet recognized that the judicial power belonged to the Lords alone. [54] It may therefore fairly be concluded that the Commons did not at the time of 25 Edw. III share in the judicial function. [55]

Let us now consider Hale's view that the *salvo* required a "bill declaratively" in which the Commons must join with the King and Lords. Although the Commons had grown considerably in importance by 1325, and though their presence in Parliament was no longer sporadic but an accepted fact, [56] they did not exert a power of enactment even by 1350. Through the medium of a petition the Commons had gained a power to initiate legislation, [57] but the power of enactment remained with the King. [58] In 1351 the King gave favorable answers to only three out of thirty-nine Commons' petitions, and it was these three that emerged as stat-

51. 4 Hatsell 51.
52. 1 Howell 91, 98, 101, 114.
53. Supra, text accompanying n. 24.
54. Supra, text accompanying n. 41.
55. The "house of commons has never claimed a share in the judicial functions of the house of lords." Pasquet, quoted in Bodet, supra, n. 9 at 48. "The commons were not and never had been judges in parliament." Carl Stephenson, "The Beginnings of Representative Government in England," in *The Constitution Reconsidered,* ed. Conyers Read 33 (New York, 1938).
56. Sir Maurice Powicke, *King Henry III and the Lord Edward* (London, 1947), in Bodet, supra, n. 9 at 45; Edwards, in Bodet, supra, n. 9 at 67; Richardson & Sayles, supra, n. 9 at 227.
57. Richardson & Sayles, supra, n. 9 at 228; Jolliffe, supra, n. 47 at 377.
58. Jolliffe, supra, n. 47 at 377. Richardson & Sayles, supra, n. 7 at 562, cite Year Book, Hil. 22 Edw. 3 (1348), for the statement that the "king makes the law with the assent of the peers and the commune, and not the peers and the commune," and they state, "The king then is the legislator, not parliament; and it is a difficult question, not only how far he is bound to consult, but how far, once parliament has been consulted, he is bound by the decision then made." They also refer to the abrogation of a statute by Edward III in 1341. Ibid. 550, 554. In his preface to Plucknett, *Statutes and Their Interpretation,* supra, n. 13 at xviii, Harold D. Hazeltine remarks about Edwardian statutes, even those of Edward III, "they are the king's acts . . . the enacting power of the king in parliament is the king's power."

utes. To others the King answered that he was pleased that the law "should be enforced as heretofore." [59] One of the Rolls of Parliament recited that "the king will ordain what seems to him should be done with the advice of his Great Council," [60] in which sat the magnates, not the Commons.[61] Jolliffe concludes that in the reign of Edward III a statute would be regarded as "law promulgated in parliament by the king's grace at the petition of the commons, and with the counsel and consent of the lords." [62] In the very petition of 1351 which eventuated in 25 Edw. III the Commons pray that it may "please the King by his Council and the great and wise men of the law, to declare what are treasons in this present Parliament," [63] striking testimony by the Commons itself that it claimed no right to participate in the making of the Declaration." The assent of the Commons to statute, states Jolliffe, "was not assumed to be necessary until the reign of Henry V" (1418).[64]

If Hale meant by a "bill declaratively" a legislative enactment, there is yet another objection to an interpretation that would require adoption of a statute to resolve each doubtful case referred by the Justices. During this period, Plucknett tells us, statutes were

59. Jolliffe, supra, n. 47 at 378.
60. Rot. Parl. ii, 320, quoted by Jolliffe, ibid. 379 n. 4.
61. Richardson & Sayles, supra, n. 9 at 230, state that the magnum concilium (1305) "does not include any representatives of the commons . . . The great council is one of magnates and ministers . . . such as had been described by Fleta a few years earlier." For Fleta, see supra, text accompanying n. 44.
62. Jolliffe, supra, n. 47 at 380. Although a statute of 15 Edw. II (1322) declared that the establishment of matters "for the estate of the realm and the people" required the assent of the barons, prelates and Commons, Jolliffe remarks that "in 1369, Edward III was able to tell parliament with justice that 'he had at all times during his reign acted with the advice by the Counsel of the magnates and commons.'" Jolliffe, supra, at 371 n. 1. Holdsworth states, "In the fourteenth and at the beginning of the fifteenth century it was the king who, with the advice of the judges and others of his council, framed and enacted the statute upon the petition of Parliament." 2 Holdsworth 438 (3d ed. 1923). Cf. Plucknett, supra, n. 13 at 31.
63. Tanner, supra, n. 5 at 375. When it was objected before Thorpe, C. J., that the Commons had not assented to the statute, he said, "when all the lords are assembled they can make an ordinance, and it shall be held for a statute." Rex v. Bishop of Chichester, Y. B. 39 Edw. III, f. 7 (1365), quoted Plucknett, Concise History 328.
64. Jolliffe, supra, n. 47 at 371 n. 1; 2 Holdsworth 440 (3d ed. 1923); Richardson & Sayles, supra, n. 9 at 423. Plucknett states that one generation "after our period closes," i.e., after the 14th century, there is a statement, "The law of the land is made in Parliament by the King and the Lords . . . and the commonality of the realm." Rot. Parl. iii 234, quoted Plucknett, supra, n. 13 at 31.

viewed as "special law," as "something extraordinary, outside the usual law, and radically different from it . . . Almost as frequently," the Year Books "contrasted 'novel law' with 'ancient law.'" In a word, statutes were thought "exceptional law . . . [and] novelties as well." [65] Since the proliferation of statutes also ran counter to the "ideal of the medieval statesman" that there "should not be too many laws," [66] it may be doubted that the *salvo* contemplated routine resort to fresh statutes in order to meet each particular referred case.

Judgments in Parliament were older, more familiar than statutes; [67] and Holdsworth states that "the judges were in the habit of consulting with the Parliament on points of law, and it is probable that the statute had this practice in view." [68] In addition, the enacting power of the King in Parliament was virtually plenary,[69] so there "was no necessity," as Stephen says, "for Parliament in 1352 to reserve the right of future parliaments to pass declaratory acts as to treasons not mentioned in the statute," [70] more especially since the power of the King in Parliament had nowise been challenged. In fine, the fact that the Commons did not participate in the judicial function, and that in 1352 its participation was not yet essential to the enactment of a statute, shows that the meaning of the *salvo* does not turn on such participation.

The seventeenth-century discussion of the *salvo* in terms of "legislative" or "judicial" functions imports a differentiation that found no clear expression in the fourteenth century. But in light of the fact that the judgment of particular cases was the older function, that there was an established practice of consultation by Justices with Parliament respecting difficult cases,

---

65. Plucknett, supra, n. 13 at 30.
66. 2 Holdsworth 436 (3d ed. 1923). "On the whole, few statutes were made or felt to be necessary. Those that were made were, in the main, administrative regulations and frequently obvious emergency matters." Max Radin, *Anglo-American History* 335 (St. Paul, Minn., 1936).
67. Supra, n. 9.
68. 1 Holdsworth 378n (3d ed. 1922).
69. Cf. supra, text accompanying nn. 58–62. Compare the abrogation or change of statute by the King after an enactment. Plucknett, *Concise History* 323.
70. 2 Stephen 252.

I incline to the view that the draftsmen of 25 Edw. III, who had enumerated described categories and then provided for the judgment of particular doubtful cases not so described, regarded the function of Parliament under the *salvo* as "judicial."

EFFECT OF SUBSEQUENT STATUTES

In the seventeenth century it was frequently argued that the *salvo* of 25 Edw. III was repealed in whole or in part by two later statutes. Then first, 1 Hen. IV, c. X (1399), provides:

Whereas in the said Parliament, holden in the said one and twentieth year of the late said King Richard, divers pains of treason were ordained by statute, in as much that there was no man which did know how he ought to behave himself, to do, speak, or say, for doubt of such pains; it is accorded and assented by the King, the Lords and Commons aforesaid, That in no time to come any treason be judged otherwise, than it was ordained by the statute in the time of his noble grandfather King Edward the third.[71]

Aimed explicitly at the treasons "ordained by statute" of 21 Rich. II (1398), this statute confirms 25 Edw. III and, as Stephen noted, it makes no mention of the *salvo.*[72] The words that treason is not to "be judged otherwise than it was ordained by the statute" 25 Edw. III do not necessitate a repeal of the *salvo,* for it was "ordained" by that statute that doubtful cases should be referred by the justices to Parliament. At most, the reference to 25 Edw. III may suggest that Parliament would now be limited to judgment of doubtful cases so referred. But it would be anomalous to construe 1 Hen. IV as preserving the "referred" jurisdiction while striking down the "original" jurisdiction of Parliament. Less equivocal language should be required to abrogate a power which the Lords had asserted so cate-

---

71. 1 Stat. at Large 402.
72. 2 Stephen 253.

gorically in the *Suffolk* case only eleven years prior to 1 Hen. IV, and that not in terms of grant to them by statute but "by ancient custom of the realm." [73] A contemporary Parliament did not consider itself hobbled by 1 Hen. IV, for in 1423 it declared in the *Mortimer* case that the escape of a prisoner held on suspicion of treason should be adjudged as equivalent to treason.[74] Subsequently there were bills of attainder for high treason of John Spynell (1487) for the slaying of divers great officers of the King, and of Lord Howard (1536) for contracting to marry the King's niece without his consent,[75] although neither offense was within the specific categories of 25 Edw. III. These cases demonstrate that Parliament did not consider that its power to deal with treason retroactively had been diminished by 1 Hen. IV.

The Act of 1 Mary ch. 1 (III) (1553), said Stephen, "is to much the same effect" as 1 Hen. IV.[76] It recites in relevant part,

Be it therefore ordained and enacted . . . That from henceforth none act, deed or offence by act of Parliament or statute made treason . . . by words, writing . . . or other-

---

73. Supra, text accompanying n. 22. See 4 Blackstone 85, quoted infra, text accompanying n. 85. In 1691, Attorney General Treby, soon to become Chief Justice of Common Pleas, said of 1 Hen. IV, "the statute is not meant of impeachments . . . it never intended taking away any impeachments." 5 *Parl. Hist.* 678, 712 (London, 1809).

74. See Rezneck, supra, n. 17 at 506–507. *Mortimer* is a curious and complex case, in which the Lords were presented with an indictment that had been confirmed by the Commons, who then requested "that the lords should do likewise and then proceed to judgment. With this demand the lords complied and gave sentence as for treason. The record suggests that the final sentence was put in the form of a regular statute." The statute "was made retroactive to the beginning of the current parliament, but was to remain in force only until the next parliament." Ibid. Rezneck considers that the statute may be accounted for by special circumstances. But in any event, it was tailored for the special case and designed to be short-lived. It would be difficult to conclude that resort was had to statute rather than judgment because 1 Hen. IV curtailed the judgment power and left the statute power untouched; and Rezneck does not consider the possibility.

75. 4 Hatsell 80–81, 83n. Although a general Act passed earlier in the same session to reach such crimes, Coke considered that the general Act had been aimed at Spinell and his adherents. Ibid. 80n. A bill of attainder "is a legislative act which inflicts punishment without a judicial trial," Charles E. Hughes, *The Supreme Court* 200 (New York, 1928), and it may therefore be thought inapposite because the statute speaks of cases "to be judged." Such a bill was in fact a "judgment." Infra, text accompanying nn. 100–103. It would be exceeding strange were Parliament bound by 1 Hen. IV not to "judge" of treasons except within the 25 Edw. III enumeration and remain free by attainder to condemn without trial for any reason whatsoever.

76. 2 Stephen 253.

wise whatsoever, shall be taken ... or adjudged to be high treason ... but only such as be declared and expressed to be treason ... in or by the Act of Parliament or statute made in [25 Edw. III] ... nor that any pains of death ... in any wise ensue ... for the doing or committing any treason ... other than such as be in the said statute [25 Edw. III] ordained or provided, any such act or acts of Parliament, statute or statutes, had or made at any time heretofore, or after the said 25th year of the reign of the late Edward the Third, or any other declaration or matter to the contrary in any wise notwithstanding.[77]

Unlike 1 Hen. IV, which seeks to govern the future by the phrase "in no time to come," 1 Mary strikes at statutes "made heretofore"; thus it speaks retroactively and does not purport to limit future action. Queen Mary herself, having shortly afterward married the Catholic Philip of Spain, procured two "ferocious new treason laws" [78] in 1555 against treason by "words." [79] Mary was a fanatical Catholic, whose "single ambition was to restore England to the papal obedience;" [80] and the treason statutes were a shuttle-cock in the deadly Catholic-Reformation struggle.[81] The first of the 1555 statutes was explicitly designed to protect the "true" Catholic faith [82] and, with the statute of 1553, was part of her design—with which Parliament "at last agreed to repeal all the anti-papal and anti-ecclesiastical legislation passed since 1529." [83] What compulsion is there to construe Mary's repeal of anti-Catholic treasons as a surrender by Parliament of its power to curb straying ministers by impeachment? [84] An affirmative answer is not writ large in the text.

The 1 Mary statute was aimed at offenses by "statute made treason," saving only those "declared and ex-

77. 2 Stat. at Large 89.
78. G. R. Elton, *England under the Tudors* 219 (London, 1960).
79. Tanner, supra, n. 5 at 380, 407–408.
80. Elton, supra, n. 78 at 215.
81. New treason laws, states Elton, were "a weapon which no effective sixteenth-century government could avoid." Ibid. 219; see infra, n. 96.
82. Tanner, supra, n. 5 at 407.
83. Elton, supra, n. 78 at 219.
84. Compare infra, n. 92.

pressed to be treason" in the statute of 25 Edw. III. Offenses by "statute made treason" do not necessarily include offenses so "declared" by Parliament. It is possible to read "expressed to be treason" as designating those specifically described in 25 Edw. III and as repealing the *salvo* provision for referral of doubtful cases to Parliament. But that reading encounters the difficulty that the power of Parliament, in the words of Blackstone, was not "originally granted by the statute of Edward III, but [was] constitutionally inherent in every subsequent parliament (which cannot be abridged of any rights by the act of a precedent one)." [85] Apart from the question of power to abridge "inherent" power of future Parliaments, there is the affirmation by the Lords in the *Suffolk* case that they were not bound by statutes, that these were established for the guidance of the inferior courts, but that the Lords would proceed according to their own course and law. If it be assumed that the Commons with the consent of the Lords could abridge the judicial power of the Lords by an act of Parliament, it remains to explain why the Lords, who later advised the Commons that the Lords "must be tender of their own judicial proceedings" and were told by the Commons that they had no thought to "intrench on their power," should voluntarily have stripped themselves by 1 Mary of their power to decide doubtful cases.[86]

This question cuts deeper when we turn to impeachment, which involves a power shared by the Lords with the Commons, who prefer charges as Grand Inquest of the Nation.[87] The "crowning achievement" of the fourteenth century, it has been said, was to devise impeachment as a procedure for trial of the King's ministers, who were otherwise not reachable.[88] In the

---

85. 4 Blackstone 85. Earlier Coke stated, "A subsequent parliament cannot be restrained by a former." 4 Coke *Inst.* 43. And see Francis Bacon, infra. n. 92.

86. Supra, text accompanying n. 41. During the impeachment of Chief Justice Scroggs, Sir Richard Temple said in the Commons, "the Lords do not use to part with those powers they once get." 8 Howell 211. Records of the conferences between the two Houses show how stubbornly both stood on their privileges. 4 Hatsell 7, 42, 388–389.

87. 4 Hatsell 103n; 1 Wilson 426.

88. Clarke, supra, n. 6 at 188, 163, 173; cf. supra, text accompanying nn. 50–53.

almost 180 years that had elapsed when 1 Mary was enacted in 1553, the stature of Parliament had grown greatly; [89] and at just this time the Commons had "a good conceit of itself." [90] The history of Parliament is a tale of accretion, of hard-won power stubbornly maintained, not of voluntary self-diminution.[91] In later days Serjeant Maynard was to urge that "an act of parliament does not bind the parliament unless the parliament be named. General words shall never take away the right of the nation, in the Judgment of Lords and Commons." [92]

Nevertheless, Serjeant Maynard had earlier concurred with those who held that the "legislative" power of Parliament is unlimited, whereas the power of Parliament to "declare" retrospective treason is not.[93] By legislative power was meant a bill of attainder, and as Oliver St. John, leading counsel for the Commons in the Strafford trial stated: "Since 1 H. 4 we have not found any such declarations made, but all At-

---

89. Elton, supra, n. 78 at 166–168.
90. Ibid. 217.
91. Cf. supra, text accompanying n. 41.
92. 8 Howell 202–203. The doctrine that the *King* is not bound by a statute unless expressly named is at least as old as Coke. Case of a Fine Levied by the King, Tenant in Tail. 7 Co. 32a–32b, 77 E. R. 459–460 (1604). See also King v. Cook, 3 Term. Rep. 519–522, 100 E. R. 710, 712 (1790). I found no parallel rule with respect to Parliament, perhaps because the normal function of Parliament is to make rules for others, not to promulgate self-denying ordinances. At an early date (1388), however, a Parliament attempted to secure its judgments and enactments against repeal "by declaring that every such effort to undo its work was to be punished as treason." Rezneck, supra, n. 17 at 512. But as Rezneck states, "In practice, of course, a subsequent parliament had in general the power to undo what another had established . . . And in the end all such safeguards proved to be futile; there was an alternation of repeal and restoration." Ibid. Not too long after 1 Mary, Francis Bacon rejected the power "by a precedent act of Parliament to bind or frustrate a future. For a supreme and absolute power can not conclude itself." 6 Bacon, *Works* 160 (London, Spedding ed. 1858), quoted Elton, supra, n. 9 at 239. See supra, n. 85. One might at least ask for a clear indication that Parliament did mean by 1 Mary to conclude itself. It remains to mention that Maynard's view hardened into a "sound rule of construction, that certain rights are not to be taken away by uncertain words." Henry v. Great Northern Ry. Co. 1 De G. & J. 606, 652, 44 E. R. 858, 877 (Ct. App. Chan. 1857) per Lord Justice Turner.
93. Sir Heneage Finch said in the Clarendon proceedings, "The power of parliament is double, legislative, which hath no bounds; declaratory, by pronouncing judgments . . . it is not in the power of parliament . . . to declare anything to be Treason, which is not in the common law felony before." 6 Howell 328. For similar remarks by Coleman, ibid. 344. Maynard said of the *salvo* of 25 Edw. III that Parliament may proceed under it by bill but not by impeachment. Ibid. 345. Compare Maynard's later statement, supra, n. 26.

tainders of Treason have been by Bill." [94] That was, I suggest, a consequence of historical accident rather than of statutory curtailment. Attainders had become a royal tool during the Tudor period, when there was "an immense increase of royal power." As Stephen remarks, "If the King himself wished to punish a minister a bill of attainder was more convenient than an impeachment, because it superseded the necessity for a trial." [95] Hatsell explained that bills of attainder "became during the civil wars between the Houses of York and Lancaster, alternately the engine of the prevailing party, to wreak their vengeance against such of their enemies, as had taken part with their competitors for the Crown." And referring to the Henry VIII attainders, he said: "The cases of Empson and Dudley, and of Cromwell Earl of Essex, are instances in which the parties accused would have been the proper objects of Parliamentary impeachment, for high crimes and misdemeanors . . . but the impatient and overbearing spirit of the sovereign . . . rendered the summary proceeding by bill of attainder the more proper for his purposes." [96] By bill of attainder, in a word, Parliament would lend an air of legitimacy to a bloodletting desired by the King.[97] But where a minister favored by the King was objectionable to Parliament, such a bill would not equally serve *its* purpose, because it required the King's consent. What emerges is that Parliament bent before the wind of Tudor power and

94. 3 Howell 1508.
95. 1 Stephen 158. Apparently attainder bills were during that period "proposed by the king;" and because "of his ability from 1461 to dominate completely the lords and the commons in parliament, his control over attainder was virtually complete." Bellamy, supra, n. 5 at 211–212.
96. 4 Hatsell 88–89. Elton, supra, n. 78 at 21, remarks upon the "true spirit of the civil wars, each stage of which had been signalled by the attainder of the defeated and the reversal of attainder previously inflicted on the victors." See supra, n. 81.
97. Elton states of the murders of Empson and Dudley, that "The first parliament of the reign (January, 1510) readily endorsed the murders by an act of attainder . . ." Elton, supra, n. 78 at 71. The potent magnates of the 14th century were greatly reduced by the Wars of the Roses, and their successors "owed their position to selection by the early Tudors, and it was only natural that under Henry VII and Henry VIII they were fawning and servile instruments of royal authority." Radin, *Anglo-American Legal History* 53–54. Bellamy rejects the conventional learning. Speaking of the early 15th century attainders, he states, "Nothing could be further from the truth than the verdict that it was judgment by means of legislation." Bellamy, supra, n. 5 at 204.

prudently refrained from confrontations with royal favorites. This is not the stuff from which repeals or abandonment of a power are fashioned. Certainly Parliament had no thought in the early seventeenth century that it had relinquished the power of impeachment, for it launched on a notable series of impeachments when it felt strong enough to confront the Stuarts.[98]

Three great seventeenth-century impeachments, as we shall see, eventuated for one reason or another in bills of attainder; and opponents of impeachment in the House of Commons urged that the power to "declare" treasons had been curtailed while the power to "legislate" fresh treasons was left intact. By legislation they referred, not to general enactments for the future, but to bills of attainder, which are in reality no less "judgments" of conviction than are convictions on impeachment. Erskine May states that "a bill of attainder is undoubtedly the highest form of parliamentary judicature . . . in passing bills of attainder the Commons commit themselves by no accusation [as they do in filing impeachment charges] . . . they are judges of equal jurisdiction and with the same responsibility as the Lords." [99] Explaining the bill of attainder against Strafford, Hatsell states that "in the judgment of Parliament, these offenses charged against the Earl of Strafford were by them adjudged to amount to the crime of high treason." [100] By an attainder, said Chafee, "the legislature, all by itself, determines guilt and inflicts punishment upon an individual by name" [101] and without trial.[102] Such an act is only by courtesy labelled

---

98. See Swinfen's remark, infra, n. 199. The cases are abstracted in Simpson 91 et seq. It may be objected that attainders ran only to treason so that impeachment for "other high crimes and misdemeanors" was unaffected. But no such impeachments were brought during the circa 160 year attainder period, so that on St. John's reasoning that power had also been abandoned through disuse. Coke stated that no "Act of Parliament by non-use can be antiquated or lose his force." Coke on Littleton 81b. A fortiori, this is true of a "constitutional," "inherent" power of Parliament.

99. Quoted in 1 Holdsworth 328n. (3d ed. 1922).

100. 4 Hatsell 220n. Hallam states that the Lords "voted upon the articles judicially, and not as if they were enacting a legislative matter". 2 Hallam 105 n. See infra, text accompanying nn. 166–167.

101. Chafee 93.

102. In 1540, Thomas Cromwell "was never heard in his own defence, being condemned for treason and heresy—and guilty of neither—by an

"legislative," for it is a judgment of individual guilt in everything but name. For this reason, perhaps, Oliver St. John explained to the Lords, "Herein the legislative power is not used against my Lord of Strafford in the Bill; it is only the jurisdiction of the parliament." [103] To infer, therefore, that the sixteenth-century draftsmen of the "repeal" statutes drew a vital distinction between a retroactive "judgment" by impeachment and one by bill of attainder is to conclude that they consciously engaged in spinning cobwebs. And it would attribute to both Lords and Commons action that was at war with their own interests. Why should the Lords relinquish the sole power to *try* a fellow peer—peers were predominantly the subjects of impeachment—in favor of a drumhead proceeding without trial in which the Commons had an equal voice, and thereby weaken the protection of every peer? And why should the Commons renounce the tremendous power to lodge articles of impeachment in a proceeding not dependent upon the King's consent? Some explanation should be forthcoming before we read into 1 Mary a gratuitous surrender of an important parliamentary power.[104] The Act can be sufficiently explained by Queen Mary's desire to repeal the anti-Catholic treasons.[105]

A number of seventeenth-century impeachments should be considered, both for the light they shed on Parliament's own view of its powers and for the manner in which these powers were employed to advance important political ends.

---

act of attainder without trial . . ." Elton, supra, n. 78 at 158. Coke was told by one of the Justices that Henry VIII pressed them to tell him that one "might be attained of high treason by Parliament, and never called to his answer." 4 Coke, *Institutes* 37–38. See also, Hughes, supra, n. 75.

103. 3 Howell 1508.

104. Supra, n. 92.

105. Conrad Russell considers that "the question of the salvo ["whether it was still in force"] is probably unanswerable, since the treason statutes of 1399 and 1533 [1 Hen. and 1 Mary] are insolubly ambiguous on this point." Russell, "The Theory of Treason in the Trial of Strafford," 80 *Eng. Hist. Rev.* 30, 45 (1965). Repeal of a prior statute requires a clear intention to do so, and if the subsequent statutes "are insolubly ambiguous on this point," the prior statute is unaffected. Compare Henry v. Great Northern Ry., supra, n. 92.

IMPEACHMENT OF THE EARL OF STRAFFORD
(1642)

The impeachment of Strafford [106] is of interest not
alone because of the diverse treason theories that were
advanced, but because it constitutes a great watershed
in English constitutional history of which the Founders
were aware.[107] Strafford's downfall was rooted in a
conflict between the view of Charles I that "the will
of the Prince was the source of law" and that of Coke
and his followers that law had "an independent existence of its own, set above the King as well as above
his subjects." [108] His impeachment may be regarded as
the opening gun in the struggle whereby the Long
Parliament "prevented the English monarchy from
hardening into an absolutism of the type then becom-
ing general in Europe." [109]

Absolutism nakedly appears in the words Charles
addressed to both houses in 1626: "Parliaments are

---

106. 8 John Rushworth, *Historical Collections* (London, 1721). A less
trustworthy account by a purported eyewitness was published in 3 Howell
1382. Hallam, vol. 2 at 105n, says, "The account in the new edition of the
State Trials, I know not whence taken, is curious, as coming from an eyewitness, though very partial to the prisoner; but it can hardly be so accurate as the others." Lest this be taken as another illustration of "Whig-
gish" coloration, let me briefly muster some evidence of the eyewitness'
partiality. He writes, "I was so afraid of my own affection to the gentleman, that I . . . have set down his defenses rather to his disadvantage
by my rude pen, than in the native color, to his eternal glory, and the
confusion of his enemies." 3 Howell 1468. He states that Strafford
"carr[ied] himself with that constancy and resolution, which his innocence
and brave parts do promise," ibid. 1420. At every turn the prosecution
is unfavorably compared with Strafford: Strafford "spoke with no less
moderation and wisdom" than Pym "with heat and passion," ibid. 1418.
Counsel for the Managers speak with a "flourish," with "hyperboles,"
they reply "bitterly," ibid. 1421, 1417, 1425, whereas Strafford makes
"honest and witty defences." Ibid. 1469.
107. In an article published in the *Boston Gazette*, January 4, 1768, Josiah
Quincy, Jr., called attention to the English impeachments "for high treason
in subverting the fundamental laws and introducing arbitrary power,"
including that of Strafford, and concluded with a ringing call to follow
those examples. Reprinted in *Quincy's Mass. Reports 1761–1772*, App. IV,
pp. 581, 583, 584 (1865). See also, supra, Introduction, n. 21; infra, Chapter
IV, n. 4.
108. Trevelyan 401. "Consciousness of what happened abroad, of what
absolutism meant in practice, was one factor which made Englishmen
think it necessary to fight a civil war." J. P. Cooper, "Differences between
English and Continental Governments in the Early Seventeenth Century,"
in *Britain and the Netherlands*, ed. J. S. Bromley & E. H. Kossman 73
(Oxford, 1960). See Christopher Hill, *The Century of Revolution 1603–
1714*, 73, 187 (New York, 1961). If it was only the men of property who
"won freedom," Hill 310, the seeds for the wider dissemination of liberty
were then sown.
109. Trevelyan 391.

altogether in my power for the calling, sitting and dissolution. Therefore as I find the fruits of them to be good or evil, they are to continue or not to be." [110] When he pressed the King's Bench to uphold the extension of the Ship-Money Tax—theretofore levied only on seaports—to inland towns,[111] it was seen as a move "to dispense forever with the representative body of the kingdom." [112] That judgment appeared to the Venetian Ambassador to mean "royal absolutism and the end of Parliament." [113] What with the Ship-Money Tax and Strafford's reliance on government by proclamation, Parliament not unjustly feared that its monopoly of the powers to tax and to legislate were threatened; [114] and Charles's neglect to call a Parliament for eleven years did not lessen these fears.[115]

Strafford was the toughest executant of the royal policies; he would suffer no hindrance.[116] He was resolved that the King must conquer the "universal distemper of this age . . . where we are more apt wantonly to dispute the Powers which are over us." [117] He assured Archbishop Laud that he would not rest until he saw his "Master's power and greatness set out of wardship and above the exposition of Sir Edward Coke and his Year Books." [118] At a Council meeting, it was recorded by Sir Henry Vane, Strafford "advised Charles he was now absolved from law" and apparently "urged the introduction of an Irish army to compel England

---

110. Quoted Hill 73; Perez Zagorin, *The Court and the Country* 87 (London, 1969).
111. Hill 55. Chief Justice Finch, by one form of pressure or another, "had made certain of the opinions of the judges before the king had formally put his case." 6 Holdsworth 52n (1924); T. Taswell-Langmaid, *English Constitutional History* 517 (9th ed. 1929). The Ship-Money Case, The King v. John Hampden, is reported in 3 Howell 825 (1637). See Clarendon's comment on Finch, 3 Howell 835n; see also 4 Hatsell 127. And see infra, Chapter II, note 176.
112. Zagorin 102.
113. Hill 107.
114. Russell, supra, n. 105 at 38–41. Strafford sought to "make proclamations equal in authority to Acts of Parliament," to put the royal will above the protection afforded by the common law. Clayton Roberts, *The Growth of Constitutional Government in Stuart England* 93 (Cambridge, 1966).
115. Trevelyan 390.
116. G. E. Aylmer. *The Struggle for the Constitution* 96 (London, 2d ed. 1968); Zagorin 68.
117. Quoted Zagorin 68.
118. Quoted Trevelyan 396.

to obedience." [119] His "severe and unscrupulous rule" in Ireland convinced the opposition that there was no safety for them if he lived.[120] Still in being was an Irish army raised by Strafford, 9,000 Papists whom Charles refused to disband.[121] Then John Pym got wind of a plot, organized with Charles's knowledge and the encouragement of the Queen,[122] to bring the northern army to London to "overawe the parliament." Little wonder that the nation rose as one, believing that Strafford had "endeavored to destroy the excellent constitution of this kingdom." [123]

The drive against Strafford was spearheaded by two of England's greatest sons: John Pym, "perhaps the strongest Parliamentary leader in history, and [John] Hampden, the best beloved in that choice assembly of England's best." [124] Strafford was charged by the Commons with subverting the fundamental law and introducing an arbitrary and tyrannical government.[125] Thereby the Commons "intended to pass judgment on a system of government as well as the man. For to them Strafford personified more than any other the injustice and misrule they meant to end." [126]

Menacing as the acts of Strafford were, they did not amount to treason within the common understanding because they were not in the strict sense acts committed against the authority of the king: they had his

---

119. This charge is contained in Article 23, 8 Rushworth 72–73. Sir Henry Vane the younger had shown these notes to Pym, who copied them. 3 Howell 1458; Zagorin 209, 220. Strafford did not deny the utterance, but explained that by "this kingdom" he meant Scotland, not England; which Christopher Hill dismisses on the ground that if "the Scottish revolt had been suppressed by military power, there would have been small prospect of a Parliament's meeting in England." Hill 73.
120. Zagorin 69, 219. See also Aylmer, supra, n. 116 at 106.
121. Zagorin 219.
122. Ibid. 219, 226.
123. Roberts 77, 79. For popular support of the opposition, see Zagorin 106, 109, 117, 203.
124. Trevelyan 402. Zagorin 200, states that to Pym the "House of Commons owed an incalculable debt. He was a man who lived wholly for the public cause . . ." Clarendon wrote that Hampden "was indeed a very wise man, of great parts . . ." Quoted 1 T. B. Macaulay, *Critical and Historical Essays* 135 (London, 1890). Sir William Jones, himself reputed to be "a very wise man," said that Hampden was "the greatest man, for sense and foresight, that was concerned against king Charles I." 8 Howell 174–175, 176.
125. 8 Rushworth 8. This was in Article I, but it was on this charge that Pym hammered in his summation. Ibid. 661, 666; compare St. John, ibid. 678, 681. It was the gravamen to which all the charges were tied. Zagorin 217.
126. Zagorin 217.

tacit consent, if not encouragement.[127] The offense, rather, was that Strafford had "undermined the immemorial constitution of the kingdom by attacking its free institutions." [128] For this theory there was precedent. "In England during the later middle ages," J. C. Bellamy states, "there existed not one but two theories of treason side by side. One doctrine was . . . the law of treason as seen through the eyes of the king and his legal advisers. The other was the theory of the barons and to a lesser extent of the people . . . Treason was held to lie particularly in causing a division between the king and his people, thereby endangering the union which was the basis of the late medieval English state." [129] In a valuable study of the various treason theories advanced in the Strafford proceedings, Conrad Russell has pulled together early seventeenth-century instances which turned on withdrawal of the hearts of the people from the King, and has shown that the theory came to Pym stamped with the authority of Coke.[130] In his argument for the prosecution before the Lords, Pym said, "this crime of subverting the laws, and introducing an arbitrary and tyrannical government, is contrary to the pact and covenant between the King and his people . . . the legal union of allegiance and protection"; that is, the King owed protection to the people in return for their allegiance. And Pym stated, "to alter the settled frame and constitution of government is treason in any state. The laws whereby all other parts of a Kingdom are preserved, should be very vain and defective, if they had not a power to secure and preserve themselves." [131]

127. Chafee 111; Zagorin 217–218.
128. Zagorin 218; see also Russell 37–41.
129. Bellamy, supra, n. 5 at 209–210. Russell remarks, "whatever the constitution of England was believed to be, and whatever names historians give to different conceptions of it, they will all be found to preclude the development of arbitrary government." Russell 37.
130. Russell, supra, n. 105 at 31. "In 1629 members of the Parliament differentiated between treason to the King and treason to the Commonwealth . . . in 1640 the Commons impeached Lord Justice Finch 'for treason as well against the King as against the kingdom, for whatsoever is against the whole is undoubtedly against the head.' " Hill 288.
131. 8 Rushworth 666, 669. "It is the law that doth entitle the King to the allegiance and service of his people; it entitles the people to the protection and justice of the King." Ibid. 662. Russell states, "This idea of destroying allegiance by making the king's authority odious is not new; it has appeared against both Elizabeth Barton and Empson and Dudley." Russell, supra, n. 105 at 42; see also ibid. 31.

As Nathaniel Fiennes put it in the Commons debate, "if it be treason to kill the governor, then sure 'tis treason to kill the government." [132]

After the evidence had been placed before the Lords and Strafford had been heard in his own defense, after Pym had countered for the prosecution and Sir Richard Lane had replied for the defense, the Commons abandoned the impeachment and turned to a bill of attainder.[133] Before the trial, Lord Digby had suggested an attainder in order "to remove the scruples the peers might feel as judges." [134] Digby's advice was rejected, for the bulk of the Commons "did not doubt the justice of the accusation, and they desired the solemnity of a judicial condemnation." [135] Nevertheless, on the very day that Pym produced before the Lords the bombshell, Vane's recorded remarks of Strafford, Arthur Haselrig introduced a bill of attainder in the Commons. Pym perceived that to drop the impeachment would amount to a declaration of nonconfidence in the Lords, which might offend them. Although Pym, Hampden, Strode, and Selden opposed substitution of an attainder, they were voted down.[136] Pym's fears proved well founded; for the majority of the Lords were "deeply annoyed by the Commons' refusal to go on with the impeachment." Notwithstanding, they joined in the bill because they were beset by "fear of a 'rightist' reaction ["the threat of violence on the King's behalf"], fear of the mutinous people." [137] In the words of Trevelyan, the Parliament "held it necessary that the man should die who might by his vigor and genius restore the despotic power of the Crown." [138] It was a Lord, Essex, who bluntly said, "Stone-dead hath no fellow." [139]

---

132. Quoted Russell, supra, n. 105 at 38.
133. 8 Rushworth 634, 661, 671, 675.
134. Zagorin 218. When it came to the vote on the attainder, Digby (who had apparently purloined the damaging copy of the Vane notes from Whitlocke's files and forwarded them to the King, who made them known to Strafford, 3 Howell 1460n), while branding Strafford as a "most dangerous minister, the most insupportable to free subjects," yet refused to vote for the attainder. 8 Rushworth 50; 2 *Parl. Hist.* 750 (London, 1807).
135. Zagorin 218.
136. Ibid. 220–222. See also 1 Macaulay, supra, n. 124 at 461–462; 2 Lord John Campbell, *Lives of the Chief Justices of England* 117 (New York, 1874).
137. Zagorin 222, 223.
138. Trevelyan 403–404. See also Zagorin 69, 219; Aylmer, supra, n. 115 at 100.
139. 1 Macaulay, supra, n. 124 at 143.

The shift from impeachment to attainder, to my mind, remains an unsolved puzzle. The attainder proceeded on the identical charges contained in the impeachment; [140] they were carefully examined in the Commons [141] and, as Russell found, studiously considered by the Lords.[142] The shift to an attainder required the problematical consent of a hostile King. Then too, the Lords were resentful at having the matter "taken out of [their] control" [143] because, one may surmise, they were being asked to surrender the sole right to try a fellow peer and to share the right of judgment with the Commons, who on impeachment were the prosecutors, not the co-judges.

Attempts to explain the shift seem to me unsatisfactory. An eyewitness partial to Strafford stated that the Commons moved to an attainder because they "perceived a great defection of their party, and a great increase of the Lord Strafford's friends in both houses." [144] Summary votes for a death penalty would scarcely be more palatable to the "friends." Stephen said that the shift must "be taken as an admission that either by the statutes [1 Hen. IV and 1 Mary] or otherwise the proviso [*salvo*] had ceased to have effect." [145] Yet Strafford conceded at a late stage in the proceedings that the *salvo* was still in effect.[146] The proceeding, moreover, was not a reference of a doubtful case to Parliament by the Justices, which was the subject of the *salvo,* but an original proceeding in Parliament. Recently it has been stated that the Commons "could not prove the charges of treason, and were forced to

---

140. For the main charge in the impeachment, see supra, n. 125. In the preamble, the bill of attainder recites the impeachment by the Commons for "endeavoring to subvert the ancient and fundamental laws . . . and to introduce an arbitrary and tyrannical government," adduces some of the important proof, and then enacts that Strafford be attained of high treason. 8 Rushworth 756–775; 3 Howell 1518–1520. It was argued in the Commons that the Bill was "nothing but an affirmation of" the impeachment. 3 Howell 1470.
141. In the Commons debate on the attainder, "The charges in the impeachment were discussed one-by-one in a committee of the whole House which voted them to be proved and to constitute high treason." Zagorin 221.
142. Russell, supra n. 105 at 44, 48–50.
143. Chafee 112.
144. 3 Howell 1469.
145. 2 Stephen 253. He is followed by 1 Holdsworth 378 (3d ed. 1922).
146. Russell, supra, n. 105 at 44.

abandon the impeachment of Strafford. So they turned to an act of attainder, which did not require trial." [147] In substance this was the earlier view of Lord Campbell: because Strafford "was on the point of being acquitted," St. John "required that the impeachment should be dropped, and that a bill of attainder should be substituted for it, whereby the forms of law and principles of justice might more easily be violated." [148] If the issue of guilt was indeed for the Lords "a judicial question, which must be judicially proved," [149] it does them little credit to attribute to them a readiness to acquit after a full-dress trial only to turn and join in a legislative lynching.

It was left to Oliver St. John to explain the shift to the Lords. Cognizant of Pym's fears and perhaps of the Lords' resentment, he stated: "The proceeding by bill, it was not to decline your Lordships justice in the judicial way, in these exigends of the state and kingdom; it was to husband time, by silencing those doubts, [the Commons] conceived it the speediest and surest way." [150] Although this explanation satisfied Hallam,[151] it rings hollow. All the proofs were in; Strafford and his counsel had been heard; St. John's argument on the bill could as well have been made on the impeachment; and the time given by the Lords to debate on the attainder charges could equally have been devoted to the identical charges in the impeachment.

St. John's comprehensive analysis of the treason problem is marked by contradictions, in all probability because he was constrained to justify resort to attainder by arguing that a judicial declaration was barred. Let us focus on his fifth ground, the charge basic both to the impeachment and the attainder, "subverting the fundamental law," which he declared to be "treason by the common law." [152] It "was not the meaning" of 25 Edw. III, he said, "to take away any treasons that

---

147. Roberts 91-92.
148. 2 Campbell, *Chief Justices* 117.
149. J. R. Tanner, *Constitutional Conflicts of the 17th Century* 94-95 (Cambridge, 1928). In fact, the Lords found the facts on which the main charges rested as "proved." Russell, supra, n. 105 at 49-50.
150. 8 Rushworth 667; 3 Howell 1479.
151. 2 Hallam 105.
152. 8 Rushworth 678; 3 Howell 1480.

were so before, but only to regulate the jurisdiction
and manner of trial"; that is, the inferior courts were
circumscribed by the specified categories but the power
of Parliament was left intact. The statute, he explained,
left those categories to "the ordinary courts of justice";
the "others," depending "upon constructions and necessary inferences, they thought it not fit to give to the
inferior courts so great a latitude here, as too dangerous to the subject, those they restrained to the Parliament." [153]

The statute of 1 Hen. IV, St. John stated, left 25
Edw. "entire, and upon the old bottom" [154]—a bottom
which embraced judicial declarations of treason by
Parliament that fell outside the Edw. III categories,
as he acknowledged by his citation of the case of John
Imperiall (1380).[155] Nevertheless, he found it possible
to state that

it may be doubted, whether the manner of the parliamentary proceedings, be not altered by the statute of
1 Hen. 4 ... that is, whether since that statute, the parliamentary power of declaration of treasons, whereby the
inferior courts receive jurisdiction, be not taken away and
restrained only to bill, that so it might operate no further
than to that particular contained in the bill, that so the
parliamentary declarations for after-times should be kept
within the Parliament itself, and be extended no further;
since 1 Hen. 4 we have not found any such declarations,
but all attainders of treason have been by bill.[156]

In short, Parliament had renounced its power to declare treasons except by bill of attainder—apparently
both in cases arising before the Justices and impeachments arising in Parliament—so that its decisions
would not serve as precedents to the inferior courts.
So drastic an amputation was not needed to accomplish
a purpose the very Strafford bill of attainder achieved

---

153. 8 Rushworth 699–700; 3 Howell 1506. Professor Chrimes doubts that
25 Edw. III superseded the common law. Chrimes, supra, n. 22 at 383.
154. 8 Rushworth 700; 3 Howell 1508.
155. Infra, text accompanying n. 164.
156. 8 Rushworth 701; 3 Howell 1508.

by a mere proviso that the bill should not serve as a precedent for the judges.[157] In any case, St. John's statement that 1 Hen. "altered the manner of parliamentary proceedings," confining Parliament to bills of attainder, contradicts his earlier statement that 1 Hen. left the law "entire, and upon its old bottom." Like 1 Hen., St. John proceeded, 1 Mary left "the attainders in Parliament, precedent to themselves, untouched, wherein the legislative power had been exercised." [158] Although his discussion of Edw. III recognizes that the proceedings there governed arose before the Justices,[159] from which one might infer that he had no reference to impeachment proceedings which arose in Parliament, the negative implication of his remarks that the two repealing statutes left Parliament's "legislative power" untouched cuts across impeachment. His statement that "since 1 Hen. 4 we have not found any such [judicial] declarations, but all attainders have been by bill," [160] overlooked that during that period attainders had served as instruments of arbitrary *royal* policy; [161] it unnecessarily implied that Parliament had abandoned its own power, in despite of the King, to remove evil ministers. Pym, arguing the impeachment, had urged that Strafford "should perish by the justice of that law which would have subverted; neither will this be a new way of blood. There are marks enough to trace this law to the very original of this kingdom." [162]

It was this view that St. John argued in his sixth

---

157. 8 Rushworth 759; 3 Howell 1519. Chafee 112, states that "as if ashamed of the way they had stretched the word 'Treason' in order to kill their deadliest foe" the Commons inserted a proviso in the Attainder that it should not serve as a precedent to any Judge. Hallam states, however, that the proviso "seems to have been introduced in order to quiet the apprehension of some among the peers, who had gone to great lengths with the late government, and were astonished to find that their obedience to the king could be turned into treason against him." 2 Hallam 105. Such fears were recorded in the eye-witness report of the trial. Supra, n. 3 Howell 1461, 1477. Under the terms of the *salvo* Judges were not in fact authorized to apply declaratory precedents of the Parliament without a fresh referral to and declaration by it, because their power was limited to the enumerated categories of 25 Edw. III. See supra, text accompanying n. 39a.
158. 8 Rushworth 705; 3 Howell 1512. Compare St. John's explanation that resort was not had to the "legislative" power of Parliament but to its "jurisdiction." Supra, text accompanying n. 103.
159. 8 Rushworth 609; 3 Howell 1506.
160. 8 Rushworth 701; 3 Howell 1508.
161. See supra, text accompanying nn. 95–97.
162. 8 Rushworth 669–670.

point: "resort to the supreme power in Parliament."
Subversion of law was *"malum in se,* against the dictates of the dullest conscience, against the light of nature." [163] He cited the case of John Imperiall, the Genoese ambassador who came to England under a safe-conduct and was slain by a passer-by. The latter was indicted for high treason, and "the judges, it being out of the statute 25 Edw. III, could not proceed; the Parliament declared it treason . . . [I]t concerns the honor of the nation that the public faith should be strictly kept . . . they made the first man an example." [164] Then he cited a number of bills of attainder which he maintained were left "untouched, wherein the legislative power had been exercised . . . There's nothing" in 1 Hen. 4 and 1 Mary, he said, "whence it can be gathered, but that they intended to leave it as free for the future." [165] For me, St. John's disclaimer of "judicial" declarations and his reliance on a legislative bill is explained largely by his need to justify the Commons' shift from impeachment to attainder.

In the upshot the Lords adopted a theory that fitted within the "levying war" definition of 25 Edw. III. From his study of manuscript sources in the British Museum, Russell concluded, "it appears from the Lords' votes that it was almost entirely upon articles 15 and 23 that the Commons won their case in the Lords . . . They were both treasons by levying war, and so reducible to the terms of the statute. They both involved the assumption that levying war against the people was levying war against the king, but they did not involve the main body of the argument which had been put by the Commons." [166] After finding that Strafford "did counsel and advise his Majesty that he was absolved from rules of government," that "by his words counsels and actions [he] endeavored to subvert the

---

163. 8 Rushworth 703; 3 Howell 1510. Sir Richard Lane, arguing for Strafford, denied that the acts alleged amounted to the "Subversion of the Fundamental Laws," but agreed that "the crime, doubtless is unnatural and monstrous, and the punishment must keep the same proportion." 8 Rushworth 672, 3 Howell 1473–1474.
164. 8 Rushworth 704; 3 Howell 1511. For other discussion of the Imperiall case, see supra, text accompanying nn. 19–20.
165. 8 Rushworth 705; 3 Howell 1512.
166. Russell, supra, n. 105 at 44, 43.

fundamental laws of the kingdoms of England and Ireland, and to introduce an arbitrary power," that he had "exercised a tyrannous and exorbitant government above and against the laws, over the lives, liberties and estates of the subjects," the Lords resolved that "this question be put to the judges; that upon all the Lords have voted to be proved, [whether] the Earl of Strafford doth deserve to undergo the pains and forfeitures of high treason by law." [167] The reply was: "The Lord chief justice of the King's Bench delivered to the Lords, the unanimous opinion of all the judges present: 'That they are of opinion, upon all of which their lordships have voted to be proved, that the Earl of Strafford doth deserve to undergo the pains and forfeitures of high treason by law.' " [168]

Since the charges of high treason for the impeachment were identical with those in the bill there was no occasion, on this opinion, to disclaim a power of impeachment. And a treason within a definition of 25 Edw. III could be no less the subject of impeachment than of attainder. An inference that the Lords' judgment implicates that they could not act under the *salvo* is rebutted by Strafford's concession in the midst of the Lord's deliberations that the *salvo* was still in force.[169] Repeal or disclaimer of either the statutory or inherent power to declare retrospective treason cannot be rested on doubts.

In sum, St. John's gratuitous concession that the declaratory power of Parliament was now limited to attainder by bill was at odds with the views of the great leaders, Pym and Hampden, and those of Selden; it would deprive the jealous Lords of a judicial power [170] they had categorically claimed in 1386, and it would elevate a summary procedure without trial above a trial on impeachment, and this for "blood." These difficulties as well as those posed by the final judgment of the Lords require evaluation before the Strafford proceedings are accepted as a repudiation of an im-

---

167. Ibid. 49–50.
168. 2 *Parl. Hist.* 757 (London, 1807); Russell, supra, n. 105 at 30.
169. Russell, supra, n. 105 at 44.
170. See supra, text accompanying n. 41; and n. 86.

peachment for treason. And as we shall now see, St. John's renunciatory reading exerted little influence on the Commons in subsequent impeachments for non-statutory high treasons against Clarendon, Danby, and Scroggs.

IMPEACHMENT OF THE EARL OF CLARENDON (1663–1667)

As Edward Hyde, the Earl of Clarendon had voted for Strafford's attainder but afterwards became a prominent royalist,[171] went into exile with the sons of Charles I, and returned with Charles II after the Restoration to become Lord Chancellor and chief minister, while his daughter married Charles's brother, the future James II.[172] He himself recorded that the "late rebellion" had to be "extirpated and pulled up by the roots," the "usurpation" of Parliament "disclaimed and made odious."[173] He advised Charles not to fear the power of Parliament, "which was more or less, or nothing, as he pleased to make it,"[174] an echo of the absolutist pretensions that had cost Charles I his head.[175] His fall was due in large part, said Christopher Hill, to "his failure . . . to accept the fact that, in his own outraged words, 'the House of Commons was the fittest judge of the necessities and grievances of the people.'"[176] He was the moving figure in the sale of Dunkirk, conquered by Cromwell, to the French—an affront to the pride of the people.[177] He had caused men to be imprisoned outside of the kingdom in order to evade the writ of habeas corpus;[178] he solicited money from France so that the King could "elude the control of Parliament by help of French money."[179] Certainly

---

171. Zagorin 225.
172. Chafee 115.
173. 2 Hallam 332.
174. Ibid. 367n.
175. Supra, text accompanying n. 109.
176. Hill 228. Moreover, "Clarendon was no longer firmly supported by Charles, who had grown tired of him and perhaps felt that he had to be made a scapegoat." Aylmer, supra, n. 116 at 183.
177. 2 Hallam 353, 369; Hill 194; Aylmer, supra, n. 116 at 180.
178. 2 Hallam 367–368.
179. Ibid. 371.

these acts demonstrate his "unfitness for the government of a free country"; [180] and what with his royal son-in-law "working in his favor," and his own steadfast supporters,[181] the Commons invoked high treason "to put him away for good, to bar a return to office." [182]

As in the Strafford proceedings, the Commons now sought to have Clarendon sequestered on a general charge of treason, promising to exhibit articles against him "in convenient time." [183] But the Lords declined to follow the Strafford precedent; "it was not allowable, being in an ill-time, and branded by an act of repeal" after the Restoration.[184] The Lords demanded particular charges,[185] thereby touching off a prolonged altercation culminating in a resolution by the Commons that this was an "obstruction to the public justice." [186] Word now came that Clarendon had decamped; according to Clarendon himself, upon the advice of some Lords who now, knowing full well that he was already in Calais, moved "to stop the ports, so that he might be apprehended." [187] Then the Lords joined in a bill banishing Clarendon to "perpetual exile" and, if he returned, to suffer the "pains and penalties of treason." [188] By adoption of the bill the Lords agreed that the facts added up to high treason.[189]

---

180. Ibid. 367.
181. Chafee 116.
182. Roberts 157. In large part, it has been said, his downfall was attributable to his opponents' hunger for the fruits of office, ibid. 155, intensified by the fact that he had made implacable enemies of "very eminent men" and had offended the "dignity and privileges" of the Commons. 2 Hallam 366. Clarendon himself "virtually admitted the political necessity of his sacrifice." Christopher Hill, *Puritanism and Revolution* 201 (London, 1958).
183. 6 Howell 351.
184. Ibid. 364. 2 Hallam 376n, points out that the Commons made out a stronger case than in the Strafford proceedings. The repeal to which the Lords referred was that of the Strafford attainder in 13–14 Charles II (1663), which also repealed all the impeachment proceedings against Strafford. 6 Howell 364. The repeal is reported in 3 Howell 1525. Among other things it refers to "the late King Charles I of glorious memory." Ibid. 1527. Alas for such attempts to turn back the clock, for in July 1698, the Lords restrained the repeal to the bill of attainder and ordered that "whatsoever stands crossed upon the Journals, relating to the proceedings on the impeachment of the said Earl, ought not, nor shall be looked on as obliterated." 4 Hatsell 218n.
185. 6 Howell 351.
186. Ibid. 374.
187. Ibid. 374, 381–382n.
188. Ibid. 391.
189. In the Commons Vaughan explained that the "bill is grounded upon his flight after his impeachment, and his flying implies some guilt." Ibid. 390. In Respublica v. Doan, 1 Dallas 86, 91 (Pa. 1784), the court

The issue of high treason had been earnestly debated in the Commons. Some, like Heneage Finch and Coleman, declared the legislative power to be unlimited but not so the declaratory power.[190] In this view Serjeant Maynard, who had been a Manager for the Strafford impeachment, now joined,[191] though he was once more to plump for the declaratory power in later impeachments. Finch urged that treason ought to be confined to one "who literally offended" 25 Edw. III,[192] whereas Coleman insisted that the declaratory power was limited to a "resemblance to some other like case,"[193] possibly meaning like one of those specified in the Act. Maynard recognized the *salvo* but limited it to attainder by bill.[194] On the other side, Sir Thomas Littleton stated that the Edward Act was made "to bound inferior courts, not themselves,"[195] that is, Parliament. Sir Edward Thurloe said that Parliament had "declaratory power," as "in the case of the Genoa Ambassador."[196] John Vaughan, later chief justice, read the *salvo* to provide that the "doubtful case" would "pass from court to court, at last they come to the Lords."[197]

Proponents of the declaratory power carried the day; the articles of impeachment were voted and the com-

---

said, "By refusing to take his trial [flight], he tacitly seems to have admitted himself guilty," citing 2 Hawkins, fo. 170, ch. 23, sec. 53; 2 Sir Matthew Hale, *History of Pleas of the Crown* 208 (London, 3d ed. 1739). It may be suggested that the Lords cynically engaged in a harmless gesture, but this ill comports with the view that they were "sentinels of the law." Roberts 436.

190. 6 Howell 328, 344.

191. Ibid. 345.

192. Ibid. 328. Goodrick also asserted that treason must come "within the words of the statute." Ibid. 343.

193. Ibid. 344. Hallam stated that it is "impossible to justify the charge of high treason," 2 Hallam 367, 373, which is true if by treason is meant the offenses *specified* in 25 Edw. III. But Parliament had adjudged the slayer of John Imperiall guilty of high treason for the murder of a Genoese minister, and it had impeached de la Pole (Earl of Suffolk), though both cases fell outside the statutory enumeration. If that power remained in Parliament then it could declare the acts of Clarendon treason. The issue therefore is whether that power continued to reside in Parliament. Hallam noted in the Clarendon case "one of the articles did actually contain an unquestionable treason." 2 Hallam 412.

194. 6 Howell 345–346.

195. Ibid. 344.

196. Ibid. 344–345. In a footnote to the Thurloe remark, the report states: "Killing the King's Ambassador had formerly at the common law been adjudged treason . . . and may still be so by Parliament, for the statute of 25 E. 3, is a restraint only upon the Judges, but not upon the Parliament." Ibid. 345.

197. Ibid. 347. Finch insisted that action by King, Lords and Commons, i.e., by bill, was required. Ibid. 348.

mittee which had been directed to "draw reasons" reported that the "proceedings of inferior courts . . . is bounded and limited by the discretion of the parliament" (in other words, by statute) but that the "discretion of parliament . . . is, and ought to be unconfined for the safety and preservation of the whole." [198] And "what can or ought to be done by either house of parliament is best known by the customs and proceedings of parliament in former times." [199] The broad view taken by the committee is more solid historically, in my opinion, than reliance on the *salvo* which was designed to govern "doubtful" cases that arose before the Justices, not impeachments arising in Parliament.

IMPEACHMENT OF THE EARL OF DANBY (1678)

By the whirligig of politics, one of the leaders in the impeachment of Clarendon, Sir Thomas Osborne, was himself impeached for high treason in 1678; he was then Earl of Danby and chief minister of Charles II.[200] The country feared the "suspected pro-French and Papist leanings of the King and his entourage." [201] Rumors of a secret Treaty of Dover (all too well founded) whereby Charles II "undertook to restore the Roman Catholic religion" and "Louis XIV undertook to provide money and other support" fed the alarm.[202] Though Danby was himself anti-French and sought rather to give members of the established church "a permanent monopoly of every branch of politics and public life" [203] (a course not calculated to endear him to non-Anglicans), a mounting campaign against the Catholics and the King's pro-French policy found its center in Danby.[204] That his impeachment

---

198. Ibid. 355–356. Sir R. Howard had said, "Though common law has its proper sphere, 'tis not in this place, we are in a higher sphere." Ibid. 336.
199. Ibid. 355. Swinfen recalled the precedents of "Michael Delapool and in the Long Parliament." The paucity of precedent, he explained, was because "The parliament was wont to proceed formerly by bill." Ibid. 356.
200. Chafee 116, 118–119.
201. Hill 195.
202. Aylmer, supra, n. 116 at 184, 191; Hill 195.
203. Aylmer, supra, n. 116 at 188.
204. Ibid. 197.

was politically motivated can hardly be doubted,[205] but he himself supplied the trap-door to ruin. A letter written by him to Ralph Montagu, the go-between in Paris, empowered Montagu to make an offer to neutrality to France for the price, paid to Charles, of 6,000,000 livres "yearly for three years" because Parliament would be in no humor "to give him supplies after the having made any peace with France." [206] This letter was written upon Charles's express order, attested by his signature in a postscript.[207] When it came to light on the heels of the Popish Plot and the "disclosures" of Titus Oates, the Commons was aflame.[208] As the King was "beyond their reach, they exercised a constitutional right in the impeachment of his responsible minister." [209] If the power of Parliament to declare treason was untrammeled, the disgraceful occasion afforded provocation for its exercise—remembering that Danby, just prior to the Clarendon impeachment, had asserted that "if the Chancellor were not hanged for high treason, he would be hanged himself." [210]

After the articles of impeachment were delivered to the Lords, the Commons requested that Danby be committed to safe custody.[211] At this juncture the King came into the House of Lords and stated that the letter had been written by his order, that he had given Danby a pardon, and that Danby had already been

---

205. Chafee 120–121; for the underlying realities, see Trevelyan 460–463.
206. 11 Howell 608–611; 2 Hallam 410–411. Charles had secretly received 500,000 crowns from France for the long prorogation of Parliament, from November 1675, to February 1677, in which Danby was likewise concerned. 2 Hallam 401n. "In the beginning of the year 1676 the two kings bound themselves, by a formal treaty (to which Danby and Louderdale . . . were privy) not to enter on any treaties but by mutual consent; and Charles promised, in consideration of a pension, to prorogue or dissolve parliament, if they should attempt to force such treaties upon him." Ibid. As Lord Treasurer Danby was personally responsible for receiving "the French money . . . from Louis XIV and overseeing the use made of it." Aylmer, supra, n. 116 at 189.
207. 11 Howell 725; 2 Hallam 410.
208. Trevelyan 461–463.
209. 2 Hallam 410. He was impeached, said Roberts 218, because "Englishmen now believed it intolerable for a minister, not merely to give unlawful advice, but to continue to serve a king whose policies were hateful to the nation and whose commands threatened to make the Crown independent of Parliament."
210. Chafee 116. Danby was to render great service to England. Although a Tory, he "did more than any Whig to prepare the way for the Revolution and the reign of William III." Trevelyan 460, 471.
211. 11 Howell 622, 725.

dismissed.[212] A storm blew up, for as Sir Francis Winnington, late Solicitor General, said, "An impeachment is of no purpose when a pardon shall stop our mouths." [213] Under the law, said Winnington, one who takes a pardon "confesses the crime he stands charged with." [214] Danby went into hiding; the Commons introduced a bill of attainder which the Lords proposed to reduce to a bill of banishment, much to the Commons' displeasure.[215] At length the bill of attainder, first passed by the Commons, also passed in the Lords, and Danby surrendered himself.[216] A protracted quarrel between the two Houses about matters connected with the treatment of the pardon followed [217] and was terminated by the King's prorogation, shortly followed by dissolution, of the Parliament.[218] But Danby remained in prison because the King "could not enlarge him." [219]

For present purposes two remarks in the Commons debate are significant. Powle said, "It is the greatest mistake in the world, to tie us up with arguments of inferior courts." [220] And Winnington stated, "Should a minister of state have endeavoured to subvert the government, parliaments have power by 25 Edw. 3, to declare that treason, and it is the wisdom of the government to leave that declaratory power to parliament." [221] Hallam, who was no friend to this impeachment, sums up:

The house of commons faintly urged a remarkable clause in the act of Edward III, which provides that, in case of any doubt arising as to the nature of an offence charged to amount to treason, the judges should refer it to the sentence of parliament; and maintained that this invested

---

212. Ibid. 725, 766.
213. Ibid. 775. That view is expressed in our own Constitution, Article II, §2, which exempts impeachment altogether from the President's pardoning power.
214. 11 Howell 729. Lord Chancellor Campbell described Winnington as a "great lawyer." 4 Lord John Campbell, *Lives of the Lord Chancellors* 68 (London, 1849).
215. 11 Howell 750.
216. Ibid. 752, 763.
217. Chafee 130–131.
218. 11 Howell 830.
219. Ibid. 832.
220. Ibid. 806.
221. Ibid. 730.

the two houses with a declaratory power to extend the penalties of the law to new offenses which had not been clearly provided for in its enactments. But, though something like this might possibly have been in contemplation with the framers of that statute, and precedents were not absolutely wanting to support the construction, it was so repugnant to the more equitable principles of criminal law which had begun to gain ground, that even the heat of faction did not induce the commons to insist upon it. They may be considered, however, as having carried their point; for, though the prorogation and subsequent dissolution of the present parliament ensued so quickly that nothing more was done in the matter, yet, when the next house of commons revived the impeachment, the Lords voted to take Danby into custody without any further objection.[222]

The infiltration of more equitable principles of criminal law, noted by the great historian, exerted little influence on the bill of attainder passed by the Commons and Lords. In pressing afresh for impeachment and in passing an attainder on grounds that fell outside the specific categories of 25 Edw. III, the Commons acted either under the declaratory power in the *salvo,* relied on by Winnington,[223] or under the inherent power of Parliament to declare fresh treasons to which the Lords had laid claim in 1386.

IMPEACHMENTS OF CHIEF JUSTICE SCROGGS AND OTHERS

The impeachment of Chief Justice Scroggs in 1680 was perhaps the last notable occasion on which Parliament asserted the power to declare retrospective treasons. Scroggs, said Lord Ellenborough, was a "monster," [224] guilty of "abominable cruelties" and "judicial murders," whose name, said Lord Campbell,

---

222. 2 Hallam 413.
223. Winnington's reliance on 25 Edw. III for Parliament's power to declare subversion to be treason is, in my opinion, mistaken because the power was inherent. See supra, text accompanying nn. 8–27, 89.
224. 4 Campbell, *Chief Justices* 205.

will ever "call up the image of a base and bloody-minded villain." [225] At length fortune wearied of him, and the Commons by a large majority impeached him for high treason. Once more the main charge was that Scroggs had "wickedly endeavoured to subvert the fundamental laws, and . . . to introduce . . . arbitrary and tyrannical government against law." [226] Among the particulars were that he had arbitrarily discharged a grand jury before they had made their presentments of Papists, that he made an illegal order to prevent publication of an anti-Popery book, that he oppressively granted general warrants for the attachment of persons and property, and the like.[227] "It would have been difficult," said Campbell, "to make out that any of the charges amounted to *high treason;* but in those days men were not at all nice about such distinctions, and a dangerous but convenient doctrine prevailed, that, upon impeachment, the two Houses of Parliament might retrospectively declare anything to be treason, according to their discretion and punish it capitally." [228] Assertion of that power in the proceedings is plain. A few, Knight, Finch, and Temple, argued that Parliament could proceed only by bill; and both Finch and Temple urged the Commons not to set precedents that might haunt them in time to come.[229] Sacheverell and Winnington pointed out that there were already precedents, that men had been impeached and hung "for less crimes than these." [230] When Finch sought to discredit these precedents as coming from the "unquiet time" of Richard II,[231] Powle retorted, "I take them always to be unfortunate times when

225. 2 ibid. 259, 272. Campbell states: "I must not run the risk of disgusting my readers by a detailed account of Scroggs' enormities on the trials" of victims allegedly implicated in the Popish Plot. Ibid. 260–261.
226. 8 Howell 197–198; 2 Campbell, *Chief Justices* 269. Roberts 220, states: "many Parliaments had extended the concept of treason to comprehend the subversion of the law."
227. 8 Howell 198–201.
228. 2 Campbell, *Chief Justices* 270. Scroggs himself had said that a petition "to the King, for calling a parliament, was high treason"; and when his colleague, Chief Baron Atkyns, demurred that the people might lawfully petition the King, "if it was done with modesty and respect," Scroggs reported his "treasonable language" to the King and Atkyns was superseded. Ibid. 266; 8 Howell 193.
229. 8 Howell 202, 205, 211.
230. Ibid. 182, 208.
231. Ibid. 209.

there is occasion of such precedents." [232] Serjeant
Maynard declared that "enormous offenses may be
impeached by the name of treason, notwithstanding
the statutes," and that by 25 Edw. III "the judgment
of treason in doubtful cases, is expressly reserved to
parliament." And he asked, what if "there should be
a contrivance to destroy the Lords and Commons; is
that comparable to the treason of coining a shil-
ling? . . . take that power away of declaring treason
in parliament, and you may have all your throats
cut." [233] Sir Thomas Lee concurred that Parliament "is
not so bound up" by statute as to prevent it from
declaring "enormous offenses" to be treason, though
he expressed doubts on some particulars.[234] Paraphrasing Maynard, Winnington said that "what is committed
to the destruction of the government deserves as much
punishment as those treasons in the statute . . . to subvert the government, that is a parliament treason." [235]
And Sir William Jones stated, "in one in high place,
where he does obstruct justice, and change the law, [it]
is treason at common law." [236] These views prevailed
and the articles were adopted by the Commons; but
again the Lords denied the Commons' request for
commitment and instead let Scroggs go on bail of
10,000 pounds.[237] Soon after, Parliament was prorogued; and before long Scroggs was dismissed.[238] Thus
"he escaped the full measure of retribution which he
deserved." [239] In the Lords, remarked Campbell, "the
anti-exclusionists could not have defended or palliated
the infamous conduct of Scroggs; had his case come

---

232. Ibid.
233. Ibid. 202–203. Holdsworth labelled Maynard's views as "monstrous,"
1 Holdsworth 384n (3d ed. 1922), but they reflected a long-continued
assertion of power. In contrast, Lord Campbell stated: "It would have
been consolatory to us, in reading an account of the base action of Scroggs,
if we could have looked forward to his suffering on the scaffold like
Tresilian." 2 Campbell, *Chief Justices* 268.
234. 8 Howell 203–204.
235. Ibid. 206.
236. Ibid. 212. Jones was then Attorney General, an "honest and wise
man," according to Burnet. Sir William Temple noted that he was reputed
to be "the greatest lawyer of England" and "a very wise man." Ibid.
174–175n.
237. Ibid. 211–212. A considerable number of dissenting Lords wished
Scroggs committed. Ibid. 212.
238. Ibid. 216.
239. 2 Campbell, *Chief Justices* 268.

to a hearing, he could not have got off without some
very severe and degrading punishment." [240]

No departure from this course of Parliament is to
be found in two impeachments that Dwight cites to
demonstrate "that the court of impeachment must administer the same law as the criminal court . . . Thus
the Earl of Orrery was not tried in A.D. 1669, as the
offence charged was thought not sufficient to constitute
treason, and the case was directed to be heard in a
court of law." [241] It is true that the Commons voted
that this accusation "be left to be prosecuted at
law"; [242] but this was not because the charge was
deemed legally insufficient, but because it was not
deemed of sufficient moment to occupy the Parliament.
Serjeant Maynard said, "considering the time, and the
thing, if ever it was, and the petitioners must go to
Ireland for their witnesses . . . [I] would have it referred to the law." Sir Thomas Clifford stated that he
"would not have the sword of this house of impeachments be blunted upon offenses of this nature . . .
Would have impeachments . . . upon great and considerable occasions." [243] Dwight's citation to the impeachment of Sir Adam Blair in 1689 stands no better.[244] Blair was charged with distributing a seditious
and treasonable paper; Serjeant Maynard, now nearing
the close of his fifty-year span in the Commons, said,
"These papers are high treason; an impeachment may
walk long before it comes to issue. Prosecute them by
way of indictment." And he added significantly, "I
would not go before the Lords, when the law is clear,
and may be tried by juries." [245] Hampden the younger,
who had himself been condemned to death for treason,
stated, "I would not have it pass for doctrine, that
there is no treason but what is declared by 25 Edw.
3. If you take not that for granted, we shall never be
safe, nor any government, if you cannot declare trea-

---

240. Ibid. 271.
241. Theodore Dwight, "Trial by Impeachment," 6 *Am. L. Reg.* (N.S.)
257, 266 (1867).
242. 6 Howell 920.
243. Ibid. 919.
244. Dwight, supra, n. 241 at 266, citing to 12 Howell 1213, without
naming Blair.
245. 12 Howell 1211, 1212.

son." [246] And Hawles said, "I do not think this to be a plain case of treason, by 25 Edw. 3. I do say, no court can judge this offence to be treason . . . The proper way is to judge this high treason, and therefore I am for proceeding by impeachment." [247] For Maynard this was a "clear" case best left to the courts, reserving application to the Lords for cases when the law is not clear; for Hawles the case was outside the statute and therefore required impeachment. Dwight's citation of *Orrery* and of *Blair* to demonstrate that "the law was settled . . . that the court of impeachment must administer the same law as the criminal court" [248] is unsupported by these cases. Instead, they exhibit recognition of Parliament's power to declare treasons that go beyond those administered by the courts. And the testimony of Serjeant Maynard—who had participated in the leading impeachments, from Strafford in 1640 to Blair in 1689—goes far to establish the power. [249]

---

246. Ibid. 1208–1209. John Hampden was the son of the great leader in the Long Parliament, and had himself been condemned to death on a charge of treason. Bishop Burnet described him as "one of the learnedest gentlemen I ever Knew." *Encyclopedia Britannica* "John Hampden" (London, 14th ed. 1929).

247. 12 Howell 1212–1213.

248. Dwight, supra, n. 241 at 266.

249. Maynard himself had been impeached in 1648 for high treason far removed from the Edwardian categories. 4 Campbell, *Chancellors* 12.

In his pioneer study of impeachment proceedings (1796), Hatsell stated: Above four hundred years ago, the Lords claimed it to be their acknowledged franchise, "That matters moved in Parliament shall be managed, adjudged and discussed by the course of Parliament; and in no way sort by the law civil, or by the common law of the land, used in other lower courts of this Kingdom." Sir Edward Coke says, "As every court of justice hath laws and customs for its direction, some by the common law, some by the civil and canon law . . . It is by the *Lex et consuetodo Parliamenti*, that all weighty matters concerning the peers of the realm, or commons in Parliament assembled, ought to be discussed, adjudged, and determined." Indeed all the wisest statesmen and greatest lawyers, through a long succession, from Sir Edward Coke and Mr. Selden to the Earl of Hardwicke, have, whenever an opportunity has been offered to them, constantly repeated this doctrine. Nor is the authority of the Judges in Westminster wanting in its support.
4 Hatsell, Preface vi. See also Theodore Plucknett, "Impeachment and Attainder," *R.H.S.* (5th Ser. v. 3, 1953) 145, 147. Holdsworth remarks of the "idea" expressed in the 1388 Suffolk case that it "was long-lived." 1 Holdsworth 380n (3d ed. 1922).

Feerick states about the position "espoused in 1388" in the Suffolk case that "it had formally been rejected by the Lords as early as 1709," citing Hatsell 282–283. J. J. Feerick, "Impeaching Federal Judges: A Study of the Constitutional Provisions," 39 *Fordham L. Rev.* 1, 35n (1970). Hatsell does not confirm this reading. At the cited pages, Hatsell quoted a resolve of the Lords in the Sacheverell impeachment, "That they will proceed to the determination of the impeachment according to the law of the land, and the 'law and usage of Parliament.'" Hatsell 282. But after a search of the precedents, the Lords resolved to act "by the law and usage of

Some of the cases, as already observed, did not come to issue because the King prorogued or dissolved the Parliament; but although such royal interference balked conviction, it did not rob the parliamentary utterances of effect. Where such interference cut deep, as when Charles's pardon of Danby pending impeachment threatened to eviscerate the power, the Commons in due course embodied their protest in the Act of Settlement.[250] It is the long "course of Parliament" in disregard of royal interventions that should serve as the criterion. At times the Lords backed and filled, embracing attainder rather than impeachment, but it is not easy to evoke from the actions of the Lords an image of that body as the bulwark of liberties.[251] As Trevelyan noted of the Long Parliament—the cradle of English liberties—"it was the Commons who led, and the Lords who followed."[252] The resolute opposition of the Commons to royal absolutism and fawning favorites, its leadership in the struggle for freedom and parliamentary government (in no small part through the instrumentality of impeachment), plus the fact that it spoke for the commonality, lend to its charges a weight far beyond that ordinarily accorded to charges by a prosecutor.[253]

Parliament." Hatsell 283. In pronouncing judgment for the Lords, Lord Chancellor Cowper took account of the latter resolution and stated that "in their Lordships opinion (the law and usage of the High Court of Parliament 'being a part of the law of the land'.)" Hatsell 283n. This is also set forth in the record of the proceedings, 15 Howell 473 (1710). It scarcely adds up to repudiation of the 1388 (actually 1386) claim; and Hatsell's own preface regards the power as alive. Supra. It may be added that in 1811 Lord Ellenborough, C. J., stated, "if the *lex consuetodo Parliamenti* be, as Lord Coke and all the writers on the law have held that it is, a part of the law of the land in its large and extended sense." Burdett v. Abbott, 14 East. 1, 135, 104 E. R. 50, 553. Consequently there is no conflict between the "law of the land" and the *lex parliamentaria*.

250. Thereby they "removed the last barrier to Parliamentary control of ministers." Hill 277.

251. Roberts 436, regards the Lords as "standing sentinels to the law." Compare Tanner, supra, text accompanying n. 149. But see infra, Chapter II, n. 104.

252. Trevelyan 401. The consequence was that after the Restoration the place of the Lords "in the constitution could never be the same." Hill 223. The Commons again were in the vanguard in 1688: "The Commons were almost unanimously for dethroning James [II], and disregarding the claims of his son, while a majority of the Lords, with a strong feeling in favor of the divine right of kings, were desirous of some expedient whereby the immediate danger to religion and liberty might be warded off, without violating the order of succession to the crown." 4 Campbell, *Chancellors* 89. Compare supra, n. 109.

253. In the Clarendon proceedings Vaughan declared, "What this House shall charge is of more authority than the oaths of ordinary witnesses; peers, though not upon oath, are supposed to do right; so are we upon

This discussion of impeachment for high treason may fittingly close with the remarks of Solicitor General Somers, who was to become a noted Lord Chancellor and who spoke in an atmosphere removed from the turmoil and strife of an impeachment proceeding. The occasion was a debate on a proposed amendment by the Lords to a "Bill regulating Trials for High Treasons" adding a proviso which was objected to on the ground that it would interfere with the right of the Commons to proceed by impeachment for other treasons than those specified in 25 Edw. III. Somers said, "The security of your constitution is lost when you lose this power. The statute of 25 Edw. III did foresee that men would be above the law, and, I believe, did not take away those that were treasons at common law. *Seductio Regis* can be punished no otherwise than in Parliament." [254]

In sum, 25 Edw. III did not purport either to confer upon Parliament or to diminish its power judicially to declare retroactive treasons. Various reasons were advanced in the seventeenth-century Parliaments for the exercise of the power, but that the Commons steadily laid claim to the power, with the acquiescence in one form or another of the Lords, is fairly clear. Plainly an indictable treason was not the prerequisite of impeachment.

---

the reputation of our honesty and discretion." 6 Howell 328. The Lords themselves noted that impeachments by the Commons "are the groans of the people . . . and carry with them a greater supposition of guilt than any other accusation." Quoted 4 Hatsell 343, 333, 342.
254. *5 Parl. Hist. of England* 678, 712 (1691). Hampden the younger stated in the same debate: "The Lords are content that there should be no limitation of impeachment in parliament." Ibid. 676.

Chapter II

"HIGH CRIMES AND MISDEMEANORS"

When Congressman Gerald R. Ford proposed the impeachment of Justice William O. Douglas in April 1970, and asserted that an "impeachable offense" is whatever the House, with the concurrence of the Senate, "considers [it] to be",[1] he laid claim to an illimitable power that rings strangely in American ears. For illimitable power is alien to a Constitution that was designed to fence all power about.[2]

---

1. "What, then, is an impeachable offense? The only honest answer is that an impeachable offense is whatever a majority of the House of Representatives considers it to be at a given moment in history; conviction results from whatever offense or offenses two-thirds of the other body considers to be sufficiently serious to require removal of the accused from office . . . there are few fixed principles among the handful of precedents." 116 *Cong. Rec. H.* 3113–3114 (daily ed. April 15, 1970). Much earlier Judge Thomas Cooley stated that the offenses for which an officer "may be impeached are any such as in the opinion of the House are deserving of punishment under that process." 1 Thomas Cooley, *The General Principles of Constitutional Law* 205 (Boston, 4th ed. 1931). Benjamin Butler had made the same claim in the Andrew Johnson impeachment. Infra, Chapter IX, text accompanying n. 85.

2. James Iredell, "mastermind" of the North Carolina Ratification Convention, 2 George Bancroft, *History of the Formation of the Constitution of the United States of America* 348 (New York, 1882), and later a Justice of the Supreme Court, stated in an address published in 1786 respecting the formation of the North Carolina Constitution,

It was, of course, to be considered how to impose restrictions on the legislature . . . [to] guard against the abuse of unlimited power, which was not to be trusted, without the most imminent danger, to any man or body of men on earth. We had not only been sickened and disgusted for years with the high and almost impious language from Great Britain, of the omnipotent power of the British Parliament, but had severely smarted under its effects. We . . . should have been guilty of . . . the grossest folly, if in the same moment when we spurned at the *insolent despotism* of Great Britain, we had established a *despotic* power among ourselves.

Griffith J. McRee, *Life and Correspondence of James Iredell* 145–146 (New York, 1857–1858). The colonists were unceasingly concerned with the aggressiveness of power, "its endlessly propulsive tendency to expand itself beyond legitimate boundaries." Bailyn 56–57. George Mason stated in the Virginia Ratification Convention, "considering the natural lust for power so inherent in man, I fear the thirst for power will prevail to oppress

56

Article II §4 of the Constitution provides that "the President, Vice President and all civil officers of the United States, shall be removed from office on impeachment for, and conviction of, treason, bribery, or other high crimes and misdemeanors." Despite a plethora of discussion, the scope of the power thus conferred has not received adequate analysis.[3] Many questions remain unanswered. Did the Framers intend to confer unlimited power to impeach? Do the words "high crimes and misdemeanors" presuppose conduct punishable by the general criminal law, an indictable crime? Does the Constitution contemplate that impeachment shall be a criminal proceeding in any sense? Criminal or not, do the words "high crimes and misdemeanors" have ascertainable limits? If they have such limits, is an impeachment and conviction outside these limits reviewable by the courts? Impeachment is too important in the constitutional scheme to be left to the politicians; beyond the Senate's own precedents, the roots and constitutional history of impeachment need to be explored.

To understand what the Framers had in mind we must begin with English law, for nowhere did they more evidently take off from that law than in drafting the impeachment provisions. The very terms "impeachment . . . treason, bribery, or other high crimes and misdemeanors" were lifted bodily from English law. The age-old division of functions which assigned the role of prosecutor to the Commons while the Lords sat in judgment was the "model" of the parallel division of functions between the House of Representatives and the Senate.[4] Aware, in the words of James Wilson, that "numerous and dangerous excrescences" had disfigured the English law of treason, the Framers delimited and defined treason and thereby, as Wilson told the Penn-

---

the people." 3 Elliot 32. In his Farewell Address, President Washington adverted to the "love of power and proneness to abuse it." 1 Edwin Williams, *Addresses and Messages of the Presidents of the United States* 69, 74 (New York, 1846). Jefferson said, "173 despots would surely be as oppressive as one . . . An *elective despotism* was not the government we fought for." 3 Thomas Jefferson, *Writings* 222–224 (New York, Ford ed. 1892–1899). Madison quoted these remarks in *Federalist* No. 48 at 324. For similar remarks by other Founders, see Berger, *Congress v. Court* 34–35, 8–15.
3. See supra, Introduction, n. 35.
4. *Federalist* No. 65 at 425.

sylvania Ratification Convention, put it beyond the power of Congress to "extend the crime and punishment of treason." [5] They banned the related bill of attainder and corruption of blood; [6] they replaced an unimpeachable King with an impeachable President. Profiting from Charles II's pardon of the Earl of Danby,[7] they withheld from the President power to pardon an impeached officer. And of far-reaching importance, they separated impeachment from subsequent criminal prosecution [8] so that political passions no longer could sweep an accused to his death. As the Framers proceeded in the task of adapting impeachment to the American scene, the common law was for them indeed a "brooding omnipresence." [9]

The view that impeachment must rest upon a violation of existing criminal law [10] has the imprimatur of Blackstone; an impeachment, he stated, "is a prosecu-

5. 2 Wilson 663; 2 Elliot 469.

6. Constitution, Article I, §9 (3); Article III, §3 (2). For discussion of bills of attainder, see Chafee 9 et seq.; J. G. Bellamy, *The Law of Treason in England in the Later Middle Ages* 177–205 (Cambridge, 1970).

7. In the midst of his impeachment proceeding, the Earl of Danby produced a pardon from Charles II. The incident is recounted in Chafee 129, 132. The Commons were outraged, for, as Sir Francis Winnington, but lately Solicitor General, said, "An impeachment is of no purpose when a pardon shall stop our mouths." 11 Howell 751, 775. In 1700 the Act of Settlement, 12 & 13 Will. III, c. 2, §3, barred the pleading of a pardon to an impeachment, but not a pardon issued after conviction. 1 Joseph Chitty, *Criminal Law* 763 (New York, 5th Amer. ed. 1847).

8. Constitution, Article II, §2 (1).

9. James A. Bayard's great statement on behalf of the Managers in the impeachment of Senator William Blount (1797) deserves to be remembered: "On this subject, the Convention proceeded in the same manner it is manifest they did in many other cases. They considered the object of their legislation as a known thing, having a previous definite existence. Thus existing, their work was solely to mould it into a suitable shape . . . And, therefore, . . . it remains as at common law, with the variance only of the positive provisions of the Constitution . . . That law was familiar to all those who framed the Constitution. Its institutions furnished the principles of jurisprudence in most of the States . . . The members of the south would never have agreed to receive the local institutions of the north, as the common law of the States. But the first source from which all the colonies originally derived the principles of their law, was the only point of resort to which it could be expected that all would have recourse. We accordingly find many terms which cannot be understood, and many regulations which can not be executed without the aid of the common law of England." Wharton 264. See also Robert G. Harper and Jared Ingersoll, ibid. 299, 292; compare, infra, Chapter IV, n. 97.

10. This argument was made in the English treason impeachments which turned on the effect of the treason statute, 25 Edw. III. See supra, Chapter I, text accompanying nn. 192, 193. No comparable statute purported to define "high crimes and misdemeanors," either in England or the United States; and I found no English impeachment for "high crimes and misdemeanors" in which it appeared that the impeachment must fail for lack of an indictable crime. But compare the argument of Theodore Dwight, infra, Appendix A.

tion of the already known and established law." [11] His successor as Vinerian lecturer, Richard Wooddeson,[12] said that impeachments "are not framed to alter the law, but to carry it into more effectual execution"; they "are founded and proceed upon the law in being." [13] On the eve of President Andrew Johnson's impeachment, Theodore Dwight put the matter more sharply: "The decided weight of authority is, that no impeachment will lie except for a true crime . . . a breach of the common or statute law, which . . . would be the subject of indictment." [14] This, as we have seen, was not true of impeachments for high treason.

It is quite clear that the Dwight view has not won the assent of the Senate in impeachments for "high crimes and misdemeanors," for in a succession of "guilty" verdicts it has tacitly "settled" that impeachment lies for nonindictable offenses. Let the impeachment of district judge Halsted Ritter in 1936 serve as an example. Ritter was acquitted of charges under Articles I through VI, two of which (V and VI) charged income tax evasion made unlawful by statute. He was then convicted under Article VII, which charged that the consequence of his conduct was "to bring his court into scandal and disrepute, to the prejudice of said court and public confidence in the administration of justice." The conduct of which Article VII complained was "detailed in Articles I, II, III and IV hereof, and by his income tax evasion as set forth in articles V and VI. Wherefore the said Judge Halsted L. Ritter was and is guilty of high crimes and misdemeanors in office." Thus misconduct which fell sort of a specific criminal offense (for so the specific aquittals are to be

---

11. 4 Blackstone 259.
12. 2 Wooddeson 619 devoted a chapter to impeachment, which he thought the first "methodical compilation . . . on this subject." There were the Vinerian Lectures, commencing in 1777. He was much cited in our country.
13. 2 Wooddeson 611–12.
14. Theodore Dwight, "Trial by Impeachment," 6 *Am. L. Reg.* (N.S.) 257, 264 (1867). And, he continued, "It is asserted without fear of successful contradiction, both upon authority and principle, notwithstanding a few isolated instances apparently to the contrary, that no impeachment can be had where the King's Bench would not have held that a crime had been committed . . ." Ibid. He relied chiefly on the treason cases. Supra, n. 10. Chafee 148, stated, "so far as I know the Senate has faithfully adhered to the criminal character of impeachments when trying members of the Cabinet and judges."

understood) could yet constitute a "high crime and misdemeanor" because it degraded the court.

Were this doubtful, there is the statement of Hatton Sumners, chairman of the House Judiciary Committee, who was the leading Manager of the impeachment for the House: "We do not assume the responsibility . . . of proving that the respondent is guilty of a crime as that term is known to criminal jurisprudence. We do assume the responsibility of bringing before you a case, proven facts, the reasonable and probable consequences of which are to cause people to doubt the integrity of the respondent presiding as a judge." [15] It would be a

---

15. 80 *Cong. Rec.* 5469, 5602–06 (74th Cong. 2d Sess. 1936). In a "Memorandum on Impeachment of Federal Judges" filed by Simon H. Rifkind as counsel for Justice William O. Douglas with the Special Subcommittee on H. Res. 920 of the House Committee on the Judiciary (91st Con. 2d Sess. August 11, 1970) (hereinafter cited as Rifkind Memo), Mr. Rifkind cites the Ritter case to illustrate "our practice . . . to impeach only on the basis of charges which state criminal offenses," stating, "although the Senate narrowly failed to convict him on the specific criminal charges, it did convict him on a blanket charge which asserted that he was guilty of 'high crimes and misdemeanors in office,' specifically including 'income tax evasion.' " The acquittal of "specific criminal charges . . . including income tax evasion" under Articles V and VI, speaks against importation of criminal content into Article VII, which merely cites the preceding charges as illustrating conduct that brought the court into "scandal and disrepute."

Mr. Rifkind puts so strange a construction on several Senate precedents that it would be remiss to refrain from comment. He states of the 1803 impeachment and conviction of district judge John Pickering that "Although Judge Pickering had been hopelessly insane for three years, was an incurable drunkard, and had misconducted himself on the bench," the leaders of the impeachment "felt it necessary to couch their charges under the rubric "high Crimes and Misdemeanors." Rifkind Memo 26. Of course! Lacking "treason" or "bribery," impeachment can be brought only for "high crimes and misdemeanors." Mr. Rifkind begs the question when he regards such charges as proof of a "practice . . . to impeach only on the basis of charges which state criminal offenses." Rifkind Memo 26. That reading is refuted by the specific charges themselves. According to Mr. Rifkind, Pickering was charged "with three counts of wilfully violating a Federal statute relating to the posting of bond in certain attachment situations, and the misdemeanors of public drunkenness and blasphemy." Rifkind Memo 26. No federal statute made violation of the bond-posting statute a crime; nor did a federal statute make either drunkenness or blasphemy a crime. To assume that either drunkenness or blasphemy might be a crime by State law would make impeachment turn on whether a judge blasphemed or was drunk in one State rather than another. A system which did not provide for removal of a demented judge because insanity was not a "crime" would be sadly wanting. See infra, Chapter V.

The impeachment of Justice Samuel Chase in 1805, Mr. Rifkind states, "made it clear that to warrant impeachment actual criminal conduct must be shown . . ." Rifkind Memo 27. The Senate's verdict of "not guilty" is far from giving a "clear" indication that impeachment required an "indictable crime." So to read the cryptic verdict is to attribute to it an intention to overrule the Pickering impeachment of 1803, made the more difficult by the subsequent noncriminal convictions of judges Ritter and Archbald. For a detailed examination of the Chase impeachment, see infra, Chapter VIII.

In 1912, Judge Robert W. Archbald, was "charged with inducing railroads with cases pending before him to sell or lease to him certain coal properties; with accepting $500 from a coal operator

queer criminal jurisprudence that would permit the tribunal to find an accused guilty of a crime after the prosecution said it had no intention of proving a crime. The great preponderance of authority, including extrajudicial statements by Chief Justice Taft and Justice Hughes, regards "high crimes and misdemeanors" as not confined to criminal conduct.[16]

Nevertheless, to derive from the undeniably criminal terminology of the impeachment and associated provisions the proposition that impeachment may be based on noncriminal conduct is somewhat startling; [17] one

for seeking to persuade another railroad with a matter before him to lease certain coal properties to the operator, with generally speculating in coal properties while a member of the Commerce Court." Rifkind Memo 28–29. Manifestly such speculation did not constitute a "crime": nor did acceptance of the $500 to induce a lease to a third person. The inducement of leases to himself by railroads having cases pending before him trenches on "bribery," but the fact that "bribery" was not charged suggests that the House considered that the misconduct did not amount to that crime. The Constitution provides for impeachment for "bribery, or other high crimes and misdemeanors," thus differentiating between the two, and it is not for us to convert a charge of "high crimes and misdemeanors" into one for "bribery." Senator Elihu Root's explanation that he voted for conviction of a "high crime and misdemeanor" because Archbald used his office "to secure favors of money value for himself and his friends," Rifkind Memo 29, leaves unanswered whether he considered the misconduct to be a "criminal offense." When so accomplished a lawyer avoids use of the obvious terms "criminal offense" and restrains himself to the statutory "high crimes and misdemeanors" the implication is that he does not equate the two. For Chief Justice Taft's broad reading of the Archbald conviction, see infra, nn. 16 and 187. A catalogue of American impeachments may be found in Simpson 81 et seq.

16. Chief Justice Taft, in an address to the American Bar Association in 1913, said, "By liberal interpretation of the term 'high misdemeanors' which the Senate has given there is now no difficulty in securing removal of a judge for any reason that shows him unfit." Quoted by Merrill Otis, "A Proposed Tribunal: Is It Constitutional?" 7 *Kan. City L. Rev.* 3, 22 (1938). So too, Charles E. Hughes, *The Supreme Court of the United States* 19 (New York, 1928) stated: "According to the weight of opinion, impeachable offenses include, not merely acts that are indictable, but serious misbehavior which may be considered as coming within the category of high crimes and misdemeanors." Most commentators are in accord: Rawle 273; Joseph Story, *Commentaries on the Constitution of the United States* §800 (5th ed. Boston, 1905); 2 George Curtis, *History of the Formation of the Constitution of the United States* 260–261 (New York, 1861); Simpson 41–45; Otis 33; C. S. Potts, "Impeachment as a Remedy," 12 *St. Louis L. Rev.* 15, 23–26 (1927); Jacobus Ten Broek, "Partisan Politics and Federal Judeship Impeachments Since 1903," 23 *Minn. L. Rev.* 185, 193 (1939). A recent voice to the contrary is Frank Thompson and D. H. Pollitt, "Impeachment of Federal Judges: An Historical Overview," 49 *N. Car. L. Rev.* 87, 106, 117 (1970).

17. So seasoned a scholar as Charles Warren said of the Chase proceeding, "Its gravest aspect lay in the theory which the Republican leaders in the House had adopted, that impeachment was not a criminal proceeding but only a method of removal, the ground for which need not be a crime or misdemeanor as those terms were commonly understood." 1 Charles Warren, *The Supreme Court in United States History* 293 (Boston, 1922). On the other hand, Henry Adams earlier stated that a conclusion restricting impeachment "to misdemeanors, indictable at law" is "not to be resisted if the words of the Constitution were to be understood in a legal sense," but he considered that "Such a rule would have made impeachment

may therefore be indulged in the inquiry whether the convictions by the Senate have constitutional warrant. And if impeachment be in fact the sole avenue for removal of judges, we ought to know more about its elements and scope than can be derived from the Delphic Senate verdicts of "guilty" or "not guilty." The historian, as Plucknett said, "is left heir to the lawyer's unsolved conundrums." [18]

IMPEACHMENT AND INDICTABLE CRIMES

Because "crimes and misdemeanors" are familiar terms of criminal law,[19] it is tempting to conclude that "high crimes and misdemeanors" are simply ordinary crimes and misdemeanors raised to the nth degree. Apparently this is what Christian had in mind when, in a note to Blackstone, he explained that when used in impeachments the words "high crimes . . . have no definite signification, but are used merely to give greater solemnity to the charge." [20] In this he went astray. The phrase "high crimes and misdemeanors" is first met not in an ordinary criminal proceeding but in an impeachment, that of the Earl of Suffolk in 1386.[21] Impeachment itself was conceived because the objects of impeachment, for one reason or another, were beyond the reach of ordinary criminal redress. It was "es-

worthless for many cases where it was most likely to be needed; for comparatively few violations of official duty, however fatal to the State, could be brought within this definition." 2 Henry Adams, *History of the United States of America* 223 (New York, 1962). He thought it an absurdity that "unless a judge committed some indictable offense the people were powerless to protect themselves." 2 H. Adams, supra, 155–156.

18. Theodore Plucknett, "Impeachment and Attainder," *R. H. S.* (5th Ser. 1953, vol. 3) 145, 155.

19. Blackstone stated that "Crimes and misdemeanors . . . properly speaking, are mere synonymous terms." 4 Blackstone 5. But he was speaking too loosely, for crimes comprise both felonies and misdemeanors. Felonies were anciently punishable by death, ibid. 94, "while smaller faults and omissions of less consequence [than offenses "of a deeper and more atrocious dye"] are comprised under the gentler name of 'misdemeanors' only." Ibid. 5.

20. Edward Christian's note to 4 Blackstone 5. Chief Justice Bailey Aldrich said, "I have never been able to find out what a high misdemeanor was as distinguished from some other misdemeanor." Hearings on the Independence of Federal Judges before the Senate Subcommittee on Separation of Powers 369 (91st Cong. 2d Sess. April–May 1970). See infra. n. 108.

21. 1 Howell 89, 91; Simpson 86.

sentially a political weapon," [22] an outgrowth of the fact that from an early date the King and his Council were the "court for great men and great causes." [23] Before the Commons assumed the role of accuser late in the reign of Edward III (about 1376) of those charged with "treason or other high crimes and misdemeanors" against the State, private persons had been wont to turn to the Crown to institute proceedings before the High Court of Parliament when they were aggrieved by officers of the Crown in "high trust and power, and against whom they had no other redress than by application to Parliament." Such officers were persons of the "highest rank and favor with the Crown" or they were "in judicial or executive offices, whose elevated station placed them above the reach of complaint from private individuals." Before long the Commons became the prosecutor of the "highest and most powerful offenders against the State." [24] And in 1386 the Peers categorically asserted exclusive jurisdiction to try a peer for a high crime against the realm in the landmark proceeding against the Earl of Suffolk, and this not by the common law but by the course of Parliament.[25] The House of Lords was reminded of this history by Serjeant Pengelly during the impeachment of Lord Chancellor Macclesfield in 1725:

---

22. M. V. Clarke, "The Origin of Impeachment," in *Oxford Essays in Medieval History* 164, 185 (Oxford, 1934). For its subsequent use in the struggle to make Ministers of the Crown accountable to Parliament, see supra, Introduction, text accompanying nn. 6–12.

23. 1 Holdsworth 380 (3d ed. 1922). See also supra, Introduction, n. 4, and text accompanying nn. 50–53.

24. 4 Hatsell 63. Blackstone, notwithstanding his definition of impeachment as a prosecution of the "already known and established law," supra, text accompanying n. 11, stated that an administrator of "public affairs may infringe the rights of the people, and be guilty of such crimes, as the ordinary magistrate either does not or cannot punish," for which situation impeachment furnishes the remedy. 4 Blackstone 260. See also Roberts 7; Clarke, supra, n. 22 at 166; J. P. Kenyon, *The Stuart Constitution 1603–1688*, 93 (Cambridge, 1966); Theodore Plucknett, "State Trials under Richard II," *R. H. S.* (5th Ser. vol. 2, 1952) 159. To "devise a routine procedure for the trial of the king's ministers was perhaps the crowning achievement of Parliament in the fourteenth century." Clarke, supra, at 188.

25. The Lords declared "That in so high a crime . . . perpetrated by persons who are peers . . . the cause cannot be tried elsewhere but in parliament, nor by any other law or court except that of parliament," distinguishing the "process or order used in inferior courts . . . [only] intrusted with the execution of the ancient laws and customs of the realm, and the ordinances and establishments of parliament" from the "laws and course of parliament" by which the Lords would decide. 1 Howell 113. For the full quotation, see supra, Chapter I, text accompanying n. 22.

your lordships are now exercising a power of judicature reserved in the original frame of the English constitution for the punishment of offenses of a public nature, which may affect the nation; as well in instances where the inferior courts have no power to punish the crimes committed by ordinary rules of justice; as in cases within the jurisdiction of the courts of Westminster-hall, where the person offending is by his degree, raised above the apprehension of danger, from a prosecution carried on in the usual course of justice; and whose exalted station requires the united accusation of all the Commons.[26]

At the time when the phrase "high crimes and misdemeanors" is first met in the proceedings against the Earl of Suffolk in 1386, there was in fact no such crime as a "misdemeanor." Lesser crimes were prosecuted as "trespasses" well into the sixteenth century, and only then were "trespasses" supplanted by "misdemeanors" as a category of ordinary crimes.[27] As "trespasses" itself suggests, "misdemeanors" derived from torts or private wrongs; and Fitzjames Stephen stated in 1863 that "prosecutions for misdemeanor are to the Crown what actions for wrongs are to private persons." [28] In addition, therefore, to the gap of 150 years that separates "misdemeanors" from "high misdemeanors," there is a sharp functional division between the two. "High crimes and misdemeanors" were a category of *political* crimes against the state,[29] whereas "misdemeanors" described criminal sanctions for *private* wrongs. An intuitive sense of the difference is exhibited in the development of English law, for though "misdemeanor" entered into the ordinary criminal law, it did not become the cri-

---

26. 16 Howell 1330. Almost fifty years later this was the lesson drawn from the State Trials by John Adams: "without this high jurisdiction it was thought impossible to defend the constitution against princes, nobles, and great ministers, who might commit high crimes and misdemeanors which no other authority would be powerful enough to prevent or punish." 2 Adams 330.

27. 2 Holdsworth 357, 365 (4th ed. 1936); 3 Holdsworth 263 n. 1 (1st ed. 1909); 4 Holdsworth 512 (1924). See also Plucknett, *Concise History* 458–459; cf. Sir. J. F. Stephen, *The Criminal Law of England* 58 (London, 1863).

28. Stephen, supra, n. 27 at 60.

29. For England, see infra, text accompanying nn. 32–35, 37–38, 62–91; for United States, see infra, text accompanying nn. 110–111, n. 111, and text accompanying n. 132.

terion of "high misdemeanor" in the parliamentary law of impeachment.[30] Nor did either "high crimes" or "high misdemeanors" find their way into the general criminal law of England.[31] As late as 1757 Blackstone could say that "the first and principal [high misdemeanor] is the *mal-administration* of such high officers, as are in the public trust and employment. This is usually punished by the method of parliamentary impeachment." Other high misdemeanors, he stated, are contempts against the King's prerogative, against his person and government, against his title, "not amounting to treason," in a word, "political crimes." [32] Treason is plainly a "political" crime, an offense against the State; so too bribery of an officer attempts to corrupt administration of the State. Indeed, early in the common law bribery "was sometimes viewed as high treason." [33] Later Hawkins referred to "great Bribes . . . and . . . other such like misdemeanors"; and Parliament itself regarded bribery as a "high crime and misdemeanor." [34] In addition to this identification of bribery, first with "high treason" and then with "misdemeanor," the association, as a matter of construction, of "other high crimes and misdemeanors" with "treason, bribery," which are unmistakably "political" crimes, lends them a similar connotation under the maxim *noscitur a sociis*.[35]

---

30. Appreciation of the difference was later exhibited by Governor Johnston in the North Carolina Convention: "If an officer commits an offense against an individual, he is amenable to the courts of law. If he commits crimes against the state, he may be indicted and punished. Impeachment only extends to high crimes and misdemeanors in a public office. It is a mode of trial pointed out for great misdemeanors against the public." 4 Elliot 48. See similar remarks by James Wilson, infra, text accompanying n. 111. In a fairly extensive reading of English impeachment cases, I found no argument, with the possible exception of the Macclesfield case, infra, Appendix A, that a "high crime and misdemeanor" was or was not made out because it was or was not a misdemeanor at common law.

31. At least I could turn up no instance in a search of the texts of Chitty, Holdsworth, Russell, Stephen, the *Abridgments* of Bacon and Viner, and the *Comyns' Digest*.

32. 4 Blackstone 121–123. See also infra, n. 108. Since the word "political" also appears in "political weapon," it is to be noted that the latter describes the use of impeachment by Parliament in order to make ministers accountable to it, whereas "political crimes" describes misconduct in office as distinguished from ordinary crimes.

33. 1 William Hawkins, *History of Pleas of the Crown*, Ch. 67, §6, p. 169 (London, 1716).

34. Ibid. Ch. 67, §7, p. 170; 4 Campbell, *Lord Chancellors* 55.

35. Neal v. Clark, 95 U.S. 704, 708–709 (1877); McCulloch v. Maryland, 17 U.S. (4 Wheat.) 316, 418 (1819).

In sum, "high crimes and misdemeanors" appear to be words of art confined to impeachments, without roots in the ordinary criminal law and which, so far as I could discover, had no relation to whether an indictment would lie in the particular circumstances.[36] For this Wooddeson himself furnishes collateral evidence when he states that impeachments are framed to execute the law where it is "not easily discovered in the ordinary course of jurisdiction by reason of the peculiar quality of the alleged crimes." [37] What lends a "peculiar" quality to these crimes is the fact that they are not encompassed by criminal statutes or, for that matter, by the common law cases, as his own illustrations disclose:

if the judges mislead their sovereign by unconstitutional opinions . . . where a lord chancellor has been thought to put the seal to an ignominious treaty . . . a privy councillor to propound or support pernicious or dishonorable measures, or a confidential adviser of his sovereign to obtain exorbitant grants . . . these imputations have properly occasioned impeachments; because it is apparent how little the ordinary tribunals are calculated to take cognizance of such offences, or to investigate and reform the general policy of the state.[38]

---

36. The Solicitor General reminded the Lords in the trial of Lord Arundel (1678) that the "trial of a Peer in Parliament is more ancient than by indictment." 4 Hatsell 141n. In the 14th century redress for "wrongs done by the king's servants" was "outside the sphere of the common law." Parliament was dissatisfied with the niceties of an indictment and a "system which served to shelter offenders who were either highly placed or guilty of offenses beyond the plain man's understanding." Clarke, supra, n. 22 at 166, 173. See also supra, n. 24. The analogy of trial by Parliament to "trial upon indictment," remarks Plucknett, was "clearly" not obvious to the 14th century lawyer. Theodore Plucknett, "The Impeachments of 1376," *R. H. S.* 153 (5th Ser. vol. 1, 1951). In Grantham v. Gordon, 1 Peere Williams 612, 616, 24 E. R. 539, 541 (1719), the court stated, "impeachments in Parliament differed from indictments, and might be justified by the law and course of Parliament." Wooddeson suggests that this refers solely to matters of procedure, 2 Wooddeson, supra, n. 12 at 606n, a matter that is by no means clear. My own study of the treason trials convinced me that the hotly debated issue was whether the power of Parliament extended to retrospective declarations of treason, i.e., substantive law. In fourteenth-century treason cases, Parliament laid claim to "a supreme jurisdiction, in which it was bound by none of the law and rules which restricted the *power* and regulated the procedure of the other courts." Samuel Rezneck, "The Early History of the Parliamentary Declaration of Treason," 42 *Eng. Hist. Rev.* 497, 510 (1927) (emphasis added). See also supra, Chapter I.
37. 2 Wooddeson 611–612.
38. Ibid. 602–603.

One would search in vain for a statute that made it a crime to render an "unconstitutional" opinion, or to obtain large grants such as an overindulgent sovereign was wont to make to a spoiled favorite, for example, the Duke of Buckingham.[39] And there were no common law cases which declared such acts to be criminal if only because the circumstances involved great ministers who were in the parliamentary preserve.

The cases which declared misconduct in office to be criminal are not to the contrary. Misconduct in office is first met as a common law crime late in the seventeenth century,[40] but the crime was apparently confined to lesser officials who were almost never the subjects of impeachment. No case turned up in my search of the Abridgments in which a minister had been indicted for misconduct in office; one may fairly conclude that indictability was not the test of impeachment of a minister.[41] Nor was it the test of impeachment of a Justice. Caesar Rodney could justly twit counsel for Justice Chase with not having "adduced a single case where a judge of one of their [England's] superior courts has been indicted for any malconduct in office," and "defy them to show an example of the kind," [42] for Luther Martin had in truth failed to make out the contrary.[43] In part, this may be traced to the fact that the Justices were a very small "elite group," originally a part of the King's entourage, who accompanied him on his travels; only later did they come to rest at Westminster Hall [44] and, like the ministers of the King, they were deemed

39. See Article 12 of the articles of impeachment of the Duke of Buckingham, 2 Howell 1307, 1316–1318; Simpson, 101, 104.
40. "If a man be made an officer by Act of Parliament, and misbehave himself in his office, he is indictable for it at common law; and any public officer is indictable for misbehavior in his office." Anonymous, 6 Mod. 96, 87 E. R. 853 (1704). See also Regina v. Wyat, 1 Salk. 380, 91 E. R. 331 (1706) (neglect of duty); Rex & Regina. v. Barlow, 2 Salk 609, 91 E. R. 516 (1694); Rex v. Davis, Sayer 163, 96 E. R. 839 (1754).
41. The treason cases do not, in my view, shake this proposition. See supra, Chapter I. For discussion of two "high crimes and misdemeanors" cases see infra, Appendix A.
42. 14 Ann. Cong. 599–600 (1805); the point had earlier been made by Congressman G. W. Campbell, ibid. 343.
43. For analysis of Martin's citations, see infra, Appendix B.
44. The early judges "were not ministerial officers of low rank, but the men closest to the king, so close, indeed, that they could readily embody his most characteristic function of doing justice." Radin, Anglo-American History. John P. Dawson, Oracles of the Law 1–2 (Ann Arbor, Mich., 1968).

triable only by the Lords.[45] In part, the continuing absence of such indictments may be due to over-broad dicta of judicial immunity uttered by Coke in *Floyd v. Barker*. That was a private action against a judge of assize for conspiring to injure the plaintiff, and it was held that neither such a Judge, nor "any other Judge . . . of record" could be charged for "that which he did openly in Court as Judge." His conduct could not be drawn in question "at the suit of the parties" nor, said Coke by way of dictum, "before any other Judge at the suit of the King." Although Coke put to one side the case of a judge who had conspired "out of court" as "extra-judicial," although he leaned heavily on the sanctity of the record—"records are of so high a nature, that for their very sublimity they import verity in themselves"—he undercut his circumspection by saying that "for any surmise of corruption" the judge should be answerable only "before the King himself." [46] Complaint should be made to Parliament, later said Chief Justice Vaughan, for "corrupt and dishonest judgments," [47] a view reaffirmed still later by Chief Justice Wilmot.[48] Coke's "verity of the record" was translated into a rule that no indictment of a judge could be allowed to "defeat the record," a phrase anticipated by Fitzherbert's "it seemeth he might be indicted for taking of money . . . which doth not destroy and defeat the Record. *Quaere*." [49]

One might therefore expect to find indictments against High Court Justices for bribery, particularly because statutes had from earliest times penalized judicial bribery; [50] indeed for a long time the offense

---

45. Supra, text accompanying nn. 23–26; and see infra, text accompanying n. 52.
46. 12 Co. 23–25, 77 E. R. 1305–1307 (Star Chamber, 1608).
47. Bushell's Case, Vaughan 135, 139, 124 E. R. 1006–1008 (1673).
48. Rex v. Almon, Wilm. 243, 259, 97 E. R. 94, 101 (1765). See also Hammond v. Howell, 2 Mod. 218, 220, 221, 86 E. R. 1035, 1036–1037 (1678) (per Hale, C. J.). In an extensive review of the cases, Taafe v. Downs (1813), published as a note to Calder v. Halkett, 3 Moo. P. C. 37, 48, 13 E. R. 16, 23 (1839), concluded that the judges of the superior courts are "only answerable for their judicial conduct in the high Court of Parliament."
49. Anthony Fitzherbert, *Natura Brevium* *243 (1534) (Eng. trans. 1652), p. 605.
50. It is one of the curiosa of history that these statutes were probably ineffective, so that Stephen justifiably states that there is "no statute against" bribery, but that "it has ever been an offense against common law." 3 Stephen 250. The statutes are discussed infra, Appendix C.

was criminal only when judges and judicial officers were involved.[51] But here too I found no indictments against Justices of the high courts. Two of the earliest cases, of Chief Justice Hengham (1289) and Chief Justice Thorpe (1349), which antedate the use of impeachments, were brought before the Lords,[52] as was then customary in the case of high officers of the Crown. Broad statements by Hawkins and others that bribery was punishable by fine and imprisonment will be found to refer to impeachments,[53] as when Lord Chancellor Bacon was charged with bribery.[54]

While the protection of "the Superior Courts is absolute and universal," said Chief Justice Grey in 1764, "with respect to the inferior [courts], it is only while they act within their jurisdiction." [55] Lesser judges, and among that category were some we should scarcely recognize as such today—for example, censors of the College of Physicians, a coroner— [56] were prosecutable for acts outside their jurisdiction.[57] Even when they

---

51. Bribery, stated Coke, 3 *Institutes* 147, is "only committed by him that hath a judicial place." And see 1 Hawkins ch. 67, §§1, 2, p. 168.

52. 1 Campbell, *Justices* 76, 91–92.

53. 1 Hawkins ch. 67, §7, p. 170. Among Hawkins' citations is John Rushworth's *Historical Collections*, pt. 1, fol. 31 (1659), which deals with the impeachment of Francis Bacon for bribery. Jenkins 162, 145 E. R. 104 (Exch. Ch. undated), states that "if a judge of record takes bribes, he shall be indicted for it," citing *FNB* 243, 8 H. 6, cap, 12, and 27 E. 3. *Fitzherbert* (*FNB*), supra, text accompanying n. 49 cites no case for the statement that in a case which does not "defeat the record" "it seemeth" the offense is indictable, and himself adds a "Quaere." 8 Hen. VI, ch. 12 (3) makes the stealing of a judicial record by a "Clerk, or by other person," indictable, the judges to hear such cases; but Coke, 3 *Institutes* 72, states: "This act does not extend to any judge of the court." Nothing contained in 27 Edw. III has any bearing on the indictment of a judge for bribery.

54. 2 Howell 1087. Apparently the current shifted in the 19th century. When Sir Jonah Barrington, Judge of the High Court of Admiralty in Ireland, was under investigation by the House of Commons, his counsel, Thomas Denman, later Chief Justice, urged that a criminal information "could have been filed." The Solicitor General explained that no criminal prosecution was instituted because of the "advanced age and . . . many infirmities" of the judge. 24 Parl. Debates 966, 968 (Hansard, N. S. 1830). Holdsworth states that the offices of the Judges of the High Court who hold during good behavior, "may, it is said, be determined, for want of good behavior, without an address to the Crown, either by scire facias . . . criminal information or impeachment." Part VI of 6 Halsbury, *Laws of England* 609 (Hailsham ed. 1932). This section on "Constitutional Law" is attributed to Holdsworth.

55. Miller v. Seare, 2 W. Bl 1141, 1145, 96 E. R. 673, 675 (1764); cf. Calder v. Halkett, 3 Moo. C. P. 28, 35, 13 E.R. 12, 15 (1839).

56. Groenevelt v. Burwell, 1 Salk. 396, 91 E. R. 343 (1701) (censors "are Judges of Record because they can fine and imprison"); "The Court of the Coroner is a Court of Record of which the Coroner is the Judge." Garnett v. Ferrand, 6 B. & C. 611, 625, 108 E. R. 576, 581 (1827); cf. Ashby v. White, 6 Mod. 46, 47, 87 E. R. 810, 811 (1704) (vote-counting sheriff is "quasi a judge").

57. Rex v. Jones, 1 Wils. K. B. 7, 95 E. R. 462 (1743); cf. King v. Holland & Forster, 1 Term. R. 692, 99 E. R. 1324 (1787).

acted within their jurisdiction, lesser judges were punishable at the suit of the King if they had acted corruptly; [58] and if what they did was illegal, they were indictable "without the addition of any corrupt motives," despite the presence of jurisdiction.[59] Additionally they were punishable by attachment. King's Bench, said Bacon's Abridgment, "exercises a superintendency over all inferior courts, and may grant an attachment against the Judges of such courts for oppressive, unjust, or irregular practice contrary to the obvious rules of natural justice." [60] Such conduct was viewed as a contempt; and Chief Justice Holt recalled that "the Mayor of Hereford was laid by the heels for sitting in judgment in a cause where he himself was lessor of the plaintiff in ejectment [and "gave judgment for his own lessee"] though he by the Charter was the sole Judge of the Court." [61] Thus it results that Justices, who were *not* the subject of indictment, were impeachable and in fact impeached, whereas the indictable lesser judges, so far as I could find, were not impeached. What the Framers might have made of this dichotomy is hereafter discussed.

THE SCOPE OF "HIGH CRIMES AND MISDEMEANORS"

Although English impeachments did not require an indictable crime they were nonetheless criminal proceedings because conviction was punishable by death, imprisonment, or heavy fine. The impeachable offense, however, was not a statutory or ordinary common law crime but a crime by "the course of Parliament," the *lex Parliamentaria*. The following charges drawn from impeachment cases disclose that impeachable miscon-

58. 2 Hawkins ch. 13, §20, p. 85. In 1827 Tenterden, C. J., stated: "Corruption is quite another matter, so also are neglect of duty and misconduct in it. For these I trust there is always will be some due course of punishment by public prosecution." Garnett v. Ferrand, 6 B. & C. 611, 626, 108 E. R. 576, 582 (1827).
59. King v. Saintsbury, 4 Term. R. 450, 457, 100 E. R. 1113, 1117 (1791).
60. 3 Bacon's *Abridgment*, "Offices and Officers" (N) p. 744 (London, 3d ed. 1768).
61. Anonymous, 1 Salk. 396, 91 E. R. 343 (1699); Anonymous, 1 Salk. 201, 91 E. R. 180 (1702).

duct was patently not "criminal" in the ordinary sense; they furnish a guide to the "course of Parliament"; and they give content to the phrase "high crimes and misdemeanors."

Chancellor Michael de la Pole, Earl of Suffolk (1386), high crimes and misdemeanors: applied appropriated funds to purposes other than those specified.[62]

Duke of Suffolk (1450), treason and high crimes and misdemeanors: procured offices for persons who were unfit and unworthy of them; delayed justice by stopping writs of appeal (private criminal prosecutions) for the deaths of complainants' husbands.[63]

Attorney General Yelverton (1621), high crimes and misdemeanors: committed persons for refusal to enter into bonds before he had authority so to require; commencing but not prosecuting suits.[64]

Lord Treasurer Middlesex (1624), high crimes and misdemeanors: allowed the office of Ordnance to go unrepaired though money was appropriated for that purpose; allowed contracts for greatly needed powder to lapse for want of payment.[65]

Duke of Buckingham (1626), misdemeanors, misprisions, offenses, and crimes: though young and inexperienced, procured offices for himself, thereby blocking the deserving; neglected as great admiral to safeguard the seas; procured titles of honor to his mother, brothers, kindred.[66]

Justice Berkley (1637), treason and other great misdemeanors: reviled and threatened the grand jury for presenting the removal of the communion table in All Saints

---

62. 1 Howell 89, 93, Art. 3. In each of the listed cases, the charge or charges are selected from a group.
63. 4 Hatsell 60n. Several treason charges are included because charges that fell short of treason might yet amount to misdemeanor. Charles I, attempting to save Strafford from the deadly charge of treason, told the assembled Lords and Commons, "I cannot condemn him of High-Treason; yet I cannot say I can clear him of Misdemeanor . . . for matter of Misdemeanor, I am so clear in that . . . that I do think my Lord of Strafford is not fit hereafter to serve Me or the Commonwealth in any place of trust." 8 Rushworth 734.
64. 2 Howell 1136, 1137, Art. 1 and 6.
65. Ibid. 1183, 1239.
66. Ibid. 1307, 1308, 1310, 1316, Art. 1, 4 and 11.

Church; on the trial of an indictment, he "did much discourage complainants' counsel" and "did overrule the cause for matter of law." [67]

Sir Richard Gurney, lord mayor of London (1642), high crimes and misdemeanors: thwarted Parliament's order to store arms and ammunition in storehouses.[68]

Viscount Mordaunt (1660), high crimes and misdemeanors: prevented Tayleur from standing for election as a burgess to serve in Parliament; caused his illegal arrest and detention.[69]

Peter Pett, Commissioner of the Navy (1668), high crimes and misdemeanors: negligent preparation for the Dutch invasion; loss of a ship through neglect to bring it to mooring.[70]

Chief Justice North (1680), high crimes and misdemeanors: assisted the Attorney General in drawing a proclamation to suppress petitions to the King to call a Parliament.[71]

Chief Justice Scroggs (1680), treason and high misdemeanors: discharged grand jury before they made their presentment, thereby obstructing the presentment of many Papists; arbitrarily granted general warrants in blank.[72]

Sir Edward Seymour (1680), high crimes and misdemeanors: applied appropriated funds to public purposes other than those specified.[73]

Duke of Leeds (1695), high crimes and misdemeanors: as president of Privy Council accepted 5,500 guineas from the East India Company to procure a charter of confirmation.[74]

---

67. 3 Howell 1283, 1287, 1288.
68. 4 Howell 159, 162–163, Art. 4.
69. 6 Howell 785, 789, 790–791, Art. 1 and 5.
70. Ibid. 865, 866, 867, Art. 1 and 5.
71. 4 Hatsell 115–116. For details, see 3 Campbell, *Chancellors*, 460–461.
72. Originally Scroggs was charged only with "high Misdemeanors," among them brow-beating witnesses, prejudicing the jury against them by disparaging remarks. 8 Howell 163–169, Art. 2 and 3. The charges were enlarged to "High Treason and other Great Crimes and Misdemeanors," ibid. 197.
73. Ibid. 127–131, Art. 1.
74. 13 Howell 1263, 1269, Art. 1.

In addition to the foregoing, there is the familiar summary by Wooddeson, paraphrased by Story in his discussion of impeachment: [75]

lord chancellors and judges and other magistrates have not only been impeached for bribery, and acting grossly contrary to the duties of their office, but for misleading their sovereign by unconstitutional opinions and for attempts to subvert the fundamenal laws, and introduce arbitrary power. So where a lord chancellor has been thought to have put the great seal to an ignominious treaty; [76] a lord admiral to have neglected the safeguard of the sea; [77] an ambassador to have betrayed his trust; a privy councillor to have propounded or supported pernicious or dishonorable measures; [78] or as confidential adviser to his sovereign to have obtained exorbitant grants or incompatible employments; [79] these have all been deemed impeachable offenses.

The foregoing examples by no means exhaust the list which could be adduced to illustrate that English impeachments did proceed for misconduct that was not "criminal" in the sense of the general criminal law.[80]

These charges fulfill an even more important purpose —they serve, broadly speaking, to delineate the outlines of "high crimes and misdemeanors." For they are reducible to intelligible categories: misapplication of funds (Earl of Suffolk, Seymour), abuse of official

75. 1 Story §800; 2 Wooddeson 602. In some of these cases the charge was treason.
76. Lord Chancellor Somers sealed the Partition Treaties at the King's command. 4 Campbell, *Chancellors* 142; Roberts 311 (high crimes and misdemeanors).
77. Duke of Buckingham as Great Admiral, 2 Howell 1267, 1307, 1310, Art. 4 (1626) (misdemeanor).
78. Infra, text accompanying n. 91. "The author of The Method of the Proceedings in the Houses of Lords and Commons in Cases of Impeachment for High Treason (3d ed. 1715) observed 'That almost in every considerable and legal impeachment since Charles the First, the giving of "evil advice" to the Prince has been the foundation of the accusation and has bore hardest upon the person accused.'" Roberts 396 n. 1.
79. Duke of Buckingham, 2 Howell 1308, Art. 1. So too, the Duke of Suffolk was impeached for advising the grant of a peerage to the husband of his niece, for procuring offices for persons who were unfit and unworthy of them. 4 Hatsell 59–60 (treason).
80. Other charges of similar import may be found in Simpson's convenient summary of English impeachments. Simpson 81–190. See also infra, Chapter VI, text accompanying nn. 9–17.

power (Duke of Suffolk, Buckingham, Berkley, Yelverton, Mordaunt, Scroggs), neglect of duty (Buckingham, Pett),[81] encroachment on or contempts of Parliament's prerogatives (Gurney, North, the Ship-Money Tax opinions).[82] Then there are a group of charges which can be gathered under the rubric "corruption," as when Lord Treasurer Middlesex was charged with "corruption, shadowed under pretext of a New Year's-Gift," and with "using the power of his place, and countenance of the king's service, to wrest [from certain persons] a lease and estate of great value." [83] So too, Middlesex, and much earlier the Earl of Suffolk, were charged with obtaining property from the King for less than its value.[84] Buckingham, Danby, the Earl of Arlington, Earl of Orford, Lord Somers, and Lord Halifax were charged with procuring large gifts from the King to themselves.[85] Buckingham, Sir William Penn, Seymour, and Orford were charged with conversion of public property.[86] Lord Chancellor Macclesfield was charged with the sale of public offices.[87] Lord Halifax was accused of "opening a way to all manner of corrupt practices in the future management of the revenues" by appointing his brother to an office which had been designed as a check on his own, the profits to be held in trust for Halifax.[88] There were charges of betrayal of trust, as when Buckingham put valuable

---

81. The Earl of Orford was charged in 1701 with neglect of duty in that he permitted French ships to return safely to their harbors. 14 Howell 241, 243–244, Art. 8.

82. Justice Berkley and other Justices were impeached for uttering opinions that Charles I could obtain "Ship Money Taxes" without resort to Parliament. 3 Howell 1283, 1285–1286, Art. 4–7 (1637); and see infra, note 175. See also the impeachment of Sir Thomas Gardiner, Recorder of London, 4 Howell 167, Art. 1 (1642). Other encroachments may be exemplified by Gardiner's efforts to hinder the calling of Parliament, Art. 5, and his threats against those who sought to petition Parliament, Art. 6, ibid. 169; and by Sir Richard Halford's resistance to arrest under a warrant of Parliament. 4 Howell 171 (1642).

83. 2 Howell 1228, 1199 (1624). There is also a charge of corruption in that Middlesex bought assets conveyed by the King for the benefit of creditors at much less than their value. Ibid. 1233–1244.

84. Ibid. 1230; Suffolk, 1 Howell 89, 91, Art. I (1388).

85. Buckingham: 2 Howell 1307, 1316–1318, Art. 12 (1626); Arlington: 6 Howell 1053, 1055, Art. 2 (1674); Danby: 11 Howell 599, 626, Art. 6 (1678); Orford: 14 Howell 241, Art. 1 (1701); Somers, 14 Howell 250, 255–258, Art. 8 (1701); Halifax: 14 Howell 293–295, Art. 1 and 3 (1701).

86. Buckingham: 2 Howell 1307, 1311–1312, Art. 5 (1626); Penn: 6 Howell 873–874, Art. 1–3 (1668); Seymour: 8 Howell 127, 136–137, Art. 4 (1680); Orford: 14 Howell 241–242, Art. 2–4 (1701).

87. Supra, n. 41.

88. 14 Howell 293, 296–297, Art. 5 (1701).

ships within the grasp of the French,[89] and when Orford weakened the navy while invasion threatened.[90] And there were charges against Orford, Somers, Halifax, Viscount Bolingbroke, the Earl of Strafford, and the Earl of Oxford of giving pernicious advice to the Crown.[91]

Broadly speaking, these categories may be taken to outline the boundaries of the phrase "high crimes and misdemeanors" at the time the Constitution was adopted.[92] The importance of these categories for American law derives from two facts: (1) when the Framers employed language having a common law meaning it was expected that those terms would be given their common law content; [93] (2) they considered that the phrase had a "limited," "technical meaning." [94]

Today impeachment and severe punishment for giving "bad advice" seems extravagant. It derived in part from the postulated inviolability of the King, which compelled attribution of his misdeeds to his ministers.[94a] In course of time it became a weapon in the struggle to make ministers accountable to the Parliament rather than the King, to punish them for espousing policies disliked by the Parliament. And it was watered by a deep distaste for "favorites," understandable enough when one views the luckless adventures upon which Buckingham, for example, had embarked the nation.[95]

---

89. 2 Howell 1307, 1313–1314, Art. 7 (1626).
90. 14 Howell 241, 243, Art. 6 (1701); see also charges of betrayal of trust against the Earl of Arlington, 6 Howell 1053–1056, Art. 3 (1674).
91. Orford: 14 Howell 241, 244, Art. 9 (1701); Somers: ibid. 250, 252, Art. 1; Halifax: ibid. 293, 297–298, Art. 6 (1701); Bolingbroke: 15 Howell 994, 997, Art. 2 (1715); Strafford: ibid. 1013, 1023–1024, Art. 6 (1715); Oxford: ibid. 1045, 1063–1065, Art. 2–3 (1717). Additionally Bolingbroke and Oxford were charged with high treason. See supra, n. 78. In the North Carolina Ratification Convention James Iredell noted that the King could be reached and that "Everything . . . that the king does, must be by some *advice*, and the adviser of course answerable." 4 Elliot 109. See also infra, text accompanying n. 169.
92. Although the bulk of the foregoing examples involve "official" misconduct, I do not suggest that impeachment did not lie for out-of-office misconduct. See infra, Chapter VI. Setting aside several cases in which no charges exist, several impeachments of non-officers, and some combined charges of "high treason and high crimes and misdemeanors" which stress traitorous conduct, there were in all eighteen impeachments for high crimes and misdemeanors listed by Simpson in what purports to be a complete list of impeachments. Simpson 81 et seq.
93. Infra, text accompanying n. 160; and nn. 160, 161.
94. Infra, text accompanying nn. 157–159.
94a. Supra, Introduction, n. 7. See Iredell, supra, n. 91.
95. The dissolute Duke of Buckingham, whose "boundless influence over both James I and Charles I was one of the greatest calamities which ever

When Oxford, Bolingbroke, and Strafford were impeached (1715) [96] for giving "bad advice" to the King, the Commons "really sought to condemn policies which they believed pernicious to the realm," [97] the negotiation of a separate "treacherous peace," the Treaty of Utrecht.[98] The nation, said Trevelyan, "little liked the secret negotiations with France behind the back of the allies . . . the disgrace of Marlborough, and the withdrawal of the British armies from the field in the face of the enemy." [99]

Not all of the cited impeachments eventuated in verdicts of guilty by the House of Lords. Some did result in convictions; [100] in some cases the accused were saved by the intervention of the King, who prorogued or dissolved Parliament. The odious Scroggs was thus rescued by the abrupt dissolution of Parliament, as were Mordaunt, Seymour, and Buckingham. Is the impeachment of Buckingham robbed of precedential value because it was thwarted by a foolishly obstinate King who was beating his own path to the scaffold? [101] On a number of occasions the Commons stayed its hand, as when Chief Justice Kelynge groveled in abject apology before its bar; [102] or when it referred the trial of the Earl of

hit the English throne," Chafee 46, illustrates why "favorites have always been highly odious." 2 Thomas B. Macaulay, *Critical & Historical Essays* 817 (London, 1890). His domination "brought the royal regime into hatred and contempt." Zagorin 59. He sought to promote a match between Charles I and the Spanish Infanta, which the English heartily disliked for they "saw in Spain the national enemy and the supreme menace to continental Protestantism," ibid. 63, let alone that it "would lead to Spanish heirs and Catholic Kings who would endeavor to undo the work of Elizabeth." Trevelyan 388, 389. The "monopolisation of patronage by Buckingham did much to cause . . . the split in the ruling class, which made possible the Civil War." Hill 71.

96. Oxford: 15 Howell 1045 (1717); Bolingbroke: ibid. 994 (1715); Strafford: ibid. 1013 (1715).

97. Roberts 395.

98. Ibid. 385.

99. Trevelyan 499; Winston Churchill, *Marlborough: His Life and Times* 890 (New York, abr. ed. 1968), states: "Forty years later, William Pitt . . . feeling the odium which still clung to England and infected her every public pledge, pronounced the stern judgment that 'Utrecht was an indelible reproach to the last generation.'"

100. Earl of Suffolk: supra, text accompanying n. 62; Lord Treasurer Middlesex: supra, text accompanying n. 65; Sir Richard Gurney: supra, text accompanying n. 68; the Duke of Suffolk was banished by the King. 1 Howell 271, 274 (1451).

101. Scroggs: 8 Howell 216; Mordaunt: 6 Howell 806; Seymour: 8 Howell 162; Buckingham: 2 Howell 1446–1447. In Buckingham's case, "Charles preferred to invite a challenge to his sole control of executive power than to surrender a favorite." Roberts 441.

102. 2 Campbell, *Justices* 170; Churchill, supra, n. 99 at 861. So too, the Commons turned down a proposal to impeach the Duke of Leeds, Lord Treasurer. 4 Hatsell 235n.

Orrery to the criminal courts,[103] evidence that it did not automatically grind out impeachments. If the House of Lords did not always see eye to eye with the Commons, it was not so much because the Lords were worthier sentinels of the law [104] as because of factional differences that arose from time to time. In a moment untroubled by political agitation, the Lords noted that impeachments by the Commons "are the groans of the people . . . and carry with them a greater supposition of guilt than any other accusation." [105] For the most part the Lords parted company with the Commons in cases that proceeded "for blood," "high treason"; such acquittals do not cast doubt on the charges of "high crimes and misdemeanors" here collected.[105a]

The American Scene

Article II §4 of the Constitution provides:

> The President, Vice President and all civil officers of the United States, shall be removed from office on impeachment for, and conviction of, treason, bribery, or other high crimes and misdemeanors."

The path by which the Framers arrived at this language is traceable in the records of the Convention.[106] In-

---

103. 6 Howell 913, 920 (1669).
104. For example, it has been indicated that the Commons moved from the impeachment of the Earl of Strafford, 3 Howell 1381 (1640), to a bill of attainder, because the issue of guilt was for the Lords "a judicial question, which must be legally proved." J. R. Tanner, *English Constitutional Conflicts of the Seventeenth Century* 94–95 (Cambridge, 1928). But see supra, Chapter I, text accompanying nn. 148–149, and nn. 251–253.
105. 4 Hatsell 343, 333, 342. 2 Wooddeson 620, concluded that impeachments "have been too often misguided by personal and factious animosities, and productive of alarming dissensions between two branches of the legislature." See also supra, Chapter I, text accompanying nn. 239–241. As Trevelyan, 401, noted of the Long Parliament—the cradle of English liberties—"it was the Commons who led, and the Lords who followed." The pioneer Wooddeson, and Story, who followed in his path, included impeachments that did not eventuate in convictions. See supra, Somers, text accompanying n. 76; Buckingham, text accompanying n. 79; the impeachments of Orford, Oxford, et al. for giving pernicious advice, text accompanying n. 91, and n. 91. (In the Virginia Convention Francis Corbin and Edmund Pendleton considered that the giving of "bad advice" was impeachable, infra, n. 169); the obtention of exorbitant grants from the King, Buckingham, supra, text accompanying n. 79, Danby et al. supra, text accompanying n. 83.
105a. When Charles I appeared before the House of Lords to plead for Strafford, he stated, "I cannot condemn him of High-Treason; yet I cannot say I can clear him of Misdemeanor." 8 Rushworth 734; cf. 3 Howell 1513.
106. In this enterprise both the Colonial materials and the early State

itially, impeachment was to be based upon "malpractice or neglect of duty." In the Committee of Detail this became "treason, bribery or corruption," and was then reduced by the Committee of Eleven to "treason or bribery." When George Mason suggested on the floor of the Convention the addition of "maladministration," Madison remarked that it was "so vague," whereupon Mason substituted "high crimes and misdemeanors," which was adopted without demur.[107] The special nature of "high misdemeanors" had already been recognized by the Convention. As reported by the Committee on Detail, Aricle XV provided that a fugitive from justice charged with "treason, felony or high misdemeanor" should be returned to the state from which he had fled. In the Convention, "the words 'high misdemeanor' were struck out, and 'other crime' inserted, in order to comprehend all proper cases; it being doubtful whether 'high misdemeanor' had not a technical meaning too limited" [108]—limited, inferably, to an impeachable offense as distinguished from a misdemeanor ordinarily coupled with a felony in criminal law. Except for a few early statutes directed at "political" crimes,[109] "high misdemeanors" found no place in the criminal law of this country. Like Blackstone, James Wilson referred

---

constitutions played a slight role. For the Colonial materials, see Mary P. Clarke, *Parliamentary Privilege in the American Colonies* 39–43 (New Haven, Conn., 1943). The State constitutional provisions are discussed in Martha Ziskind, "Judicial Tenure in the American Constitution: English and American Precedents," in *Supreme Court Rev.*, 138–147 (1969). See also Gordon Wood, *The Creation of the American Republic, 1776–1787*, p. 142 (Chapel Hill, N.C., 1969); infra, Chapter III, text accompanying nn. 87–104, 182–183.

107. 1 Farrand 230. 2 Farrand 64, 172, 186, 495, 545, 550. In his Philadelphia Lectures (1791), Justice James Wilson, who had been a leading Framer, referred to "malversation in office, or what are called high misdemeanors." 1 Wilson 426.

108. 2 Farrand 174, 443. This confirms that the word "high" in "high crimes and misdemeanors" modifies both "crimes and misdemeanors." See also King, ibid. 348; Blackstone's definition of "high misdemeanor," supra, text accompanying n. 32; James Wilson, supra, n. 107; infra, n. 110; see also infra, Chapter IV, n. 178.

109. Statutory "high misdemeanors": Act of June 5, 1794, ch. 50 §1 (3d Cong. 1st Sess.) 1 Stat. 381–382 (1861), acceptance by a citizen of a commission to serve a foreign state; Act of June 14, 1798, ch. 74 (5th Cong. 2d Sess.) 1 Stat. 596, Alien & Sedition Act, unlawful combination to oppose measures of government; Act of January 30, 1799, ch. 1 (5th Cong. 3d Sess.) 1 Stat. 613, correspondence by citizens with a foreign government in order to influence its measures in disputes with the United States. The practice of law by a federal judge, and his failure to reside at the place required by law were made "high misdemeanors," 28 U.S.C. §1, §373. Jud. Code. 1, 258.

to "malversation in office, or what are called high misdemeanors." [110] Impeachments, he states, "and offenses
and offenders impeachable, come not, in those descrip-
tions, within the sphere of ordinary jurisprudence. They
are founded on different principles, are governed by
different maxims, and are directed to different objects."
Again, "impeachments are confined to political characters, to political crimes and misdemeanors, and to
political punishments." [111]

Indictability of judges in English law, as we have
seen, posed a special problem. Assuming that the learning respecting judges that is pulled together above [112]
was available to the Framers, [113] and that they had occasion to collate the authorities or did so out of
scholarly curiosity, they would have found that lesser
judges were held to strict account criminally; whereas
Justices of the High Courts, according to dicta uttered
by judges of great distinction, were deemed accountable only to Parliament. Since the Justices were not
indictable, and since they had been impeached, the
Framers might conclude that indictability was not the
test of their impeachment. [114] The federal judges were
from the outset more numerous than the early English

---

110. I Wilson 426. In 1797 Senator William Blount was expelled from the
Senate for a "high misdemeanor entirely inconsistent with his public trust
and duty as a Senator." Wharton 202. For the nature of his offense, see
infra, n. 147. In the Trial of John Fries, Justice Chase charged that "if a
body of people . . . opposed the execution of any statute of the United
States by force, that they are only guilty of a high misdemeanor . . ." as
compared with treason. Wharton 634.

111. 1 Wilson 324, 426. For a similar statement by Story, see infra, text
accompanying n. 132. In the Virginia convention, George Mason presumably noticed the distinction. After animadverting on the provisions that
the Senators try themselves for impeachable crimes, he inquired as to "what
court the members of the government were to be tried for the commission
of indictable offences," 3 Elliot 402, thus distinguishing between impeachable and indictable offences. That impeachment is not coterminous with
common law crimes was also noticed by James Iredell in the North Carolina Convention: "the person convicted is *further liable* to a trial at common law, and may receive such common-law punishment as belongs to a
description of such offenses, *if it be punishable by that law.*" 4 Elliot 114
(emphasis added).

112. Text accompanying nn. 42–61. See Charles Warren, *History of the
American Bar* 160 n. 10, 181, 185 (Boston, 1911). Bacon's *Abridgement,*
Comyn's *Digest,* and Hawkins' *Pleas of the Crown* seem to have been
available, ibid. 170, 171, 172, 181, 183.

113. Cf. Julius Goebel, "Ex Parte Clio," 54 *Colum. L. Rev.* 450, 455
(1954). For examples of pre-1787 citaitons of English cases in Pennsylvania,
see Doan v. The Commander, 1 Dallas 95 (1784); Van Hornes Lessee v.
Harrison, ibid. 137 (1785).

114. Cf. dictum of Justice Field in Bradley v. Fisher, 13 Wall. (80 U.S.)
335, 350 (1872).

Justices [115] and more widely dispersed than the Justices settled in Westminster Hall,[116] with whom they were not altogether assimilable; but still less were they to be classed with the minor English judges who *were* indictable. It can hardly be postulated, however, that the Framers would demand a more stringent standard of impeachment (indictability) for district judges than for Supreme Court Justices.

In the United States the problem is futher complicated by the doctrine that there is no federal common law of crimes, so that to constitute a "high crime or misdemeanor," it has been maintained, there must be a statute which creates an indictable crime.[117] One of the components of impeachment, "treason," is defined in the Constitution; "bribery" is not.[118] The Framers were content to look to the common law for a definition of bribery. So too, when the Convention adopted Mason's substitution of "high crimes and misdemeanors" for the "vague" "maladministration" he had at first suggested, the Framers inferably had the English cases in mind as giving content to the phrase.[119] A striking assumption by the Founders that English law would be applicable is exhibited by the First Congress' prohibition of resort to "benefit of clergy" as an exemption from capital punishment, an exemption first afforded by the common law to the clergy and then to such of the laity as could read.[120] Then too, the doctrine that there was no

---

115. Section 1 of the Judiciary Act of 1789 (ch. 20) (1st Cong. 1st Sess.) 1 Stat. 72–73 (1861), provided for a Chief Justice and five Associate Justices of the Supreme Court; sections 2 and 3 provided for thirteen district judges.

116. For centuries the Justices of the High Courts—Common Pleas, King's Bench, Exchequer—numbered seven or eight. As late as 1800, "the permanent judges of the central courts of common law and Chancery, all taken together, rarely exceeded fifteen." John P. Dawson, *The Oracles of the Law* 2–3 (Ann Arbor, Mich., 1968).

117. As "there are under the laws of the United States no common-law crimes, but only those which are contrary to some positive statutory rule, there can be no impeachment except for a violation of a law of Congress ... English precedents concerning *impeachable crimes* are consequently not applicable." Dwight, supra, n. 14 at 268–269.

118. In the Act of April 30, 1790, §21 (1st Cong. 2d Sess.) 1 Stat. 117 (1861), Congress made punishable acceptance by a judge of money "or any other bribe" to influence his judgment in a pending cause, the common law definition of bribery.

119. See infra, text accompanying notes 167–171.

120. Max Radin, *Anglo-American Legal History* 230–231 (St. Paul, 1936). Act of April 30, 1790, §31, 1 Stat. 119 (1861).

federal common law of crimes was a child of a later time. Leonard Levy justly states that "all the early cases, excepting one in which the court split,[121] are on the side of the proposition that there was a federal common law of crimes." [122] According to Chief Justice Taft, six Justices and two Chief Justices of the Supreme Court shared this view—two of whom, Justices James Wilson and William Paterson, were Framers,[123] presumably attuned to the thinking of the Convention. The Supreme Court, to be sure, reversed this current of opinion in 1812; but there is little warrant for the conclusion that as the Framers, twenty-five years earlier, drafted the impeachment provisions they intended to circumscribe them by an as yet unborn limitation.[124]

Both William Rawle and Story rejected the limitation on the ground that it "renders impeachment a nullity . . . until Congress pass laws, declaring what shall constitute the other 'high crimes and misdemeanors'." [125] Theoretically, it was open to Congress immediately to enact a complete code of impeachable offenses, and given room for leisurely analysis it might have perceived that the English precedents were reducible to manage-

---

121. In that case, United States v. Worrall, 2 Dall. (2 U.S.) 384 (1798), Justice Chase held there is no federal common law of crimes; District Judge Richard Peters was of the contrary opinion. Said Levy, "Chase's opinion remained unique until it was later adopted by the Supreme Court in 1812." Leonard Levy, *Legacy of Suppression* 241 (Cambridge, Mass., 1960).

122. Levy, supra, n. 121 at 239.

123. In Ex Parte Grossman, 267 U.S. 87, 114–115 (1925), Chief Justice Taft stated, "It is not too much to say that, immediately after the ratification of the Constitution, the power and jurisdiction of federal courts to indict and prosecute common law crimes within the scope of federal judicial power was thought to exist by most of the then members of this Court," among them Chief Justice Jay, and Justices Wilson and Iredell. Taft also quoted Charles Warren, "in the early years of the Court, Chief Justice Ellsworth, and Justices Cushing, Paterson and Washington had also delivered opinions or charges of the same tenor. Justices Wilson and Paterson were members of the Constitutional Convention . . ." Ibid. 115. Ellsworth and Iredell were leading proponents of ratification in the Connecticut and North Carolina Conventions, respectively, and presumably had an informed opinion. See the encomium of Wharton on the early opinions as reflecting the "united opinion of the day." 1 Francis Wharton, *Criminal Law* 121 (Philadelphia, 6th ed. 1868).

124. United States v. Hudson & Goodwin, 7 Cranch (11 U.S.) 32 (1812). For the view that the case was politically inspired, see 2 W. W. Crosskey, *Politics and the Constitution in the History of the United States* 770–784 (Chicago, 1952). United States v. Barnett, 376 U.S. 681; 693 (1964): "our inquiry concerns the standard prevailing at the time of the adoption of the Constitution, not a score or more years later."

125. Rawle 273; Story §798. For an earlier critique of the view that there was a federal common law of crimes, see 1 St. George Tucker, ed., *Blackstone's Commentaries* (part I), App. 378 (Philadelphia, 1803).

able categories.[126] But the Congress was engaged in weightier tasks, in erecting a novel structure of government, in fleshing out the bare bones of the Constitution. The meager role that criminal legislation played in this endeavor can be gathered from the negligible handful of criminal statutes that were enacted by a succession of early Congresses. Whatever the merits of the no-federal-common-law-crimes doctrine the Senate, itself the tribunal for impeachments, has not embraced it, as its Delphic verdicts of guilty in the absence of statutory offenses indicate.[127] Nor has the Congress, the alter ego of the Senate as impeachment tribunal and the House as Grand Inquest, ever felt called upon to supply a code of impeachable offenses—a tacit judgment that it does not deem such a code necessary. These verdicts and that judgment seem to me to rest upon a sound historical basis.

IS IMPEACHMENT A CRIMINAL PROCEEDING?

A more arresting question, and one that has not received the attention it deserves, is whether the constitutional impeachment provisions, particularly when viewed in the context of the Fifth and Sixth Amendments, set up a criminal proceeding at all. Undoubtedly English impeachments were criminal, though by the *lex Parliamentaria,* because conviction could be followed by death, imprisonment, or heavy fine. Our

---

126. Supra, text accompanying nn. 82–92. I would therefore differ with Story's statement that "political offenses are of so various and complex a character, so utterly incapable of being defined or classified, that the task of positive legislation would be impracticable, if it were not almost absurd to attempt it." Story §797.

Nevertheless, Congress has never undertaken the task. So too, although authorized by Article I §8 (10) "To define and punish piracies and felonies committed on the high seas," Congress left the task to the courts. The Act of March 3, 1819, c. 77, §5 (1st Cong. 2d Sess.) 3 Stat. 513–514 (1846), provides a death penalty for one who is found "on the high seas [to] commit the crime of piracy, as defined by the law of nations." Thus it is left to the courts to select from the "law of nations." Again, "From 1799 to the present, Congress has made no definitive statement concerning grand jury powers." United States v. Cox, 342 F.2d 167, 186 (5th Cir. 1965) (Wisdom, J., concurring), again illustrating the exercise of power left undefined.

127. These verdicts also indicate that no indictable crime whatsoever is necessary. Supra, n. 15, and text accompanying nn. 15–16.

impeachment provisions may seem to point in the direction of criminality because they employ criminal terminology. For example, Article II §4 provides for removal from office on "conviction of treason, bribery, or other high crimes and misdemeanors." Article III §2(3) provides that "the trial of all crimes, except in cases of impeachment, shall be by jury." And Article II §2(1) empowers the President to grant "pardons for offences against the United States, except in cases of impeachment"; the function of a pardon is to exempt from punishment for a crime.[128] Then there are the references by the Founders to impeachment in terms of punishment.[129]

But Article I §3(7) sharply separates removal from office from subsequent punishment after indictment, in contrast to the English practice, which wedded criminal punishment and removal in one proceeding. From the text of the Constitution there emerges a leading purpose: partisan passions should no longer give rise to political executions.[130] Removal would enable the government to replace an unfit officer with a proper person, leaving "punishment" to a later and separate proceeding, if indeed the impeachable offense were thus punishable. The distinction was drawn in the Virginia Convention by George Nicholas between disqualification from office and "further punishment if [the President] has committed such high crimes as are punishable at common law," the implication being that some "high crimes" were *not* thus punishable.[131] Anomalies remain:

---

128. United States v. Wilson, 7 Pet. (32 U.S.) 150, 159 (1833). So too, the "word 'offense' in its usual sense means a crime or misdemeanor, a breach of the criminal law." United States v. Krebs, 104 F. Supp. 670 (D. Neb. 1951); W. J. Dillner Transfer Co. v. International Brotherhood, 94 F. Supp. 491, 492 n. 2 (D. W. Pa. 1950); cf. Moore v. Illinois, 14 How. (55 U.S.) 13, 19–20 (1852).

129. Thomas McKean, Pennsylvania Ratification Convention, 2 Elliot 538; James Iredell, North Carolina Convention, 4 Elliot 32; Archibald Maclaine, ibid. 34; Elias Boudinot, First Congress, 1 *Ann. Cong.* 375 (Gales & Seaton ed. Washington, D.C., 1834; print bearing running-page head "History of Congress"); Samuel Livermore, ibid. 478 (conviction of some crime); Thomas Hartley, ibid. 480.

130. As Vice President, Jefferson noted that "history shows, that in England, impeachment has been an engine more of passion than of justice." Quoted Wharton 315n.

131. 3 Elliot 240. Speaking of the President in the North Carolina Convention, James Iredell also stated: "If he commits any misdemeanor in office, he is impeachable, removable from office ... If he commits any crime, he is punishable by the laws of his country," 4 Elliot 109, again drawing a distinction between an impeachable "misdemeanor" and an in-

why the pardon, why the exemption from "trial of all crimes . . . by jury"; but the starting point, to borrow from Story, is that impeachment is "a proceeding purely of a political nature. It is not so much designed to punish an offender as to secure the state against gross official misdemeanors. It touches neither his person nor his property, but simply divests him of his political capacity," [132] that is, it disqualifies him to hold office.

In a statement which anticipated Story, James Wilson came close to saying that the problem posed by double jeopardy is met by reading impeachment in noncriminal terms: "Impeachments . . . come not . . . within the sphere of ordinary jurisprudence. They are founded on different principles; are governed by different maxims, and are directed to different objects; for this reason, the trial and punishment of an offense on impeachment, is no bar to a trial of the same offense at common law." [133] In a word, the separation of removal from criminal prosecution poses the problem of double jeopardy unless the removal proceeding is read in noncriminal terms. If impeachment is not criminal, it may be asked, why was it deemed necessary to have a saving clause for subsequent indictment and punishment. Possibly the saving clause was designed to preclude an inference from the unmistakable criminal nature of English impeachment that an impeachment could be pleaded in bar to a subsequent criminal prosecution, an excess of caution.[134] To read impeachment in criminal

dictable crime. That impeachable offenses might be noncriminal is further illustrated by Iredell's reference to "impeachment for concealing important intelligence" from the Senate respecting foreign relations, 4 Elliot 127. See also supra, n. 111, and the remarks of Madison, Corbin and Pendleton, quote infra, text accompanying nn. 168–169.

132. Story §803. This was borrowed from Congressman James Bayard's remarks in the Blount impeachment. Infra, text accompanying n. 148.

133. 1 Wilson 324. The townspeople of Sutton criticized the proposed Massachusetts constitution of 1780 on the ground that impeachment involved double jeopardy because the impeached official could subsequently be tried in a court of law. Oscar and Mary Handlin, eds. *The Popular Sources of Political Authority: Documents on the Massachusetts Constitution of 1780*, 236 (Cambridge, Mass., 1966).

134. In *Federalist* No. 65, p. 426, Hamilton asks, "Would it be proper that the persons who had disposed of his fame and his most valuable rights as a citizen, in one trial, should, in another trial, for the same offence, be also the disposers of his life and his fortune?" But the House of Lords had long decided both issues in one trial, and I see no impropriety in dividing the issues for two trials before the same tribunal. Courts frequently hear civil cases which may be damaging to the defendant's reputation and then turn to the criminal side to try charges arising from the same facts.

terms is to raise a constitutional doubt whether a subsequent indictment and trial offends against the Fifth Amendment ban of double jeopardy, a doubt which the courts are under a duty to avoid.[135]

Although Wilson tacitly assumed that but for the noncriminal nature of impeachment double jeopardy would apply, at common law *autre fois acquit* and *autre fois convict* were confined to jeopardy of life.[136] The Fifth Amendment also provides "nor shall any person be subject for the same offense to be twice put in jeopardy of life or limb"; and early district courts therefore excluded "mere misdemeanors," and even an "infamous and severely punishable offense," from its protective scope.[137] But in 1873 the Supreme Court, noting inter alia that Joseph Chitty, a noted English commentator, had dropped "life and limb" and substituted "placed in peril of legal penalties upon the same accusation," concluded that the "constitutional provision must be applied in all cases." [138] To the extent that impeachment retains a residual punitive aura, it may be compared to deportation, which is attended by very painful consequences but which, the Supreme Court held, "is not a punishment for a crime . . . It is but a method of enforcing the return to his own country of an alien who has not complied with the conditions" laid down for his residence,[139] precisely as impeachment is designed to remove an unfit officer for the good of the government. It is not here suggested that the Founders conceived of "double jeopardy" in its present broadened sense, but rather that, were a court now confronted with the nature of an impeachable crime, it would be apt to read

---

135. Richmond Screw Anchor Co. v. United States, 275 U.S. 331, 346 (1928); United States v. Jim Fuey Moy, 241 U.S. 394, 401 (1916).

136. 2 Hawkins ch. 36, §10, p. 377; 4 Blackstone 335–336.

137. United States v. Gibert, 25 Fed. Cas. No. 15,204, pp. 1287, 1296–97 (C. Ct. Mass. 1834), per Story, Cir. J.; United States v. Keen, 26 Fed. Cas. No. 15,510, pp. 686, 687 (C. Ct. Ind. 1839).

138. Ex parte Lange, 18 Wall. (85 U.S.) 163, 172–173 (1873). Judge Friendly stated: "The Fifth Amendment guarantees that when the government has proceeded to judgment on a certain fact situation, there can be no further prosecution of that fact situation alone." United States v. Sabella, 272 F. 2d 206, 212 (2d Cir. 1959). See also Abbate v. United States, 359 U.S. 187, 196–98 (1959), Brennan, J., concurring.

139. Fong Yue Ting v. United States, 149 U.S. 698, 730 (1893).

"double jeopardy" in present-day terms for the protection of the accused.[139a]

Another problem is presented by the Sixth Amendment: "In all criminal prosecutions, the accused shall enjoy the right to a speedy and public trial by an impartial jury." If impeachment be deemed a "criminal prosecution," it is difficult to escape the requirement of trial by jury. Earlier, Article III §2(3), had expressly exempted impeachment from the jury "Trial of all Crimes"; and with that exemption before them, the draftsmen of the Sixth Amendment extended trial by jury to "all criminal prosecutions," without exception, thereby exhibiting an intention to withdraw the former exception.[140] Either we must conclude that the Founders felt no need to exempt impeachment from the Sixth Amendment because they did not consider it a "criminal prosecution," or that jury trial is required if impeachment be in fact a "criminal prosecution." One who would make "all" mean less than "all" has the burden of proving why the ordinary meaning should not prevail.[141] Speaking in another context of the Article III

139a. Is there inconsistency in principle in declining to read back into the impeachment provisions the later formulated "no federal common law crimes" doctrine while reading "life and limb" in the later and broader judicial fashion? First, James Wilson understood the removal provisions to be noncriminal and consequently considered the double jeopardy principle to be inapplicable. Second, the impeachment provisions conferred upon Congress an essential curative removal power which a subsequently *self-limiting* judicial doctrine, "no federal common law crimes," cannot curtail. Third, over the years Congress has tacitly considered the doctrine inapplicable to its impeachment function. The guarantee against double jeopardy, on the other hand, is for the benefit of the individual; it does not purport to cut down an essential power conferred upon one of the branches, and like other constitutional guarantees, e.g., due process, it has been broadened over the years.

140. Simpson 34, states that the "use of the word 'crimes' in Article III . . . tells for neither side of the controversy, for the reason that inasmuch as the proceedings in impeachment are a trial, and that a 'trial' may be for a 'crime,' it was necessary therein to exclude 'impeachments' in order to avoid the implication, which otherwise might arise, that criminal impeachments should be tried by a jury." But the exclusion of jury trial for impeachment posits that it proceeds for a "crime."

141. Henry Hart, Book Review, "Professor Crosskey and Judicial Review," 67 *Harv. L. Rev.* 1456, 1465 (1954). Simpson 66, dismisses the impact of the Sixth Amendment on the ground that it was adopted to secure jury trials "in the ordinary civil and criminal suits." He is plainly mistaken as to "criminal suits," for express provision had earlier been made by Article III, §2(3) for the "trial of all crimes, except in cases of impeachment . . . by jury," and it was that provision which triggered the drive for the Seventh Amendment provision for jury trial in civil cases. For citations see infra, Chapter IV, text accompanying nn. 73–75. Provision for "ordinary *civil*" suits did not require a departure from the exception made for "cases of impeachment" in Article III in favor of the all-inclusive "In all *criminal* Prosecutions" of the Sixth Amendment. Moreover, as the debate in the North Carolina convention revealed in the very context of impeachment,

and Sixth Amendment jury trial provisions, the Supreme Court said: "If there be any conflict between these two provisions, the one found in the amendment must control, under the well-understood rule that the last expression of the will of the lawmaker prevails over the earlier one." [142] If impeachment be deemed criminal in nature, the problem is not to be solved by reading an exception from "criminal prosecution" into the Sixth Amendment. The companion Fifth Amendment clause —"No person shall be held to answer for a capital, or otherwise infamous crime, unless on a presentment or indictment of a Grand Jury, except in cases arising in the land or naval forces"—shows that the draftsmen knew well enough how to carve out exceptions. It is not for us to interpolate exceptions that they withheld. No need exists to read "exceptions" into the Sixth Amendment if impeachment is regarded merely as a removal procedure rather than a criminal trial, as the structure of the Article I §3(7) impeachment provision itself indicates. And if, contrary to my view, impeachment is indeed a criminal proceeding, the task of reading an exception into the Amendment is not for the Senate but for the Supreme Court.

Simpson regards the point as settled by the Senate: the point "that criminal impeachments should be tried by a jury" was "made and overruled in the impeachment of Senator William Blount." [143] To my mind, the question was left open. True, Jefferson, then Vice President, noted that a motion would be made to incorporate into a proposed bill for regulating impeachments in the Senate "a clause for the introduction of juries into these trials. (Compare the paragraph in the Constitution which says, that all crimes, *except in cases of impeachment,* shall be by jury, with the eighth amendment [the Sixth], which says, that in *all* criminal prosecutions, the trial shall be by jury.) There is no

there was distrust of Congress' "dangerous latitude of construction." Infra, Chapter III, text accompanying n. 63. On the eve of the first impeachment, Jefferson thought the Sixth Amendment relevant to impeachment trials. Infra, text accompanying n. 144. All this, of course, on the debatable assumption that impeachment envisaged a "criminal prosecution."
142. Schick v. United States, 195 U.S. 65, 68 (1904).
143. Simpson 34.

expectation of carrying this, because the division in the Senate is two to one." [144] Apparently the motion failed,[145] but this by no means disposes of the issue. Many months after failure of the motion [146] Blount filed what was in fact a plea to the jurisdiction, based on three points: (1) a right to trial by jury under the Sixth Amendment; (2) a Senator is not a "civil officer" within the meaning of the impeachment provision; and (3) he was not charged with malconduct in office,[147] but with actions in his private capacity. Opening for the Managers of the prosecution, Congressman James A. Bayard ironically pointed out that from the jury-trial claim "it must necessarily follow that the whole of [the Senate] judicial authority is abolished." Then he showed it was not at all a "necessary" deduction when he made his final observation on the point, "impeachment is a proceeding purely of a political nature. It is not so much designed to punish an offender, as to secure the State. It touches neither his person nor his property, but simply divests him of his political capacity [office]." [148]

In short, lacking punishment or impact on life or property, the proceeding was not the trial of a "crime"; hence the judicial authority of the Senate could be maintained and exercised. For whatever reason, A. J. Dallas, counsel for Blount, did not argue the jury-trial point but confined himself to the other two.[149] The Senate was persuaded by the plea "that this court ought not to hold jurisdiction," [150] a statement that, as regards the jury-trial point, is to say the least equivocal. Virtual abandonment of that point on argument removed the necessity of ruling on it; and the Senate ruling is compatible with Bayard's argument that impeachment is

---

144. Quoted Wharton ·314–315. Parenthetically, Jefferson confirms my reading of the Sixth Amendment if impeachment be indeed criminal.
145. Cf. ibid. 315n.
146. The motion was made in February, 1798, ibid. 314–315n; the trial opened in December, ibid. 259.
147. Ibid. 260. The most serious charge was that Blount had conspired to launch a military expedition to wrest Florida and Louisiana from Spain and to deliver it to England. Ibid. 253. Before the impeachment, the Senate, by a vote of 25 to 1, expelled him as "guilty of a high misdemeanor, entirely inconsistent with his public trust and duty as a Senator." Ibid. 251–252.
148. Ibid. 262–263.
149. Ibid. Closing for the Managers, Robert G. Harper followed suit and confined himself to those two points. Ibid. 296.
150. Ibid. 316.

unaffected by the Sixth Amendment because it is a non-criminal proceeding.[151]

Yet another difficulty is presented by the Article II §2 provision that excepts impeachments from the presidential power to grant "pardons for offenses." Blackstone treats "offenses" as virtually synonymous with "crimes";[152] and a pardon comes into play to exempt from punishment for a crime.[153] Let me attempt an explanation of this confusing cross-current. The Framers had the English practice constantly before their eyes; doubtless they were aware that the Act of Settlement (1700) foreclosed the plea of pardon to an impeachment, though it remained open to the King to issue a pardon after conviction.[154] Since the Framers were following the English pattern in important respects, it was the counsel of prudence to bar a pardon after impeachment and conviction, notwithstanding that separation of removal from subsequent indictment and conviction had rendered it unnecessary.[155]

Quite possibly the Framers did not pause to think through the impact of this "pardon" exception upon the division they had instituted between impeachment and subsequent indictment. In the crowded effort to

---

151. Subsequent convictions by the Senate show that it does not regard the jury-trial requirement as a bar.

152. 4 Blackstone 5; see also 1 Sir William Russell, *Crimes and Misdemeanors* 58 (London, 1819); and supra, n. 128.

153. See supra, n. 128. Simpson 34, stated, "The only inference that can be fairly drawn from the use of the word 'offenses' in Article II, Section 2, instead of the word 'crimes,' is that it was recognized that there were 'offenses' against the United States' which were not crimes, and all those, including fines, penalties, and forfeitures, could be pardoned by the President; but for 'offenses' resulting in a conviction upon impeachment, the President was not to be permitted to pardon." Apparently Simpson considers that impeachment is grounded upon an "offense" that is not a crime. See also Simpson 32–37, 40–41. Like Simpson, I consider that the American impeachment process is not criminal, but I can not as easily deprive "offenses" of its normal "criminal" connotations. Supra, n. 128; text accompanying note 152. Simpson furnishes no evidence for the assignment of a double meaning to "offenses," no explanation why penalties such as "fines and forfeitures" should be excluded from the norms of criminal sanctions. Where they were clearly "civil" in nature, the likelihood that a "pardon" would come into play was remote. The exemption of impeachment, in a word, is not explicable on the Simpson analysis.

154. Act of Settlement, 12 & 13 Will. III, ch. 2, § 3 (1700); 1 Chitty, supra, n. 7 at 763; see supra, n. 7.

155. Other instances of superabundant caution are the prohibition of bills of attainder, Article I, § 9 (3), the bar to suspension of the writ of habeas corpus, Article I § 9 (1), which arguably were unnecessary given the prevailing view that the Constitution created a government of enumerated and limited powers. See Berger, "Executive Privilege" 1075–1076. The point was raised by Thomas Tredwell in the New York Ratification convention. 2 Elliot 398–399.

erect an unprecedented structure of government, the Framers might well have overlooked some lack of harmony in detail. Marks of haste are apparent on the face of the instrument: for example, the provision which enables Congress to punish treason is not found in Article I, the Legislative Article, but in the Judicial Article III; the provision for impeachment of judges is inferentially included in the phrase "all civil Officers" in the Executive Article II. Words like "offenses," "convict," "high crimes" had been employed in the English impeachment process; and a thoroughgoing attempt to clarify the nonpenal aspect of removal would have required the Framers to coin a fresh and different vocabulary, perhaps an insuperable task in all the circumstances. They were content to furnish practical answers to manifest problems, to prevent, for example, a presidential pardon from undoing the impeachment of a presidential favorite. One need not be completely persuaded by such explanations and yet prefer them to the difficulties presented by the double jeopardy and trial by jury Amendments. It is not given to the historian retrospectively to impose a tidy scheme upon the unruly facts; instead he must be content to take account of anomalies and to try to resolve ambiguity by making what appears to him to be the best available choice.

THE LIMITS OF "HIGH CRIMES AND MISDEMEANORS"

Pressing for the impeachment of Justice Douglas, Congressman Ford, it will be recalled, asserted that an "impeachable offense" is whatever House and Senate jointly "consider [it] to be." [156] The Records make quite plain that the Framers, far from proposing to confer illimitable power to impeach and convict, intended to confer a *limited* power.

Before Mason moved to add "maladministration" to "treason, bribery," he explained that "Treason as de-

---

156. Supra, n. 1.

fined in the Constitution will not reach many great and dangerous offenses. Hastings is not guilty of Treason. Attempts to subvert the Constitution may not be Treason as above defined . . . it is the more necessary to extend the power of impeachments." [157] Thus Mason proposed to "extend the power of impeachment" to reach "great and dangerous offenses," "attempts to subvert the Constitution," by adding "maladministration." But Madison demurred because "so vague a term [as maladministration] will be equivalent to a tenure during the pleasure of the Senate," and "high crimes and misdemeanors" was accepted in its place. Manifestly, this substitution was made for the purpose of limiting, not expanding the initial Mason proposal.[158]

Shortly before, the Convention had rejected "high misdemeanors" in another context because it "had a technical meaning too limited," [159] so that adoption of "high crimes and misdemeanors" exhibits an intent to embrace the "limited," "technical meaning" of the words for purposes of impeachment. That consequence would attach in any event, for use of a technical term, "fully ascertained by the common or civil law" would require reference to that law "for its precise meaning." [160] If "high crimes and misdemeanors" had an

---

157. 2 Farrand 550. For Warren Hastings see infra, Index.

158. 2 Farrand 550. Earlier George Mason had said in the Convention that the President as well as his coadjutors should be punished "when great crimes were committed." Ibid. 65.

159. Supra, text accompanying n. 108. When Benjamin Butler, arguing for the prosecution in the impeachment of President Andrew Johnson, cited the broad claims of the House of Lords in the impeachment of 1386 (see supra, Chapter I, text accompanying n. 22), and maintained that the Senate likewise was "bound by no law," but was "a law unto" itself, infra, Chapter IX, text accompanying n. 85, he overlooked two important facts. The power of Congress in treason cases was sharply limited by the narrow definition of treason in Article III, § 3 (1), so that unlike Parliament, Congress has no power to declare retrospective treasons. And its power to label any conduct whatsoever as a high misdemeanor was circumscribed by the adoption of the phrase "high crimes and misdemeanors," a phrase thought to have a "limited" and "technical meaning" and adopted in order to insure that the tenure of neither President nor judiciary would be reduced to service "at the pleasure of Congress." In reading the "technical meaning" associated with "high misdemeanors" into the phrase "high crimes and misdemeanors," I relied on the fact that I found no reference to "high crimes" separately; the references were to "high misdemeanors." See supra, nn. 32 and 110, and text accompanying nn. 102, 108, 110; and infra, Chapter IV, n. 178.

160. United States v. Jones, 26 Fed. Cas. No. 15,494, pp. 653, 655 (C. Ct. Pa. 1813), per Justice Bushrod Washington. Chief Justice Marshall said of the word "robbery" in a statute that "it must be understood in the sense in which it is recognized and defined at common law." United States v. Palmer, 3 Wheat. (16 U.S.) 610, 630 (1818). So too, "the word 'jury' and the words 'trial by jury' were placed in the Constitution . . . with refer-

ascertainable content at the time the Constitution was adopted, that content furnishes the boundaries of the power. It is no more open to Congress to stray beyond those boundaries than it is to include in the companion word "bribery" an offense such as "robbery," which had a quite different common law connotation.[161] The design of the Framers to confer a limited power is confirmed by their rejection of removal by Address which knew no limits.[162]

---

ence to the meaning affixed to them in the law as it was in this country and in England at the adoption of the Constitution." Thompson v. Utah, 170 U.S. 343, 344 (1898).

This was the common view, as is illustrated by Jefferson's transmittal of a draft of a Virginia criminal code to George Wythe, in which he explained that he sought to preserve "the very words of the established law, whenever their meaning has been sanctioned by judicial decisions or rendered technical by usage," in order, as he added in a subsequent "Note," "to give no occasion for new questions by new expressions." Quoted Willard Hurst, "Treason in the United States," 58 *Harv. L. Rev.* 226, 253–254 (1944).

It is reasonable to infer that the Framers were familiar with English impeachment trials. As early as 1734, William Smith, in an opinion rendered to the New York Assembly, quoted Art. 3 of the Clarendon impeachment. Quoted Joseph Smith, *Cases & Materials on Development of Legal Institutions* 440, 442 (St. Paul, Minn. 1965). Several Colonial libraries in New York had various collections of the State Trials. Paul A. Hamlin, *Legal Education in Colonial New York* 188, 193, 196 (New York, 1939). For his *Manual of Parliamentary Practice,* reprinted in Senate Manual (55th Cong. 1899) 61–153, Vice-President Jefferson combed the debates in Parliament and the State Trials. For impeachment materials see ibid. 149–153. In a letter to the *Boston Gazette,* January 4, 1768, Josiah Quincy, Jr., directed attention to the scope of impeachment in England and to the impeachment of leading English statesmen across the centuries, drawing on Selden's *Jur. Parl.,* Rushworth's *Historical Collections,* the *Lords' Journal.* Quincy's *Mass. Repts. 1761–1772,* App. 580–584 (1865).

Of the fifty-five members of the Federal Convention, "Four had studied in the Inner Temple, five in the Middle Temple . . ." Hughes, supra, n. 16 at 11. And it is not to be presumed that they were ignorant of the famous State Trials. See also infra, n. 169; John Adams, supra, n. 26; infra, chapter IV, text accompanying n. 95; and n. 97. "The history of Seventeenth Century England—the Long Parliament, the Puritan Revolution, the 'Glorious Revolution' all that was no closed book to eighteenth century Americans . . ." G. W. Ross, " 'Good Behavior' of Federal Judges," 12 *U. Kan. City L. Rev.* 119, 122 (1944). See also Bailyn, supra, n. 2; and infra, n. 170.

161. As Story stated, "The doctrine, indeed would be truly alarming that the common law did not regulate, interpret, and control the powers and duties of the court of impeachment. . . . If the common law has no existence, as to the Union as a rule or guide, the whole proceedings are completely at the arbitrary pleasure of the government and its functionaries . . ." Story §798. Since, he said, "high crimes and misdemeanors" are not defined by any statute of the United States (nor, it may be added, by any English statute) "Resort, then, must be had either to parliamentary practice and the common law, in order to ascertain what are high crimes and misdemeanors, or the whole subject must be left to the arbitrary discretion of the Senate . . ." Id. §§ 796, 798. Compare Marshall, C. J., in United States v. Wilson, 7 Pet. (32 U.S.) 150, 159 (1833).

162. 2 Farrand 428. Speaking of the Act of Settlement (1700), Todd properly remarks that the removal by address "is, in fact, a qualification or exception from, the words creating a tenure during good behavior, and not an incident or legal consequence thereof." The power "may be invoked upon occasions when the misbehavior complained of would not constitute a legal breach of the conditions on which the office is held," i.e., when they do not amount to "misbehavior" in law. 1 Alpheus Todd, *Parliamentary Government* 193 (London 1892). The terms of the Act confirm Todd's con-

Even so, some uneasiness apparently was excited by the breadth of the power, for there were repeated assurances that impeachment was meant only for "great injuries," "great misdemeanors." James Iredell, later a Supreme Court Justice, told the North Carolina Convention that the "occasion for its exercise [impeachment] will arise from acts of great injury to the community." [163] Impeachment, said Governor Johnston in that Convention, "is a mode of trial pointed out for great misdemeanors against the public." [164] From James Wilson's expression of hope in the Pennsylvania Convention that impeachments "will seldom happen," [165] it is inferable that he too was concerned only with serious misconduct. In this the Founders were but reflecting English sentiment, as was well put by Solicitor General, later Lord Chancellor, Somers, who stated in Parliament in 1691 that "the power of impeachment ought to be, like Goliath's sword, kept in the temple, and not used but on great occasions." [166]

The peaks of the English practice were evidently familiar to the Founders. In the Federal Convention George Mason said "corruption" would be impeachable; Gouverneur Morris agreed that "corruption and some few other offenses" ought to be impeachable. Madison added that protection against the "negligence or perfidy of the Chief Magistrate" were "indispensable." The President, said Madison, "might pervert his administration into a scheme of peculation or op-

---

struction: "Judges' Commissions [to] be made *Quamdiu se bene gesserint* . . . but upon the Address of both Houses of Parliament it may be lawful to remove them." 12 & 13 Will. III, c. 2, §3. The "but" clause seems to me to carve out an exception. For fuller discussion, see infra, Chapter IV, text accompanying nn. 131–34.
163. 4 Elliot 113.
164. Ibid. 48. In the Federal Convention George Mason said impeachment was to be for "great crimes." 2 Farrand 65.
165. 2 Elliot 513.
166. 5 New Parl. Hist. 678 (1691). His view was immediately paraphrased by Attorney General Treby, later Chief Justice of Common Pleas: "Impeachments are seldom used, as not fit on common occasions." Ibid. So too, when the impeachment of the Earl of Orrery was proposed, Sir Thomas Clifford said he "Would not have the sword of this House of Impeachments be blunted upon offenses of this nature . . . Would have impeachments of this nature upon great and considerable occasions." The Commons voted that the accusation "be left to be prosecuted at law." 6 Howell 913, 919, 920 (1669). In this country, Story said that impeachment is "intended for occasional and extraordinary cases, where a superior power, acting for the whole people, is put into operation to protect their rights, and to rescue their liberties from violation." Story §751.

pression. He might betray his trust to a foreign power."
Morris added that he "may be bribed . . . to betray
his trust," and recalled that "Charles II was bribed by
Louis XIV." [167]

In the Virginia Ratification Convention Madison
stated that "if the President be connected, in any suspicious manner with any person, and there be grounds
to believe that he will shelter him" he may be impeached. He also stated that "were the President to
commit anything so atrocious as to summon only a
few States [that is, Senators to consider a treaty]" he
would be impeached for a "misdemeanor." [168] Francis
Corbin and Henry Pendleton considered the giving of
"bad advice" by ministers impeachable.[169] In North
Carolina James Iredell said, "I suppose the only instances, in which the President would be liable to
impeachment, would be where he had received a bribe,
or had acted from some corrupt motive or other." [170]
General C. C. Pinckney said in South Carolina that
those are impeachable "who behave amiss, or betray
their public trust." An abuse of trust by the President,
said Edward Rutledge there, was impeachable.[171]

The net effect of these remarks, it seems to me, is
to preclude resort to impeachment of the President for
petty misconduct. Hamilton's reference to "the awful
discretion which a court of impeachment must necessarily have, to doom to honor or to infamy the most
confidential and the most distinguished characters of
the community," goes beyond the presidency; but as
will shortly appear, the restriction of "high crimes and
misdemeanors" to "great offenses" for others than the

---

167. 2 Farrand 68–69. For the bribe Louis paid to Charles, which came
out in the impeachment of Danby, see Chafee 120; and see supra, Chapter I, text accompanying nn. 206–207.
168. 3 Elliot 498, 500.
169. Francis Corbin noted in the Virginia convention that a British
minister who advises an "abuse of this royal prerogative" is impeachable.
3 Elliot 516. In South Carolina, Henry Pendleton said that "In England
. . . ministers that advised illegal measures were liable to impeachment, for
advising the king." 4 Elliot 263. See Iredell, supra, n. 91. Referring to
written opinions Cabinet officers are to furnish the President, Iredell told
the North Carolina Convention that "the necessity of their opinions being
in writing, will render them more cautious in giving them, and make them
responsible should they give advice manifestly improper." 4 Elliot 108;
see Gerry, 1 Farrand 71.
170. 4 Elliot 126; and see Iredell, supra, text accompanying n. 163.
171. 4 Elliot 281, 276.

President raises still other problems.[172] In any event, Senate power was not designed to be unlimited; rather, as Story said, "what are what are not high crimes and misdemeanors is to be ascertained by a recurrence" to English law.[173]

One case of impeachable conduct in England mentioned by Story, the rendering of unconstitutional opinions,[174] merits special notice. The subservient judges of Charles I had held that the Ship Money Tax was constitutional,[175] a judgment rejected by an outraged Commons, which later impeached the judges.[176] Under our Constitution, however, the determination whether a measure is constitutional was left to the final determination of the judiciary. When it was objected in the Pennsylvania Ratification Convention that the security allegedly provided by an independent judiciary was dubious because the judges could be impeached if they declared an act null and void, the suggestion was flatly rejected by James Wilson: "What House of Representatives would dare to impeach, or Senate to commit, judges for the performance of their duty?" [177] A similar statement was made by Elbridge Gerry; [178] and that conclusion is inherent in the very nature of

---

172. *Federalist* No. 65 at 426. See also supra, text accompanying nn. 163–165. Apparently Story, §786, conceived of removal by impeachment "upon the mere ground of political usurpation or malversation in office, admitting of endless varieties, from the slightest guilt up to the most flagrant corruption." But he did not explain his "slightest guilt" nor take note of the assurances in the several conventions, e.g., respecting "great offenses," including the history of the adoption of the phrase "high crimes and misdemeanors." Nor did he seek to reconcile it with his statement in § 751, quoted supra, n. 166.

173. Supra, text accompanying n. 76.

174. Supra, text accompanying n. 76.

175. See supra, Chapter I, text accompanying nn. 110–112. The Ship-Money Case, The King v. Hampden, is reported in 3 Howell 825 (1637).

176. The Commons called the judges to account for their opinions, 3 Howell 1260; Finch's solicitation was stressed, ibid. 1264; the legality of the opinion was challenged, ibid. 1263, 1266, 1268; the judgment was declared void by the Lords, ibid. 1300; and the judges were convicted, ibid. 1283, 1301. The core of Justice Berkley's impeachment, supra, text accompanying n. 63, was his participation in the Ship-Money matter. See Art. 5–8, 3 Howell 1285–1287. He was fined 20,000 pounds and made incapable of any place in the judicature. 4 Hatsell 173n.

177. 2 Elliot 478.

178. Elbridge Gerry, 1 *Ann. Cong.* 537. In New Hampshire the court had declared the "Ten Pound Act" unconstitutional, and although the Representatives by a vote of 44 to 14 then declared the Act constitutional, they approved by a vote of 56 to 21 a committee report that the judges were "not impeachable for maladministration as their conduct [was] justified by the constitution" of New Hampshire. 2 W. W. Crosskey, *Politics and the Constitution in the History of the United States* 970 (Chicago, 1953).

judicial review. Once it is granted that judges were empowered to declare an act void that is not "in pursuance" of the Constitution, it defeats the Framers' purpose to conclude that they authorized Congress to impeach judges for rendering such decisions.[179]

The Founders' almost exclusive concern with impeachment of the President led them to speak of the "technical" phrase "high crimes and misdemeanors" in terms of "great offenses." [180] Does it necessarily follow that the terms must be similarly restricted when applied to judges? Influenced by the difficulty of giving the words both a narrow and a broad construction, I initially concluded that they must be given one meaning only; [181] further study has led me to alter my view. Judges were added to the impeachment provision at the last minute, presumably by inclusion in the words "all civil officers," without any reference whatsoever either to judges or to governing standards.[182] There was no intimation that the restrictive standards deemed appropriate for removal of the President were likewise to apply on removal of judges. And there are good reasons for differentiating between the two.

Charles Pinckney reminded the Framers that a faction-ridden Congress could "throw [the President] out of office"; and it was to reduce that possibility, I suggest, that they emphasized "great offenses." [183] Removal of the President must generate shock waves that can rock the very foundations of government, as will appear in the discussion of Andrew Johnson's impeachment. Johnson also illustrates the frustrations that may accumulate when succession to a President, selected by the people at a nationwide election, falls to one whom the electorate did not really contemplate in the presidency.[184] Removal of a district Judge, or

---

179. Berger, *Congress v. Court* 289–96.
180. Supra, text accompanying nn. 157–73; 1 Farrand 230; 2 Farrand 39, 64–69, 111, 172, 500, 550–51, 606; 3 Farrand 611. Cf. infra, text accompanying nn. 213–18, 223–24.
181. Raoul Berger, "Impeachment of Judges and 'Good Behavior' Tenure," 79 *Yale L. J.* 1475, 1511–12 (1970); Raoul Berger, "Impeachment for 'High Crimes and Misdemeanors,'" 44 *So. Calif. L. Rev.* 395, 458 (1971).
182. Infra, Chapter IV, text accompanying nn. 111–17.
183. 2 Farrand 551.
184. Infra, Chapter IX, text accompanying nn. 11–55.

even of a single Justice, does not have nearly the same impact. Then too, if the President brings disgrace upon his office by a lesser offense, for example, by openly associating with notorious corruptionists, the people can remove him at the polls. Judges are not thus removable; and their tenure "during good behavior" indicates that the Framers did not intend to shelter those who indulged in disgraceful conduct short of "great offenses." This is not to import the standards of "good behavior" into "high crimes and misdemeanors" but to indicate that serious infractions of "good behavior," though less than "great offenses," may yet amount to "high crimes and misdemeanors" at common law.[185] In sum, it is difficult on removal of judges to attribute to the Founders an intention to curtail the common law scope of "high crimes and misdemeanors" (which they employed with consciousness of their "technical" meaning) merely because they had good reason, not present in the case of judges, to stress that removal of the President required "great offenses."

The difficulty of construing the same words differently for different purposes was met head-on by Judge Edmund Pendleton of the Virginia Court of Appeals, the venerable presiding officer of the Virginia Ratification Convention. Speaking in another context he said: "In the construction of general words of this sort, they will apply concurrently to different purposes. We give them that distributive interpretation, and liberal explication, which will not make them mischievous."[185a]

Two convictions of judges rest on offenses that fell short of the "great offenses" contemplated for impeachment of the President. District Judge Halsted Ritter (1936), though acquitted of specific criminal charges, was nonetheless convicted for bringing his court "into scandal and disrepute," in part because he accepted substantial gifts from wealthy residents of his district, notwithstanding they had no cases pending

---

185 The relation of "good behavior" to "high crimes and misdemeanors" is considered infra, Chapter IV.
185a. 3 Elliot 550.

before him.[186] The conviction of Judge Robert W. Archbald (1912) falls in the same category, to mention only the charge of speculating in coal properties while a member of the Commerce Court.[187] These convictions did not take account of the problem here considered; indeed it has been all but unnoticed. But they are explicable, it seems to me, only on the theory that the "great offenses" applicable to the impeachment of the President do not limit the common law scope of "high crimes and misdemeanors" when the subject of impeachment is a judge.

Having first espoused the view that the words "high crimes and misdemeanors" should be given one and the same meaning in either case, I am sensible of the difficulties involved in adoption of the view that impeachment of judges requires a less restricted reading of those words than does that of the President. Perhaps a better solution is to take a more hospitable approach to removal of judges *by judges* for infractions of "good behavior"; although that would not account for the *Archbald* and *Ritter* impeachments, nor permit the desirable impeachment of judges who bring disgrace upon the courts by offenses that fall short of "high misdemeanors" when the judiciary fails to clean its own house.

Mention should here be made of an associated problem: both the *Archbald* and *Ritter* impeachments turned on misconduct outside of court, and the Senate assumed rather than inquired whether such conduct is impeachable. That assumption presents still other difficulties, which will be discussed in Chapter VI. In short, the conclusion that "high crimes and misdemeanors" was adopted as a "technical," limiting phrase leaves perplexing problems; and it is to be hoped that my reflections will stimulate further study and investigation.

---

186. Supra, n. 15. The Senate convicted Ritter on the charge that he brought "his court into scandal and disrepute, to the prejudice of said court and public confidence in the administration of justice therein, and to the prejudice of public respect and confidence in the Federal judiciary." 80 *Cong. Rec.* 5606 (74th Cong. 2d Sess. 1936).
187. Supra, n. 15.

THE ROLE OF POLITICS—
MOTIVATION OF THE FRAMERS

In a comment on the Resolution for the impeachment of Justice Douglas introduced in the House on April 16, 1970, by Congressman Gerald R. Ford, Milton Viorst states: "the 110 sponsors of the anti-Douglas resolution are all conservative Republicans and Dixiecrats. This seems persuasive evidence in support of the hypothesis which virtually everyone in Washington accepts: that the undertaking seeks not simply to impeach William Orville Douglas but to discredit the liberalism inherent in the domestic programs of Democratic Administrations since the New Deal." [188]

Congressman Ford all but conceded that his Resolution was in retaliation for the Senate's rejection of two of President Nixon's nominees to the Supreme Court.[189] 'Twas ever thus; impeachment was "essentially a political [factional] weapon" from its inception in 1386; [190] and so it continued to be when it was revived in the reign of James I in order to bring his corrupt and oppressive ministers to heel.[191] What was the impeachment of Strafford, where the rising forces of parliamentary government defeated Stuart absolutism, but "political"? Post-Restoration impeachments were unabashedly "political." [192] Commenting on the Warren Hastings impeachment, which was dragging its weary way while the Constitutional Convention was sitting, Macaulay spoke bitingly of the political motivation of the tribunal: "Whatever confidence may be

---

188. Viorst, "Bill Douglas Has Never Stopped Fighting the Bullies of Yakima," *N.Y. Times Mag.* June 14, 1970, pp. 8, 32.
189. Facing up to the view of his resolution as retaliation for the "rejection of the [Nixon] nominees for the Supreme Court, Judge Haynsworth and Judge Carswell," Ford said, "In a narrow sense, no. But in a larger sense, I do not think there can be two standards for membership on the Supreme Court, one for Mr. Justice Fortas [who, Ford implies, resigned under pressure], another for Mr. Justice Douglas." 116 *Cong. Rec.* H3118–3119 (daily ed. April 15, 1970).
190. Clarke, supra, n. 22 at 184.
191. Roberts 23–28; see also Jefferson, supra, n. 130.
192. Roberts 32. True, the Ford charges resemble the partisanship which characterized post-Restoration impeachments, supra, Introduction, text accompanying nn. 11–12, rather than the high issues of constitutional policy which brought about the downfall of Strafford.

placed in the decision of the Peers on an appeal arising out of ordinary litigation, it is certain that no man has the least confidence in this impartiality, when a great public functionary, charged with a great state crime, is brought to their bar. They are all politicians. There is hardly one among them whose vote on an impeachment may not be confidently predicted before a witness has been examined." [193]

Impeachment did not change color in this country. When John Adams proposed in 1774 to impeach, and the Massachusetts Assembly filed charges against, the Justices because they had declined to renounce royal salaries in place of those theretofore paid by the Assembly's appropriation, it was in the hope of reaping political benefits.[194] In the Convention Charles Pinckney warned that Congress "under the influence of heat and faction" would "throw [the President] out of office," [195] a prophecy which barely fell short of realization eighty years later when the conviction of Andrew Johnson was narrowly defeated.[196] Explaining impeachment to the People, who were being asked to adopt the Constitution, Hamilton stated that the prosecution of impeachments "will seldom fail to agitate the passions of the whole community, and to divide it into parties more or less friendly or inimical to the accused. In many cases it will connect itself with the preexisting factions . . . and in such cases there will always be the greatest danger that the decision will be regulated more by the comparative strength of the parties, than by the real demonstrations of innocence or guilt." [197]

193. Quoted in J. H. Dougherty, "Inherent Limitations upon Impeachment," 23 *Yale L. J.* 60, 69 (1913). In the impeachment of President Andrew Johnson, "Prejudgment on the part of most Senators . . . was brazenly announced." John F. Kennedy, *Profiles in Courage* 133 (New York, 1961).

194. Herbert Johnson, "William Cushing," in 1 Leon Friedman & Fred Israel, ed. *The Justices of the United States Supreme Court* 57–58 (New York, 1969); 2 Adams 329–331. See also infra, Chapter III, text accompanying n. 95.

195. 2 Farrand 551.

196. Senators who sought to vote according to the dictates of conscience rather than of politics were subjected to intolerable pressure, and some were later hounded out of office. Julius Marke, *Vignettes of Legal History* 141–168 (South Hackensack, N.J., 1965); Kennedy, supra, n. 193 at 126, 133, 135, 142.

197. *Federalist* No. 65 at 424.

From the outset, the impeachment of the insane Judge John Pickering in 1804 became a political football.[198] The Federalists were entrenched in the Judiciary, which was practically an arm of the party;[199] judges, as in the case of Justice Samuel Chase, were making intemperate attacks on the Jefferson administration in harangues to the grand jury,[200] and they all but goaded the infuriated Jeffersonians to launch a number of impeachments.[201] Chase was impeached, and he was saved from retribution not so much by innocence of the charges as by a solid Federalist phalanx aided by a disaffected Republican swing-group who blocked a two-thirds vote.[202] In a study of the role of partisan politics in the impeachment of judges since 1903, Ten Broek found a correlation between votes and party affiliations; at times the voting split along party lines.[203] The impeachment of Judge Ritter in 1936 is thus described by Gerald Ford: "Judge Ritter was a transplanted conservative Colorado Republican appointed to the bench in solidly Democratic Florida by President Coolidge. He was convicted by a coalition of liberal Republicans, New Deal Democrats, and Farmer-Labor and Progressive Party Senators in what might be called the northwestern strategy of that era."[204] Notwithstanding, it may be added, Ford unhesitatingly borrowed the explanatory utterances of

---

198. 3 Albert E. Beveridge, *The Life of John Marshall* 164–167 (Boston, 1919). Pickering was convicted "by a strictly partisan vote." Ibid. 167. Dumas Malone states that "Members of the Judge's own party strongly opposed his resignation for purely political reasons." 4 D. Malone, *Jefferson and His Time* 463 (Boston, 1970). For corroborative details, see Lynn Turner, "The Impeachment of John Pickering," 54 *Am. Hist. Rev.* 485, 488, 490, 496, 505 (1949).

199. The "national judiciary, [a little earlier] one hundred per cent. Federalist, amounted to an arm of the party." 4 Malone 458.

200. 1 Warren 274–276. For example, Chief Justice Dana of Massachusetts "in a charge to the Grand Jury denounced the Vice-President [Jefferson] and the minority in Congress as 'apostles of atheism and anarchy, bloodshed and plunder.'" Ibid. 275.

201. E.g., The Trial of Alexander Addison (Lancaster, Pa. 1803). See infra, Chapter VIII, nn. 23, 29.

202. 4 Malone 479–480. Six days before the trial ended, it was announced that Jefferson and Clinton had been elected President and Vice President. Aaron Burr, who presided at the Chase trial, had been "'dumped' by Jefferson in favor of Burr's arch political rival, George Clinton . . . the Republican Senators who voted against impeachment were from the Burr strongholds." Frank Thompson & D. H. Pollitt, "Impeachment of Federal Judges: An Historical Overview," 49 *N. Car. L. Rev.* 87, 99 n. 79 (1970).

203. Ten Broek, supra, n. 16 at 193; see also Potts, supra, n. 16 at 35–36.

204. 116 *Cong. Rec.* H3114 (daily ed. April 15, 1970).

several Senators in that proceeding for his own proposal to impeach Justice Douglas.

In evaluating the uses of impeachment, therefore, we should not close our eyes to its political inception and continued political coloration, even in the cases of the English Justices who had offended Parliament by assisting the King to carry out detested policies.[205] The drawing of political lines goes to the *motivation* behind the given impeachment; and here we need to recall that in the great English impeachments the charges were often the sheerest facade for a "politically" motivated proceeding. But be the motivation what it may, in this country impeachment must proceed within the confines of "high crimes and misdemeanors" as exhibited by the prior English practice. No judicial impeachment, it may be added, aroused anything like the furious factionalism exhibited in the impeachment of President Andrew Johnson,[205a] which also lacked the normal braking action of conviction by a two-thirds vote because of the overwhelming representation of Republicans in both Houses. The critical focus, in sum, should be not on political animus, for that is the nature of the beast, but on whether Congress is proceeding within the limits of "high crimes and misdemeanors" and affording a fair trial, as was emphatically not the case in the Johnson impeachment.

Why, one asks, did the Framers take up this faction-ridden mechanism, which long before the Hastings trial had seen its best days?—for with the achievement of ministerial accountability early in the eighteenth century, the prime purpose of impeachment had been accomplished, and thenceforth it found but infrequent use.[206] Then too, the successful struggle for ministerial accountability to Parliament, as has been noted, was not really relevant to a system which set up three separate, independent departments and made Cabinet members responsible to the President, not to Con-

---

205. Supra, nn. 175 and 176.
205a. Infra. Ch. IX.
206. Holdsworth remarks that between 1621 "and 1715 there were fifty cases of impeachment brought to trial. Since that date there have been only four." 1 Holdsworth 382 (3d ed. 1922). See also Roberts 413. For 18th century impeachments, see ibid. 380 n. 1.

gress.[207] Chafee considered that "the British situation is obvious to us, but it was not obvious to the men who framed our Constitution . . . They thought of the King as the Chief Executive and replaced him by the President . . . You cannot get rid of a King by a hostile vote in the legislature, and perhaps their minds stopped there. The importance of a majority vote in Parliament for getting rid of the King's main advisers was overlooked." [208] To my mind, there was no confusion on this score. Gouverneur Morris reminded the Convention that the President "is not the King, but the prime-Minister," and that in England the prime Minister was "the real King." [209] James Iredell adverted to the maxim that the King can do no wrong and exulted in the "happier" American provision which made the President himself triable.[210] Thus they made sure to reach the topmost executive by impeachment. Nor did the Framers overlook "the importance of a majority vote in the Parliament for getting rid of the King's main advisers." In setting up an independent President who was to serve for a term, and in making cabinet officers a part of the executive branch, the Framers surely were aware that a mere vote of no confidence could not, as in England, topple a Secretary.[211] Indeed they rejected legislative removal by Address of judges, members of another independent branch.[212] It was

---

207. For example, Article II, § 2(1) provides that the President "may require the Opinion, in writing, of the principal officers in each of the Executive departments, upon any subject relating to the duties of their respective offices."
208. Chafee 141.
209. 2 Farrand 69, 104.
210. 4 Elliot 109. See also George Nicholas and Francis Corbin in the Virginia Convention, 3 Elliot 17, 516.
211. Consider Pierce Butler's remark in the Convention on May 30th, when Edmund Randolph proposed three separate departments, that he had "opposed the grant of powers to Congrs. [under the Articles of Confederation], heretofore, because the whole power was vested in one body. The proposed distribution of the powers into different bodies changes the case." 1 Farrand 34. That Congress, Butler surely knew, appointed the Secretary of Foreign Affairs. And the suggestion, rejected by the Convention, that the national legislature appoint the President, 2 Farrand 56–58, again indicates some awareness that the Prime Minister owed his office to Parliament. The Framers knew the English practice and consciously diverged from it. Cf. Madison, 2 Farrand 56. Further awareness of details of English practice is disclosed by Hamilton's distinction in the New York convention between representatives of the "rotten boroughs" "in the possession and gift of the king," from the "knights of the shire" in the Commons, who "have been generally esteemed a virtuous and incorruptible set of men" and "have uniformly supported and strengthened the constitutional claims of the people." 2 Elliot 264–265.
212. 2 Farrand 428–429.

because the separation of powers left no room for removal by a vote of no confidence that impeachment was adopted as a safety valve, a security against an oppressive or corrupt President and his sheltered ministers.

In truth, the gaze of the Framers was concentrated on the struggles with royal oppression during the seventeenth century rather than on the system of parliamentary government fully achieved in the eighteenth.[213] Like the Colonists, the Founders were haunted by the threat to liberty of illimitable greed for power.[214] Before them marched a procession of ghostly despots; [215] they were familiar with absolutist Stuart claims; many dreaded that a single Executive might tend to monarchy.[216] Benjamin Franklin asked, "What was the

213. Supra, Introduction, n. 28. Compare the comments of Corbin and Pendleton on impeachment of ministers for giving pernicious "advice." Supra, n. 169.

214. See supra, n. 2; cf. Berger, *Congress v. Court* 8–14. Speaking of the earlier State constitutions, Professor Gordon Wood stated: "Nothing indicates better how thoroughly Americans were imbued with Whig apprehensions of misapplied ruling power than their rather unthinking adoption of this ancient English proceeding enabling 'the grand inquest of the Colony,' the representatives of the people, to pull 'over-grown criminals who are above the reach of ordinary justice' to the ground." Wood, supra, n. 106 at 141.

The records of the Federal and Ratification Conventions indicate that the adoption of impeachment was anything but "unthinking." The objective of the Framers, I suggest, was like that outlined by an English barrister in 1791, who, writing long after the achievement of ministerial accountability, adverted to the "obvious and great" advantage "which impeachments afford, as a check and terror to bad Ministers," and cited as an additional reason "why it ought to be cherished by Englishmen" that "it furnishes the most effectual preservative against the corrupt administration of justice ... That Ministers are not now violating the principles of the constitution, or that the administration of justice is now free from the slightest stain or suspicion or corruption, furnishes no reason for abolishing this mode of trial, for it is impossible to know, how much the security, with which we now enjoy our constitution and liberties, and how much of the satisfaction, with which we now confide in these unsuspected characters, that now grace the seats of justice, may be derived from the existence of this very institution." Quoted 4 Hatsell 69–70, 253n. The Founders were very much aware of the lessons of the past. See text accompanying nn. 4–9, 214–224, 229–230, and n. 169.

215. See supra, introduction, n. 29. Compare John Dickinson's review of Charles I's reign, quoted Bailyn 145; James Alexander's criticism of the despotic Charles I in Alexander, *A Brief Narrative of the Case and Trial of John Peter Zenger* 28, S. N. Katz ed. (Cambridge, Mass. 1963); and a reference to James I's claim to make judges who were subservient to his will. *Pennsylvania Gazette* (1737), quoted ibid. 181, 184; and a recital that "Charles II had entered into a secret league with France to render himself absolute, and enslave his subjects." Ibid. 188. See also supra, n. 167. C. C. Pinckney adverted to the fact that Charles II was bribed. 4 Elliot 264. Patrick Henry referred to Stuart usurpations till they were banished. 3 Elliot 316.

216. 1 Farrand 66, 83, 90, 96, 101, 113, 119, 152, 425; 2 Farrand 35–36, 101, 278, 513, 632, 640. In the North Carolina Convention, which rejected the Constitution Rawlin Lowndes said, "as to our changing from a republic, it was what everybody must naturally expect. How easy the transition! No

practice before this in cases where the chief Magistrate rendered himself obnoxious? Why, recourse was had to assassination." [217] Impeachment was preferable. Fear of presidential abuses prevailed over frequent objections that impeachment threatened a President's independence.[218] "No point," said George Mason, "is of more importance than that the right of impeachment should be continued." [219]

This may seem strange in light of Madison's warning that all power tended to be drawn into the "legislative vortex." [220] It is true that the Framers had come to fear legislative excesses as a result of the states' post-1776 experience; [221] and they fenced the Congress about with a number of restraints, for example, a presidential veto and judicial review. But the Colonial Assemblies—elected by themselves, not thrust upon them by a distant King, as were judges and Governors, had been the darling of the Colonists.[222] At the end of the Colonial period the prevalent belief, said Corwin, was that " 'the executive magistracy' was the natural enemy, the legislative assembly the natural friend of liberty." [223] To the radical Whig mind, a potent influence on Colonial thinking, "the most insidious and powerful weapon of eighteenth century despotism" was the "power of appointment to offices." The Executive, it was feared, could fasten his grip on the community by placemen scattered strategically over the nation.[224] Such suspicions died hard; and when a choice had to be made the Framers preferred the Congress to the President, for as Madison explained in the *Federalist*,

---

difficulty in finding a king: the President was the man proper for the appointment." 4 Elliot 311. In Virginia, Patrick Henry said, "your President may easily become king." 3 Elliot 58; and see ibid. 60.

217. 2 Farrand 65.
218. Ibid. 64–69.
219. Ibid. 65.
220. Ibid. 35; see also *Federalist* No. 48 at 322.
221. Berger, *Congress v. Court* 10–12, 82, 182; and ibid. 12 n. 21.
222. Thus it was that James Wilson explained the predilection for the legislature. 1 Wilson 292–293. The persistence of this feeling may be gathered from his admonition in 1791 that it was time to regard Executive and judges equally with the legislature as representatives of the people. Ibid. 293. See Madison, supra, Introduction, n. 25.
223. Edward Corwin, *The President: Office and Powers* 4 (3d ed. New York, 1948).
224. Wood, supra, n. 106 at 143; see also Bailyn 102–103.

"in republican government, the legislative authority necessarily predominates." [225]

One thing is clear: in the impeachment debate the Convention was almost exclusively concerned with the President.[226] The extent to which the President occupied center stage can be gathered from the fact that the addition to the impeachment clause of the "Vice President and all civil officers" only took place on September 8, shortly before the Convention adjourned.[227] But the Founders were also fearful of the ministers and favorites whom Kings had refused to remove,[228] and they dwelt repeatedly on the need of power to oust corrupt or oppressive ministers whom the President might seek to shelter. "Few ministers," said George Nicholas in the Virginia Convention, "will ever run the risk of being impeached, when they know the King cannot protect them by a pardon," [229] and how much less against impeachment itself. No friend of the Constitution, Patrick Henry deplored the absence of "blocks and gibbets, those necessary instruments of justice." But he too looked to impeachment; Blackstone, he said, "tells you that the minister who will sacrifice the interest of the nation is

---

225. *Federalist* No. 51 at 338. In the preceding sentence Madison stated, "it is not possible to give to each department an equal power of self-defense." Justice Brandeis referred to the deep-seated conviction of the English and American people that "they must look to representative assemblies for protection of their liberties." Myers v. United States, 272 U.S. 52, 294–295 (1926) (dissenting opinion: Holmes, J., concurring). But I would not intimate that Congress was given unlimited power over the President. To the contrary, the power was carefully hedged about. See supra, text accompanying nn. 157–160, 167–170.
226. 2 Farrand 64–69; and see supra, text accompanying nn. 167–171.
227. 2 Farrand 552.
228. The Founders' concern with removal of "favorites" emerges most clearly in the First Congress. Madison stated: "It is very possible that an officer who may not incur the displeasure of the President may be guilty of actions that ought to forfeit his place. The power of this House may reach him by means of an impeachment, and he may be removed even against the will of the President." 1 *Ann. Cong.* 372. He made the point again, ibid. 498; see also supra, text accompanying n. 168. Abraham Baldwin, also a Framer, put the matter more sharply: a "bad man" "can be got out in despite of the President. We can impeach him and drag him from his place." 1 *Ann. Cong.* 558. "It is this clause," said Elias Boudinot, "which guards the rights of the House, and enables them to pull down an improper officer, although he should be supported by all the power of the Executive." Ibid. 468. Similar remarks were made by Egbert Benson, ibid. 382; Samuel Livermore, ibid. 478; John Lawrence, ibid. 377, 482; and Benjamin Goodhue, ibid. 534. The nagging fear of "favorites" testifies that the Founders had studied the lessons of 17th century experience. See supra, n. 95.
229. 3 Elliot 17.

subject to parliamentary impeachment. This has ever been effectual." [230]

Should application of "high crimes and misdemeanors" to ministers (Secretaries) be read in terms of the "great offenses" emphasized with respect to the President? Some of the same considerations are present. Secretaries are readily removable by the President; and disgraceful conduct which discredits the administration makes their retention a political liability. For the rare case of stubborn presidential retention of a Secretary whose misconduct falls short of a "great offense," his tenure will expire with the term of the President.

In contrast to references to impeachment of ministers in the Ratification Conventions, no mention of impeachment of judges is to be found.[231] This may in part be due to confidence in their "preeminent integrity." [232] But that confidence carried with it a recognized responsibility for conduct that comported with the office.[233] If tenure "during good behavior" was designed to set them apart from "every successive tide of party," [234] it still carried the implication that "good behavior" was the condition of tenure.

---

230. Ibid. 512. See also the remarks of Corbin and Pendleton, supra, text accompanying n. 169.
231. The one exception is Wilson's rejection of the argument that judicial review was a hollow reed because judges could be impeached for holding an act unconstitutional. Supra, text accompanying n. 174.
232. Berger, *Congress v. Court* 117–119. St. George Tucker referred in 1803 to the "preeminent integrity which amidst surrounding corruption, beams with genuine lustre from the English courts." 1 Tucker App. 356 (part 1). Madison said in the Virginia Convention, "Were I to select a power which might be given with confidence, it would be the judicial power." 3 Elliot 535. Edmund Randolph there said, "No man says anything against them." 3 Elliot 205. See also, infra, Chapter III n. 78; Berger, *Congress v. Court* 185–186.
233. See infra, Chapter VI, nn. 38, 43, and text accompanying n. 44.
234. 1 Wilson 297.

Chapter III

JUDICIAL REVIEW

"The Constitution," said Charles Evans Hughes, "is what the judges say it is." [1] If "treason, bribery, and other high crimes and misdemeanors" likewise are what the Senate say they are, Congressman Gerald Ford did not err in asserting that "impeachable offenses" are what House and Senate jointly "consider [them] to be." [2] From Story onward it has been thought that in the domain of impeachment the Senate has the last word; [3] that even the issue whether the charged misconduct constitutes an impeachable offense is unreviewable, because the trial of impeachments is confided to the Senate alone. [4] This view has the weighty approval of Professor Herbert Wechsler: "Who . . . would contend that the civil courts may properly review a judgment of impeachment when article I, section 3 declares that the 'sole power to try' is in the Senate? That any proper trial of an impeach-

---

1. 1 Merlo Pusey, *Charles Evans Hughes* 204 (New York, 1951). This was uttered in 1907 in the course of an address delivered in Elmira. Later Hughes explained, "The inference that I was picturing constitutional interpretations by the courts as a matter of judicial caprice . . . was farthest from my mind." Ibid.

2. Supra, Chapter II, n. 1.

3. Story § 805, said with respect to impeachments, "the true exposition of the Constitution" is a matter, "the final decision of which may reasonably be left to the high tribunal constituting the court of impeachment when the occasion shall arise." See also, ibid. § 802; Rawle 219. G. W. Ross, " 'Good Behavior' of Federal Judges," 12 *Univ. Kan. City L. Rev.* 119, 125–126 (1944); 1 Thomas Cooley, *The General Principles of Constitutional Law* 206 (Boston, 4th ed. 1931).

4. In Ritter v. United States, 84 Ct. Cl. 293 (1936), cert. den. 300 U.S. 668 (1937), the court dismissed the suit of a judge who contended that the Senate had exceeded its jurisdiction in trying him on charges which did not constitute impeachable offenses under the Constitution, saying that the provision that conferred upon the Senate "the sole power to try all impeachments," Article 1, §3 (6), meant that "no other tribunal should have any jurisdiction of the cases tried under the provisions with reference to impeachment." Ibid. 296.

ment may present issues of the most important constitutional dimension . . . is simply immaterial in this connection. What is explicit in the trial of an impeachment or, to take another case, the seating or expulsion of a Senator or Representative, may well be found in others." [5] On one branch of his assertion, the "seating" of a Representative, Wechsler has since been repudiated by the Supreme Court in *Powell v. McCormack,* which reviewed and set aside the exclusion of Congressman Adam Clayton Powell from the House for serious misconduct.[6] That decision calls for reconsideration of the scope of the Senate's "sole" right to try impeachments.

At issue in *Powell* were Article I, §2 (2), which describes three qualifications that must be met by a Representative, and Article I, §5 (1), which provides that "each House shall be the judge of the . . . qualifications of its own members." In a suit against the Speaker of the House, Powell maintained that the exclusion was unconstitutional because exclusion was limited to the requirements of age, citizenship, and residence contained in Article I, §2.[7] The House invoked the Article I, §5, provision empowering it to "be the judge of the . . . qualifications of its own members," and went on to "note that under Art. I, §3, the Senate has the 'sole power' to try all impeachments." And it argued that "these delegations (to 'judge,' to 'punish' and to 'try') to the Legislative Branch are explicit grants of 'judicial power' to the Congress and constitute specific exceptions to the general mandate of Article III that the 'judicial power' shall be vested in the federal courts." [8] In consequence, the House maintained, the Court could do no "more than to declare its lack of jurisdiction to proceed." [9] The Court rejected the contention and found that the

5. Wechsler, "Toward Neutral Principles of Constitutional Law," 73 *Harv. L. Rev.* 1, 8 (1959).
6. 395 U.S. 486 (1969). The Committee reported that Powell "had wrongfully diverted House funds for the use of others and himself, that he had made false reports on expenditures of foreign currency [belonging to the United States] to the Committee on House Administration." Ibid. 492.
7. Ibid. 489.
8. Ibid. 513–514.
9. Ibid. 514.

"political question" turned on an inquiry whether the claimed power had been committed to the House by the Constitution.[10]

The Court began with the established proposition that "it is the province and duty of the judicial department to determine . . . whether the powers of any branch of the government . . . have been exercised in conformity to the Constitution; and if they have not to treat their acts as null and void." [11] And it concluded that "in judging the qualifications of its members Congress is limited to the standing qualifications prescribed in the Constitution." Consequently "the House was without power to exclude [Powell] from its membership" on grounds of misconduct.[12] In other words, the power to "judge" does not permit the Senate to add to the Constitutional "qualifications." The point was made admirably by Senator Murdock in the debate on the unsuccessful attempt to exclude Senator William Langer in 1941: "whoever heard the word 'judge' used as meaning the power to add to what already is the law." [13] The Senate, he stated, has no right "to add to the qualifications" enumerated in the Constitution; and, said Justice Douglas, concurring in *Powell v. McCormack,* Murdock "stated the correct constitutional principle governing the present case." [14]

Like the three qualifications of Article I, §2(2)— age, residence, and citizenship—to which exclusion is limited, impeachment, by Article II, §4, is confined to three grounds, "treason, bribery, or other high crimes and misdemeanors," which circumscribe the Senate's "sole power to try all impeachments." The "sole power to try all impeachments" does not enlarge these three grounds. For the "power to try" is limited by the power to "convict"; and by the express terms of Article II, §4, only "on impeachment for, and conviction of, treason, bribery, or other high crimes and misdemeanors" may the President "be removed."

A threshold question is whether a misconstruction

---

10. Ibid. 519–521.
11. Ibid. 506.
12. Ibid. 550.
13. Quoted ibid. 557.
14. Ibid. 559.

of "treason," for example, is the equivalent of adding a fourth category, as was "misconduct" in *Powell*. Let us test the analogy. The Senate may convict for "treason"; by Article III, §3, "treason" is defined as levying war against the United States or giving aid and comfort to its enemies. Suppose the Senate convicts the President of treason on the ground that he attempted to subvert the Constitution, a favorite formula of Parliament.[15] Whether this be labeled as a "construction" or a "factual determination," it plainly amounts to an attempt to add an omitted category to the Constitutional definition.[16] When George Mason suggested the addition to "treason, bribery" of the word "maladministration," he explained to the Convention that "treason . . . will not reach many great and dangerous offenses . . . Attempts to subvert the Constitution may not be treason as above defined." [17] And James Wilson stated in the Pennsylvania Ratification Convention that "it has not been left to the legislature to extend the crime and punishment of treason so far as they thought proper." [18] To impeach for "treason" on grounds that are outside the constitutional definition, therefore, lies beyond the powers conferred. Nor does a freewheeling senatorial power to expand the common law definition of "bribery" stand any better.[19]

The phrase "high crimes and misdemeanors" is not as sharply defined as "treason" or "bribery," but it does have an ascertainable content in English practice.[20] If the phrase leaves more latitude for judgment to the Senate, this is not equivalent to unbridled discretion. The last thing intended by the Framers was

---

15. Compare Wilson's remarks, supra, Chapter II, text accompanying n. 5. It "will not do to say that the argument is drawn from extremes. Constitutional provisions are based on the possibilities of extremes." General Oil Co. v. Crain, 209 U.S. 211, 226–227 (1908).

16. Consequently the Court's reservation in *Powell* of the issue whether under the "political question" doctrine review would be barred of "the House's factual determination that a member did not meet one of the standing qualifications," 395 U.S. at 591 n. 42, is inapposite.

17. 2 Farrand 550.

18. 2 Elliot 469.

19. Compare supra, Chapter II, text accompanying n. 160, and n. 160.

20. Supra, Chapter II, text accompanying nn. 81–92. The alternative, as Story stressed, was to leave "the whole proceedings . . . completely at the arbitrary pleasure" of the Congress. Supra, Chapter II, n. 161; see also Story § 799.

to leave the Senate free to declare any conduct whatsoever a "high crime and misdemeanor." Madison
rejected "maladministration" because "so vague a term
will be equivalent to a tenure during the pleasure of
the Senate"; [21] and "high crimes and misdemeanors"
was adopted in its place with knowledge that it had
a "limited" and "technical meaning," a meaning to be
sought by recurrence to English practice.[22]

It may be objected that this analysis is too pat, that
the three categories of *Powell v. McCormack,* age,
citizenship, and residence, are quite clear, whereas
"high crimes and misdemeanors" lacks definite con-
tours—that the Court would have no standards, no
criteria whereby to settle the boundaries of the power
thus conferred. The problem of "standards" was much
greater in *Baker v. Carr,* the "reapportionment" case,
where there were no precedents whatever to serve as
guidelines. Yet despite the "enormously difficult problem of working out standards for utilizing the equal
protection provision in the apportionment cases" the
Supreme Court entered the field.[23] The "standards"
problem posed by "high crimes and misdemeanors"
is very considerably less; the English practice, if impre-
cise, may yet be reduced to recognizable categories
that serve as an outline such as was altogether lacking
in "apportionment."

When the constitutional boundaries of a power are
in issue, the problem of "criteria," I suggest, is not
really apposite. The "lack of criteria" test derives from
Luther v. Borden, which arose out of the Dorr Rebellion in Rhode Island. In the aftermath, "two groups
laid competing claims to recognition as the lawful government," invoking the guarantee of a republican form
of government.[24] The Court dwelt on the practical and
evidentiary difficulties of determining whether the
Rhode Island government sponsored by the Dorr faction was adopted by the authorized voters.[25] In sub-

---

21. 2 Farrand 550.
22. Supra, Chapter II, text accompanying nn. 157–165.
23. 369 U.S. 186 (1962). The quotation is from Thomas I. Emerson,
"Malapportionment and Judicial Review," 72 *Yale L. J.* 64, 65 (1962).
24. 7 How. (48 U.S.) 1 (1849). So the Court explained at 369 U.S. 218.
25. 7 How. at 41–42; cf. Coleman v. Miller, 307 U.S. 433, 453–454
(1939).

stance, the Court refused to become involved in factual findings in a political struggle for power between competing state factions; it held that whether a state had changed its form of government was a question for the "political power," the Congress. Even so, it took care to differentiate and reserve

the high power ... of passing judgment upon the acts ... of the legislative and executive branches of federal government, and of determining *whether they are beyond the limits of power* marked out for them respectively by the Constitution.[26]

In the performance of this function the Court has undertaken massive tasks of interpretation without any standards to guide it, as *Baker v. Carr* illustrates, and as the related path of case law pricking out the boundaries between state and federal powers under the "commerce clause," for example, again demonstrates.[27]

Another criterion of "political question," in the words of Justice Frankfurter, is the difficulty of "finding appropriate modes of relief." [28] A Court which did not boggle at the refractory remedial difficulties [29] posed by reapportionment [30] should not shy from entering a decree, in a suit to recover salary or in a quo warranto action (to challenge title to office of a successor) ordering payment of the salary or restoration of the suitor to office.

The "political question" doctrine, in my judgment,

---

26. 7 How. at 47 (emphasis added).
27. Justice Douglas remarked, "Adjudication is often perplexing and complicated. An example of the extreme complexity of the task can be seen in a decree apportioning water among several States . . . The constitutional guide is often vague, as the decisions under the Due Process and Commerce Clauses show." Baker v. Carr, 269 U.S. at 245 (concurring opinion).
28. 369 U.S. at 278 (dissenting opinion).
29. Bickel points out that "the decisive factor in Colegrove could not well have been the difficulty or uncertainty that might attend enforcement of a judicial decree. A judicial system that swallowed *Brown v. Board of Education* and *Cooper v. Aaron* could hardly strain at *Colegrove v. Green* or *Baker v. Carr.*" Alexander M. Bickel, "The Durability of Colegrove v. Green," 72 *Yale L. J.* 39, 40 (1962). The Court itself acknowledged in Brown v. Board of Education, 347 U.S. 483, 495 (1954), that "the formulation of decrees in these cases presents problems of considerable complexity."
30. Emerson, supra, n. 23 at 75–78. Cf. Allen P. Sindler, "Baker v. Carr; How to 'Sear the Conscience' of Legislators," 72 *Yale L. J.* 23, 32–38 (1962).

has been seriously undermined by *Baker v. Carr* and *Powell v. McCormack*. That doctrine was a self-denying judicial construct without roots in constitutional history. No mention is made in the debates of the Framers or Ratifiers that "political questions" should be excluded from the ambit of judicial review. Constitutional questions are inescapably political.[31] In at least one pre-1787 case, *Commonwealth v. Caton*,[32] Judge George Wythe took for granted the justiciability of a dispute between the Virginia Senate and the House of Delegates. That dispute lay at the bottom of an appeal from a conviction for treason; and Wythe unhesitatingly assimilated the duty "to protect one branch of the legislature, and, consequently, the whole community, against the usurpations of the other" to the judicial duty to protect "a solitary individual against the rapacity of the sovereign." It speaks volumes on whether a dispute between different branches of government was deemed justiciable in 1782 that so eminent a scholar and jurist should not have experienced the slightest qualm on that score.

No case has thus far held that a legislative-executive conflict is nonjusticiable. On the contrary, the Supreme Court has already acted "as umpire between the Congress and the president"[33] in *Myers v. United States*[34] and *United States v. Lovett*.[35] In *Myers* the Court permitted the Attorney General to attack a

---

31. "From the beginning the Court had to resolve what were essentially political issues—the accommodation between the states and the central government." Felix Frankfurter & James M. Landis, *The Business of the Supreme Court* 318 (New York, 1927). It needs to be borne in mind that a "Constitution is a political instrument. It deals with government and governmental powers . . . It is not a question whether the considerations are political, for nearly every consideration arising from the Constitution can be so described." Melbourne v. Commonwealth of Australia, 74 *Commw. L. R.* 31, 82 (1947) (per Dixon, J.) This had been anticipated by de Tocqueville: "The American judge is brought into the political arena independently of his own will . . . The political question which he is called upon to resolve is connected with the interest of the suitors and he cannot refuse to decide it without abdicating the duties of his post." 1 Alexis de Tocqueville, *Democracy in America* 101 (New York, 1899).
32. 4 Call. 5, 8 (Va. 1782).
33. Nathaniel L. Nathanson, "The Supreme Court as a Unit of National Government: Herein of Separation of Powers and Political Questions," 6 *J. Pub. L.* 331, 332 (1957). In the Congressional debate on the President's "removal" power, which involved the question whether the Senate should share in the "removal" of officers to whose appointment it "consented," Elbridge Gerry, one of the Framers, said that "Judges are the Constitutional umpires on such questions." 1 *Ann. Cong.* 473.
34. 272 U.S. 52 (1926).
35. 328 U.S. 303, 312 (1946).

congressionally enacted statute that limited the President's removal power; and as Justice Frankfurter remarked, "on the Court's special invitation Senator George Wharton Pepper, of Pennsylvania, presented the position of Congress [in opposition to the Attorney General] at the bar of this Court." [36] In *United States v. Lovett,* which involved a statute designed to force certain agencies to discharge respondents, the Court rejected the argument of counsel for Congress [37] that "since Congress under the Constitution has complete control over appropriations, a challenge to the measure's constitutionality does not present a justiciable question in the courts, but is merely a political issue over which Congress has final say." [38]

In form, to be sure, both *Myers* and *Lovett* were private suits for recovery of salary, but in fact they were vigorous contests between Congress and the President. And in the teeth of a Congressional attempt to deprive the Supreme Court of jurisdiction to review a provision curtailing the effect of a presidential pardon, the Court held in *United States v. Klein* that the provision "impairs the executive authority," [39] thus jumping into a political thicket with both feet. If the central "power" issue was "political," the curse was not removed because it was presented in a "private" litigation. "Some arbiter," said Justice Jackson, "is almost indispensable when power . . . is balanced between different branches, as the legislative and execu-

---

36. Wiener v. United States, 357 U.S. 349, 353 (1958).
37. 328 U.S. at 304.
38. Ibid. 313, 314. Nathanson, supra, n. 33 at 337, says that United States v. Lovett "in one sense . . . was a protection of the executive power over personnel against unwarranted intrusions by Congress." See also 328 U.S. at 312. The Court found no "need" to decide whether the statute was an "unconstitutional encroachment on executive power," for it held against Congress on another Constitutional ground. Ibid. 307.

In Youngstown Sheet & Tube Co. v. Sawyer, 343 U.S. 579 (1952), the President had directed the Secretary of Commerce to seize and operate most of the nation's steel mills on the ground that a strike called by the steel union would jeopardize the continued production of steel indispensable to the national defense. The seizure was held invalid because Congress had "refused to adopt that method of settling labor disputes," ibid. 586, 602, 603, 657, because, in the words of Justice Burton, concurring, the President "invaded the jurisdiction of Congress." Ibid. 660. Citing *Youngstown* (infra, n. 40), Berk v. Laird, 429 F. 2d 302, 304–305 (2d Cir. 1970), held that the courts were empowered to make a "constitutional decision involving the division of powers between the legislative and executive branches."
39. 13 Wall. (80 U.S.) 128, 145, 148 (1871).

tive . . . Each unit cannot be left to judge the limits
of its own power." [40] The courts, said *Baker v. Carr,*
"cannot reject as 'no law suit' a bona fide controversy
as to whether some action denominated 'political'
exceeds constitutional authority." [41] For, said Chief
Justice White in another "political question" case, it
is the "ever present duty" of the courts "to enforce
and uphold the applicable provisions of the Constitution as to each and every exercise of governmental
power." [42]

Another argument against judicial review of impeachment is that the power to "try" and to issue a
"judgment," Article I, §3(7), is itself "judicial" and,
in consequence, the Court may not substitute its "judicial power" for that of the Senate. On this view,
there is an exception from Article III, §2(1), which
provides that "the judicial power shall extend to all
cases . . . arising under this Constitution." [43] If there
be indeed a conflict between the judicial jurisdiction
in "all cases" and the Senate's "sole power to try all
impeachments," our course has been marked out by
Chief Justice Marshall: "When two principles come in
conflict with each other, the court must give them both
a reasonable construction, so as to preserve them both
to a reasonable extent," a canon earlier cited by

---

40. Robert H. Jackson, *The Struggle for Judicial Supremacy* 9 (New
York, 1941). Justice Frankfurter said: "The judiciary may, as this case
proves, have to intervene in determining where the authority lies as between the democratic forces in our scheme of government," i.e., between
Congress and the President. Youngstown Sheet & Tube Co. v. Sawyer, 343
U.S. 579, 597 (1952) (concurring).
In the words of Professor Willard Hurst, "An institution which wields
practical power—which controls men's wills or behavior—must be accountable for its purposes and its performance by criteria not wholly in
the control of the institution itself . . . [A]n institution with power must
be accountable to some judgment other than that of the power holders
. . ." J. W. Hurst, *The Legitimacy of the Business Corporation in the
Law of the United States* 58 (Charlottesville, Va., 1970).
41. 369 U.S. at 217. Compare, supra, text accompanying n. 38.
42. Pacific States Tel. & Tel. Co. v. Oregon, 223 U.S. 118, 150 (1912).
43. See supra, text accompanying n. 8; and infra, n. 46. In his charge
to the jury in the Trial of John Fries (1799), Justice Iredell, who had
fought for ratification of the Constitution in the North Carolina Convention, said, "The whole judicial power of the government is vested in the
judges of the United States . . . to themselves it belongs to explain the law
and the Constitution; and Congress have no more right nor authority over
the judicial exposition of these acts, than this court has to make a law
to bind them." Wharton 588. See also his remarks, quoted supra, Chapter
II, n. 2.

Elbridge Gerry in the First Congress.[44] We need only read the power to "try" as a grant of jurisdiction to try a case in the first instance, leaving untouched an appeal to the Supreme Court from action in excess of jurisdiction—a case "arising under" the Constitution. For there is good reason to conclude that in 1787 the word "try" connoted a trial rather than a hearing on appeal.[45] An accommodation of a "trial" by the Senate with an appeal from violation of constitutional boundaries would harmonize with the *Powell* holding that the Article I, §5(1) provision that "each House shall be the *Judge* of the . . . qualifications of its own members" does not bar inquiry into action in excess of jurisdiction. Surely the power to "try" is not more comprehensive or final than the power to "judge"; [46]

---

44. United States v. Burr, 25 Fed. Cas. No. 14,692e, pp. 38, 39 (C. Ct. Va. 1807). Gerry asked, "Why should we construe any part of the Constitution in such a manner as to destroy its essential principles when a more consonant construction can be obtained?" 1 *Ann. Cong.* 473.

How far Marshall went to preserve the integrity of the word "all" is illustrated by United States v. Burr, 25 Fed. Cas. No. 14,692d (C. Ct. Va. 1807). He sustained a subpoena to the President because the Eighth Amendment gives to the accused "in all criminal prosecutions, a right to compulsory process for obtaining witnesses in his favor," saying that in these provisions "there is no exception whatever . . . no person could claim an exemption from them, but one who could not be a witness." Ibid. 34. He rejected the English practice whereunder it was thought "incompatible" with the dignity of the King "to appear under the process of the court," pointing out that the President was impeachable. In short, the right to summon witnesses "in all criminal prosecutions" rose above a claim of Executive privilege.

45. The related word "trial" was defined by Blackstone as "the examination of matters of fact in issue," 3 Blackstone 330. Probably this was over-narrow, for it had earlier been deemed to include the trial of issues of law. John Rastall, Termes de la Ley, "Trial" (London, ed. 1742). But that it was thought of as the *initial* determination appears from Dr. Samuel Johnson's *Dictionary of the English Language* (London, 3d ed. 1765): "*Trial* is used in law for the examination of all causes . . . the trial is the issue, which is tried upon the indictment . . ." The affinity between "tried" (try) and "trial" weaves through the old examples cited under "trial" and "try" in the *Oxford English Dictionary*. True, Gouverneur Morris stated that the Supreme Court "was to try the President [on indictment] after the trial of the impeachment," 2 Farrand 500, but this was a layman's misuse of legal terms, for the Court would not "try" the criminal charges but would only hear an appeal from the trial. So too, when Hamilton, explaining the choice of the Senate, asked, "Would it be proper that the persons who had disposed of his fame . . . in one trial, should in another trial, for the same offense, be also the disposers of his life and his fortune," *Federalist* No. 65 at 426, he was employing shorthand for quick grasp by laymen rather than attempting to alter the accepted meaning of the word "try." Thomas Dawes was closer to the mark in the Massachusetts Convention: "When people, in common language talk of a trial at the Court of Common Pleas . . . do they not include . . . the jurors as well as the judges?" 2 Elliot 113.

46. In Powell v. McCormack, the House analogized its exclusion power to the power "to try all impeachments," and characterized both as "explicit grants of 'judicial power' to the Congress [which] constitute specific exceptions" to the Article III grant of "judicial power" to the courts. 395 U.S. at 513.

nor is protection of the other branches from wrongful congressional onslaughts more intrusive than review of "qualifications of [each House's] own members." In sum, my suggested accommodation is between the initial power to "try" a case and an appeal from a case "arising under this Constitution," which presents a question of constitutionality—of "law" as distinguished from questions of fact settled by the triers of the facts.[46a]

Perhaps the most formidable argument against review is the fact that the trial of impeachments was originally entrusted to the Supreme Court but was at length transferred to the Senate over the objections of Charles Pinckney and Madison.[47] The reason for the change, Gouverneur Morris explained, was that the Supreme Court "was to try the President [upon indictment] after the trial of the impeachment."[48] At a later point he added, "no other tribunal than the Senate could be trusted. The Supreme Court were too few in number and might be warped or corrupted."[49] So too, Roger Sherman "regarded the Supreme Court as improper to try the President because the judges would be appointed by him"[50] and inferentially would therefore be partial to him. These views were expanded by Hamilton in *The Federalist;* he emphasized that where-

---

46a. The distinction was taken by the Supreme Court in Luther v. Borden. Supra, text accompanying n. 26.

47. 1 Farrand 22; 2 Farrand 186, 493, 547. For the Madison objection, see ibid. 551, 612; Edmund Randolph also objected, ibid. 563. Charles Pinckney warned the Convention that the two Houses would combine against the President "under the influence of heat and faction," 2 Farrand 551, a prophecy later realized in the impeachment of Andrew Johnson.

48. Ibid. 500.

49. Ibid. 551. There is good reason not to read into the Morris words an insulation of arbitrary convictions by the Senate. Initially he had opposed impeachment altogether because it would "render the Executive dependent on those who are to impeach." 2 Farrand 65. When he was convinced of the desirability of impeachment, he cautioned that in making the President amenable to justice, "we should take care to provide some mode that will not make him dependent on the legislature." Ibid. 69. And he declared that "If the Legislature is . . . to impeach or to influence the impeachment, the Executive will be the mere creature of it." 2 Farrand 103. One who held such views would hardly have maintained, for example, that there was no protection for the President against the arbitrary Senate substitution of a verdict by majority rather than the two-thirds vote Article II, § 3 (7) requires for conviction. In his own words, addressed to the power of the judiciary to declare legislative acts unconstitutional, "A control over the legislature might have its inconveniences. But view the danger on the other side . . . Encroachments of the popular branch . . . ought to be guarded against." 2 Farrand 299.

50. 2 Farrand 551. Said Madison in *Federalist* No. 51 at 336: "the permanent tenure by which the [judicial] appointments are held . . . must soon destroy all sense of dependence on the authority conferring them."

as the Senate would be "unawed" by the fact that the House lodged charges, it was doubtful whether the Supreme Court would be "endowed with so evident a portion of fortitude" to execute "so difficult a task." [51] But he himself later explained that judicial tenure was made secure in order that the courts would have the "fortitude" to set aside unconstitutional statutes. Such decisions would defy *both* Houses, as well as the President who signed the bill; and on a state level they had generated no little political excitement.[52] It was the part of wisdom to shield the courts from participation in a trial crackling with political lightning. But the trial by the Senate would draw much of the lightning; and as the lawyers among the Founders knew from their own law practice, appellate tribunals generally do not operate in a superheated atmosphere.

This is not to say that the prospect of reviewing an impeachment as passion-laden as that of President Andrew Johnson might not give the Court pause. At that point the prestige of the Court, badly tarnished by the *Dred Scott* decision, was at its nadir,[53] and any attempt at judicial intervention might well have invited harsh reprisals by the inflamed Reconstruction Congress. But in the intervening century the Court has been restored to its high position in the regard and loyalty of the American people—witness the reaction to President Franklin Roosevelt's "Court-Packing Plan"

---

51. *Federalist* No. 65 at 425.

52. *Federalist* No. 78 at 507–509. This was a main objective of judicial independence, for there had been pre-1787 threats of impeachment against State judges who declared statutes unconstitutional. See Berger, *Congress v. Court* 42–43, 117–119. Writing about the aftermath of Marshall's opinions subordinating the States to the Nation, Beveridge said, "So it came to pass that John Marshall and the Supreme Court became a center about which swirled the forces of a fast-gathering storm that raged with increasing fury until its thunders were the roar of cannon, its lightning the flashes of battle." 4 Albert J. Beveridge, *The Life of John Marshall* 370 (Boston, 1919).

Hamilton's choice of the Senate over the Court prompted St. George Tucker to say, "If that court could not be relied on for the trial of impeachments, much less would it seem worthy of reliance for the determination of any question between the United States and any particular State; much less to decide upon the life and death of a person whose crimes might subject him to impeachment but whose influence might avert a conviction." 1 Tucker App. 335 (part I).

53. Dred Scott v. Sandford, 19 How. (60 U.S.) 393 (1857). The "grave injury that the Court sustained through its decision has been universally recognized. Its action was a public calamity." The "widespread and bitter attacks upon the judges who joined in the decision undermined confidence in the Court." Charles E. Hughes, *The Supreme Court of the United States States* 50 (New York, 1928).

notwithstanding popular discontent with the Court's anti-New Deal decisions—[54] and vindictive reprisals by the Congress would be almost unthinkable. If there be indeed power to review impeachments in excess of jurisdiction, we may expect of the Court the fortitude exhibited by the aged Chief Justice Taney when Lincoln's suspension of habeas corpus was brought before him at the outbreak of the Civil War.[55] Then too, the far more frequent impeachments of lesser figures, for example, district judges, would be unlikely to whip up a storm of such dimensions as might a direct confrontation between President and Congress. If we are to test judicial review by practical considerations, let the focus be not on the solitary Johnson impeachment but on the humdrum impeachments of district judges, the usual fare. And such considerations are at best prudential, a counsel of judicial self-restraint rather than a denial of jurisdiction to declare that constitutional bounds have been transgressed.

Another Hamilton argument drawn from Morris was that it would be improper for one and the same tribunal to hear both the impeachment and the criminal prosecution.[56] Historically, however, the House of

---

54. See Berger, *Congress v. Court* 291, 292.

55. Ex parte Merryman, Fed. Cas. No. 9,847 at p. 153 (Cir. Ct. Md. 1861). A military officer seized a citizen upon "vague charges" and conveyed him to Fort McHenry. The commanding officer rejected service of a writ of habeas corpus and stated that the President had authorized him to suspend the writ at his discretion. Taney held that only Congress could suspend the writ, and stated, "my duty was too plain to be mistaken. I have exercised all the power which the constitution and laws confer upon me, but that power has been resisted by a force too strong for me to overcome."

56. *Federalist* No. 65 at 426. Apparently he did not regard the Article I, § 3 (6) provision that "When the President . . . is tried, the Chief Justice shall preside" as a disqualification. Archibald Maclaine explained this provision in the North Carolina Convention in part on the ground that on removal of the President the office "devolves on the Vice-President . . . if the Vice-President should be judge, might he not look at the office of President, and endeavor to influence the Senate against him?" 4 Elliot 44. Should the Justices review the impeachment of a fellow Justice? They could scarcely refuse to sit in review on his conviction for a criminal offense, and it is hard to differentiate a conviction on impeachment. The Justice is no less entitled to review by the Court than any other citizen; since no other tribunal is furnished for the purpose the Justices must hear the case. Under the "rule of necessity" a judge may not disqualify himself on ground of bias where no other can hear the cause. Evans v. Gore, 253 U.S. 245 (1920). The need that a Justice be protected from impeachment on grounds not authorized by the Constitution rises above any embarrassment the Justices might feel on review. The case is easier when the Chief Justice presides over the Senate on the impeachment of the President. He may disqualify himself on review by the Court, leaving his brethren to hear the cause.

Lords tried both issues, that is, a removal and criminal punishment, in the same proceeding; whereas the Supreme Court would try neither, but would hear appeals on two different records of trials by two different triers of fact, the Senate and a jury, attended by all the limitations that surround such review. For me, the Hamilton arguments have an air of post hoc rationalization. A preference for the Senate based upon the Sherman-Morris fear of judicial corruptibility or Hamilton's fear that the Court would lack fortitude is hardly reconcilable with representations made to secure judicial tenure, or with the widespread confidence in the judiciary as constrasted with pervasive distrust of Congress.[57]

Whatever the effect of the Morris-Sherman-Hamilton remarks, their force seems to me counteracted by relevant representations made in the Ratification Conventions; for as Jefferson and Madison emphasized, the meaning of the Constitution is to be sought in the explanations made to those who adopted it.[58] There the fear of congressional excesses, of oppression and tyranny, found its sharpest expression; and proponents of adoption repeatedly assured the Ratifiers that Congress was "fenced" about with "limits," and that judicial review would confine Congress within bounds.[59] To be sure, no express mention of judicial review was made with respect to impeachment, but the same may be said

57. In weighing the words of Hamilton, we may bear in mind Marshall's statement: "No tribute can be paid [to the authors of *The Federalist*] which exceeds their merit; but in applying their opinions to the cases which may arise in the progress of our government, a right to judge of their correctness must be retained." McCulloch v. Maryland, 4 Wheat. (17 U.S.) 316, 431 (1819).

58. For Madison, the meaning of the Constitution was to be looked for "in the State Conventions which accepted and ratified the Constitution." Quoted Charles Warren, *Congress, the Constitution and the Supreme Court* 67 n. 1 (Boston, 1925). As president, Jefferson declared that he read the Constitution with the "meaning contemplated *by the plain understanding of the people at the time of its adoption*—a meaning to be found in the explanation of those who advocated it." Quoted in 4 Elliot 446. See also for Madison, 9 Madison, *Writings of James Madison* 191, 372 (New York, G. Hunt ed. 1900–1910); and 3 Farrand 518, letter of December 1831; and 3 Farrand 534.

It needs to be remembered that the Constitution, as it left the hands of the Framers, was, in the words of Archibald Maclaine in the North Carolina Convention, "only a mere proposal . . . If the people approve of it it becomes their act . . . It is no more than a blank till it be adopted by the people." 4 Elliot 24–25. The explanations made in the Ratification Conventions, designed to allay their fears, are therefore of prime importance.

59. The citations are collected in Berger, *Congress v. Court* 12–16, 124–129, 131–134, 136–140.

of other equally important functions, "To what quarter," asked John Marshall in the Virginia Convention, "will you look for protection from infringement on the constitution, if . . . not . . . to the judiciary? There is no other body that can afford such protection." [60] Similar remarks were made by others in the Virginia and other Conventions. [61]

It was never intended that Congress should be the final judge of the boundaries of its own powers. [62] Not an inkling is to be found in the records of the Ratification Conventions that the area of impeachment was to constitute an exception, that here Congress was left free to rampage at will. To the contrary, when Archibald Maclaine sought in the North Carolina Convention, by construction of the impeachment power, to allay certain fears expressed by Timothy Bloodworth, Bloodworth commented: "I do not distrust him, but I distrust them [Congress]. I wish to leave no latitude of construction." And Joseph Taylor, speaking to Congress' power to impeach, stated that the Senators are "one of the branches of power [of Congress] which we dread under this Constitution." [63] So intense was such distrust that North Carolina rejected the Constitution notwithstanding its ratification by ten states. [64] In no Convention was a claim of illimitable power made with respect to any function of Congress. Astonishment would have greeted a claim that the structure so carefully reared upon the separation of powers [65] could be

---

60. 3 Elliot 554. Compare G. Morris, supra, text accompanying n. 49. Thirty-one years later Marshall again asked, "To whom more safely than to the judges are judicial questions to be referred? . . . *No* tribunal can be less liable to be swayed by unworthy motives from a conscientious performance of duty. . . . [I]f the judge be personally disinterested, he is as exempt from any political opinion that might influence his opinion, as imperfect human institutions can make him." Gerald Gunther, *John Marshall's Defense of McCulloch v. Maryland* 211–212 (Stanford Univ. Press 1969).

61. Supra, n. 59.

62. After his remarks in *Federalist* No. 65, Hamilton himself stated in No. 78 at 506, that it "cannot be the natural presumption" that the "legislative body are themselves the constitutional judges of their own powers . . . It is far more rational to suppose that the courts were designed . . . to keep the [legislature] within the limits assigned to their authority." See also Berger, *Congress v. Court* 186–187.

63. 4 Elliot 50, 33.

64. Berger, *Congress v. Court* 131–132.

65. Wilson stated in the Pennsylvania Ratification Convention that "To have the executive officers dependent upon the legislative, would certainly be a violation of that principle, so necessary to preserve the freedom of re-

shaken to bits whenever Congress chose to resort to an unlimited power of impeachment. Instead there was a constant drumfire of warnings against congressional oppression.[66] Bearing in mind that ratification was touch and go,[67] I daresay that, had such claims been made, ratification would have foundered.[68]

Although impeachment was chiefly designed to check Executive abuses and oppressions,[69] there was no thought of delivering either the President or the Judiciary to the unbounded discretion of Congress. This is attested by the Framers' rejection of the unfettered removal by Address,[70] by their rejection of "maladministration" because that was "so vague" as to leave tenure "at the pleasure" of the Senate,[71] and by the substitution of "high crimes and misdemeanors" with knowledge that it had a "limited" and "technical meaning." Nothing less than a limited power of impeachment would have satisfied the opposition, who regarded impeachment as a threat to presidential independence.[72] Impeachment was a carefully limited exception to the

---

publics, that the legislative and executive powers should be separate and independent." 2 Elliot 511–512. Madison regarded the separation of powers as "a fundamental principle of our Government," 2 Farrand 56, as did Mason, ibid. 86, and Randolph, ibid. 256. And Wilson was "most apprehensive of a dissolution of the Government from the legislature swallowing up all the other powers." Ibid. 300. An utterly uncontrolled and unlimited power of impeachment would go far to realize that fear.

66. Supra, n. 59.

67. There were narrow majorities in Virginia, Massachusetts, New Hampshire, and New York. Berger, *Congress v. Court* 17–18.

68. As Alexander White of Virginia stated in the First Congress, insisting that the federal government must adhere to the limits described in the Constitution: "This was the ground on which the friends of the Government supported the Constitution . . . it could not have been supported on any other. If this principle had not been successfully maintained by its advocates in the convention of the State from which I came, the Constitution could never have been ratified." 1 *Ann. Cong.* 515.

69. Cf. supra, Chapter II, text accompanying nn. 167–171. See also 2 Farrand 64–69; cf. 1 Farrand 78, 85, 92, 230; 2 Farrand 61, 116, 172, 185–186, 495, 499.

70. 2 Farrand 428, 429; see also infra, Chapter IV, text accompanying nn. 131–135.

71. Supra, Chapter II, text accompanying n. 158. In a discussion of the "removal" power in the First Congress, William Smith stated: "It would be improper that [judges] should depend on this House for the degree of permanency which is essential to secure the integrity of judges." 1 *Ann. Cong.* 508. See also John Lawrence, ibid. 377. Judges, said James Wilson, could not be "made to depend on every gust of faction which might prevail in the two branches of our Government." 2 Farrand 429. Cf. Hamilton, *Federalist* No. 78 at 509; Berger, *Congress v. Court* 117–119.

George Mason "opposed decidedly making the Executive the mere creature of the Legislature as a violation of the fundamental principle of good government." 1 Farrand 86. See also Charles Pinckney, ibid. 66; Rufus King, ibid. 67; Edmund Randolph, ibid. 67; Madison, ibid. 551. See also supra, n. 65.

72. See preceding note.

separation of powers,[73] tolerable only if exercised strictly within bounds. "Limits" on Congress determined by Congress itself would be no limits at all.[74]

To this it may be answered that just as the ultimate guarantee that the judiciary will not step out of bounds is the self-restraint of the Court, so the Senate too must be trusted to exercise self-restraint. It is one thing, however, to expect self-restraint of judges schooled to disciplined, dispassionate judgment, and not subject to the gusts of faction, and something else again to expect self-restraint of a body predominantly political in character and which both in England and the United States has been unable to shake off partisan considerations when sitting in judgment.[75] Self-restraint could be relied upon with respect to the judiciary because, in the words of Hamilton, they "have neither FORCE nor WILL, but merely judgment," and were "therefore the least dangerous to the political rights of the Constitution." [76] But the vast powers to prescribe the rules under which we live—to initiate action, as is the case even in impeachment—cast Congress in a very different role, one toward which there was pervasive distrust. The fact is that the Ratifiers feared Congress and trusted judges. Said Madison in the Virginia Convention, "Were I to select a power which might be given with confidence it would be judicial power" [77]—a sentiment echoed in the several Conventions.[78] The courts, said Hamilton in *The Federalist,* were "the bulwark of a limited constitution against legislative encroach-

---

73. Elias Boudinot said in the First Congress that impeachment was one of the "exceptions to a principle," i.e., to the separation of powers. 1 *Ann. Cong.* 527. Compare George Mason, supra, n. 71; see also Michael Stone, 1 *Ann. Cong.* 564–565.

74. See supra, n. 62.

75. Supra, Chapter II, text accompanying nn. 188–204.

76. *Federalist* No. 78 at 505. Compare Hamilton's recognition that impeachment would be colored by political passions, supra, Chapter II, text accompanying n. 197.

77. 3 Elliot 535. Compare Madison's statement in the First Congress that the legislative power is the "most likely to be abused," 1 *Ann. Cong.* 437. William Smith, too, stated that the legislative power "is perhaps more liable to abuse than the judicial." Ibid. 816.

78. Patrick Henry, who wished to "see Congressional oppression crushed in embryo," declared it "the highest encomium on this country, that the acts of the legislature, if unconstitutional, are liable to be opposed by the judiciary." 3 Elliot 546, 325. See also the remarks of John Marshall, supra, text accompanying n. 60; Berger, *Congress v. Court* 186–188.

ments" [79]—a statement anticipated by Jefferson.[80] In recommending adoption of the Bill of Rights, Madison stated in the First Congress that the courts would be "an impenetrable bulwark against every assumption of power in the Legislative and Executive." [81]

Constitutional limits, as *Powell v. McCormack* again reminds us, are subject to judicial enforcement; and I would urge that judicial review of impeachments is required to protect the other branches from Congress' arbitrary will. It is hardly likely that the Framers, so devoted to "checks and balances," who so painstakingly piled one check of Congress on another,[82] would reject a crucial check at the nerve center of the separation of powers. They scarcely contemplated that their wise precautions must crumble when Congress dons its "judicial" hat, that then Congress would be free to shake the other branches to their very foundations. Before we swallow such consequences, the intention of the Framers to insulate congressional transgressions of the "limits" they imposed upon impeachment should be proved, not casually assumed. The Constitution, said the Supreme Court, condemns "all arbitrary exercise of power;" [83] "there is no place in our constitutional system for the exercise of arbitrary power." [84] The "sole power to try" affords no more exemption from that doctrine than does the sole power to legislate, which, it needs no citation, does not extend to arbitrary acts.

Finally, if it be assumed that the "sole power to try" conferred insulation from review, it must yield to the subsequent Fifth Amendment provision that "no person" shall "be deprived of life, liberty, or property without due process of law." If the Constitution does in

---

79. *Federalist* No. 78 at 508.
80. In 1787, when Jefferson welcomed the "check" which a Bill of Rights "puts in the hands of the judiciary," he added. "This is a body, which if rendered independent . . . merits confidence for their learning and integrity." 5 Jefferson, *The Writings of Thomas Jefferson* 81 (New York, Ford ed. 1892–1899).
81. 1 *Ann. Cong.* 439.
82. Berger, *Congress v. Court* 20–21.
83. ICC v. Louisville & N.R.R. 227 U.S. 88, 91 (1913).
84. Garfield v. United States ex rel. Goldsby, 211 U.S. 249, 262 (1908); Yick Wo v. Hopkins, 118 U.S. 356, 370 (1886); and see Raoul Berger, "Administrative Arbitrariness: A Synthesis," 78 *Yale L. J.* 965, 980–981 (1969).

fact place limits upon the power of impeachment, action beyond those limits is without "due process of law" in its primal sense: "when the great barons of England wrung from King John . . . the concession that neither their lives nor their property should be disposed of by the crown, except as provided by the law of the land, they meant by 'law of the land' the ancient and customary laws of the English people." [85] In our system the place of the "ancient and customary laws" was taken by the Constitution; and Article VI, §2, expressly makes the Constitution "the supreme law of the land." Injurious action not authorized by the Constitution is therefore contrary to the "law of the land" and is forbidden by the due process clause. "Due process" has been epitomized by the Court as the "protection of the individual against arbitrary action." [86] One who enters government service does not cease to be a "person" within the Fifth Amendment; and an impeachment for offenses outside constitutional authorization would deny him the protection afforded by "due process." It would be passing strange to conclude that a citizen may invoke the judicial "bulwark" against a twenty-dollar fine [87] but not against an unconstitutional impeachment, removal from and perpetual disqualification to hold federal office.[88] Here protection of the individual coincides with preservation of the separation of powers; and the interests of the assaulted branch, as Judge George Wythe perceived, are one with the interest of the "whole community." Those interests counsel us to give full scope to the "strong American bias in favor of a judicial determination of constitutional and legal issues," [89] and to deny insulation from review of impeachments in defiance of constitutional bounds.

---

85. Davidson v. New Orleans, 96 U.S. 97, 102 (1877).
86. Ohio Bell Tel. Co. v. Public Service Commn., 301 U.S. 292, 302 (1937).
87. Frank v. Maryland, 359 U.S. 360 (1959).
88. In Vitarelli v. Seaton, 359 U.S. 535 (1959), and Service v. Dulles, 354 U.S. 363 (1957), it was held that the government must comply with gratuitous regulations governing the dismissal of federal employees, notwithstanding the regulations were required by neither the Constitution nor statute. Can it be that in impeaching a Justice or a Cabinet officer Congress may dispense with a requirement contained in the Constitution?
89. Louis L. Jaffe, "Standing to Secure Judicial Review: Public Actions," 74 *Harv. L. Rev.* 1265, 1302 (1961).

Chapter IV

EXCLUSIVITY
OF IMPEACHMENT
AND JUDICIAL
"GOOD BEHAVIOR" TENURE

The Founders conceived impeachment chiefly as a "bridle" upon the President and his coadjutors; [1] and they would in all probability have been astonished to learn [2] that impeachment would sink to the ouster of little judges soiled by corruption. [3] Deeply versed in English history, [4] and familiar with the State Trials, [5] they may be taken to know that impeachment was so heavy a "piece of artillery" as to "be unfit for ordinary use." [6] Was the provision of artillery to deal with presidential usurpation or oppression intended to forbid

---

1. Chapter II, text accompanying nn. 167–172, 213–230; *Federalist* No. 65 at 425.
2. Cf. Chapter II, n. 32.
3. Borkin passim; infra, text accompanying nn. 193–197. I would not suggest that impeachment is unavailable for that purpose but rather that it should be employed only if other means of removal fail or are not exercised.
4. Among the frequent references to English history in the Ratification Conventions are: Virginia: George Nicholas, 3 Elliot 19; Francis Corbin, ibid. 111–112; Edmund Randolph, ibid. 123, 400–401; Patrick Henry, ibid. 174–175, 316; William Grayson, ibid. 275, 281. North Carolina: David Caldwell and Archibald Maclaine, 4 Elliot 62–63; Governor Samuel Johnston, ibid. 64; James Iredell, ibid. 148, 197. South Carolina: C. C. Pinckney, 4 Elliot 264; Rawlins Lowndes, ibid. 271.
   See also infra, n. 97; and supra, Introduction, n. 21; Chapter II, text accompanying n. 167; nn. 169 and 215; H. T. Colbourn, *The Lamp of Experience* 19, 25, 156, 183, 185 (Chapel Hill, N.C., 1965); Bailyn, passim.
5. Infra, n. 97.
6. Viscount James Bryce, *The American Commonwealth* 233 (New York, 1908): "It is like a hundred-ton gun which needs complex machinery to bring in into position, an enormous charge of powder to fire it, and a large mark to aim at." Woodrow Wilson said of the impeachment process, "it requires something like passion to set them agoing; and nothing short of the grossest offenses against the plain law of the land will suffice to give them speed and effectiveness. Indignation so great as to overgrow party interest may secure a conviction; nothing else can." Woodrow Wilson, *Congressional Government* 275–276 (Boston, 1901).

use of a pistol to lay low a thief?[7] Did the Framers require that the wheels of a great nation[8] must grind to a halt so that Congress, and Congress alone, could oust a venal judge?[9]

The claim that impeachment is the exclusive means for removal of judges rests on three propositions. First, the express provision for impeachment in the Constitution bars all alternatives; second, judges enjoy "absolute independence," not only from Congress and the Executive, but from other judges as well; third, the Article III provision that judges "shall hold their offices during good behavior" affords them special insulation from removal except by impeachment. Contemporary interest is heightened by Congressman Gerald Ford's proposal, in which 109 other Representatives joined, to impeach Justice William O. Douglas for "high crimes and misdemeanors." Apparently aware that the alleged misconduct may fall short of "high crimes and misdemeanors," Ford maintains that impeachment comprehends departures from "good behavior."[10] If judges are removable only by impeachment, as Justice Douglas asserted in his

---

7. Coincident with the impeachment of Justice Chase there was talk of impeaching district judge Richard Peters, who sat with him on circuit. When this came to Peters' ears, he wrote, "I think they are charging a cannon to shoot a mosquito." 1 Warren 289 n. 1.

8. The Framers were highly conscious that they were drafting for posterity. 1 Farrand 424, 431, 490, 515. See also Edward S. Corwin, *Court over Constitution: A Study of Judicial Review as an Instrument of Popular Government* 222–223 (New York, 1938).

9. In the First Congress, John Vining declared that impeachment is "insufficient to secure the public safety," pointing to the ongoing trial of Warren Hastings: "With what difficulty was that prosecution carried on! What a length of time did it take to determine!" 1 *Ann. Cong.* 373. The Hastings impeachment was begun in May 1787, infra, n. 222. Subsequently Vining termed impeachment "circuitous," "dilatory and inefficient," "what delays and uncertainties," ibid. 465, 571. To the same effect, James Madison, Elias Boudinot, Thomas Hartley, and Peter Sylvester, ibid. 497, 375, 480, 562.

"Impeachment trials have averaged from sixteen to seventeen days, and the case of Judge Archbald ran for six weeks." Borkin 195. The trial of Justice Samuel Chase ran for about a month, and the printed account occupies almost 600 pages. 14 *Ann. Cong.* 80 (8th Cong. 2d Sess. 1805).

After the trial of district judge Halsted Ritter, Congressman Chauncey W. Reed said that Senators should not thus "be required to set aside their legislative duties, paralyzing for weeks the lawmaking function . . ." 81 *Cong. Rec.* 6175 (1937). In the midst of World War II, Professor J. W. Moore wrote, "it is absurd to think that large national interests during the war . . . must wait upon the trial of Judge X." J. W. Moore, "Judicial Trial and Removal of Federal Judges: H.R. 146," 20 *Tex. L. Rev.* 352, 356 (1942). See also infra, text accompanying nn. 199–200.

10. 116 *Cong. Rec.* H3113–3114 (daily ed. April 15, 1970); Viorst, "Bill Douglas Has Never Stopped Fighting the Bullies of Yakima," *N. Y. Times Mag.*, June 14, 1970, § 6 at 8, 32.

Chandler dissents,[11] and if "high crimes and misdemeanors" does not include all "misbehavior," it follows that judges guilty of misbehavior not amounting to impeachable misconduct are sealed into office, notwithstanding the teaching of the common law that tenure "during good behavior" is terminated by bad behavior. Three major questions emerge. First, does impeachment furnish the exclusive mode for removal of judges; second, do impeachable offenses—"high crimes and misdemeanors"—embrace all infractions of "good behavior"; and third, if they do not, what alternative method of removal for nonincluded infractions is available?

It will serve to clarify analysis if we bear in mind the differences in provenance, objectives, and procedures between "high crimes and misdemeanors" and "good behavior." The former phrase is found in Article II, §4, the Executive Article of the Constitution: "The President, Vice President and all civil officers of the United States shall be removed from office on impeachment for, and conviction of, treason, bribery, or other high crimes and misdemeanors." "High crimes and misdemeanors," we have seen, fell into recognizable categories at common law; and the Framers adopted the phrase in its "limited" and "technical meaning" and contemplated that at least with respect to the President it would be employed only for "great offenses." [12] At common law, impeachment was a criminal proceeding, brought by the House of Commons before the House of Lords (under the "course of Parliament" as distinguished from the general criminal law), which resulted in removal from office and in severe penalties.[13] Generally speaking, it was employed to remove great officers whom the King refused or neglected to remove. The provision for judicial tenure "during good behavior" is located in Article

---

11. Chandler v. Judicial Council of the Tenth Circuit, 398 U.S. 74, 136 (1970) (Douglas, J., dissenting) (hereinafter cited as Chandler II); Chandler v. Judicial Council of the Tenth Circuit, 382 U.S. 1003, 1005–1006 (1966) (Black, J., dissenting, with Douglas, J., concurring) (hereinafter cited as Chandler I).
12. Supra, Chapter II, text accompanying nn. 82–92, 157–160; n. 159. See also infra, text accompanying nn. 183, 187–189.
13. Supra, Chapter II, text accompanying nn. 25–39, 62–80.

III, §1, the Judicial Article. Derelictions from "good behavior," on the other hand, were reachable in the English courts by a proceeding to forfeit one's office. This was brought by one who appointed, to either private or public office, and its sole object was to remove the misbehaving appointee. Apparently, the standard of misbehavior was broader than that of "high crimes and misdemeanors." In sum, at common law there was a civil forfeiture proceeding for "misbehavior" brought in a court, and a criminal impeachment proceeding brought by and in the Parliament. Never, so far as I could discover, did an English impeachment charge a breach of "good behavior"; instead the stock charges were "high treason and other high crimes and misdemeanors." The intermixture of these quite distinct common law procedures and doctrines has bred analytical confusion in the United States.

GOOD BEHAVIOR

Its Common Law Connotations

Only judges "hold their offices during good behavior"; no other officer has such tenure. The President and Vice President are elected for a term; civil officers, who with the President and Vice President are the subjects of impeachment, are appointed for indeterminate terms. "Good behavior" is commonly associated with the Act of Settlement (1700),[14] which granted judges tenure *quamdiu se bene gesserint,* that is, for so long as they conduct themselves well, and also provided for termination by the Crown upon the Address (formal request) of both Houses of Parliament.[15] The origin of "good behavior," however, long

---

14. John Taylor of Caroline stated of "good behavior" tenure, "It was invented in England to counteract the influence of the crown over the judges." Quoted in William S. Carpenter, "Repeal of the Judiciary Act of 1801," 9 *Am. Pol. Sci. Rev.* 519, 525 (1915). See also G. W. Ross, " 'Good Behavior' of Federal Judges," 12 *U. Kan. City L. Rev.* 119 (1944); Robert Kramer & Jerome A. Barron, "The Constitutionality of Removal and Mandatory Retirement Procedures for the Federal Judiciary: The Meaning of 'During Good Behavior,' " 35 *Geo. Wash. L. Rev.* 455, 456 (1967).

15. The Act of Settlement, 12 & 13 Will. 3, c. 2. §3. For further discussion of the Act see infra, text accompanying nn. 131–35.

antedates the Act. Judge St. George Tucker, a pioneer commentator on the Constitution, noted in 1803 that "these words (by a long train of decisions in England even as far back as the reign of Edward the third) in all commissions and grants, public and private, imported an office or estate, for the life of the grantee, determinable only by his death, or breach of good behavior." [16] So it had been indicated by Coke; [17] and in 1693 Chief Justice Holt understood Coke to refer to "an estate for life determinable upon misbehavior" and declared that "'during good behavior' is during life; it is so long as he doth behave himself well." [18] In the Pennsylvania Ratification Convention, Chief Justice McKean explained that "the judges may continue for life, if they shall so long behave themselves well"; [19] and citations can be multiplied. When Hamilton stated that "good behavior" was copied from the English model he stated the obvious. [20]

It only confuses matters to set life tenure apart from tenure "during good behavior," as Robert Kramer and Jerome Barron have done, and to read various shorthand references to judicial tenure as "life tenure," which, "taken at face value . . . appear to preclude judicial removal," that is, removal by judges. [21] For at common law "life tenure" itself was conditioned on "good behavior" and was determined by the grantee's misbehavior. [22] "Good behavior," said Coke, "is no more than the law would have implied, if the office had been granted for life." [23] Bacon's *Abridgment* explains more fully. "If an office be granted to a Man to have and enjoy so long as he shall behave himself well in it; the Grantee hath an Estate of Freehold in the Office; for since nothing but his Misbehavior can

---

16. 1 Tucker, App. 353. For an early "good behavior" statute, see 37 Hen. 8, c. 1 (1545).
17. Coke on Littleton 42a.
18. Harcourt v. Fox, 1 Show. K. B. 426, 506, 536, 89 E. R. 680, 720, 736 (1693).
19. 2 Elliot 359.
20. *Federalist* No. 65 at 425; No. 78 at 511 (Alexander Hamilton).
21. Kramer & Barron, supra, n. 14 at 455.
22. Kramer & Barron notice "some cases" which utter such learning but apparently regard them as one of two conflicting lines of authority. Ibid.
23. 4 Coke, *Institutes* 117.

determine his Interest, no Man can prefix a shorter
term than his Life; since it must be by his own Act
(which the Law does not presume to foresee) which
only can make his Estate of shorter Continuance than
his Life." And, Bacon continues, under "a grant to a
man for so long time as he shall behave himself
well . . . his misbehavior in each case determines his
Interest." [24]

Scire Facias to Determine
Misbehavior: The Judicial Role

When an office held "during good behavior" is terminated by the grantee's misbehavior, there must be an
"incident" power "to carry the law into execution" if
"good behavior" is not to be an impotent formula.[25]
English law provided a proceeding to forfeit the office
by a writ of scire facias.[26] An act "contrary to what
belongs to his office" resulted in forfeiture of the office,
as appears in the *Abridgments* of Viner and Bacon
and in the *Digest* of Comyns,[27] which faithfully reflect
the cases.[28] The writ of scire facias, said Blackstone,

---

24. 3 Matthew Bacon, *A New Abridgment of the Laws of England*,
"Offices and Officers" (H) 733 (London, 3d ed. 1768).
25. Speaking in Rex v. Richardson, 1 Burr. 517, 539, 97 E. R. 426, 438
(1758), of the power to remove an officer unfit for office, Lord Mansfield
declared, "It is necessary to the good order and government of corporate
bodies, that there should be such a power . . . Unless the power is incident,
franchises or offices might be forfeited for offences; and yet there would
be no means to carry the law into execution." To the same effect, Lord
Bruce's Case, 2 Str. 819, 820, 93 E. R. 870 (1728). In 1862, the English
crown law officers rendered an opinion with reference to judicial "good
behavior" tenure that "when a public office is held during good behavior,
a power [of removal for misbehavior] must exist somewhere; and when
it is put in force, the tenure of the office is not thereby abridged, but it
is forfeited and declared vacant for nonperformance of the condition on
which it was originally conferred." 1 Todd 192.
26. 3 Bacon (M) 741; 4 Baron John Comyns, *A Digest of the Laws of
England*, "Officer" (K) 259 (London, 1766); and see infra, n. 30. The writ
of *quo warranto* has replaced *scire facias*. Burke Shartel, "Federal Judges:
Appointment, Supervision, and Removal—Some Possibilities under the
Constitution," 28 *Mich. L. Rev.* 870, 887–888 (1930).
27. 16 Charles Viner, *General Abridgment of Law and Equity*, "Officers
and Offices" (N) 122 (1743); 3 Bacon, (M) 741; 4 Comyns, preceding
note, (K) 255.
28. "[E]very voluntary act done by an officer contrary to that which
belongs to his office is a forfeiture of his office . . ." Earl of Pembroke v.
Sir H. Barkeley, Popham 116, 118, 79 E. R. 1223, 1224 (1597); Earl of
Shrewsbury's Case, 9 Co. 46b, 50a, 77 E. R. 798, 804 (1611); Regina v.
Bailiffs of Ipswich, 2 Salk. 435, 91 E. R. 378 (1707).

was the remedy to repeal a patent in case of forfeiture.[29] It is true that this procedure found employment with respect to lesser officials—rising no higher than a Recorder, a lesser judge [30]—and Judge Merrill Otis correctly stated that there is no English case wherein a judge comparable to a federal judge was removed in a judicial proceeding.[31] Since there was admittedly an established judicial procedure to forfeit an office upon "misbehavior," the Otis argument is merely that there is no precise precedent for application of that procedure to judges. That argument does not vitiate the "judicial power"; for that power, as will appear, turns on quite other considerations. At most the argument goes to the absence of a special *remedy,* and this despite the historical growth of the common law by application of a principle to analogous circumstances when the situation presented itself. There was little or no occasion to remove judges by scire facias because for the most part they were appointed "at pleasure" [32] and could be unceremoniously removed, as James's dismissal of Coke testifies.[33] When rare "good behavior" appointees were threatened by arbitrary royal removal, they insisted on the protection of scire facias where the issue of misbehavior could be tried judicially.

Among the exceptional judicial appointments for "good behavior" was that of the Chief Baron of the Exchequer.[34] In 1628 the post was occupied by Sir John Walter; Charles I "was dissatisfied with his opinion in the case of parliament men imprisoned for seditious speechs in parliament, and ordered him to surrender his patent [of appointment]. He refused to do so, on the ground that his grant was for good behavior, and

---

29. 3 Blackstone 260–261.
30. The cases are set forth in Martha Ziskind, "Judicial Tenure in the American Constitution: English and American Precedents," in *Supreme Court Rev.* 135, 153–154 (1969).
31. Otis 49. Shartel 882, mistakenly cites 4 Coke, *Institutes* 117 for the proposition that judges "holding 'during good behavior' . . . were removable on scire facias." All that appears at the cited page is that the Chief Baron of the Exchequer has "good behavior" tenure in contrast to other judges who held "at pleasure."
32. Charles H. McIlwain, "The Tenure of English Judges," 7 *Am. Pol. Sci. Rev.* 217, 218 (1913); 7 Edward Foss, *The Judges of England* 4 (London, 1864); 6 Holdsworth 503–510 (1924).
33. 5 Holdsworth 430–440 (2d ed. 1937).
34. 4 Coke 117.

that he ought not to be removed without a proceeding on a *scire facias* to determine 'whether he did *bene se gerere* or not,' as Whitelocke says." [35] Thus a highly placed judge affirmed that his office could be forfeited for misbehavior in a scire facias proceeding. At a time when impeachments were humming around the heads of Charles's ministers,[36] Chief Baron Walter wisely preferred trial by judges to the political ordeal of impeachment. In 1672 Charles II, following his father's example, tried to dismiss Sir John Archer, a Justice of Common Pleas, a court which ranked with King's Bench. Justice Archer also "refused to surrender his patent without a scire facias." [37] Both the Walter and Archer cases were cited in 1692 before Chief Justice Holt and his associate Justices by Serjeant Levinz, who had himself been a Justice; and Holt made the significant remark that "our places as Judges are so settled, only determinable upon misbehavior." [38]

That scire facias could be employed for removal of a judge was again indicated in an opinion rendered in 1753 by Attorney General Dudley Ryder and Solicitor General William Murray—both later to be Chief Justices, Murray to become better known as Lord Mansfield. Governor Clinton of New York had improvidently made a grant to Chief Justice De Lancey of a commission for "good behavior" instead of the customary "at pleasure" appointment, and subsequently the two were at odds. Ryder and Murray stated: "We think the Governor should not have granted this commission

---

35. McIlwain, supra, n. 32 at 221; 6 Foss, supra, n. 32 at 372 (1857); cf. Vandam v. Deconell, W. Jones, 228, 82 E. R. 120 (1631).

36. E.g., from the impeachment of Lord Chancellor Bacon in 1620 to that of the Duke of Buckingham in 1626. See Simpson 91–95.

37. "Justice Archer was amoved from sitting in the Court of Common Pleas, *pro quibusdam causi mihi incognitis;* but the judge having his patent to be judge *quamdiu se bene gesserint* refused to surrender his patent without a *scire facias,* and continued justice of that Court, though prohibited to sit there." T. Raym. 217, 83 E. R. 113 (1674). See also McIlwain, supra, n. 32 at 223; 7 Foss, supra, n. 32 at 52–53.

38. Harcourt v. Fox, 1 Show. K. B. 426, 506, 514, 535, 89 E. R. 680, 720, 722, 724, 734 (1692–1693). This was a suit to restore to office a Clerk of the Peace who held for so long as he "shall well demean himself in his said office," ibid. 426, 680; cf. ibid. 536, 736, and who had been summarily dismissed. Holt, C. J., held that such persons were "removable" upon "misbehavior," ibid. 536, 738, and that "misbehavior should forfeit their places." Ibid. 536, 736. For this, a forfeiture proceeding, not impeachment, was the remedy, so that Holt's remark apparently refers back to the Walter and Archer refusals to surrender office without a scire facias.

different from the usage; but as the power given by the commission is general, we apprehend the grant is good in point of law, and cannot be revoked without misbehavior." [39] Ryder and Murray were too practiced to employ "revoked" for the technical term "impeached"; and it is highly improbable that they confused "misbehavior," the classic scire facias formula, with impeachment, which proceeds for "high crimes and misdemeanors." Indeed, advice that it required nothing less than a full-dress impeachment by Parliament to undo a mistaken appointment in a Colony of the far-flung Empire would have been grossly unpalatable. This view of the law was later summarized by Lord Chancellor Erskine when, in the course of a debate in the House of Lords in 1806 upon whether to employ an Address for the removal of Justice Luke Fox of Common Pleas in Ireland, he inquired, "Were their Lordships afraid to trust the ordinary tribunals upon this occasion, to let the guilt or innocence of the honorable judge be decided . . . upon a *scire facias* to repeal the patent by which he held his office?" [40]

In his "Life of Erskine" Lord Campbell, himself a Lord Chancellor and one who did not shrink from pointing out errors in the views of his predecessors, quoted this passage without comment,[41] from which we may infer that he deemed Erskine to state the law. Eminent scholars, among them Holdsworth, consider that removal of judges by scire facias remains available in England.[42] Scire facias may consequently be re-

---

39. 5 *Dictionary of American Biography*, "James De Lancey" 212 (N.Y. 1930); George Chalmers, *Opinions of Eminent Lawyers* 491 (Burlington, Vt., 1st Amer. ed. 1858); see infra, n. 93.

40. 7 *Parl. Deb.* 751, 770 (1806). Thus a great judge preferred to have the misconduct of a judge tried by other judges. A similar choice was made by Thomas Denman, later Lord Justice, when arguing in behalf of Sir Jonah Barrington, a judge of the court of admiralty of Ireland, to avert removal by address, he stated, "a *scire facias* could have been sued out to abrogate the patent of office." 24 *Parl. Deb.* 966 (Hansard, New. Ser. 1830).

In Floyd v. Barker, 12 Co. 23, 77 E. R. 1305 (Star Chamber, 1608), a suit against a judge or acts performed in his judicial capacity, Coke delivered himself of an over-broad dictum that for such acts a judge could not be tried before "any other judge" but only before the King. But this dictum exerted no influence on the views of the judges and jurists mentioned above as to the availability of *scire facias*.

41. 6 Campbell, *Chancellors* 559–560.

42. This Holdsworth statement appears in the chapter on "Constitutional Law," credited to him, in 6 Halsbury, *Laws of England* 609 (London, 1932). See also R. M. Jackson, *The Machinery of Justice in England* 289 n. 1

garded as an established medium for the determination that an office held "during good behavior" was terminated by misbehavior; and leading judges had recognized its availability for the trial of judicial misbehavior.

When the Framers employed "good behavior," a common law term of ascertainable meaning, with no indication that they were employing it in a new and different sense, it might be presumed that they implicitly adopted the judicial enforcement machinery that traditionally went with it.[43] For as Madison explained in the Virginia Ratification Convention, "where a technical word was used all the incidents belonging to it necessarily attended it," an explanation in which John Marshall, Judge Edmund Pendleton, and Edmund Randolph concurred.[44] Minimally, if "good behavior" would be ineffectual without scire facias to try misbehavior, it may be posited that the Framers would not have excluded the writ's employment. For this there is the test laid down by Chief Justice Marshall, who, be it remembered, had himself been a vigorous participant in the

(London, 5th ed. 1967); Herbert Broom, *Constitutional Law Viewed in Relation to the Common Law*, 789, 791 (London, 1866); McIlwain, supra, n. 32 at 225; 2 Sir William Anson (Part 1), *Law and Custom of the Constitution* 235 (Oxford, 4th ed. 1935); 1 Todd 192–193; cf. infra, n. 132.

The arguments for judicial proceedings have been deemed "inconclusive . . . since no cases involving an attempted use of such process have arisen in England since the Act of Settlement." Note, "The Exclusiveness of the Impeachment Power under the Constitution," 51 *Harv. L. Rev.* 330, 335 (1937). But since provision in that Act for removal by Address, there also has been but one such attempt, in 1830. H. R. W. Wade, *Administrative Law* 281 (Oxford, 2d ed. 1967). Impeccable conduct, not atrophy of process, may be the answer.

A number of expressions are contrary to those of Holdsworth *et al.* So 8 Halsbury, supra at 590 (1933) stated that judges holding during good behavior are "only removable on an address." This chapter on "Courts" by Messrs. Inskip and Bridgman takes no account of Holdsworth's statement to the contrary in vol. 6, supra. So too, Frederic Maitland, *The Constitutional History of England* 313 (London, 1913), states that the provision of the Act of Settlement bars removal except upon "conviction for some offense or on the address of both houses." In his preface to this work, H. A. L. Fisher, ibid. vi, states that it is an early work which "does not claim to be based upon original research; for much of his information [Maitland] was confessedly content to draw upon the classical text-books." For reasons hereinafter set out, I consider the majority view stands more firmly. Infra, text accompanying nn. 131–135.

43. Cf. supra, n. 25; and supra, Chapter II, n. 160. In United States v. Wilson 7 Pet. (32 U.S.) 150, 160 (1833), Chief Justice Marshall stated respecting a "pardon," "As this power has been exercised from time immemorial by the executive of that nation . . . to whose judicial institutions ours bear a close resemblance; we adopt their principles respecting the operation and effect of a pardon, and look into their books for the rules prescribing the manner in which it is to be used."

44. 3 Elliot 531, 546, 558–559, 573. The issue was whether the provision for jury trial carried with it as an incident the right to challenge jurors.

Virginia Ratification Convention. He said in the *Dartmouth College Case,* "It is not enough to say, that this particular case was not in the mind of the Convention, when the article was framed . . . It is necessary to go farther, and to say that, had this particular case been suggested, the language would have been so varied, as to exclude it." [45] There is little or no basis for attribution to the Framers of an exclusory purpose that would deprive "good behavior" of meaning.

Thus far I have considered the matter in the narrow compass to which prior discussions have been confined. But it is a mistake to stop with the inquiry whether or not scire facias was available at common law for the enforcement of "good behavior" against judges. When the Constitution limited judicial tenure to "during good behavior," the Framers self-evidently did not intend that a judge who behaved badly and thus violated the condition of his tenure should be continued in office. So much the common law teaches us with respect to "good behavior" tenure in general; indeed, it represents plain common sense.[46] If, contrary to my view, "high crimes and misdemeanors" is to be restricted to "great offenses" for judges as well as the President or if, as I propose to demonstrate, impeachment for "high crimes and misdemeanors" did not embrace removal for "misbehavior" which fell short of "high crimes and misdemeanors," [47] some other means of removal must be available,[48] unless we attribute to the Framers the Dickensian design of maintaining a "misbehaving" judge in office.

There are no dead words in the Constitution, said Hatton Sumners, chairman of the House Judiciary Committee,[49] in championing removal by judges of judges

---

45. Trustees of Dartmouth College v. Woodward, 4 Wheat. (17 U.S.) 518, 644 (1819).
46. Justice Frankfurter reminded us to read all enactments "with the saving grace of common sense," Bell v. United States, 349 U.S. 81, 83 (1955); and United States v. Cook, 384 U.S. 257, 262 (1966), stated that the canon that penal statutes should be strictly construed "is not an inexorable command to override common sense."
47. Infra, text accompanying nn. 183, 187–189.
48. See supra, n. 25.
49. 81 *Cong. Rec.* 6164 (1937). Speaking to the "Judicial Good Behavior Bill" in 1937, Sumners said, "If the Senate cannot make vital the 'good behavior' provision in the judicial tenure clause, and clearly it cannot do

who misbehaved. That every word in the Constitution must be given effect is the rule.[50] To give meaning to a tenure limited to "good behavior" there must be a means of termination for misbehavior. It is of no moment that no express provision was made, for as Madison said: "No axiom is more clearly established . . . than that wherever the end is required, the means are authorized." [51] Were it therefore assumed that scire facias was not and is not available for the removal of judges, it would be open to Congress, under the "necessary and proper" clause, to provide a *remedy* for effectuation of the constitutional design.

Given common law judicial determinations of forfeitures upon breach of condition subsequent, the most that can be claimed by Otis and his followers is that the common law provided no *remedy* for forfeiture of *judicial* office—an omission that, as has been noted, was fortuitous [52] and that is curable under the common law principle of growth by analogy. Remedies were not frozen by the Constitution to those extant in 1788. Marshall laid claim in *Marbury v. Madison* to the common law power to fashion a remedy for every right.[53] And Congress, over the years, has provided an array of

---

it, what agency of government can do it? The historical background precludes any notion that the President can effectuate those words, because those words went into the framework of the English constitution, from which we appropriated them, in order to prevent the Executive from having anything to do with it. So by process of elimination we come to a court as the only agency of government that can keep those words from being dead words in the Constitution." Ibid.

50. "It cannot be presumed that any clause in the constitution is intended to be without effect; and therefore such a construction is inadmissible, unless the words require it." Marbury v. Madison, 1 Cranch (5 U.S.) 137, 174 (1803). "No word in the instrument . . . can be rejected as superfluous . . . or unmeaning." Holmes v. Jennison, 14 Pet. (39 U.S.) 540, 571 (1840) (per Taney, C. J.).

51. *Federalist* No. 44 at 294. This was also stated in the Massachusetts Convention by Christopher Gore, 2 Elliot 66. The classic expression is that of Marshall, C. J.: "Let the end be legitimate, let it be within the scope of the constitution, and all means which are appropriate, which are plainly adapted to that end, which are not prohibited, but consist with the letter and spirit of the constitution, are constitutional." McCulloch v. Maryland, 4 Wheat. (17 U.S.) 316, 421 (1819). See also Prigg v. Commonwealth of Pennsylvania, 16 Pet. (41 U.S.) 539, 619, 615 (1842). Moreover, "A constitutional provision should not be construed so as to defeat its evident purpose, but rather so as to give it effective operation." Jarrolt v. Moberly, 103 U.S. 580, 586 (1880). Compare Lord Mansfield, supra, n. 25.

52. See supra, text accompanying nn. 32–33.

53. 1 Cranch (5 U.S.) 137, 163 (1803). That we are merely dealing with the question of "remedy" is confirmed in 3 Blackstone 260–261: "where the patentee hath done an act that amounts to a forfeiture of the grant . . . the remedy to repeal the patent is by writ of *scire facias*." See also supra, n. 26.

remedies unknown to the common law; were a new remedy required, it is open to Congress to provide it.

Enabling legislation may also be viewed as an additional grant of *subject matter* jurisdiction: forfeitures of judicial office, quite different from an attempt to expand the Article III "judicial power." In a grudging concession, Judge Merrill Otis stated: "It can well be argued that an action to forfeit the office of a judge for misconduct . . . is a true 'case' or 'controversy.' " [54] Certainly the contrary cannot be maintained. A grant "during good behavior" is simply an estate on a condition subsequent, which is defeated or forfeited by nonperformance of the condition.[55] Thereupon the grantor is free to claim the forfeited estate; if the grantee controverts the charge of "misbehavior" there is a "case or controversy," a "real dispute between the plaintiff and defendant." [56] Existence of an exact precedent for the particular dispute, for example, forfeiture of *judicial* office, is not the test of Article III "judicial power." Were that the test, many unprecedented "disputes" could never have been adjudicated. Instead, "judicial power" is activated when an actual dispute between adverse parties is presented.

In sum, since the judicial power to declare a forfeiture on breach of a condition subsequent existed at the adoption of the Constitution, and since a dispute whether the condition was breached constitutes a "case or controversy," it falls within the "judicial power." Consequently, legislation that would set up a special court within the judiciary branch to adjudicate disputes whether a judge breached the "good behavior" condition would merely entail a grant of fresh *subject matter* jurisdiction or, on the dubious assumption that forfei-

---

54. Otis 36.
55. 2 Blackstone 155; cf. ibid. 152–153. Blackstone refers to "all forfeitures which are given by law [see infra, n. 174] of life estates . . . for any acts done by the tenant himself, that are incompatible with the estate which he holds," and instances "a grant . . . to a man of an office." Ibid. 153. See also Todd quotation, supra, n. 25.
56. Lord v. Veazie, 8 How. (49 U.S.) 251, 254 (1850) (per Taney, C. J.). There is a "controversy" where there is "a dispute between parties who face each other in an adversary proceeding . . . [parties who] had taken adverse positions with respect to their existing obligations." Aetna Life Ins. Co. v. Haworth, 300 U.S. 227, 242 (1937).

tures of judicial office were unavailable at common law, the creation of a new *remedy*.

The exercise of the "judicial power" is required because it was the design of the Framers to limit presidential and congressional interference with the judiciary.[57] Outside the impeachment clause, Congress enjoys no "judicial" power to remove a judge from office.[58] Given a "case or controversy," the congressional grant of fresh subject matter jurisdiction or the creation of a new remedy would not represent a delegation of congressional power. Such a grant would instead constitute action to supplement the "judicial power" under the "necessary and proper" clause or under the power of Congress to regulate the jurisdiction of the inferior courts.[59]

---

57. See infra, text accompanying nn. 227–231. In 1783 a petition was filed with the Virginia Council of State, an executive body, to remove a justice of the peace, J. P. Posey, from office for "misdemeanors, disgraceful to the Character . . . [of] a Justice of the peace." The Council declined to act, saying that "the Law authorizing the Executive to enquire into the Conduct of a Magistrate and determine whether he has or has not committed a certain fact is repugnant to the Act of Government, contrary to the fundamental principles of our constitution and directly opposite to the general tenor of our Laws." 3 *Journals of the Council of the State of Virginia* 222 (Richmond, 1952). For this citation I am indebted to Timothy C. Perry, Esq.

58. See infra, nn. 127, 146, 149; and text accompanying nn. 148, 227–231. The impeachment power is manifestly "judicial." Art. I, §3 (6) empowers the Senate to "try all impeachments"; Art. II, §4 provides for removal on "impeachment for, and conviction of, treason" etc.; Art. I, §3 (7) provides that "Judgment in cases of impeachment" etc.; Art. III, §2 (3) refers to "The trial of all crimes, except in the case of impeachment"; all of which plainly imply a judicial trial. Such was the view that was spread before the Senate by Jefferson's *Manual*, Thomas Jefferson, *Manual of Parliamentary Practice*, reprinted in Senate Manual 69–160 (55th Cong. 1899) at 149–153. The record of the Blount impeachment (1797) recites that "the Senate formed itself into a High Court of Impeachment, in the manner directed by the Constitution." Francis Wharton, *State Trials of the United States* 257 (Philadelphia, 1849).

Judge Otis had an "easy answer" to Shartel's view that impeachment constitutes the "only way in which Congress" may remove. Impeachment, said Otis, was not "legislative" but "judicial." Otis 27–28. The decisive fact, however, is that this is the only grant of power *to Congress* to interfere with the "good behavior" tenure. It is the limited grant, underscored by rejection of legislative removal by Address, not the nature of the granted power, which is conclusive.

59. Article I, §8 (18) empowers Congress "To make all Laws which shall be necessary and proper for carrying into Execution the foregoing Powers, and all other Powers vested by this Constitution in the Government of the United States, or in any Department or Officer thereof." For the power of Congress over the jurisdiction of the inferior federal courts, see Sheldon v. Sill, 8 How. (49 U.S.) 440 (1850).

The question has been put whether the "good behavior" clause constitutes a grant of power, either to Congress or to the courts. In my judgment, it constitutes no grant to either, but merely describes the *duration* of the granted tenure. When the condition subsequent of the grant is breached, and the breach is disputed, there exists Article III "judicial power" to determine the "case," subject to a Congressional grant of *subject matter* jurisdiction. At common law tenure "during good behavior"

Since the unavailability of impeachment to enforce "good behavior" is pivotal to this reading, it is necessary to examine the two opposing claims: (1) impeachment is the exclusive means provided by the Constitution for removal of judges, and (2) impeachment for "high crimes and misdemeanors" embraces infractions of "good behavior" so that an alternative remedy is superfluous. Of these in turn.

THE "IMPEACHMENT IS EXCLUSIVE" ARGUMENT

The government which has a right to do an act . . . must . . . be allowed to select the means; and those who contend that it may not select any appropriate means, that one particular mode of effecting the object is excepted, take upon themselves the burden of establishing that exception.[60]

As Chief Justice Marshall's remarks in *McCulloch v. Maryland* indicate, those who would dispute the availability of an "appropriate means"—in other words, an alternative to impeachment—for the removal of a judge guilty of bad behavior must "take upon themselves" the burden of proof. And, as a guide to consideration of the "exclusivist" argument, I suggest another Marshall statement in the same case: "Can we adopt that construction (unless the words imperiously require it), which would impute to the framers of that instrument, when granting these powers . . . the intention of impeding their exercise by withholding a choice of means?" [61] In terms of "good behavior," a power to declare that the tenure was terminated by bad behavior is reasonably implied, and "what is reasonably implied is as much a part of [the Constitution] as what is expressed." [62] Where are "the words [which] imperiously

did not allow arbitrary dismissal but required a trial, and in adopting the common law phrase, the Framers presumably had the same trial in view.
60. McCulloch v. Maryland, 4 Wheat. (17 U.S.) 316, 409–410 (1819).
61. Ibid. 408.
62. Dillon v. Gloss, 256 U.S. 368, 373 (1921): "That the Constitution contains no express provision on the subject is not itself controlling; for with the Constitution . . . what is reasonably implied is as much a part of it as what is expressed."

require" that impeachment be the sole means for removal of judges, once it is accepted that impeachment cannot reach all breaches of "good behavior"?

The Constitutional Test

No express terms making impeachment the exclusive means of removal are contained in the Constitution. Judge Otis sought to locate them in the Article I, §2, provision granting the House "the sole Power of Impeachment" and the Article I, §3, provision giving the Senate "the sole Power to try all Impeachments." He labored mightily to prove that "sole" means sole,[63] a proposition no one would deny, but he merely proved that *no other body* can bring or try *impeachments*. His deduction from "sole" that "the House of Representatives has the sole power to charge civil officers of the United States with misconduct for the purpose of securing their removal" [64] begs the question: *is* impeachment the "sole" means of removal? The fact that Congress has the sole right to bring and try *impeachments* does not answer the question whether there are *other methods* of removal. Judge Otis himself read into "the sole power to charge civil officers . . . with misconduct" a "necessarily implied exception to the otherwise all exclusive meaning of the word 'sole' . . . *It does not exclude another method of removing those civil officers whose appointment is at the absolute or conditional pleasure of the officer appointing them.*" [65] This "necessarily implied exception" is merely an accommodation to an uncomfortable datum—the First Congress' rejection of impeachment as the exclusive means for removal of executive civil officers; it is an abandonment of an interpretive canon run over by a brutal fact. Common sense counsels against freezing countless officials into lifetime appointments, for it would be utterly imprac-

63. Otis 24–28. Kurland quotes, presumably with approval, Congressman Celler's deduction from the "sole power" provisions, "The use of the word 'sole' in those two particulars undoubtedly is most significant . . . [T]he conclusion is inescapable that the only way you can try these judges is by the method that the Constitution allows us." Philip Kurland, "The Constitution and the Tenure of Federal Judges: Some Notes from History," 36 *U. Chi. L. Rev.* 665, 692 (1969).
64. Otis 24.
65. Ibid. (Otis' italics).

ticable to require congressional trials for such a multitude.[66] But common sense also may be revolted by insistence that trials of judicial misconduct, though much fewer in number, must, come what may, be conducted by Congress alone. For Congress has more pressing and important tasks, which it alone can and must perform, and which should not be deferred while it sits in judgment for from three to six weeks on charges of judicial misconduct. Weighed against the crucial and tormenting national interests which occupy the congressional stage, such issues are really too picayune.[67] We are no less free than Judge Otis to read another "necessarily implied exception" into the allegedly exclusive word "sole," for such a reading does not turn on the demands of remorseless logic but on practical considerations to which others may attach more weight than did Otis. "Sole," of course, does not have the effect claimed for it by him.

Expressio Unius, Exclusio Est Alterius

A second "exclusive" argument drawn from the face of the Constitution reflects the maxim *expressio unius, exclusio est alterius.* Hamilton gave it its most noted formulation: "The precautions for their [judges'] responsibility are comprised in the article respecting impeachments . . . This is the only provision on the point, which is consistent with the necessary independence of the judicial character, and is the only one which we find in our own constitution in respect to our own judges." [68] That view has recently been espoused by Justices Black and Douglas in notable dissents.[69] To

---

66. The inapplicability of impeachment to "petty" officers was stressed in the North Carolina Ratification Convention, infra, text accompanying n. 182; compare infra, text accompanying n. 183, and n. 181; and see infra, n. 89.

67. See supra, nn. 9 and 6, and text accompanying nn. 198–199; cf. supra, n. 7.

68. *Federalist* No. 79 at 513–514.

69. Chandler II, 398 U.S. at 136, Douglas, J., dissenting; Black J., dissenting, ibid. 141–142. Such expressions overlook Chief Justice Marshall's explanation in Cohens v. Virginia, 6 Wheat. (19 U.S.) 264, 395 (1821): "It is admitted, that 'affirmative words are often, in their operation, negative of other objects than those affirmed'; and that where 'a negative or exclusive sense must be given to them, or they have no operation at all,' they must receive that negative or exclusive sense. But where they have full operation without it; where it would destroy some of the most important

one who for the first time encounters the argument that the express provision for impeachment excludes all other means of removal, it comes as a surprise that a canon of construction should be exalted to an impassable constitutional bar.[70] Such canons, the Supreme Court has repeatedly indicated, merely express rules (and not "inescapable" rules) of construction, not of law.[71] "Nothing," said a great judge, Learned Hand, "is so likely to lead us astray as an abject reliance upon canons of any sort; so much the whole history of verbal interpretation teaches, if it teaches anything." [72]

Indeed, Hamilton himself refused to regard the maxim as conclusive where its application "would be unnatural and unreasonable": "Is it natural to suppose that a command to do one thing, is a prohibition to the doing of another, which there was a previous power to do, and which is not incompatible with the thing commanded to be done? If such a supposition would be unnatural and unreasonable, it cannot be rational to maintain, that an injunction of the trial by jury in certain cases [criminal] is an interdiction of it in others." [73] In this he was echoed by the Ratification Conventions, where a vigorous campaign was waged for an express provision for jury trial in civil cases on the ground that otherwise it was likely to be barred by the express provision for jury trial in criminal cases. The doubters were reassured by John Marshall, Edmund Pendleton,

---

objects for which the power was created; then, we think, affirmative words ought not to be construed negatively." In sum, "The court may imply a negative from affirmative words, where the implication promotes, not where it defeats the intention." Ibid. 397. See infra, text accompanying nn. 73–75. See infra, n. 73.

70. Black and Douglas ally it to a theory of "absolute independence," of which more anon.

71. United States v. Barnes, 222 U.S. 513, 519 (1912); Jarecki v. G. D. Searle & Co., 367 U.S. 303, 307 (1961).

72. Van Vranken v. Helvering, 115 F. 2d 709, 711 (2d Cir. 1940); cf. United States v. Universal C. I. T. Credit Corp., 344 U.S. 218, 221 (1952): rules of construction "do not solve the special difficulties in constructing a particular statute."

73. Federalist No. 83 at 540. As Elias Boudinot said in the First Congress: "it is nowhere said that officers shall never be removed but by impeachment; but it says they shall be removed on impeachment." 1 Ann. Cong. 468.

Hamilton had submitted to the Convention a provision that Judges should be "removable only by impeachment." 3 Farrand 617, 625 (emphasis added). The omission of the word "only" in Article II, § 4, speaks against an interpolation of "only" into the Article, particularly when the consequence is partially to defeat the words "during good behavior." See Marshall, C. J., supra, n. 69.

Edmund Randolph, C. C. Pinckney, and James Wilson.[74] Wilson stated in Pennsylvania, "It is very true that trial by jury is not mentioned in civil cases . . . it is very improper to infer from hence that it was not meant to exist under this government." [75] Manifestly, *exclusio unius* was no fetish for the Founders. And even with the "necessary independency" of the judiciary in mind, Hamilton made yet another breach in the maxim: insanity of judges, he said, "without any formal or express provision, may be safely pronounced to be a virtual disqualification" [76] and presumably, therefore, should justify removal. Disqualification "without any formal or express provision" implies that "high crimes and misdemeanors" does not embrace insanity, for that is the only "express" removal provision. Unless, therefore, Hamilton contemplated some alternative means of removal, his "virtual disqualification" is empty verbiage.

That practical considerations weighed more heavily with the Founders than an interpretive canon was immediately demonstrated by the First Congress, which rejected the Hamiltonian "only provision" argument as an alleged bar to presidential removal of executive officers. "Show me," said William Smith in the House, "where it is said that the President shall remove from office . . . as the Constitution has not given the President the power of removability, it means he should not have that power," [77] a persuasive argument under the widely held doctrine of enumerated powers.[78] And he continued, "this inference is supported by that clause . . . which provides that all civil officers . . . shall be removed from office on impeachment." [79] Although this view was strenuously maintained by a number of other

---

74. Pendleton, 3 Elliot 546; Randolph, ibid. 573; C. C. Pinckney, 4 Elliot 307; Marshall, 3 Elliot 561.

75. 2 Elliot 488. In North Carolina, James Iredell explained that although the Constitution "does not provide expressly for a trial by jury in civil cases, it does not say there shall not be such a trial." 4 Elliot 145; and see ibid. 171.

76. *Federalist* No. 79 at 514.

77. 1 *Ann. Cong.* 457. Compare Justice Black's nothing in the Constitution "gives any indication that any judge was ever to be . . . removed from office except" by impeachment. Chandler II, 398 U.S. at 142.

78. The debates were reminded of the rule by Richard B. Lee: "This Government is invested with powers for enumerated purposes only, and cannot exercise any others whatever." 1 *Ann. Cong.* 524. For other citations see Berger, *Congress v. Court* 13–14, 377 n. 52.

79. 1 *Ann. Cong.* 457.

members, including Elbridge Gerry, himself a Framer,[80] it was overcome by the argument of Madison and others, that such a restrictive reading would be destructive of good government,[81] that, as Theodore Sedgwick said, impeachment was a "tardy, tedious, desultory road" for the accomplishment of needed removals.[82] The Madison view prevailed,[83] ostensibly on the theory that the power of removal was a necessary correlative of the power of appointment, though many argued that the Senate therefore should participate in removals as in appointments.[84]

Impeachment, Madison explained, had a special purpose: it was designed to reach a bad officer sheltered by the President, who "could be removed even against the will of the President; so that the declaration in the Constitution was intended as a *supplemental security* for the good behavior of the public officers." [85] This point was made again and again. Impeachment, said Elias Boudinot, enables the House "to pull down an improper officer, although he should be supported by all the power of the Executive." [86] "Favoritism," said Abraham Baldwin, also a Framer, could not protect a man from the power of the House "in despite of the President" to "drag him from his place." [87] The point bears emphasis because it reveals, first, that the Founders had learned from English history of the need for power to remove evil favorites, presidential no less

---

80. Benjamin Huntington, ibid. 459; Elbridge Gerry, ibid. 473, 536.
81. Madison, ibid. 496; Peter Sylvester said the doctrine was "big with mischief, and likely to drive the whole Government into confusion." Ibid. 562. Thomas Hartley said the exclusivist argument "would be attended with very inconvenient and mischievous circumstances." Ibid. 480.
82. Ibid. 460; see also John Vining's remark, quoted supra, n. 9. For similar remarks by Madison, Boudinot, Hartley, and Sylvester, see ibid. 497, 375, 480, 562.
83. As Chief Justice Taft noted, "Hamilton changed his view of this matter," quoting, "This method of construing the Constitution has indeed been recognized by Congress in formal acts upon full consideration and debate; of which the power of removal from office is an important instance," citing 7 J. C. Hamilton, *Works of Hamilton* 80–81, in Myers v. United States, 272 U.S. 52, 137, 139 (1926).
84. Theodorick Bland, 1 *Ann. Cong.* 374; Samuel Livermore, ibid. 381, 478; Alexander White, ibid. 456, 467; John Page, ibid. 491; William Smith quoted Hamilton's statement in *Federalist* No. 77 that "The consent of [the Senate] would be necessary to displace as well as appoint;" ibid. 456; but here too the First Congress rejected Hamilton's interpretation.
85. Ibid. 372 (emphasis added); similiter Vining, ibid. 373; Bland, ibid. 374.
86. Ibid. 468; similiter Livermore, ibid. 478.
87. Ibid. 588; John Lawrence, ibid. 482.

than royal, and also that impeachment was in essence not an exclusive medium of removal but a breach in the separation of powers for the purpose of "supplemental security," "an exception to a principle." [88]

The implication of removal power drawn from the presidential power of appointment seems to me a weaker argument for breaching exclusivity than that which associates "good behavior" tenure with its traditional termination by scire facias. Despite the emphasis on the relation between the power of appointment and that of removal, the motive power, in my opinion, was furnished by the exigencies of government. It simply made no sense to freeze hundreds of "civil officers" into what in effect would become life tenure, terminable only by the arduous impeachment procedure.[89] There were, however, other remarks in the First Congress noting the special position of judges; but before examining the bearing of those remarks on the intention of the Founders, it will serve chronological coherence to examine that intention first.

The Intention of the Framers

A search for the intention of the Framers may seem gratuitous in light of Professor Philip Kurland's statement that "it has been made pellucidly clear by Martha Ziskind that the intention was to make impeachment the sole means of removal of federal judicial officers." [90] But in my opinion, her demonstration does not stand up. Referring to Burke Shartel's view that the Constitution does not bar judicial removal of judges by scire facias, she put her case in a nutshell: "The clearest rejection of Shartel's argument lies in the fact that no

---

88. Boudinot, ibid. 527.

89. Boudinot rejected "perpetuity in office," ibid. 469; Sylvester said, if impeachment is "the only way of removing officers, they have all of them in inheritance in office." Ibid. 562; and see Egbert Benson, ibid. 373. Compare infra, text accompanying n. 182.

90. Kurland, supra, n. 63 at 668. Assistant Attorney General (now Justice) William H. Rehnquist testified before the Senate Subcommittee on Separation of Powers on the Independence of Federal Judges (Hearings, 91st Cong. 2d Sess., April–May 1970), p. 330, that it is "the opinion of the Department of Justice" that the provisions of the Tydings Bill (S.1506) relating "to a new judicial commission to remove judges in cases of failure to conform with the good behavior standards of the Constitution are constitutionally permissible."

colonial or state constitution provided for such a use for the *scire facias,* nor was a proposal made to include it during the Constitutional Convention. Even in the unreformed common law, there was a distinction between precedents and fossils." [91] Erskine, Holdsworth and others regarded scire facias as vital rather than fossilized; [92] and, as we shall see, at least two of the states Ziskind cites provided for removal by courts for misbehavior, which was the purpose of the scire facias proceeding.

The reason why "no colonial constitution" provided for removal of judges by scire facias can be simply stated: almost without exception judicial appointments in the Colonies were made at the King's pleasure, terminable at *his* will.[93] On one occasion in New York, a good behavior appointment was made in violation of instructions: when the advice of the Attorney General and Solicitor General in England was sought as to the manner of dismissal, they regretfully pointed out that a forfeiture proceeding (by scire facias) would be required [94]—a proceeding, we may be sure, that would be brought in the name of the King, not of the colony. Indeed, one of the grievances recited in the Declaration of Independence was that the King "made judges dependent on his will alone for the tenure of their offices,"

---

91. Ziskind, supra, n. 30 at 138.

92. See supra, text accompanying nn. 35–43, and n. 42.

93. Samuel Eliot Morison, *The Oxford History of the American People* 135, 178 (New York, 1965); Bailyn 105–106; Gordon Wood, *The Creation of the American Republic 1776–1787* at 106 (Chapel Hill, N.C., 1969). The English Board of Trade explained that an independent colonial judiciary would be "subversive of the policy by which alone colonies can be kept in a just dependence upon the government of the mother country," quoted in Milton M. Klein, "Prelude to Revolution in New York: Jury Trials & Judicial Tenure," 17 *Wm. & Mary Q.* (Ser. 3) 439, 448 (1960). The "King in Council, disturbed with the growing colonial movement for judicial independence, had ordered the issuance of new instructions absolutely forbidding governors to grant judicial offices during good behavior." Ibid. 452.

The background of the instructions appears in 9 Archives of the State of New Jersey (N.J. 1st Ser. 1885). Governors were cautioned that judicial "Commissions are granted during pleasure only, agreeable to what has been in ancient practice and usage in our said Colonies." Ibid. 321–326, 329–330. See also supra, text accompanying n. 39; cf. Ziskind, supra, n. 30 at 138.

94. Supra, text accompanying n. 39. In 1760, a similar "good behavior" appointment was made in New Jersey, when R. H. Morris was made Chief Justice. Later the Attorney General of England declared the appointment invalid because the Governor was limited to "at pleasure" appointments. 9 Archives, supra, n. 93 at 207–209, 216, 349–351, 380–381.

recognition of colonial powerlessness to interfere with their tenure.

In a lively, oft cited passage, John Adams painted the astonishment of his colleagues in 1774 when he suggested impeachment of judges who accepted Lieutenant Governor Hutchinson's substitution of royal salaries for the existing payment by legislative appropriations. Adams admitted that the thing was "without precedent . . . in this Province" but said that there were precedents in England, pointing to the State Trials on his shelves.[95] In later years he was to claim that his was the only copy of the set in Boston, indeed, "that there was not another copy . . . of those works in the United States." [96] It was not, however, ignorance of impeachments [97] but rather lack of power to impeach that accounts for the nonuse and the absence of colonial precedents. Given the "English point of view that the judges needed protection from the caprice and parsimony of colonial assemblies," [98] it is hardly to be presumed that the Crown would countenance impeachment of a royal appointee. Appreciation of the lack of power to impeach royal appointees bobs up in the colonial

---

95. 2 Adams 329–30; Herbert Johnson, "William Cushing," in 1 Leon Friedman and Fred Israel, eds. *The Justices of the United States Supreme Court 1789–1969* at 57–58 (New York, 1969).

96. 10 Adams 239.

97. Adams overlooked that Josiah Quincy, Jr., had published a letter in the *Boston Gazette*, January 4, 1768, wherein he directed attention to the scope of impeachment in England and to the impeachments of leading figures across the centuries, drawing on Selden's *Jud. Parl.*; Rushworth's *Collections* and the Lords' *Journal*. *Quincy's Mass. Repts. 1761–1772* at 580–584 (Boston, 1865). Several colonial libraries in New York had various collections of the State Trials. Paul A. Hamlin, *Legal Education in Colonial New York* 188, 193, 196 (New York, 1939). John Rushworth's *Historical Collections* (1721), which reported a number of noted impeachments— including that of the Earl of Strafford, reported in 775 folio pages of volume 8—were liberally sprinkled throughout the libraries of the Thirteen Colonies. For citations see Colbourn, supra, n. 4, Index, "Rushworth."

In 1734 William Smith rendered an opinion to the New York Assembly in which he quoted Article 3 of the Clarendon impeachment. Joseph Smith, *Cases and Materials on Development of Legal Institutions* 440, 442 (St. Paul, Minn., 1965). State Trials were referred to in the 1736 Zenger proceedings. James Alexander, *A Brief Narrative of the Case and Trial of John Peter Zenger* 28, 46, 49, 72 (Cambridge, Mass., S. N. Katz ed. 1963). References, Professor Katz tells us, were to the 2d edition of 1730, the Emlyn edition, ibid. 215. In 1737, a letter to the *Pennsylvania Gazette* analyzed the case of the Seven Bishops, reported in the State Trials, ibid. 193.

98. Morison 179. When the Pennsylvania Assembly sought to punish one Moore for an indignity to a *prior* Assembly, a matter of its own privilege, they were advised in 1759 that the English Attorney General Pratt and Solicitor General Yorke considered that "this unusual power could not be tolerated in inferior assemblies in the Colonies." Mary Clarke, *Parliamentary Privilege in the American Colonies* 220 n. 34 (New Haven, Conn., 1943); cf. supra, n. 93.

records. So, the South Carolina House rejected a suggestion by the Council to impeach Chief Justice Nicholas Trott, stating that the "governor and council . . . were not a House of Lords nor a proper jurisdiction before whom any impeachment will lie." [99] Something of the sort also emerged in Pennsylvania in 1706 when the unicameral Assembly brought impeachment charges against the agent of the Proprietor, and the Governor refused to try him, insisting that the Parliament of England had a " 'transcendent power and original jurisdiction in itself' whereas the assembly had no power except as it was specifically granted in the charter." [100] Adams harbored no illusions as to the efficacy of an impeachment by the Assembly; he freely acknowledged that there was no precedent in the province, that the Council would refuse to act on the impeachment, but urged nevertheless that the impeachment be set afoot to reap the political benefit of the consequences. Events confirmed his judgment. The House impeached, the "Council would do nothing," and he recorded that the "royal government was from that moment laid prostrate in the dust." How could an impeachment be effective when, as Adams himself recognized, the Governor was "possessed of an absolute negative on all acts of the legislature," [101] and when disallowance by the Privy

---

99. Quoted in Clarke, supra, n. 98 at 42. John Adams, however, recorded in his 1774 diary that when asked "whence can we pretend to derive such a power?" he replied, "From our charter, which gives us in words as express, as clear, and as strong as the language affords all the rights and privileges of Englishmen." 2 Adams 329. Only eye aglow with revolutionary fervor could discern in a Crown charter a grant of power to remove Crown appointees.

100. Clarke, supra, n. 98 at 40–41. In January 1736, Lewis Morris wrote to James Alexander relative to Alexander's disbarment by Chief Justice De Lancey in the Zenger trial, "The thing is ridiculous, but your misfortune is . . . it is difficult to attack a court otherwise than by impeachment, or act of Assembly, which, as we stand in New York, is hardly to be come at." Vol. 2, Rutherford ms. N.Y. Hist. Soc. 171.

101. 2 Adams 330, 331; 10 Adams 236–238, 241. So far as the Convention records reveal, the colonial experience ultimately did not exercise as much influence as the English practice. When removal by Address was proposed, references were made, not to the four early State constitutions which provided for such removal, infra, text accompanying n. 104, but to the English Act of Settlement. 2 Farrand 428–429. John Dickinson remarked in the Federal Convention, respecting the English practice of originating money bills in the Commons: "Shall we oppose to this long experience, the short experience of 11 years which we had ourselves." 2 Farrand 278. So too, when Vice-President Jefferson was preparing a Manual of Parliamentary Practice for the Senate some ten years later, "he went back to the [English] prototype, not contenting himself with such modifications of the historic practices as had been made in particular legislative bodies." 3 Dumas Malone, *Jefferson and His Times* 454 (Boston, 1962).

Council loomed ahead? [102] Against this background it is little wonder that the several state constitutions later went off in different directions.

As Mrs. Ziskind notes, the state constitutions drafted after 1776 exhibited "no uniform pattern"; [103] but they can be categorized.

(1) Removal by Address [104] without regard to misbehavior: Maryland, Massachusetts, New Hampshire, and South Carolina. A variant was supplied by the Georgia provision that every officer shall be liable to be called to account by the house of the Assembly. Maryland also provided for removal for misbehavior on conviction in a court of law, which may allude either to a criminal prosecution for misconduct or to a civil removal proceeding.

(2) Impeachment: Delaware, New Jersey, New York, Pennsylvania, Vermont, and Virginia. Alternatives were provided by Delaware, conviction of misbehavior at common law; New Jersey and Pennsylvania, removal for maladministration; Vermont, removal of lesser judges for maladministration. In Virginia the impeached judges were to be tried by the Court of Appeals.

(3) North Carolina provided for prosecution on the impeachment of the General Assembly or presentment for maladministration, that is, a judicial criminal proceeding.[105]

This distribution hardly supports Mrs. Ziskind's statement that "in all but a few states, judges held office during good behavior and could be removed only by impeachment." [106] The States were pretty evenly divided between impeachment and removal by Address: four States provided for Address and a fifth, Georgia, provided for a variant; six states provided for impeachment and four of these supplied an alternative, removal

---

102. Morison 135.
103. Ziskind, supra, n. 30 at 139.
104. In England an Address was a formal request made by both Houses of Parliament to the King, asking him to perform some act. By the Act of Settlement (1700), judges were made removable by the Crown only upon an Address by both Houses. Infra, text accompanying nn. 131–133.
105. The various provisions are digested in Ziskind, supra, n. 30 at 139–147.
106. Ibid. 152.

for misbehavior or maladministration, which suggests that impeachment may have been reserved for special cases.[107] The Delaware and Maryland provisions for court removal upon misbehavior preclude an inference that there was total ignorance of judicial forfeiture. If the writ of scire facias was not expressly mentioned, it is not the function of a Constitution to detail the relevant writs.[108]

Why then was no similar alternative incorporated in the Constitution? For Mrs. Ziskind the fact that no "proposal [was] made to include" scire facias apparently constitutes a conclusive constitutional bar. The test rather is that of Chief Justice Marshall, who required a showing that had "this particular case" been suggested —for present purposes, removal by scire facias to effectuate "good behavior"—the Framers would have rejected it.[109] And if "misbehavior" does not in fact constitute impeachable misconduct unless it rises to the level of "high crimes and misdemeanors" or, as in the case of the President, still higher, to a "great offense," and if we cannot attribute to the Framers an intention to maintain judges in office notwithstanding lesser "misbehavior," the means are available, under orthodox rules of construction, to effectuate the manifest purpose of "during good behavior." [110]

Viewed from the standpoint of the Framers, who were hard pressed to complete their extraordinary labors, the various state remedial provisions must have seemed a tangled thicket.[111] Then too, removal of judges was of minor concern to the Framers. We have become so wrapped up in the impeachment of judges that the place of their impeachment in the minds of the Framers has become distorted. The Framers were

---

107. The Pennsylvania constitution provided for impeachment of an officer "either when in office, or *after* . . . removal for maladministration." Ziskind, ibid. 141 (emphasis added), as did Vermont, 2 Ben. Poore, *Federal and State Constitutions, Colonial Charters* 1863 (1877).

108. In the words of Chief Justice Marshall, "A constitution, to contain an accurate detail of all the subdivisions of which the great powers will admit, and of all the means by which they may be carried into execution, would partake of the prolixity of a legal code, and could scarcely be embraced by the human mind." McCulloch v. Maryland, 4 Wheat. (17 U.S.) 316, 407 (1819); cf. id. at 415.

109. Supra, text accompanying n. 45.

110. Supra, text accompanying nn. 47–59.

111. See Madison, supra, n. 64.

troubled almost entirely by transgressions of the President and his advisers; the misbehavior of judges was all but unmentioned. The Framers began with and long debated the impeachment of the President; at first the judges were to constitute the impeachment tribunal; [112] transferral of that function was vigorously debated and was only accomplished at the last minute, September 8.[113] Late in the day, on August 20, the Committee of Five was directed to report "a mode of trying the supreme Judges in case of impeachment," and it reported back on August 22 that "the Judges of the Supreme Court shall be triable by the Senate." [114] Although provision for the establishment of inferior court judges had been made,[115] no mention was made of *their* impeachment, suggesting that no consideration had been given to the impeachment of lesser judges. When they were at last caught up, it was as an unarticulated afterthought, tucked away in the last-minute insertion "civil officers," which itself was added without comment to the Executive Department Article II provision for impeachment of the President.[116] Remarking on the absence of a provision for removal of the Judiciary Article, Mrs. Ziskind states, "There is a legitimate textual question whether judges were included in the impeachment provisions of Article II." [117] This "legitimate textual question," plus the fact that no word was said about the impeachment of lesser judges, cautions against attribution to the Framers of an undebatable intention to bar removal of judges save by impeachment.

---

112. President: 1 Farrand 78, 85, 91, 250; 2 Farrand 61, 64–69, 116, 172, 185, 186, 495, 499. Judges: 1 Farrand 223–224, 231, 244; 2 Farrand 186.
113. 2 Farrand 42, 423, 500, 522–523, 551.
114. Ibid. 337, 367.
115. 1 Farrand 124–125; June 11th.
116. 2 Farrand 552; September 8th.
117. Ziskind, supra, n. 30 at 151. The *only* suggestion that was made to deal *directly* with removal of judges was Dickinson's proposal on August 27th, to add after the provision for "good behavior" in Article II, the Judicial Article, the proviso that judges "may be removed by the Executive on the application [by] the Senate and House of Representatives." 2 Farrand 428. Not a word that the problem was covered by impeachment.
   Ziskind's "textual question" is pointed up by the Virginia Plan proposal for inclusion of "impeachments of any national Officer" in the "jurisdiction of the national Judiciary," while the Paterson-New Jersey Plan proposed inclusion of "federal officers." 1 Farrand 22, 244. See also 2 Farrand 186. Presumably such jurisdiction would not include trial of themselves, for impeachment of Justices (not inferior judges) was mooted much later. Supra, text accompanying nn. 114–115.

The almost absent-minded inclusion of judges among "civil officers" undercuts the assumption that the Framers designed impeachment to enforce judicial "good behavior." Even more plainly, the records of the Convention preclude the notion that "the constitutional antecedent of the phrase 'good behavior' is the impeachment clause. Presumably 'good behavior' was the term chosen because by that wording the tenure of Article III judges was wedded to the strictures of the impeachment clause." [118] Judicial tenure "during good behavior" appeared at the very outset of the Convention on May 29, in the Virginia Plan submitted by Edmund Randolph; it was likewise contained in the substitute New Jersey Plan offered two weeks later by William Paterson,[119] long before the request was made for a tribunal to try impeachments of Justices. In truth, the paramount concern with impeachment of the President had all but crowded out thought of removal of Justices until the tardy reference to a committee of a tribunal for their trial. Instead therefore of a considered "wedding" of judicial "good behavior" to impeachment, the records reflect a hurried clean-up job, in the course of which, let us hope, judges and Justices could be caught up and lumped with "all civil Officers" who had no "good behavior" tenure.

One man, Rufus King, did attempt to link "good behavior" with impeachability: "the judiciary hold their places not for a limited time, but during good behavior. It is necessary therefore that a forum should be established for trying misbehavior. Was the Executive to hold his place during good behavior? . . . He ought not to be impeachable unless he hold his office during good behavior." [120] King's attempt to make "good behavior"

---

118. Kramer & Barron, supra, n. 14 at 460–461. They also state that "the judges were deliberately tied to the impeachment clause" because "They alone are to serve 'during good Behavior'." Ibid. 460.
119. 1 Farrand 21, 244.
120. 2 Farrand 66–67. In 1802 Gouverneur Morris said, "Misbehavior is not a term known in our law; the idea is expressed by the word misdemeanor; which word is in the clause respecting impeachments. Taking, therefore, the two together . . . the Constitution says: 'The judges shall hold their offices so long as they demean themselves well; but if they shall misdemean, if they shall, on impeachment, be convicted of misdemeanor, they shall be removed.'" 11 Ann. Cong. 90 (1802), quoted in Kurland, supra, n. 63 at 676. Morris was mistaken in stating that "misbehavior is not a term known to our law"; as misbehavior was expressly

tenure the test of impeachability did not meet with favor, and the Convention provided for impeachment of "President, Vice President and all civil officers," who, but for the judges, had no such tenure. Thus the Convention itself rejected the inference that "good behavior" is necessarily wedded to impeachability. And in the upshot the "forum" was not to "try misbehavior" but "high crimes and misdemeanors," a quite different standard, as will appear.

Nevertheless, the notion that there was a special relation between "good behavior" tenure and impeachment turned up in the First Congress "removal" debate. Although insistence that impeachment was the sole means for removal of "civil officers" in the executive branch was overridden, several speakers distinguished the case for removal of judges on the ground that they had tenure "during good behavior." [121] Viewed against the above historical background, and the proof yet to come that "high crimes and misdemeanors" was not meant to comprehend infractions of "good behavior," such remarks were simply mistaken and entitled to no more respect than would be loose statements that "bribery" comprehends payments to judges by those who do not seek to influence disposition of a pending case. Since the Framers employed common law terms of accepted meaning,[122] something more than passing assertions in the halls of Congress, not essential to disposition of the point under discussion, should be required to alter that meaning.

These were tangential remarks in a debate devoted to the *President's* power to remove *executive* officers. At issue was whether the President could remove those appointed by him; the operative considerations were laid bare by Roger Sherman, himself a Framer: "I consider it an established principle, that the power which appoints can also remove, unless there are express

---

made triable in the early Delaware and Maryland constitutions; supra, text accompanying n. 105; and the Framers opted for "high crimes and misdemeanors" instead because it was a phrase of "limited" meaning. Supra, text accompanying nn. 187–189. For the relation of "misdemean" and "high misdemeanor" see infra, text accompanying nn. 175–178.
121. George Thatcher, 1 *Ann. Cong.* 376; Alexander White, ibid. 465–466.
122. See supra, Chapter II, n. 160.

exceptions made. Now the power which appoints the judges cannot displace them, because there is a constitutional restriction [good behavior] in their favor." [123] Michael Stone chimed in that "good behavior" limited "the exercise of the power *which appoints*. It is thus in the case of judges." [124] That was the view of Abraham Baldwin, likewise a Framer: "The judges are appointed by the President but they are only removable by impeachment. The President has no agency in the removal." [125] The governing principle was underlined by Elias Boudinot, who, anticipating Burke Shartel, stated that impeachment was one of the "exceptions to a principle," to the separation of powers.[126] But for that exception Congress also was blocked from removal of executive officers and of judges as well.[127]

The First Congress itself furnished the best of reasons for not attaching overmuch weight to the several utterances by its members: when it came face to face with a problem affecting judges, its action repudiated their "exclusive" remarks. In the Act of 1790 the First Congress provided that upon conviction in court for bribery a judge shall be "forever disqualified to hold any office." [128] Since the impeachment clause provides for disqualification upon impeachment and conviction, the Act is unconstitutional if the clause indeed provides the "exclusive" method of disqualification. The First Congress will scarcely be charged with misconstruing the Constitution; hence the 1790 statute must be regarded as a construction that the impeachment clause does not constitute the "only" means for the disqualification of judges. As with "disqualification" so with "removal," for the two stand on a par in the impeachment provision.[129] And the statute also illustrates the familiar

123. 1 *Ann. Cong.* 491.
124. Ibid. 492.
125. Ibid. 557.
126. Ibid. 527; cf. Michael Stone, ibid. 564–565.
127. John Lawrence: the provision that "the Judges should continue during good behavior . . . was to render them independent of the Legislature." Ibid. 377. William Smith said, "It would be improper that [judges] should depend on this House for the degree of permanency which is essential to secure the integrity of judges." Ibid. 508. See Berger, *Congress v. Court* 117–119.
128. Act of 1790, ch. 9, §21, 1 Stat. 117.
129. Article I, §3 (7): "Judgment in Cases of Impeachment shall not extend further than to removal from Office, and disqualification to hold" any office.

proposition that broad dicta (here by only a few individuals) respecting a situation not presented for determination cannot be conclusive when the situation is actually presented.[130] What the First Congress *did* when it had to deal with "disqualification" of judges thus speaks against reliance upon some earlier utterances by a few of its members when the removal of judges was not involved.

In evaluating a nonexclusive interpretation of the impeachment provisions we can profit from the parallel English experience. The Act of Settlement (1700) provided for judicial tenure during "good behavior," but judges could be removed by the Crown upon an Address by both Houses of Parliament.[131] The decided preponderance of authority, Lord Chancellor Erskine, Holdsworth, and others, consider that this provision did not exclude other means of removal, that is, by impeachment, scire facias, or criminal conviction.[132] That Act

---

130. When some of Chief Justice Marshall's own remarks in Marbury v. Madison were later pressed upon him, he said, "It is a maxim not to be disregarded, that general expressions, in every opinion . . . ought not to control the judgment in a subsequent suit when the very point is presented for decision. The reason of the maxim is obvious. The question actually before the Court is investigated with great care, and considered in its full extent. Other principles which may serve to illustrate it, are considered in their relation to the case decided, but their possible bearing on all other cases is seldom completely investigated. Cohens v. Virginia, 6 Wheat. (19 U.S.) 264, 399–400 (1821).

131. Act of Settlement, 12 & 13 Will. 3, c. 2, §3 (1700), is entitled "An Act for further limitation of the Crown" and provides that "Judges Commissions be made *Quamdiu se bene gesserint*; . . . but upon the Address of both Houses of Parliament, it may be lawful to remove them." The Address is not conditioned upon misbehavior, and the "but" phrase may be read as "notwithstanding" the commission during good behavior judges may be removed upon Address. The implication of "but" as "notwithstanding" is heightened by 1 Geo. 3, c. 23 (1760), which insured the continuation of judicial tenure despite the demise of the Crown, "Provided always . . . that it may be lawful for his Majesty . . . to remove any Judge or Judges upon the address of both Houses of Parliament." A respected authority states that the removal by address "is, in fact, a qualification of, or exception from, the words creating a tenure during good behavior, and not an incident or legal consequence thereof;" the power "may be invoked on occasions when the misbehavior complained of would not constitute a legal breach of the conditions on which the office is held." 1 Todd 193.

132. Supra, text accompanying n. 42. Edmund Burke stated in the Commons, "it is in our choice by an address to remove an improper judge; by impeachment before the peers to pursue to destruction a corrupt judge." Quoted 1 Todd 194. Not long after, in 1791, a pamphleteer, supposedly the barrister Spenser Percival, extolled the advantages of impeachment and saw "no reason for abolishing this mode of trial." Quoted 4 Hatsell 69–70n, 253n. In 1806, Lord Grenville urged that if the Commons "think the charges are matter of high crime . . . it is their duty to impeach." 7 *Parl. Deb.* 758 (1806). The "right to impeach [judges] . . . according to the ancient law and usage, is a matter of right to those who may suffer from their corruptions or oppressions." Taafe v. Downs, 3 Moo. P. C. 35, 68n, 13 E. R. 15, 31n (1813). A recent English writer states that "the

was designed to curb *royal* interference with judges, not to restrict Parliament.[133] And as McIlwain pointed out, neither the Act of Settlement, which provides that the King "may remove," nor any other Act "forces the king to remove or even gives the houses authority to force him to comply with their request for removal." [134] It follows that, were the Act given "exclusive" effect, and were the King to refuse to remove a corrupt judge upon an Address, Parliament would be powerless to remove him. It was precisely this power to remove those whom the King sought to shelter for which Parliament had fought; therefore, to give the Act "exclusive" effect would be to erect surrender of a hard-won power upon an artificial canon of construction. Reason and the great weight of authority seem to me to run counter to an "exclusive" reading of the Act of Settlement.

The argument for exclusivity of the Act of Settlement is in pertinent detail much stronger than can be made under our Constitution. In that Act, the "good behavior" and removal provisions are contained in the very same section, whereas in the Constitution the "good behavior" and impeachment provisions were spatially and temporally separated. "Good behavior" appeared from the outset, and it was embodied in Article III, while the separate provision for impeachment must be located in the belated insertion of "civil Officers" in Article II. No indication is found in the Convention records that the insertion was in any way associated with the earlier provision for "good behavior" tenure.[135] Instead, when we come to examine the relation between "good behavior" and "high crimes

---

power to remove after an address is additional to the common law. It is a principle of construction that judicial process is not abolished except by clear words. R. M. Jackson, *The Machinery of Justice in England* 289 n. 1 (London, 5th ed. 1967).

133. Story §1623 stated: "The object of the act of Parliament was to secure the judges from removal at the mere pleasure of the crown; but not to render them independent of the action of Parliament." See also McIlwain, supra, n. 32 at 226; and compare Stone, supra, text accompanying n. 124.

134. The point was nicely made in Pennsylvania when the House sent up an address to Governor Thomas McKean (formerly Chief Justice), who refused to remove. When a committee urged that the term in the constitution "may remove" meant "must remove" he replied "that he would have them know that 'may' sometimes meant 'won't.' " William Loyd, *The Early Courts of Pennsylvania* 147 (Boston, 1910).

135. Supra, text accompanying nn. 118–119.

and misdemeanors" more closely, we shall discover weighty reasons against the attribution of such an intention to the Framers.

For Judge Otis, the Framers' rejection of removal by Address was all but conclusive proof that there was an intention to bar other means of removal as well.[136] But special considerations led to rejection of removal by Address. Both in England and in the newly independent states removal by Address was untrammeled;[137] its adoption would have placed judges utterly at the mercy of Congress. Gouverneur Morris justly objected that the Address was "fundamentally wrong" and "arbitrary" because it contemplated removal "without a trial."[138] The Framers were aware of and condemned the sorry spectacle of legislative chastisement of state judges who had dared to question the constitutionality of legislation.[139] To leave the judiciary at the unbridled pleasure of Congress would have defeated the Framers' purpose to curb legislative excesses by judicial review.[140] Legislative interference was confined to trial by impeachment, under a standard (high crimes and misdemeanors) of narrow, technical meaning, and even then a two-thirds vote was required for conviction. Nor would impeachment, said James Wilson, be used to remove judges who had declared statutes unconstitutional.[141] Judges who would be at the mercy of "every

---

136. Otis 29, 30.
137. For England, supra, n. 131. Section 30 of the Maryland constitution (1776), provided "Judges shall be removed for misbehavior, on conviction in a court of law, and may be removed by the Governor [without reference to misbehavior], upon the address of the General Assembly." 1 Poore 819. Chapter III, Article I of the Massachusetts constitution (1780) provided, "All judicial . . . officers shall hold their offices during good behavior. . . . *Provided, nevertheless,* The governor . . . may remove them upon the address of both houses of the legislature." Ibid. 968. The New Hampshire provisions (1784) were identical with those of Massachusetts, 2 Poore 1290. Inferably the "Provided, nevertheless" constituted a gloss upon the English statute. Section XX of the South Carolina constitution (1776) provided that judges were to be commissioned "during good behavior, but shall be removed on the address of the general assembly and legislative council," 2 Poore 1619, following in the footsteps of the Act of Settlement.
138. 2 Farrand 428. Edmund Randolph also opposed the address "as weakening too much the independence of the Judges," ibid. 429; and John Rutledge regarded it as an "insuperable objection" that "the supreme Court is to judge between the U.S. and particular States," ibid. 428, again going to independence of the Congress.
139. Berger, *Congress v. Court* 117–118, 38–39.
140. Ibid. 13–16, and *passim.*
141. 2 Elliot 478. This was likewise the view of Elbridge Gerry, 1 *Ann. Cong.* 537. In New Hampshire, the court had declared the "Ten Pound

gust of faction which might prevail in the two branches
of our Government" could not be trusted to exhibit the
fortitude needed to set aside an Act of Congress.[142]
None of the factors which led the Framers to block legislative retaliation against judges by Address had any
applicability to removal of judges by judges. Judges enjoyed a respect withheld from the legislature [143] and
could be counted on to weigh the misconduct of a judge
as dispassionately as that of an ordinary citizen.

The Argument for Absolute Independence

To buttress their view that impeachment is the sole
avenue for removal of judges, Justices Black and
Douglas assert that the solicitude of the Founders for
judicial independence was all-encompassing, that it included independence even from judicial control and
demanded nothing other than "the admittedly difficult
method of impeachment." [144] The correlation between
judicial tenure and impeachment, as we have seen, was
virtually nil.[145] And all the remarks in the several Conventions that bear on judicial independence, so far as I
could find, referred to freedom from legislative and
executive encroachments.[146] No one suggested that
judges must be immune from traditional judicial control
which, minimally, included attachments that King's

Act" unconstitutional, and although the legislature by a 44 to 14 vote
then declared the act constitutional, the representatives overwhelmingly
approved a committee report that the judges were "not impeachable for
maladministration as their conduct [was] justified by the constitution" of
New Hampshire. 2 W. W. Crosskey, *Politics and the Constitution in the
History of the United States* 960–970 (Chicago, 1953).
142. James Wilson, 2 Farrand 429; cf. *Federalist* No. 78 at 509.
143. See infra, n. 160.
144. Chandler II, 398 U.S. at 136–141, Douglas, J., dissenting; Black,
J., dissenting, ibid. 142. This is also the view of Kurland: "certainly there
is no point in tinkering with the independence of federal judges by sub-
jecting their tenure to control of other federal judges appointed by the
same defective process. Without their independence, the federal judges will
have lost all that separates them from total subordination to the political
processes from which they ought to be aloof." Kurland, supra, n. 63 at 667.
As if impeachment has not been shot through with political partisanship!
See infra, n. 153, and text accompanying nn. 152–158. See also supra,
Chapter II, text accompanying nn. 188–205.
145. Supra, text accompanying nn. 112–120.
146. The materials are collected in Berger, *Congress v. Court* 117–119.
In *Federalist* No. 78 at 503, Hamilton stated: "The standard of good
behavior" is an "excellent barrier to the encroachments and oppressions
of the representative body." See also supra, n. 127, and infra, n. 149. It
was from the state legislatures that threats to the judiciary had come.
Berger, supra, at 38, 42–43, 117.

Bench had long issued against lesser judges for misconduct and oppression.[147] To the contrary, Justice Wilson, a leading Framer, stated in his 1791 Lectures.

The independence of each power consists in this, that its proceedings . . . should be free from the remotest influence, direct or indirect, of either of the other two powers. But further than this, the independency of each power ought not to extend.[148]

This was the view of judicial independence taken by Judge St. George Tucker in 1803,[149] and it may be discerned in Jefferson's recognition that judges can remove judges.[150]

The emphasis of Justices Black and Douglas upon the exclusivity of impeachment suggests a preference for congressional over judicial trial, surely a strange preference in a Justice. Congressional trial suffers from serious defects. Fresh illustration of the political partisanship that has characterized impeachment has recently been furnished by Congressman Gerald Ford's proposal to impeach Justice Douglas.[151] As Macaulay

---

147. By virtue of its "general superintendency over all inferior Courts," King's Bench could punish judges of lesser courts by attachment for contempt "for acting unjustly, oppressively or irregularly," for "any practice contrary to the plain rules of natural justice . . . as for denying a defendant a copy of the declaration against him . . . or for compelling a defendant to give exorbitant bail." 2 Hawkins, ch. 22, §§ 25–26 at 149–150 (1716); and "putting the subject to unnecessary vexation by colour of a judicial Proceeding wholly unwarranted by law." Ibid. § 25. So too, 3 Bacon (N) 744, states: "the Court of Kings Bench, by the plenitude of its power, exercises a superintendency over all inferior courts, and may grant an attachment against the judges of such courts for oppressive, unjust or irregular practice, contrary to the obvious rules of natural justice."
148. 1 Wilson 299.
149. "That absolute independence of the judiciary for which we contend is not, then, incompatible with the strictest responsibility . . . but such an independence of the other *coordinate* branches of the government as seems absolutely necessary to secure them the free exercise of their constitutional functions, without the hope of pleasing or the fear of offending. And as from the natural feebleness of the judiciary it is in continual jeopardy of being overpowered, awed or influenced by its coordinate branches who have the custody of the purse and sword." Tucker App. 359.
150. Writing in 1816, Jefferson lamented that judges had been made "independent of the nation itself. They are irremovable, *but by their own body*, for any depravities of conduct." Quoted in Ross, supra, n. 14 at 123–124 (emphasis added). In 1825 Rawle wrote that in England "Judges are held liable to trial for every offense before their brethen." Rawle 214.
151. In a comment on this proposal Milton Viorst states that "the 110 sponsors of the anti-Douglas resolution are all conservative Republicans and Dixiecrats. This seems persuasive evidence in support of the hypothesis which virtually everyone in Washington accepts: that the undertaking seeks not simply to impeach William Orville Douglas but to discredit the liberalism . . . inherent in the domestic programs of Democratic Administrations

said of the Hastings impeachment: "no man has the least confidence in [the Peers'] impartiality, when a great public functionary, charged with a great state crime, is brought to their bar. They are all politicians." [152] That statement was amply verified on our own soil in the impeachment of President Andrew Johnson; and impeachment has continued to be colored by political partisanship.[153]

Justice Douglas states, however, that "our tradition even bars political impeachments as evidenced by the highly partisan, but unsuccessful, effort to oust Justice Samuel Chase of this Court in 1805." [154] Chase's acquittal was no less partisan than his impeachment. When Jefferson became President, the "national judiciary, one hundred per cent Federalist, amounted to an arm of that party." [155] Chase, after the fashion of his Federalist brethren, made intemperate attacks on the Jefferson administration in harangues to a grand jury.[156] Not unnaturally the incensed Jeffersonians took out after Chase. The Federalists "supported Chase completely in every test," and with the aid of a group of Jeffersonians whom John Randolph, leader of the impeachment, had alienated, saved Chase from the retribution he richly deserved.[157] So too, the bitterly partisan impeachment of Andrew Johnson narrowly failed; and partisanship has continued to dominate impeachments.[158]

Apart from partisanship there is the glaring inade-

---

since the New Deal." Viorst, supra, n. 10 at 32. Representative Gerald Ford all but conceded that his Resolution was in retaliation for the Senate's rejection of two of President Nixon's nominees to the Supreme Court. See supra, Chapter II, n. 189.

152. More fully quoted supra, Chapter II text accompanying n. 193.

153. See supra, Chapter II, text accompanying nn. 188–205; infra, Chapter VIII, text accompanying nn. 9–16. See also Jacobus Ten Broek, "Partisan Politics and Federal Judgeship Impeachments Since 1903," 23 *Minn. L. Rev.* 185 (1927).

154. Chandler II, 398 U.S. at 136 (Douglas, J., dissenting).

155. 4 Malone 158. By the time of the Chase impeachment in 1805, Jefferson had been afforded the opportunity of making several appointments in the lower echelons. See chronological list of judges, 1 Fed. Cas. xiii–xxviii.

156. 1 Warren 274–276. For example, Chief Justice Dana of Massachusetts, "in a charge to the Grand Jury denounced the Vice President [Jefferson] and the minority in Congress as 'apostles of atheism and anarchy, bloodshed and plunder.' " Ibid. 275.

157. 4 Malone 479–480. There was at least one solid ground for conviction of Chase. See infra, Chapter VIII.

158. See references in n. 153, supra.

quacy of a tribunal at which attendance is so sporadic that more than a handful of Senators are rarely present at any given time; and they simply cannot find time to study and digest the bulky record.[159] Contrast with this the constant attendance of judges schooled to listen to evidence and to grasp complex issues, trained (one hopes) in more dispassionate judgment than a politician. In comparing legislative with judicial trial, it may be noted that the Founders had more confidence in the judiciary than in the legislature.[160] Then too, a number

159. After the 1936 impeachment of Judge Halsted Ritter, Congressman John Robsion said, "Any one who has been a Member of that body knows it is humanly impossible to have all the Senators present all the time for a period of 10 days, 2 weeks or more, sitting as a jury. If they did, momentous and pressing interests of the Nation . . . would suffer." 81 *Cong. Rec.* 6183 (1937). See also Hatton Sumners, ibid. 6165. "It is absurd," wrote Moore in the midst of World War II, "to think that large interests during the war, for example, must wait upon the trial of Judge X . . . As a matter of fact, the Senate continues with the nation's business at the expense of Judge X. Senators troop in to answer the roll call when lack of a quorum is suggested and then troop out to the attendance of larger affairs." Moore, supra, n. 9 at 356–357. For other examples of sparse Senatorial attendance, see Potts, supra, n. 153 at 34–35; and see infra, n. 199. Chafee recorded, "I remember how my uncle, who was a Senator from Rhode Island, complained that the impeachment of a federal judge was disorganizing the work of the Senate while it had ever so much normal business before it." Chafee 148. After the Ritter impeachment, Congressman Chauncey Reed stated, "The Senate is composed of busy men, who cannot and will not divest themselves of the time they must necessarily devote to their lawmaking activities and concentrate, analyze and digest the intricate testimony . . ." 81 *Cong. Rec.* 6175 (1937).

160. Madison said in the Virginia Ratification Convention, "Were I to select a power which might be given with confidence, it would be the judicial power." 3 Elliot 535. "No man says anything against" the judges, stated Edmund Randolph, ibid. 205. When Jefferson welcomes the "check" which a Bill of Rights "puts into the hands of the Judiciary," he added, "This is a body, 'which if rendered independent & kept strictly to their own department merits great confidence for their learning and integrity.' " 5 Thomas Jefferson, *The Writings of Thomas Jefferson* 81 (New York, Ford ed. 1892–1899).

Contrast Madison's statement in the First Congress that the legislative power is the "most likely to be abused," 1 *Ann. Cong.* 437. William Smith also stated that the legislative "power is perhaps more liable to abuse than the judicial." Ibid. 816. In the Convention Madison stated that the legislature "was the real source of danger." 2 Farrand 74. See also Berger, *Congress v. Court* 8–13, 132–137. Wilson said in the Convention that "The English courts are hitherto pure, just and incorrupt, while their legislature are base and venal." 1 Farrand 261. In 1803, 1 Tucker App. 356, praised "that preeminent integrity, which amidst surrounding corrruption, beams with genuine luster from the English courts of judicature." At another point Tucker said, "in a republic . . . the violence and malignity of party spirit, as well in the legislature, as in the executive, requires not less the intervention of a calm, temperate, upright and independent judiciary, to prevent that violence and malignity from exerting itself?" Ibid. 355. Again, he stated: "The judiciary, therefore, is that department of the government to whom the protection of the rights of the individual is by the constitution especially confided, interposing its shield between him and the sword of usurped authority . . . and the shafts of faction and violence." Ibid. 357.

Finally, when Chief Baron Walter and Justice Archer were threatened by the King's arbitrary conduct, they did not invoke the protection of impeachment but of scire facias. Supra, text accompanying nn. 35–37. And in commending to Parliament remission of a judge's trial to the courts, Lord Chancellor Erskine hardly considered that he would be less fairly tried. Supra, text accompanying n. 40.

of the prior state constitutions contained provisions for removal of judges by judges, including the Virginia provision for the trial of judges on impeachment by the Court of Appeals.[161]

What Justice Black mildly refers to as the "admittedly difficult method of impeachment" amounts in the words of Senator William McAdoo, spoken after participating in the trial of Judge Halsted Ritter, to a "practical certainty that in a large majority of cases misconduct will never be visited with impeachment," "a standing invitation for judges to abuse their authority with impunity." [162] No student who takes the time to study the path of impeachment will quarrel with McAdoo's assessment.[163] Against generally acknowledged present deficiencies of the impeachment process,[164] Justice Douglas would pit fears of judicial visitorial powers over judges: "The power [of other judges] to keep a particular judge from sitting on a racial case, a church-and-state case . . . a union case may have profound consequences." [165] To a Black seeking civil rights, the possibility (to follow in the path of hypothesis) that a fair-minded southern district judge may repeatedly be reversed by a racist Court of Appeals is no less serious. I would hazard that judges would find reviewing judges no less fair in judicial removal cases than they have proved in racial cases.

Perhaps we have come to rely unduly on the professionalism which tends to school and temper judgment and to teach judges to discount personal biases. But if we can safely trust the life and property of a citizen to judicial determination, if we rely on the courts to rise above personal bias on racial issues that wrack the

---

161. Supra, text accompanying nn. 105–107.
162. 80 *Cong. Rec.* 5934 (1936). See also infra, n. 200.
163. See infra, text accompanying nn. 193–205.
164. Potts, supra, n. 153 at 31–36; Shartel 870–873. Impeachment, Stolz concedes, "has a deservedly bad reputation." Preble Stolz, "Disciplining Federal Judges: Is Impeachment Hopeless?" 57 *Calif. L. Rev.* 659, 660 (1969).
165. Chandler II, 398 U.S. at 155 (Douglas, J., dissenting). In 1937, Hatton Sumners stated: "I never heard it said until today . . . that three judges of the circuit court of appeals trying a district judge might stultify themselves in order to convict an honest man and remove him from office." 81 *Cong. Rec.* 6184 (1937).

nation,[166] we should trust them no less when they come to determine the far less momentous issue whether a judge is unfit for office. Our trust should extend to confidence that courts will not suddenly yield to personal bias when they are called upon to decide whether a judge has been guilty of misbehavior or whether, by reason of insanity, senility, or other disability, he has become incapable of performing his functions adequately. Courts no less than politicians can perceive that the integrity of the judicial process is best preserved by judges who can and will adequately serve the public interest.[166a] Should a convincing showing be made that in removing a judge the visitorial court was motivated by racial-religious-economic biases, rather than a genuine need to cleanse the bench of a senile, corrupt, or negligent placeman, that court may be reversed on appeal by the Supreme Court.[167] And there remains impeachment of the removing court; for oppression or abuse of power is a recognized impeachable offense, as Madison's statement in this very context further attests: "the wanton removal of meritorious officers would subject [the President] to impeachment and removal." [168]

---

166. "Since *Brown v. Board of Education* in 1954, some of the most divisive, emotion-laden issues arising within American society have been repeatedly thrust upon the courts for resolution," Rondal G. Downing, "Judicial Ethics and the Political Role of the Courts," 35 *Law & Cont. Prob.* 94, 97 (1970). President Kingman Brewster of Yale University stated that he was "sceptical of the ability of black revolutionaries to achieve fair trial anywhere in the United States." *N.Y. Times*, April 25, 1970.

166a. "It can hardly be denied that judges are better qualified to recognize the personal equations involved in the adoption [and by the same token, the application] of standards of judicial conduct. After all, they are balancing and adjusting controversies every day without the interference of political pressures and campaign exigencies . . . Legislatures are political animals who react within the framework of their constituencies which might inject political considerations into final determinations." Justice Tom C. Clark, "Judicial Self-Regulation and Its Potential," 35 *Law & Cont. Prob.* 37, 41 (1970). Cf. Macaulay, supra, text accompanying n. 152.
Chief Judge Bailey Aldrich of the First Circuit testified: "Nobody is more conscious of the need for the independence of the judiciary than the individual judges themselves. I think it might be fairer to the judge to have his interest passed upon . . . by judges rather than by others . . . Judges would be better protected if judges were used." Hearings on the Independence of Federal Judges before the Senate Subcommittee on Separation of Powers 368 (91st Cong. 2d Sess., April–May 1970). Cf. the remarks of Chief Justice Burger and Justice Blackmun, infra, n. 235.

167. It is open to Congress to provide for an appeal to the Supreme Court from a judgment by a special court for removal of judges. See generally, infra, text accompanying nn. 235–242.

168. 1 *Ann. Cong.* 498; supra, Chapter II, text accompanying nn. 81–92.

IMPEACHMENT FOR "MISBEHAVIOR"

By a seemingly logical progression Congressman Ford has concluded that impeachment was designed to enforce "good behavior." Starting with "during good behavior," he said, "it is implicit in this that when behavior ceases to be good, the right to hold judicial office ceases also." So much is unexceptionable, as is his second step. "Naturally, there must be orderly procedure for determining whether or not a Federal judge's behavior is good." Consequently, he concludes, the Founding Fathers "vested this ultimate power . . . in the Congress" in the "seldom-used procedure, called impeachment." [169] Thereby he assumed the answer, an answer contradicted by history. But in justice to Congressman Ford, he was not breaking virgin soil; his view lurks in Rufus King's remark that impeachment was the "forum . . . established for trying misbehavior." [170] The Framers, however, went on to limit impeachment to the commission of "high crimes and misdemeanors," a standard of quite different origin and dimensions. The Ford-King view was given its most ringing affirmation by Judge Merrill Otis, in his heated defense of the "exclusivity" of impeachment. Confronted with the fact that "good behavior" might be an impotent provision if unenforceable, with the "hiatus" between "good behavior" and "high crimes and misdemeanors," Judge Otis boldly asserted that "a judge may be impeached for any misbehavior or misconduct which terminates his right to continue in office." [171]

At common law, tenure "during good behavior," as we have seen, was terminated by "misbehavior." The early law does not define "misbehavior" in so many words; rather, it states several grounds for forfeiture of an office. But these, a study of Bacon's *Abridgment* discloses, are interrelated if not equivalent, and we are justified in concluding that the several grounds of forfeiture serve to identify various forms of "misbe-

---

169. 116 *Cong. Rec.* H3113 (daily ed. April 15, 1970).
170. Supra, text accompanying n. 120. See also Judge Thomas Cooley, supra, Chapter II, n. 1.
171. Otis 33.

havior." [172] For example it was held in the *Earl of Pembroke's Case* (1597) that "every voluntary act done by an officer contrary to that which belongs to his office is a forfeiture of his office." Coke enumerated three causes for "forfeiture or seizure of offices, as for abusing, not using or refusing." As abuse of office, he instanced an escape voluntarily suffered by a jailer; nonuse was exemplified by nonattendance when the office concerned the administration of justice.[173] By 1716, Hawkins could state that "in the grant of every office whatsoever, there is this condition implied by common reason, that the grantee ought to execute it diligently and faithfully." [174] His view of the scope of forfeiture was broad indeed: "It would be endless to enumerate all the particular instances, wherein an officer may be discharged or fined; and it also seems needless to endeavor it because they are generally so obvious to common sense, as to need no explication." And he emphasized that forfeiture for neglect of duty was for the protection of the public, to make possible a replacement who would adequately perform the duties of the office.[175]

"Misdemean" and "misbehave" were sometimes interchangeable terms, but it does not follow that "misbehavior" was equated with "high misdemeanor." To "misdemean," states the Oxford English Dictionary, meant "to misbehave, misconduct one's self," and it cites a 1736 example: "Sir Luke Fitzgerald misde-

---

172. Compare 3 Bacon (H) p. 741, "Of the nature of offices as to their duration and continuance" with (M) 741, "Of the Forfeitures of an Office;" and 4 Comyns, supra, n. 26 at (B 7) 242 with (K 2) 255. Cf. 2 Anson (Part I), supra, n. 42 at 235: "Misbehavior appears to mean misconduct in the performance of official duties, refusal or deliberate neglect to attend to them."
173. Popham 116, 118, 79 E. R. 1223, 1224 (1597); Earl of Shrewsbury's Case, 9 Co. 46b, 50a, 77 E. R. 798, 804 (1611). See also Regina v. Ballivos (Serjeant Whitacre's Case), 2 Ld. Raym. 1232, 1237, 92 E. R. 313, 316 (1705); 16 Viner, supra, n. 27 at 121–124; 4 Comyns, supra, n. 26 at 255; 3 Bacon 741.
174. 1 Hawkins ch. 66, § 1, p. 167; 3 Bacon 745, also states that "the particular instances wherein a Man may be said to act contrary to the Duty of his office, tho various, are yet so generally obvious, that it seems needless to endeavour to enumerate them." Blackstone states: "if a grant be made to a man of an office, generally, without adding other words, the law tacitly annexes hereto a secret condition, that the grantee shall duly execute his office, on breach of which condition it is lawful for the grantor . . . to oust him." 2 Blackstone 152–153.
175. 1 Hawkins ch. 66 § 2, p. 168 and § 1 at 167–168. Hawkins was to be found in colonial libraries. Colbourn, supra, n. 4 at 204, 211, 223.

meaned himself before the board by uncivil words." An appointment for so long as he "shall well demean himself" in his office was considered in *Harcourt v. Fox* (1692). Serjeant Levinz construed the statute to mean "during good behavior; and that is an estate for life, unless his misbehavior in his office" made him removable for "misdemeanor." Chief Justice Holt was of this opinion, saying that *"during life,* and *during good demeanor,* are therefore synonymous phrases," and that the statute was designed to put the clerk "out of fear of losing [his office] for anything but his own misbehavior in it." [176]

The interchangeability of "misbehavior" and "misdemeanor" *for purposes of forfeiture* of an office does not, however, prove that "misbehavior" and "high crimes and misdemeanors" are equivalents for purposes of impeachment. Rather, it illustrates the familiar fact that the same word may have different meanings in different contexts.[177] "High misdemeanors" was employed in impeachment proceedings long before there was such a crime as a "misdemeanor"; and impeachment was not based on "misdemeanors" but on "high misdemeanors," a quite different breed of cat.[178] And if I may be suffered to repeat: in no case, so far as I could find, was an impeachment grounded upon a breach of "good behavior." In every case the charge was "high treason" and (in some cases "or") "high crimes and misdemeanors."

Certain categories of "high crimes and misde-

176. Harcourt v. Fox, 1 Show. K. B. 426, 510, 534, 536, 89 E. R. 680, 720, 721–722, 734, 736 (1692–1693). Cf. 1 W. & M. c. 21, § VI (1688): "if any Clerk of the peace ... shall misdemean himself in the Execution of the said office, and thereupon a Complaint and Charge in Writing of such Misdemeanour shall be exhibited against him to the Justices ... [they may] ... discharge him from the said office."
177. Lamar v. United States, 240 U.S. 60, 65 (1916) (per Holmes, J.); Atlantic Cleaners and Dyers v. United States, 286 U.S. 427, 433 (1932).
178. That "high crimes and misdemeanors" means "and high misdemeanors" may be gathered from Blackstone's statement that the principal "high misdemeanor' is "the maladministration of such high officers," "usually punished by the method of parliamentary impeachment." 4 Blackstone 121. In the impeachment of Chief Justice Scroggs, he was initially charged only with "high misdemeanors." 8 Howell 163. For references to "high misdemeanor" in the Federal Convention, see 2 Farrand 348, 443. Senator William Blount was expelled from the Senate in 1797 because of "a high misdemeanor, entirely inconsistent with his public trust and duty as a Senator." Wharton 202. See also supra, Chapter II, n. 108. For the relation between "high misdemeanor" and ordinary "misdemeanors" see supra, Chapter II, text accompanying nn. 21–38.

meanors" superficially may seem coterminous with "misbehavior"; for example, abuse of official power, neglect of duty. But a gap yawns between the "non-attendance" instanced by Coke as an example of "non-use" or neglect, and the neglect that was punished by impeachment; for example, the neglect of an admiral to safeguard the seas [179] or of a Commissioner of the Navy adequately to prepare against a Dutch invasion.[180] Moreover, the impeachable "neglect" and "abuse of office" comprehended in "high crimes and misdemeanors" was, in the view of the Founders, limited to "great offenders"; [181] impeachment of all petty officers was emphatically excluded. Maclaine's remarks in the North Carolina Ratification Convention are illustrative: "it was mentioned by one gentleman, that petty officers might be impeached. It appears to me . . . the most horrid ignorance to suppose that every officer, however trifling his office, is to be impeached for every petty offense . . . I hope every gentleman . . . must see plainly that impeachments cannot extend to inferior officers of the United States." That extension, he continued, would be "a departure from the usual and well-known practice both in England and America"; [182] and in truth both the English and the Framers were almost entirely concerned

179. Impeachment of Duke of Buckingham, 2 Howell 1307, 1310, Art. IV (1626).
180. Impeachment of Peter Pett, 6 Howell 865, 867, Art. V (1668). Judge Thomas Cooley adverts to impeachment for "inexcusable neglects of duty, which are dangerous and criminal because of the immense interests involved and the greatness of the trust which has not been kept." 1 Thomas Cooley, *The General Principles of Constitutional Law in the United States of America* 205 (Boston, 4th ed. 1931).
181. For the almost exclusive concern with the President, see supra, n. 112; for "favorites" or officers sheltered by the President, see supra, text accompanying nn. 85–87. Gouverneur Morris stated in the Convention that "certain great officers of State; a minister of finance, of war, of foreign affairs, etc. . . . will be amenable by impeachment to the public justice." 2 Farrand 53–54. And George Mason said that the President as well as his coadjutors should be punished "when great crimes are committed." Ibid. 65. In the Massachusetts Convention, Fisher Ames stated that impeachment was "to bring great offenders to justice"; 2 Elliot 11; a statement echoed by James Iredell, who added, "the occasion for its exercise will arise from acts of great injury to the community." 4 Elliot 113. Governor Samuel Johnston said that impeachment was meant to reach "men who were in very high offices." 4 Elliot 37.
Historically, said Lewis Mayers, 7 *Ency. of the Social Sciences* 600 (New York 1937), impeachment "has been reserved almost exclusively for high officers of state." Cf. 1 Holdsworth 380–382 (3d ed. 1932); 2 Wooddeson 601: "abuse of high offices of trust."
182. 4 Elliot 43–44 Maclaine: "no petty officer was ever impeachable." Ibid. 46; see ibid. 37. Impeachment was devised to reach "the highest and most powerful offenders." 4 Hatsell 63.

with "great offenders," high ministers and the President, and "great offenses." Is it conceivable that the President would be impeachable for "nonattendance"? The records of the Convention furnish a conclusive answer. When the Convention took up "the trial of impeachments against the President, for Treason and bribery," Mason pointed out that this was too narrow, that it could not reach "attempts to subvert the Constitution," "great and dangerous offenses." Such was the origin of "high crimes and misdemeanors." [183]

There is yet another and weighty argument against the Otis-Ford extension of impeachment to departures from "good behavior." [184] In adopting "high crimes and misdemeanors," the Framers departed from the provisions of the seven state constitutions that provided for impeachment, five of which made "maladministration" a ground for impeachment, while New York proceeded for "malconduct" and North Carolina for "misbehavior." [185] Plainly, the wedding of "maladministration" and "misbehavior" to impeachment in the state constitutions held no charm for the Framers. In fact "maladministration" was rejected because, said Madison, "so vague a term will be equivalent to a tenure during pleasure of the Senate." In its stead "high crimes and misdemeanors," borrowed from English, not state impeachment provisions, was substituted by the Framers [186] with knowledge that these were words of "limited" and "technical meaning." [187] Against this

---

183. 2 Farrand 550. See infra, text accompanying nn. 187–189. The Founders' concern with "great offenses," largely in the context of the President, is set forth in detail, supra, Chapter II, text accompanying nn. 163–171.

184. Otis, supra, text accompanying n. 171; Ford, supra, text accompanying n. 169.

185. Maladministration: Delaware (1776) Art. 23, 1 Poore 276–277; North Carolina (1776) Art. 23, 2 Poore 1413; Pennsylvania (1776) Sec. 22, 2 Poore 1545; Vermont (1777) Art. 33, 2 Poore 1863; New Jersey (1776) Art. 12, 2 Poore 1312.

New York (1777) Art. 33, 2 Poore 1337; New Jersey (1776) Art. 12, 2 Poore 1312. The New York provisions, prototype of the Article II separation of removal from subsequent indictment and criminal punishment, provided for impeachment for malconduct but "indictment for crimes and misdemeanors," Art. 34, 2 Poore 1337. Like the other states, New York did not employ "high crimes and misdemeanors."

186. 2 Farrand 550.

187. Earlier the Convention, in another context, had rejected "high misdemeanors" because it "had a technical meaning too limited," ibid. 443. Hence we may conclude that the Framers adopted the phrase for purposes of impeachment precisely because it had that technical, limited meaning. It is this meaning which is to be given to the constitutional phrase. Con-

background, how can we attribute to the Framers an intention to include in "high crimes and misdemeanors" impeachment for "misbehavior," a standard even more uncertain and indefinite than the discarded "maladministration"? [188] To open up "high crimes and misdemeanors" for "misbehavior" would thwart the manifest purpose of the Framers to limit the scope of impeachments and to exclude "maladministration" and by the same token "misbehavior," which did not amount to "high crimes and misdemeanors." [189]

There is, however, no evidence that the Framers tended to immunize judges whose misbehavior did not ascend to "high crimes and misdemeanors." Nor is there any evidence that they employed "good behavior" in other than its accepted sense—a tenure terminated by misbehavior. Unless, therefore, we are to conclude that the Framers intended that judges whose tenure had been terminated by misbehavior were nevertheless to continue in office, there must be, as at common law, a means of effectuating the termination. And since impeachment cannot serve as the means, the argument for its exclusivity fails. Finally, "good behavior" was

---

sequently I cannot concur in Kurland's statement that "the content of [good behavior]" is "either (1) to be derived from the definition of high crimes and misdemeanors, or (2) to be left to the decision of the Senate when sitting as a court of impeachment." Kurland, supra, n. 63 at 697. The contents of "good behavior" had no association at common law with "high crimes and misdemeanors." Supra, text accompanying nn. 12–14; cf. text accompanying nn. 172–175. Nor may the Senate exceed the "limits" contemplated by the Framers, supra, Chapter II, text accompanying nn. 157–162.

188. Nathan Dane concluded that "good behavior" and its "opposite ... 'misbehavior,'" were "equally uncertain and indefinite." 7 Nathan Dane, *Digest of American Law* 366 (Boston, 1824).

189. A word about the "dilemma" with which Judge Otis sought to saddle proponents of the view that "good behavior" was enforceable by traditional means without regard to the provision for impeachment: "The proponents of the 'hiatus' theory are confronted with this dilemma: Either they must limit the jurisdiction of the court contemplated by THE SCHEME to those cases of alleged misbehavior *for which, they say, impeachment will not lie,* or they must say that the provision of the Constitution that 'The House of Representatives . . . shall have the sole power of impeachment' and its companion 'The Senate shall have the sole power to try all impeachments' are sufficiently complied with if exactly the same powers are vested elsewhere and called by different names." Otis 33. His reference to "exactly the same powers" is in error because a forfeiture of office for misbehavior does not *disqualify* the officer ever to hold another federal office, as does impeachment. Nor is removal for "misbehavior" a "different name" for "exactly the same powers" expressed in the impeachment provisions. Impeachment is confined to "high crimes and misdemeanors" and Parliament never confused it with forfeitures for misbehavior. Otis overlooked what was perceived in the First Congress, that impeachment is a form of "supplemental security" in the event that the "executive" branch, and by the same token the "judicial" branch, neglects to remove an unfit officer. Supra, text accompanying nn. 85–87.

employed to guard against legislative and executive tampering with the judiciary, not to insulate judges from removal when they misbehaved. Judicial independence, in short, rises no higher than the "good behavior" tenure in which it is expressed. And the separation of powers only guarantees, it does not alter, the tenure secured by "good behavior"; much less does it exclude the *judiciary* from removing a judge who has misbehaved.

TWO RECENT ARGUMENTS

Professor Philip Kurland

Those who would improve the removal process, Professor Philip Kurland suggests, are overlooking the "essential problem"—the "process that has made federal judicial appointments prime patronage plums to be awarded by Senators in acknowledgement of party or personal loyalty." The cure, he states, is to entrust judicial functions "only to those who are equal to their demands." [190] This is the counsel of perfection, as he himself recognizes: "The basic difficulty is to secure recognition of the necessity for merit appointments. How this sense of responsibility is to be secured is a question that has not yet been answered. Nor is it realistic to expect such improvement" at this time.[191] No such unanswerable problems are posed by the case

---

190. Kurland, supra; n. 63 at 666. Compare with this Madison's statement in the First Congress: "The danger to liberty, the danger of maladministration has not yet been found to lie so much in the facility of introducing improper persons into office, as in the difficulty of displacing those who are unworthy of public trust." 1 *Ann. Cong.* 496. Then too, the possibility that the venality, ignorance or incompetence of appointees might come to light in removal proceedings might stir the President to exercise greater care in making appointments.

191. Kurland, supra, n. 63 at 667. There is at least a doubt whether any appointment process would screen out the corrupt judge. Borkin 11, concludes, "Nor is there a discernible type of corrupt judge. A study of thirty-two of the Federal judges against whom there was a considerable body of adverse evidence and who were the subjects of Congressional investigation, impeachment proceedings, or criminal action indicates that they were recruited from the most diverse environments . . . Many were honor graduates and became trustees of universities; one was an authority on Oriental languages; another was the brother of one of America's most distinguished historians; one entered politics as a reform candidate; and another was the daily associate of gangsters and 'ward' politicians."

for removal by judges on grounds of judicial "misbehavior"; and rejection of the exclusivist interpretation is therefore preferable to reliance upon a Utopian appointment process.

Another Kurland objection is that there is an "absence of a weighty demonstration of the need for legislation providing for removal of federal judges by means other than impeachment—a case that has not been made and, I think, cannot be made." [192] If this be so, the protracted controversy about the exclusivity of impeachment has indeed been much ado about nothing. True, in the 182 years since adoption of the Constitution only nine judges have been impeached and only four convicted and removed. That, however, does not tell the whole story. Of the fifty-five judges who were investigated by the House, "eight [and one Justice] were impeached, eight were censured but not impeached, seventeen others resigned at one stage or another in the conduct of the investigation, while the rest were absolved of *impeachable* misconduct. Added to this are the undetermined number of judges who resigned upon the mere threat of inquiry; for them there are no adequate records." [193] This after sifting "the hundreds of complaints that have been registered" over the years.[194] That the adequacy of the sifting leaves something to be desired is revealed by the House's own records. To cite only a few instances involving district judges for whom a committee of the House recommended impeachment, but where the House took no action on the charges: Aleck Borman, using court money; Philip K. Lawrence, corrupt, malicious, and dangerous abuses, intemperate use of ardent spirits; [195] Augustus Ricks, appropriating moneys of the United States to his own use; the committee recommended censure but the House took no action.[196] Grover M. Moscowitz was charged with favoritism

---

192. Kurland, supra, n. 63 at 697.
193. Borkin 204 (emphasis added). For list of convictions, acquittals, investigations, see ibid. 219–258. See also 80 *Cong. Rec.* 5934 (1936); 81 *Cong. Rec.* 6175, 6178 (1937).
194. 81 *Cong. Rec.* 6178 (1937) (statement by Congressman Sam Hobbs).
195. Borkin 224, 237.
196. Ibid. 243.

toward former law partners in awarding receiverships
and allowing excessive fees; the committee "frowned"
upon his actions but made no recommendation.[197]

Assuming that the House is persuaded of the necessity to proceed, it may yet draw back from taking the
time of the entire Senate to try a "crooked judge"; in
the words of the veteran Hatton Sumners, chairman
of the House Judiciary Committee and participant in
two of the nine impeachments,[198] to do so would take
"the time of the entire Senate . . . away from all of
the other business of a great nation, and make them
sit there for days and days . . . [We] know they will
not try district judges, and we can hardly ask them to
do so." [199] On the other side of the Capitol Senator
McAdoo stated after the conviction of Judge Halsted
Ritter, "the nature of the process is such that, as evidenced in the recent proceedings, it seriously interrupts
for long periods the necessary transaction of important
legislative business, places an almost intolerable burden
of hearing and weighing testimony upon Senators already charged heavily with other responsibilities, and
for this reason alone is always resorted to with extreme
reluctance, even in cases of flagrant misconduct." As a
result, he said, "the practical certainty that in a large
majority of cases misconduct will never be visited with
impeachment is a standing invitation for judges to

197. Ibid. 239. The pervasiveness of such practices led Senator William
McAdoo, who had served as Chairman of a Senate Subcommittee to investigate receivership and bankruptcy proceedings and thus learned of
judicial misbehavior at first hand, to sponsor a bill for judicial trial of
judicial misbehavior. McAdoo became convinced that "District Courts . . .
in the management of insolvent properties and corporations, have been in
instance after instance, revealed as too frequently taking action, the effect
of which has been to deprive creditors and investors of a proportionate
share of the assets to which they are entitled, for the benefit of lawyers
and receivers and other court officials. Favoritism and influence have too
frequently ruled the selection of receivers and trustees appointed by the
courts, and the integrity and ability of these officers of the courts have too
frequently been disregarded for other considerations." 80 *Cong. Rec.* 5933
(1936).
198. Borkin 197. Sumners was also associated with investigations of other
judges. Ibid.
199. 81 *Cong. Rec.* 6165 (1937). Sumners knew whereof he spoke. He
had participated in the impeachment of Judge Harold Louderback and
said that it was "the greatest farce ever presented. At one time only three
senators were present and for ten days we presented evidence to what was
practically an empty chamber." *Time* March 13, 1936, at 18, quoted in
Note: "Removal of Federal Judges: A Proposed Plan," 31 *Ill. L. Rev.*
631, 634 (1937). Cf. supra, n. 9.

abuse their authority with impunity and without fear of removal." [200]

McAdoo's remarks were beautifully illustrated by the subsequent case of District Judge Albert W. Johnson of Pennsylvania. His noisome practices extended over a twenty-year period of judicial service; complaints about his official conduct started soon after he took the oath of office; and criticism erupted in the press in 1931.[201] Johnson was under almost continuous investigation; a judge of his own Circuit Court of Appeals went to Washington to obtain relief.[202] Hatton Sumners gave point to Congressional reluctance to impeach, saying, "If the people of the district are satisfied with Judge Johnson, I am." [203] At last Johnson resigned under the threat of impeachment; he was then indicted but acquitted.[204]

---

200. 80 *Cong. Rec.* 5934 (1936). Woodrow Wilson said, "judging by our past experiences, impeachment may be said to be little more than an empty menace. The House of Representatives is a tardy Grand Jury, and the Senate an uncertain court." W. Wilson, supra, n. 6 at 276. Borkin's study left him with the inescapable feeling that "Congress is sometimes willing to suffer a misbehaving judge rather than stop the legislative activities of the United States." Borkin 195.
In the North Carolina Convention, Iredell stated that "A man in public office who knows there, is no tribunal to punish him, may be ready to deviate from his duty." 4 Elliot 32. Chief Judge J. Edward Lumbard, speaking of the Tydings Bill to create a Judicial Commission for removal of judges, stated that a judge's knowledge that there is "a commission . . . which has the power to act" will have "a valuable effect." Quoted Peter G. Fish, "The Circuit Councils: Rusty Hinges of Federal Judicial Administration," 37 *U. Chi. L. Rev.* 203, 240 (1970).
201. Borkin 143.
202. Judge John Biggs of the Third Circuit testified that he talked to "Chairman Hatton Sumners of the House Judiciary Committee, and then to Representative Estes Kefauver." Hearings on Judicial Fitness Before the Senate Subcommittee on Improvements in Judicial Machinery, 89th Cong. 2d Sess. 19 (1966) (hereafter cited as Hearings).
203. Borkin 145.
204. Borkin 185, 182. The object of his favors, his co-conspirator son, was convicted, but two of the witnesses who had themselves been convicted refused to repeat the testimony they had given before the Grand Jury, thereby contributing to Johnson's acquittal. Ibid. 185. Another illustration involved the relation between the aged Third Circuit Judge Joseph Buffington and his confrere, Judge Warren Davis. In 1937, Judge Biggs testified, Judge Buffington was 86 years old, blind, had great difficulty hearing and did not employ a law clerk. Hearings, supra, n. 202 at 15. Judge Davis was then Senior Judge and "was writing and selling the opinions Judge Buffington was signing." Borkin 101; Root Refining Co. v. Universal Oil Products Co., 169 F. 2d 514, 533 (3d Cir. 1948). The situation led the other circuit judges, testified Judge Biggs, to insist that Buffington and Davis should not sit together. Hearings, supra, n. 202 at 21. Twice Judge Biggs called the matter to the attention of the assistant to the Attorney General. Subsequently "a letter was written by Judge William Clark at the suggestion of Judge Maris and myself [Biggs] to Mr. Edgar Hoover, and I think that brought the FBI into the situation." Ibid.
Thereafter Attorney General Francis Biddle asked Congress to impeach Judge Davis, but Davis balked the impeachment by resigning and waiving his pension rights. Borkin 120. Tactfully Judge Biggs testified that "we persuaded these elderly gentlemen to retire," but "to put it quite frankly,

Here is a case that is documented; how many were not? How many cases of censurable conduct which rendered a judge unfit for office were screened out because of doubts whether they amounted to "high crimes and misdemeanors"? The testimony of an experienced Congressman, Hatton Sumners—who learned at first hand of the "burden" which impeachment places upon Congress, who sought only to disencumber Congress of that burden to free it for weightier and more pressing tasks, and who did not seek to encroach on the judiciary but to ask it to undertake its own housecleaning—should weigh heavily for the practical need, to borrow Senator McAdoo's phrase, of a "more certain, prompt, and effective method for dealing with" judicial abuses.[205]

Professor Preble Stolz

Conceding that impeachment has a "deservedly bad reputation," Professor Preble Stolz challenges the assumption that it is an "unworkable process" and suggests that it "be modernized to meet current needs" rather than resort to an alternative method of removal that "runs a substantial risk of being held unconstitutional." [206] He would restructure impeachment by "(1) creation of a bipartisan House Committee on Judicial Fitness [for investigation and recommendations to the House]; (2) creation of a permanent professional staff as an adjunct to the Committee; (3) use of a master

it takes a good deal of effort and quite a long time." Hearings, supra, at 15–16. Judge Biggs said that there "is not the slightest doubt" that "the present machinery for the removal of unfit judges is inadequate." Ibid. 16.

    For an unsuccessful attempt to prevail upon a Sixth Circuit district judge to retire, see Hearings upon the Independence of Federal Judges, before the Senate Subcommittee on Separation of Powers (91st Cong. 2d Sess., April–May 1970) p. 299. See also the testimony of Chief Judge Bailey Aldrich of the First Circuit, ibid. 356; and the comments on the acquittal of Judge Harold Louderback in an impeachment upon the complaint of the San Francisco Bar Association, though a majority of the Senate voted him guilty. Note, "Removal of Federal Judges: A Proposed Plan," 31 Ill. L. Rev. 631, 634 (1937).

    205. 80 Cong. Rec. 5934 (1936). In 1878, Justice Miller said, it "must be confessed that the means provided by the system of organic law for removing a judge, who for any reason is found to be unfit for his office, is very unsatisfactory . . . [and] after the experience of nearly a century . . . must be pronounced inadequate." 2 N.Y. State Bar Ass'n Rep. 40 (1878), quoted in Note, "Removal of Federal Judges—New Alternatives to an Old Problem: Chandler v. Judicial Council of the Tenth Circuit," 13 UCLA L. Rev. 1385 (1966).

    206. Stolz, supra, n. 164 at 660, 664.

or masters to conduct formal evidentiary hearings for
the Senate and to prepare proposed findings of fact
and conclusions of law which would be the basis of
argument and decision in the Senate." This, he believes,
"would be created without raising any new constitutional problems."[207]

To the contrary, he would substitute a serious constitutional doubt for what appears to be no real constitutional problem. Delegation of investigatory functions
by the House to a committee, whose report to the
House could be rejected or adopted, has historical
precedent. The House of Commons often referred
charges to a committee for investigation, then debated
the committee report and voted for or against lodging
articles of impeachment.[208] But delegation of the hearing function by the Senate is something else again.

As Hamilton remarked, the role of the Commons
as prosecutor while the Lords sat in judgment was the
"model" of the parallel distribution of functions between the House of Representatives and the Senate.[209]
Although the Lords referred sundry matters to committees, the function of hearing and trial was never delegated, and with good reason. The notable impeachments were chiefly treason trials involving peers, and
the trial of a great nobleman "for blood" could
scarcely be shunted to a committee, let alone to a
"Master." Conviction would be followed by death,
fine, or imprisonment, and although the governing
law was the "course of parliament" rather than ordinary criminal law, English impeachment was therefore
clearly criminal in nature.[210] Said Blackstone: "The
articles of impeachment are a kind of bills of indictment, found by the house of commons, and afterwards
tried by the lords."[211] Such trial was a substitute for
trial by jury in which reference to a Master—an instru-

---

207. Ibid. 667. The suggestion that the Senate should entrust the hearing
of evidence to a committee which would act as a master had been mooted
by several members of the House after the Halsted Ritter impeachment
proceedings. 81 *Cong. Rec.* 6163, 6172, 6178 (1937).
208. See 4 Hatsell 99, 110, 111, 113, 118, 121, 122, 128, 132.
209. *Federalist* No. 65 at 425.
210. *Supra*, Chapter II, text accompanying nn. 21, 25, 26, 32 and text
before n. 62.
211. 4 Blackstone 260.

ment of Chancery, not an adjunct of a criminal trial—found no place.

In the case of capital offenses and treason trials there is unmistakable evidence that trial was to be by the full House of Lords. A resolution by the Lords in 1689 recites "that it is the ancient right of the Peers of England to be tried, only in full Parliament, for any capital offenses." [212] In 1695 the Trial of Treasons Act provided "that upon the trial of any Peer or Peeress [for treason] . . . all the Peers who have a right to sit and vote in parliament shall be duly summoned . . . and that every Peer, so summoned and appearing at such trial, shall vote in the trial of such Peer or Peeress so to be tried." [213] Although impeachments for "high crimes and misdemeanors" did not involve "capital offenses" they were nonetheless criminal proceedings; and there is evidence that these too were to be heard by all the Lords. On June 23, 1701, the Lords resolved that "the Lords who absented themselves from the trial of Lord Oxford [impeached for high crimes and misdemeanors], and shall not make a just excuse for the same, are guilty of a great and wilful neglect of their duty." [214] So too, the impeachment of Lord Chancellor Macclesfield for "high crimes and misdemeanors" in 1725 was before "the Lords being seated in their House." [215] No trace of a reference to a committee of the Lords for hearing of the evidence turned up in my search of impeachment proceedings. The reason appears in a statement made by the Managers of the Lords at a conference between members of the Lords and the Commons (reported January 18, 1691) that "In the case of impeachments, which are the groans of the people . . . and carry with them a great supposition of guilt than any other accusation, there all the Lords must judge." [216]

---

212. Quoted in 4 Hatsell 277–278.
213. Trial of Treasons Act, 7 Will. 3, c. 3, § 11.
214. Quoted in 4 Hatsell 279, 420.
215. 16 Howell 767.
216. 4 Hatsell 343, 333, 342. Lord Grenville stated in the House of Lords: "When you are called upon to arraign an individual, and that individual a judge, everyone must be anxious that the attendance should be as full as possible." 7 *Parl. Deb.* 762 (1806). And see Plucknett, *Concise History* 232; cf. 1 Holdsworth 389 (7th ed. 1956).

If the American impeachment process is also criminal, the English practice furnishes the standard, for almost the entire process was lifted bodily from English practice.[217] Although the American process is not criminal,[218] English procedure nonetheless furnishes the model, as is confirmed by the *Manual of Parliamentary Practice* prepared for the Senate by Vice President Jefferson. Citing and in part quoting Wooddeson, Jefferson stated: "This trial . . . differs not in essentials from criminal prosecutions before inferior courts. The same rules of evidence, the same legal notions of crimes and punishments prevailed . . . The judgment, therefore, is to be such as is warranted by legal principles or precedents." [219] Jefferson mistakenly conceived the American impeachment to be criminal in nature, but nonetheless it was a proceeding of so high and serious a nature as to call for adoption of the earlier procedure.

Impeachment, said Hamilton, was "designed as a method of NATIONAL INQUEST into the conduct of public men"; and it could result in a sentence of doom "to a perpetual ostracism from the esteem and confidence, and honors and emoluments of his country." The trial was confided to the Senate rather than the Supreme Court because "the awful discreton which a court of impeachment must necessarily have, to doom to honor or to infamy the most confidential and the most distinguished characters of the community, forbids the commitment of the trust to a small number of persons." [220] Impeachment, it cannot be unduly emphasized, was chiefly designed for the President and his high ministers, as a "bridle" on the Executive; [221] the Framers would have been aghast had it been pro-

---

217. The formula "treason, bribery and other high crimes and misdemeanors" was, but for the word "bribery," borrowed from English law. Hamilton refers to the English "model from which the idea of this institution has been borrowed." *Federalist* No. 65 at 425; and he stated that the "experience of Great Britain affords an illustrious comment on the excellence" of "good behavior" tenure. Ibid. No. 78 at 511. The division of prosecuting and adjudicating functions between House and Senate was patently modelled on the division of functions between Commons and Lords. Ibid. No. 65 at 425.
218. Supra, Chapter II, text accompanying nn. 128–142.
219. 2 Wooddeson 611; Jefferson's *Manual* 153.
220. *Federalist* No. 65 at 426.
221. Ibid. 425.

posed that the trial, hearing, and sifting of the evidence on the impeachment of the President or of the Secretary of Foreign Affairs should be remitted to a Master, and that it would suffice for the Senate to vote on his findings and conclusions. There is no historical warrant for breaking the procedural safeguards into two modes, one for the President and another for inferior federal judges.

With the seven-year-long impeachment of Warren Hastings fresh in their memory,[222] the Senate, in the 1797 impeachment of Senator Blount,[223] embraced the Lords' practice of sitting as a body—a practice from which, despite the onerous burdens it imposes, it has never departed, and which constitutes a constitutional interpretation entirely in harmony with the constitutional design. And if an analogous proposal to lighten the burdens of the Supreme Court may furnish a guide, a shift of the Senate's hearing function to a Master is of doubtful constitutionality. At the time of the Court-Packing Plan, Chief Justice Hughes, writing on behalf of Justice Van Devanter, Brandeis, and himself, and expressing confidence that his statement was "in accord with the view" of the other Justices, advised the Senate: "I understand that it has been suggested that with more Justices the Court could hear cases in divisions . . . I may also call attention to the provisions of article III, section 1, of the Constitution that the judicial power of the United States shall be vested 'in one Supreme Court' . . . The Constitution does not appear to authorize two or more Supreme Courts, or two or more parts of a supreme court functioning in effect as separate courts." [224] It is food for thought that Hughes did not suggest that the Court could meet its problems by a wholesale delegation of its hearing function to Masters.[225] Although the Stolz proposal has

222. George Mason referred to the Hastings Trial in the Federal Convention, 2 Farrand 550. John Vining referred to it in the First Congress, 1 *Ann. Cong.* 373. The impeachment was instituted in May 1787. 4 Hatsell 242n. It took nearly seven years to try. Potts, supra, n. 153 at 33.
223. Wharton 200, 257. See supra, n. 58.
224. Quoted in S. Rep. No. 711, 75th Cong. 1st Sess. 40 (1937).
225. In the general practice, references to Masters have not been favored. Justice Fields said that a court "cannot, of its own motion, or upon the request of one party, abdicate its duty to determine by its own judgment

some superficially attractive aspects, it therefore raises
disturbing constitutional issues in its turn.

SOME DOCTRINAL CONSIDERATIONS

Messrs. Kramer and Barron ask whether "the article
III provision that judges are to serve 'during good behavior' . . . is . . . a means of prohibiting Congress
and the Executive from tampering in any way with life
tenure." [226] Historically, "good behavior" tenure was
designed to put English judges beyond the royal pleasure.[227] By rejecting removal by the President on the
Address of both Houses,[228] while granting power to
House and Senate to remove by impeachment, the
Framers excluded all other means of *executive* or *legislative* interference with the "good behavior" tenure of
judges.[229] That tenure is protected by the separation of
powers, to which impeachment is an exception.[230] And
it follows, to answer another Kramer-Barron question,
that Congress cannot "remove for service which is not
good behavior," [231] for its power is confined to impeachment for "treason, bribery and other high crimes
and misdemeanors." But it does not follow that Congress may not employ its powers under the "necessary
and proper" clause to supplement the *judicial* powers
for the purpose of effectuating a manifest constitutional
end.[232] Removal by judges, even if facilitated by enabling legislation which confers subject matter jurisdiction or fashions a new remedy, is not the same thing
as removal by Congress. And it bears repetition that a
congressional enlargement of judicial subject matter
jurisdiction does not constitute a grant of *power*, for

the controversy presented, and devolve that duty upon any of its officers."
Kimberly v. Arms, 129 U.S. 512, 524 (1889). Under the more liberal
present practice, which empowers courts to appoint masters to assist the
jury in those exceptional cases where the issues are too complicated for
the jury adequately to handle alone, the Supreme Court said that "it will
indeed be a rare case in which" the burden of such a showing "can be
met." Dairy Queen v. Wood, 369 U.S. 469, 478 (1962).
226. Kramer & Barron, supra, n. 14 at 455.
227. Supra, text accompanying nn. 131–134.
228. Supra, text accompanying nn. 136–140.
229. See supra, nn. 127, 146, 149, and text accompanying n. 148.
230. Supra, text accompanying n. 88.
231. Kramer & Barron, supra, n. 14 at 457.
232. Supra, text accompanying nn. 43–59.

"judicial power" flows from Article III and it embraces resolution of forfeiture disputes.

At common law the grantor (with respect to public office, the King) could bring an action to oust an unfit officer.[233] Federal judges are appointed by the President, but it would raise separation of powers problems were he, or the Attorney General on behalf of the executive branch, to initiate a removal action.[234] Such problems are avoided by the Tydings Bill, S. 1506,[235] which would establish a commission of judges to investigate complaints of unfitness; if the commission finds cause to believe that the accused judge's conduct was inconsistent with "good behavior" it is to conduct a hearing. But this procedure is open to the objection that has been leveled at the joinder of investigatory and adjudicatory functions in one administrative agency, where investigation has been found to conduce to prejudgment of the case.[236]

The function of investigation ought to be completely divorced from the function of hearing and judging; it ought to be removed from such a commission and lodged in a branch of the Administrative Office of the courts or some special branch of the Judiciary Department. And instead of an adjudicatory commission I would suggest a special court, resembling the Emergency Court of Appeals which heard Office of Price

---

233. "This may be brought either on the part of the king to resume the thing granted," or by some aggrieved subject. 3 Blackstone 261. See also 4 Comyns, supra, n. 26 at 259. J. P. Kenyon, *The Stuart Constitution 1623–1688*, at 90 (Cambridge, 1966) is therefore mistaken in saying that "The holder [of a patent during good behavior] could sue out a writ of *scire facias* demanding that the king show cause."

234. The Hatton Sumners Bill. H. R. 146, 75th Cong. 1st Sess. (1941) provided a variant: upon a resolution of the House, the Chief Justice was to convene a special court of appeals before whom the Attorney General would institute a civil action against the accused judge. For analysis of the bill, see Moore, supra, n. 9 at 352–354.

235. 91st Cong. 1st Sess. (March 12, 1969). During a Judicial Conference in 1969, Chief Justice Warren E. Burger, then circuit judge, stated that the Tydings Bill constituted no threat to judicial independence nor invasion of the separation of powers. Judicial Conference of the United States, Proceedings 42–43, quoted by John H. Holloman, "The Judicial Reform Act: History, Analysis and Comment," 35 *Law & Cont. Prob.* 128, 138 (1970). So too, while testifying before the Senate Judiciary Committee on his nomination to the Supreme Court, Associate Justice Harry Blackmun saw "no great danger of interfering with the independence of the judiciary" in the Tydings Bill. Ibid. 142.

236. See Raoul Berger, "Removal of Judicial Functions from Federal Trade Commission to a Trade Court: A Reply to Mr. Kintner," 59 *Mich. L. Rev.* 199, 206–211 (1960). And see remarks of Commissioner Philip Elman of the FTC. *Wall Street Journal*, August 12, 1970, at 12, col. 4.

Administration cases during World War II. It might include a mixture of circuit and district judges with perhaps one Supreme Court Justice in order to secure a cross section of judicial opinion. If a member of that court happened to be a fellow judge of the accused judge, he would withdraw, to be replaced by a judge appointed in such manner as Congress should designate. Thus personal bias for or against the accused would as far as possible be eliminated. The sole function of the special court would be to hear and determine the charges of misbehavior filed by the investigatory-accusatory branch of the Judiciary Department; and upon a finding of "misbehavior" a judgment would issue removing the offending judge, a forfeiture of the office.

In his advocacy of judicial removal of judges, Shartel stopped short of removal of Supreme Court Justices on the ground that "there is no agency in the judiciary branch to remove the Justices of the Supreme Court," though he ventured that "perhaps Congress could confer statutory authority on the Supreme Court as a whole to remove its own offending members." [237] If a forfeiture action is judicial in nature, as seems plain, this would be to add to the original jurisdiction of the Court, which lies beyond the power of Congress.[238] Once it is granted that tenure "during good behavior" premises termination by bad behavior, an implied power exists to make the termination effective. Congress may confer jurisdiction of the "subject matter" on a special court, which would have "judicial power" by virtue of the existence of a dispute, and which would be established within the judiciary branch. The special court, composed of circuit and district judges, with the possible inclusion of a Supreme Court Justice, would be removed from feelings of delicacy towards a fellow Justice, of "club spirit" or of possible animosity engendered by accumulated differences and irritations. It would be unbecoming for a Justice to complain of trial before such a court when his fellow citizens are

---

237. Shartel 897 n. 73.
238. Marbury v. Madison, 1 Cranch (5 U.S.) 137, 174–176 (1803).

daily being tried for life or deprivation of property before a solitary district judge. In any event, this is a question of mechanics for Congress, not of power.

There remains the question asked by Kramer and Barron, whether the "good behavior" provision constitutes "a grant of power to Congress to prescribe the behavior which is less than good." [239] That provision, as noted earlier, does not constitute "a grant of power"; it merely describes the duration of judicial tenure.[240] Such power as Congress has in the premises derives from the "necessary and proper" clause, and from its power over the jurisdiction of the lower federal courts; those powers cannot be exercised in derogation of the common law meaning of "good behavior." The Framers employed common law terms because they had recognizable content,[241] because they posited "limits," as we have seen in the case of "high crimes and misdemeanors." [242] Who would maintain, for example, that the impeachment for "bribery" provision authorizes Congress to define bribery to include robbery, departing sharply from its common law meaning —receipt of payment to influence judicial conduct in a pending proceeding? [243] Similarly, Congress may not give to "good behavior" a meaning utterly opposed to its common law content, for that would set the constitutional protection afforded by "good behavior" tenure at naught. It can, however, codify and illuminate that meaning so long as it remains faithful to the nature of "good behavior" at common law. Such codification, indeed, could serve a number of useful purposes: it would advise every judge on what constitutes removable cause; it would guide the special court in ascertaining whether an accused judge had violated "good behavior." As applied to judges, the definitions of good behavior by Bacon and Hawkins may be overbroad; [244]

---

239. Kramer & Barron, supra, n. 14 at 455.
240. Supra, n. 59.
241. Supra, Chapter II, n. 160; and see supra, n. 43. For further analysis of "good behavior" see infra, Chapter VI.
242. Supra, text accompanying nn. 187–188.
243. The essence of "bribery" is payment "to influence his behavior in office." 1 Sir William Russell, *Crimes and Misdemeanors* 239 (London, 1819); and see 4 Comyns, supra, n. 26 at 253.
244. See supra, text accompanying n. 175, and n. 174.

because judicial removal of judges has been so controversial it may be useful to tighten and clarify the definition. If my analysis is valid, insanity, disability including senility, alcoholism, ignorance,[245] and sustained neglect of duty might be included in such a definition. The fact that the definition will be applied by judges should be regarded as additional protection for, rather than as a threat to, an accused judge; and it is to be hoped that borderline cases would be resolved in favor of the judge. As with all legislation, experience in the course of time may persuade Congress to amplify or qualify its enabling legislation.

SUMMARY

Judicial tenure "during good behavior" was terminated at common law by bad behavior and, since impeachable offenses, that is, "high crimes and misdemeanors," are not identical with all breaches of "good behavior" but merely overlap in the case of serious misconduct, there exists an implied power to remove judges whose "misbehavior" falls short of "high crimes and misdemeanors."[246] Traditionally, forfeiture upon breach of a condition subsequent was a judicial function, and a forfeiture of judicial office therefore falls within the Article III "judicial power." Congress may add the forfeiture of a judicial office for misbehavior to the forfeiture jurisdiction or, if necessary, it may under the "necessary and proper" clause provide a new remedy for forfeiture of judicial office, in order to effectuate the implied power to remove a judge whose tenure was terminated by his misbehavior.

The argument that the impeachment provisions bar the way would sacrifice a necessary power to a canon of construction. With Chief Justice Marshall, I should want nothing less than an express prohibition to pre-

---

245. See infra, Chapter V.
246. That power extends to serious offenses which also constitute "misbehavior" notwithstanding they are comprehended by "high crimes and misdemeanors," for, as we have seen, impeachment was conceived as a "supplemental security." Supra, text accompanying n. 85.

clude beneficial exercise of an implied means.[247] Those
who would deny to Congress the right to select the
means for the termination implicit in the constitutional
text—"during good behavior"—have the burden of
establishing the preclusion. The several "exclusivist"
arguments do not sustain the burden. Having rejected
the argument that an express provision for jury trial
in criminal cases barred such trial in civil cases, the
Framers would hardly have maintained that an express
provision for impeachment excluded all other means
of removal, particularly when that would make it impossible to reach a judge who had breached "good
behavior" but could not be impeached for a "high
crime and misdemeanor." The argument of "absolute
independence" seeks to override the plain implications
of the "good behavior" provision by a concept that
found no expression either in the Constitution or in
the several Conventions.

Rarely is it given to a man to brush the accumulated dust of generations from the Constitution and to
perceive afresh its rational design.[248] Such a man was
Burke Shartel, who first saw the claim for exclusivity
of impeachment in all its nakedness and furnished an
analytical structure for judicial removal of judges that
in bold outline still stands up. His analysis is not
scornfully to be dismissed, in the manner of Congressman Celler when it was made the basis of legislation
offered in the House: "It scarcely can be believed that
the framers intended vesting Congress with an important power [to pass enabling legislation] and then so
skillfully concealed it it could not be discovered save
after 150 years." [249] The difference between "good

247. McCulloch v. Maryland, 4 Wheat. (17 U.S.) 316, 409 (1819): the
Constitution does not "prohibit the creation of a corporation, if the existence of such a being be essential to the beneficial exercise of those powers."
To make impeachment the exclusive means of removal, said Elias Boudinot
in the First Congress, "would be derogatory to the powers of Government,
and subversive of the rights of the people." 1 Ann. Cong. 468.
248. In an article, "Back to the Constitution," Justice Robert H. Jackson, then Solicitor General, compared the recent emergence of the constitutional text from beneath a laissez faire gloss to the rediscovery of an
Old Master after the retouching brushwork of succeeding generations had
been removed. 25 A. B. A. J. 745 (1939).
249. 81 Cong. Rec. 6171 (1937). Apparently Kurland shares this view,
for he quotes Celler. Kurland, supra, n. 63 at 691. Judge Otis 44, labelled
Shartel "the Galileo who discovered THE SCHEME . . . which theretofore,
like the moons of Jupiter, had been unseen and unsuspected by the most

behavior" and "high crimes and misdemeanors" was
"skillfully concealed" only from those who did not
pause to turn the pages of history, and to ask: what
becomes of "good behavior" if impeachment is restricted to "high crimes and misdemeanors." On Celler's reasoning the Copernican view of the universe
must be discarded because for several millennia astron-
omers were lost in the Ptolemaic spheres within
spheres; and Columbus should never have set forth
in the Santa Maria because, as men believed for centuries, it would fall off the edge of the world. Even
in our tradition-bound law, when it was pressed upon
Chief Justice Holt that the novelty of the claim argued
against it, he replied: "that is an argument when it is
founded upon reason, but it is none, when it is against
reason." [250] It is never too late to heed the voice of
reason, and if "reason" negates the exclusivist argument, it must prevail.

It is open to Congress, and I consider it highly
desirable, to enact legislation under its "necessary and
proper" power which would give effect of the implications of "good behavior" and confirm and facilitate
judicial removal of judges for "misbehavior." This is

---

discerning." That is an unfortunate analogy, for failure to see those moons
testified not so much to their non-existence as to a lack of discernment.
For a succession of English "Galileos" who, with judicial acceptance, perceived in long-standing statutes what for generations had been "unsuspected
by the most discerning," see Sir C. K. Allen, *Law in the Making* 318 (London, 1958). There was in fact an American "Galileo," Congressman David
Stone, who discerned in 1802 what escaped Judge Otis in 1938. See
Appendix D.

"THE SCHEME," it may be added, had been embodied in a bill to facilitate
judicial removal of judges, introduced by Hatton Sumners and Senator
William McAdoo. Ibid. 4, 10. Otis describes Sumners as a "distinguished
statesman" "to whose enlightened leadership the American people more
than once has been indebted," ibid. 10. Nevertheless, Sumners was gulled
by "THE SCHEME," which is profusely sprinkled in capital letters throughout
Otis' pages. Ibid. 4, 9, 10, 12, 13, 17, 20, 22, 29, 30, 33, 34, 35, 37, 42, 43, 44.
For Shartel's article, see supra, n. 26. Having traced almost every footstep
of Otis and Shartel, I must dissent from Stolz' coupling of their articles as
"some distinguished though partisan scholarship." Stolz, supra, n. 165 at
660. Otis' article, to my mind, is far removed from "distinguished scholarship," but is rather a hysterical piece of special pleading richly spiced
with circular reasoning and vulnerable at every joint. And it is a misnomer
to label Shartel's study as "partisan scholarship," for it lacks the "character
of blind or unreasonable adherence to a party," and indeed there was no
"party" until Shartel, like Galileo, saw what was hidden from the
undiscerning.

250. Ashby v. White, 2 Ld. Raym. 938, 957, 92 E. R. 123, 138 (1703).
Compare the startling reversal in Erie R. R. v. Tompkins, 304 U.S. 64, 77–78
(1938) of a century-long course of judicial interpretation inaugurated by
Swift v. Tyson, 16 Pet. (41 U.S.) 1 (1842).

an issue that has perennially troubled the Congress [251] and that can be set at rest once and for all by an enactment which can be presented to the Supreme Court. At worst the constitutionality of removability by judges is doubtful, and the last word on constitutional doubts is for the Court. Such judicial resolution is best initiated by legislation. On many aspects of legislation the Congress must indulge in initial constitutional construction, knowing, as the very First Congress recognized,[252] that it is subject to correction by the Court. If there be indeed a constitutional doubt, the part of wisdom is to act on the counsel of Jefferson: "it is not right for those who are only to act in a preliminary form, to let their own doubts preclude the judgment of the court of ultimate decision." [253]

---

251. For citation to various bills, see Ross, supra, n. 14; Note, "The Exclusiveness of the Impeachment Power under the Constitution," 51 *Harv. L. Rev.* 330 (1937); Moore, supra, n. 9; and S. 1506, 91st Cong. 1st Sess. (1969), a bill introduced by Senator Joseph Tydings, the Judicial Reform Act.

252. "Without such a power," said Peter Sylvester, "we could pass no law whatever;" "the Judiciary will be better able to decide the question of Constitutionality in this way than any other. If we are wrong, they can correct our error." 1 *Ann. Cong.* 562. For additional citations, see Berger, *Congress v. Court* 147.

253. Letter to James Monroe, September 7, 1797. Quoted in 3 Malone 336; 7 T. Jefferson, *The Writings of Thomas Jefferson* 173 (New York, P. Ford ed. 1896). Given the fact that the Supreme Court leans to sustaining the constitutionality of a statute, I consider with Moore that "Congress cannot legitimately refuse to enact beneficial legislation because a constitutional objection lurks in the background. Were it so timorous legislation would be at a standstill. Legislation does not have to be constitutional beyond every reasonable doubt before enactment is proper. The final answer to the constitutional issue of this legislation can only be given by the Supreme Court after enactment of the measure." Moore, supra, n. 9 at 356. Kurland, a vigorous proponent of the "exclusivist" view, states respecting disputed points, "it must be conceded that a determination by Congress that legislation on one or both of these latter points is constitutional should weigh heavily in favor of its validity if the issue comes to judicial scrutiny." Kurland, supra, n. 63 at 697.

Chapter V

INSANITY-DISABILITY-SENILITY

A perplexing and oft-discussed problem is whether removal lies for insanity, disability, or senility.[1] If impeachment be the sole method of removal, and "high crimes and misdemeanors" call for criminal offenses, how can an insane person be guilty of a crime? Assuming the noncriminality of the offense, does the serious nature of the impeachment proceeding require some volitional element of which a demented person is presumed incapable? If he is removable for "misbehavior" outside impeachment the question again arises: can such a person "misbehave" in a legal sense? It will be convenient to discuss these and other problems under two heads: impeachment; and removal for "misbehavior."

IMPEACHMENT

Let us begin with the special problem posed by the incapacity of the President, both for its intrinsic importance and for its impact on other facets of removal. When impeachment was under discussion in the Convention, Madison, contrary to the view earlier expressed by Gunning Bedford that "impeachment would reach misfeasance only, not incapacity," [2] thought it "indispensable that some provision should be made for defending the community against the incapacity . . .

---

1. E.g., Hamilton, *Federalist* No. 79; Story §§1625, 1626; Shartel 870, 903, 904; G. W. Ross, " 'Good Behavior' of Federal Judges," 12 *U. Kan. City L. Rev.* 119, 126 (1944).
2. 1 Farrand 69.

of the Chief Magistrate . . . He might lose his capacity after his appointment." Said Madison: "Loss of capacity might be fatal to the Republic." Gouverneur Morris agreed that "incapacity" of the Executive was among the "causes of impeachment." [3] But in treating the presidential succession, a separation was apparently made between a vacancy resulting from impeachment and from inability. Article II, §1(6), provides that "in case of the *removal* of the President from office, *or* of his death, resignation or inability to discharge the powers and duties of the said office, the same shall devolve on the vice president." This separation is clearer in the earlier provision reported by the Committee on Detail: the President "shall be removed from his office on impeachment . . . and conviction . . . of treason, bribery, or corruption. In case of his *removal as aforesaid,* death, resignation, or disability to discharge the powers and duties of his office." [4] The changes made in the final provision and the transplantation of the "disability" provision now in Article II, §1(6), from the impeachment provision now in Article II, §4, seem to me purely stylistic; and so I would conclude that removal of the President by impeachment was not to include his removal for "disability." That differentiation was apparently extended by Article II, §1(6), to the Vice President, by the phrase "Congress may by law provide for the case of removal, death, resignation or inability both of the President and Vice President"—leaving unanswered Dickinson's great question, "what is the extent of the 'disability' and who is to be the judge of it." [5] The paralysis and severe, protracted illness of President Woodrow Wilson adumbrates what could happen if a President went mad or was totally paralyzed during a great national crisis. England provided a regency for the mad George III; but the Framers left that problem for solution by posterity, to be met at last

3. 2 Farrand 65, 69.
4. Ibid. 185–186 (emphasis added).
5. Ibid. 427.

when the Twenty-fifth Amendment was ratified in February 1967.[6]

Do the implications of this disconnection of "removal" from presidential "inability" in Article II, §1(6), radiate beyond the presidency? In terms, it is applicable only to the President, and possibly the Vice President; and arguably when the words "civil officers" were added to the impeachment provisions of Article II, §4, after the separation,[7] those officers were unaffected by the disjunction. Since the First Congress, as we have seen, speedily placed removal of Executive "officers" altogether above the necessity of removal by impeachment,[8] accompanied by ringing affirmations that insane or paralyzed officers could not be continued in office,[9] the question that remains is what relevance the special treatment of presidential succession has for removal of demented or disabled judges.

Self-evidently, the removal of a single judge would not have consequences nearly as momentous for the nation as removal of the President. Well might the Founders and their posterity be awed by the problem how to determine the President's disability. But the concern of the Framers with presidential "inability" does not demand extrapolation of his special treatment to removal of a judge. Indeed, the fact that disability of the President was specially treated militates against extension of implications drawn from that provision to those who do not come within its terms. Then too, Hamilton, who stated in *Federalist* Number 79 that the "article respecting impeachments . . . is the only provision which we find in our Constitution in respect to our own judges," nevertheless stated in the same issue that "insanity without any formal or express provision, may be safely pronounced to be a virtual

6. Section 4 of the 25th Amendment provides that whenever the Vice President and a majority of the cabinet transmit to Congress "their written declaration" that the President is unable to discharge the duties of his office, and it is disputed by the President, the "Congress shall decide the issue" by a two-thirds vote.

7. This was late in the deliberations, on September 8th. 2 Farrand 552.

8. Supra, Chapter IV, text accompanying nn. 77–88.

9. Infra, text accompanying n. 31, and n. 31.

disqualification." [10] And in an early impeachment, that of district judge John Pickering, the Senate removed an insane judge, though the charges were not framed in such terms, probably to avoid problems of "intent." Pickering "had been hopelessly insane for at least three years . . . and had become an incurable drunkard"; [11] and he was impeached and convicted in 1804 for presiding while drunk and handing down opinions clearly contrary to the relevant statute.[12] To convict such a man of "high crimes and misdemeanors" would, in the words of Henry Adams, violate the "deep principle of law and justice that an insane man was not responsible for his acts." Nevertheless, Adams concluded that the impeachers "might reasonably assume that the people had not rendered themselves" powerless to protect themselves and to "require a removal from office for the good of the public service." [13] Hamilton's offhand assumption that insanity afforded ground for removal may be taken to foreshadow this commonsense view; and I would venture that it was doubtless shared by the Framers; and it was buttressed by the centuries-old rule that a document should be construed to avoid an unreasonable or absurd result.[14]

Hamilton's view that insanity "without any formal or express provision" is a disqualification must be understood to mean either that insanity falls within "high crimes and misdemeanors," a solecism if criminality is the core of impeachable conduct, for a mad-

---

10. *Federalist* at 514.
11. Albert J. Beveridge, *The Life of John Marshall* 164–65 (Boston, 1916). Beveridge remarks that the "Judiciary Act of 1801 covered just such cases. It provided that when a National judge was unable to discharge the duties of his office, the circuit judges should name one of their members to fill his place . . . This very thing had [once] been done in the case of Judge Pickering." Ibid. 165n. McMaster, who is cited by Beveridge, invokes § 25 of the Act for the proposition "nor was it impossible to relieve" Pickering, who was clearly "no longer fit to sit on the bench." 3 J. B. McMaster, *History of the People of the United States* 166 (New York, 1892). But the Act of 1801 had been repealed in March 1802. Felix Frankfurter and James Landis, *The Business of the Supreme Court* 24–28 (New York, 1927). Pickering's insanity was placed squarely before the Senate by his son. 13 *Ann. Cong.* 328–329 (1804).
12. 13 *Ann. Cong.* 318–322 (1804). The case is analyzed in Lynn Turner, "The Impeachment of John Pickering," 54 *Am. Hist. Rev.* 485 (1949).
13. 2 Henry Adams, *History of the United States of America* 160, 155–156 (New York, 1962).
14. United States v. Kirby, 7 Wall. (74 U.S.) 482, 487 (1868), notes the old Bolognese "blood-letting" case cited by Pufendorf, and a case in Plowden. See also 1 Blackstone 91.

man is not held criminally responsible for his acts, or that the Constitution does not bar some other means of removal "without . . . any express provision" therefor.[15] If impeachment be indeed exclusive, his statement suggests that he would not have drawn back from employing impeachment for removal of an insane judge; for, as his statement shows, he approached the problem in eminently practical terms. That practical approach is still more commendable if we accept the general view that in this country impeachment is not criminal in nature,[16] but is merely designed to remove an unfit person from office. If the seriousness of the proceeding seems still to call for some volitional element of which a demented person is in law not capable, concepts originating in the desire to protect such persons from criminal responsibility should not be carried over to impede removal from office of persons who are incapable of carrying out their public duties.[17]

Although Hamilton said that insanity "may be safely pronounced to be a virtual disqualification," he did not pursue his logic but attempted to differentiate "inability" from "insanity," not because "high crimes and misdemeanors" was more adaptable to "insanity" than to "inability," but because the task of fixing bounds between ability and inability allegedly "would much oftener give rise to personal and petty attachments and enmities than advance the interests of justice or the public good." [18] His conclusion does not rest on compulsions inherent in the constitutional text, but on debatable considerations of policy which run counter to the Madison-Morris statements in the convention. There could equally be cases where it might

---

15. The "irresponsibility" point was made in the First Congress by James Jackson, infra, text accompanying n. 22, and was noted by Henry Adams, supra, text accompanying n. 13. Hamilton's stress on "disqualification" for insanity "without any formal or express provision" suggests that the "express" "high crimes and misdemeanors" did not cover the case and hence that he had some alternative means of removal in mind.

16. Supra, Chapter II, text accompanying n. 15, and nn. 15, 130–135.

17. So far as I could ascertain, there is no English precedent for impeachment of an insane officer, but that may be because the King, who could remove all Ministers and most judges at pleasure, supra, Chapter IV, text accompanying nn. 32–33, could derive small profit from a demented tool, so that there would have been little or no occasion to impeach one who was insane. Compare infra, text accompanying n. 31.

18. *Federalist* No. 79 at 514.

be as difficult to draw the line between sanity and insanity; and as the impeachment of Judge Pickering demonstrated, insanity cases may also provoke factional clamor.[19] Experience has demonstrated that the cases of judicial senility which called for exercise of some removal power were not such as excited political passions; more often than not the judges were colorless, nonpolitical figures, and it was their fellow judges who considered retirement of the particular judge essential for the public welfare.[20] The difficulty of drawing lines pervades the entire domain of law; it does not account for the cases of incontrovertible disability; and it has no place when judges are notoriously senile and incapable of performing their duties.[21] Such inability fits as well as insanity within the Madison-Morris view that "incapacity is a ground for impeachment."

There remain the remarks during the "removal" debate in the First Congress. That debate raged round existence of a means *other* than impeachment for removal of executive officers. The opponents argued that impeachment was exclusive and, in the words of James Jackson, that "madness is no treason, crime or misdemeanor." [22] Proponents, desirous to establish an independent source of removal, in no small part because impeachment was so cumbersome,[23] readily

---

19. Cf. 3 Beveridge, supra, n. 11 at 164–166. 4 Malone 463 states: "Members of the judge's own party strongly opposed his resignation for purely political reasons." For corroborative details, see Turner, supra, n. 12 at 485, 488, 490, 496, 505.

20. Cf. Testimony of Judge John Biggs, Hearings on Judicial Fitness before the Senate Subcommittee on Improvements in Judicial Machinery (89th Cong. 2d Sess., Feb. 15, 1966) 15–16, 18, 20; see also ibid. 30, 61.

21. In 1913, Attorney General, later Justice, James McReynolds, stated that some judges "have remained on the bench long beyond the time when they were capable of adequately discharging their duties, and in consequence administration of justice has suffered." *1913, Atty. Gen. Rept. 5.* Speaking to the compulsory retirement of senile Justices, Charles Evans Hughes stated, "the importance on the Supreme Court of avoiding the risk of having judges who are unable properly to do their work and yet insist on remaining on the bench, is too great to permit chances to be taken." C. E. Hughes, *The Supreme Court* 76 (New York, 1928). Experience has disproved Hamilton's "imaginary danger of a superannuated bench," *Federalist* No. 79 at 515, at least with respect to a number of individual Justices and judges. See also supra, Chapter IV, n. 204.

22. 1 *Ann. Cong.* 487.

23. John Vining termed it "circuitous," "dilatory, and inefficient," "what delays and uncertainties," ibid. 468, 571; Madison called it a "circuitous operation," ibid. 497; compare Elias Boudinot, ibid. 375; Thomas Hartley, ibid. 480; Peter Sylvester, ibid. 562.

agree^d that impeachment did not extend to disability and insanity, and maintained that the deficiency fortified their argument that there must be an independent power of removal.[24] The upshot was that the House voted to express its "sense" that the power of removal of executive officers resides in the President,[25] thereby affirming that with respect to executive officers the impeachment clause did not exclude this power. Had the impeachment clause been deemed exclusive, it is reasonable to assume that the exigencies of government which led proponents of removal to stress that removal of incapacitated officers was imperative would have prevailed on them to overlook the verbal difficulties of stretching "high crimes and misdemeanors" to include insanity and incapacity. Not for a moment, of course, do I suggest that impeachment is the ideal way of ridding ourselves of demented or incapacitated judges, but only that if impeachment, contrary to my view, is the exclusive means of removal, it should be construed to comprehend removal both of insane and incapacitated judges.

REMOVAL FOR "MISBEHAVIOR"

Removal of an insane judge by resort to "during good behavior" does not require us to ignore the absence of "criminal" intent that some have required of impeachment.[26] Instead, stress on any volitional element would seem to be out of place; for "during good behavior" minimally must premise that the appointee is *capable* of behaving well. One who is confined in a strait-jacket, for example, is incapable of "behaving" at all within the meaning of "good behavior" in office. In Hawkins' words, the grant of an office implies that the grantee "ought to execute it diligently and faithfully" [27]—a condition impossible of fulfillment by a lunatic, so that his tenure is terminated by his insanity.

---

24. See Boudinot's statement, infra, text accompanying n. 32, and n. 32.
25. 1 *Ann. Cong.* 525, 605, 604.
26. Supra, text accompanying n. 21.
27. Hawkins ch. 66, § 1 at 167.

Inability or senility are not, in my judgment, distinguishable for removal purposes from insanity. A paralyzed officer no more than an insane one can execute his office "diligently and faithfully." Bacon's *Abridgment* states that an officer may be removed for "insufficiency," "an original incapacity which creates the forfeiture of an office." [28] Shartel quotes the statement of an English writer that "good behavior" imports an estate determinable by "incapacity from mental or bodily infirmity, or breach of good behavior," but questions whether disability is a ground of forfeiture.[29] He recognizes that "there are certain venerable lines of authority which, if pursued to their logical conclusions might involve this result." For example, "the grant of an office to a person not competent or qualified was said to be void . . . Also, a judicial office could not be granted in reversion because though never so fit, the grantee might become unfit before the grant was to take effect." [30] But Shartel does not pursue the logic of such learning because "the lack of authority in the old books and decisions recognizing disability as a ground of removal, has a strong negative significance. Indeed English decisions have often asserted . . . that a good-behavior tenure is forfeitable *only* for misbehavior." [31] On this analysis his entire argument for removal by scire facias falls, for such loose dicta and lack of specific "authority" are precisely the arguments leveled against him by his critics.

For my part, I prefer the hard common sense of Elias Boudinot in the First Congress "removal" debate:

It was asked, if ever we knew a person removed from office by reason of sickness or ignorance. If there never was such a case, it is, perhaps, nevertheless proper that they should be removed for those reasons; and we shall do well to establish the principle.

Suppose your Secretary of Foreign Affairs, rendered

---

28. 3 Bacon, "Offices and Officers" (M) at 472.
29. Shartel 903.
30. Ibid. The authorities are quoted ibid. n. 90.
31. Ibid. 903–904.

incapable of thought or action by a paralytic stroke: I ask whether there would be any propriety in keeping such a person in office, and whether the *salus populi*, the first object of republican governments, does not absolutely demand his dismission.[32]

And if no supervening disability cases are met in the old decisions, the cases for removal for original "insufficiency" furnish an analogy from which a healthy common law development may proceed. The law would indeed be an ass if it required removal of one who was insane or incompetent ab initio but would prevent removal where incompetence subsequently developed.

A last Shartel argument is that "the basic common law conception of an office as property is utterly irreconcilable with the notion that such an office is subject to termination on account of supervening disability." [33] By the time Hawkins came to state the law, the "basic common law conception of an office as property" was, in the case of public office at least, tempered by recognition that an implied condition of the grant was that the grantee would "execute it diligently and faithfully." [34] One "who neglects a public Office," stated Hawkins, "should rather be immediately displaced than, the public be in danger of suffering that damage, which cannot but be expected some time or other from his negligence." [35] In a word, the public interest in adequate performance of official duty had become a paramount consideration. In the United States, the notion of property in a public office did not take hold. "Never let it be said," Thomas Hartley stated in the First Congress, "that he has an estate in his office when he is found unfit to perform his duties." [36] And the Supreme Court declared that the "nature of the relation of a public officer to the public

---

32. The question had been asked by William Smith, 1 *Ann. Cong.* 457; and Elias Boudinot replied, ibid. 469. For similar sentiments, see Thomas Hartley, ibid. 480; Theodore Sedgwick, ibid. 460.
33. Shartel 904.
34. Supra, Chapter IV, text accompanying n. 174.
35. 1 Hawkins, supra, n. 27 at Ch. 66, § 1, p. 168.
36. 1 *Ann. Cong.* 480.

is inconsistent with either a property or a contract right." [37] Implications drawn from the early common law conception of property in an office, therefore, have no place in assessing constitutional power to remove a judge.

In a recent comment on the problem, an experienced judge, Chief Judge J. Edward Lumbard, of the Second Circuit, stated:

If the physical or mental condition of a judge is such that it is reasonably apparent that the judge is not fit to try or decided cases, why should not the judicial council secure the facts promptly and act accordingly? . . . Of course in a proper case the statute empowers the council to certify disability to the President and the President may then appoint another judge. Title 28, Section 372(b), U.S. Code. While there is no specific authority, I think it follows from this provision and from Section 332 that the judicial council may direct that the disabled judge should no longer sit or act as a judge.[38]

The fact that one of the early Congresses enacted a similar statute in the Act of 1801 [39] argues in favor of its constitutionality. If it be argued that the power to bar a judge from sitting does not amount to a power to remove, I would direct attention to the 1788 "Remonstrance" of the Virginia Court: "vain would be the precautions of the founders of our government to secure liberty, if the legislature though restrained from changing the tenure of judicial officers, are at liberty . . . by lessening the duties to render offices almost sinecures; the independence of the judiciary is in either case annihilated." [40] On this reasoning, removal by a court of judges is no less constitutional than authorization to the President to appoint a replacement for an incapacitated judge.

Consideration of removal for misbehavior must take

---

37. Taylor & Marshall v. Beckham, 178 U.S. 548, 577 (1900).
38. J. Edward Lumbard, "The Place of the Federal Councils in the Administration of the Courts," 47 *A.B.A.J.* 169, 171 (1961).
39. Supra, n. 11.
40. Quoted in Kamper v. Hawkins, 1 Va. Cas. 27, 106, 107 (1793).

into account Kurland's statement that "for every ine-
briate, senile or malfesant judge . . . there are several
dullards and sluggards immune from removal whatever
new standards and machinery are offered." [41] If "dullards" be equated with "ignorant" appointees, the common law runs to the contrary. Forfeiture of an office
would lie for "insufficiency"; that is, states Bacon's
Abridgment, "original incapacity," citing the appointment of one "who is ignorant and unskillful." [42]
Vynter's Case is illustrative. A patent to fill the office
of coroner and attorney of the King had issued "during good behavior." The Justices found that the office
requires "a discreet, learned, and expert person," that
"it is impossible that any one can properly use and
exercise these offices, unless he shall have been educated in the same," that Vynter "never was educated
in those offices" and "is altogether unfit to . . . exercise the said offices," and that the grant was "void in
law." This was rehearsed before the King and ratified
by him.[43] There are other cases.[44] As to "sluggards,"
from Coke onward an office was forfeited for "neglect," and "non-attendance"; and Hawkins refers to
the duty "diligently and faithfully" to perform the
functions of the office. In the First Congress Theodore
Sedgwick insisted that there must be some less "tardy,
tedious" roads to removal than impeachment of one in
the grasp of "incurable indolence." [45]

Against the specters raised by Justice Douglas of the
consequences that may ensue if judges were removable
by other judges for "inefficiency," there is the present
reality known to the bar of judges who neglect their

41. Philip Kurland, "The Constitution and the Tenure of Federal Judges:
Some Notes from History," 36 *U. Chi. L. Rev.* 665, 666 (1969).
42. 3 Bacon (M), p. 742. See also 37 Hen. 8, c. 1 (1545).
43. Vynter's Case (undated) is set out in a memorandum to 2 Dyer 150b-
151a, 73 E. R. 328 (1557), and apparently antedates the reign of William
and Mary.
44. Sutton, The Chancellor of Gloucester's Case, Godb. 390, 78 E. R. 230
(1625). Sutton, put out of his place for insufficiency, argued that the bishop
had appointed him after examination and "if his sufficiency should be afterwards re-examined, it would be very perilous." Justice Doddrig held: "If an
office of skill be granted to one for life who hath no skill to execute the
office, the grant is void." To the same effect, John Dorrington's Case,
Hardres 129, 145 E. R. 415 (1655-1660). In the First Congress, Theodore
Sedgwick pointed to the dire consequences if the President could not remove
"a Secretary in whom he discovers a great deal of ignorance, or a total
incapacity to conduct the business." 1 *Ann. Cong.* 522.
45. See infra, n. 47.

duties.[46] Should an "ignorant" or "incompetent" or lazy judge be shielded because "absolute independence" bars the idea that "judges can be made accountable for their efficiency or lack of it to judges just over them in the federal judicial system"? [47] Who is better equipped to make that judgment; what if every other agency is precluded from taking that action? Can we defer treatment of public ills because of fears that there may be side effects? With Serjeant Hawkins, I would hold that one "who neglects a public office . . . should rather be immediately displaced than, the public be in danger of suffering that damage, which cannot but be expected some time or other from his negligence." [48] Even the Founders, so fearful of the greedy expansiveness of power,[49] still knew that there was no escape from the delegation of power, notwithstanding the possibility that it might be abused.[50] Fear of abuses

---

46. In his testimony Judge John Biggs adverted to the "very substantial problem, as to what can be done in respect to the judge who seems to be so constituted that he is either unable or unwilling to carry his caseload . . . [T]here are very few such judges, but they present problems which are more or less constantly recurring." Hearings, supra, n. 20 at 12.

Chief Judge David L. Bazelon of the District of Columbia Circuit, stated with reference to the cognate problems of Judicial Councils: "I haven't seen anything in 20 years experience on the bench which puts me in fear of anything that either the Conference or council has done to affect the independence of the judiciary." Hearings on the Independence of the Judiciary, before the Senate Subcommittee on Separation of Powers 322 (91st Cong. 2d Sess., April–May 1970). See also the remarks of Justice Tom C. Clark and Chief Judge Bailey Aldrich, supra, Chapter IV, n. 166a, and of Chief Justice Warren Burger and Justice Harry Blackmun, Chapter IV, n. 235.

47. Chandler I, 382 U.S. at 1006 (1966) (Black and Douglas, JJ., dissenting). By 1970 the indignation of Justice Douglas had mounted so that he called upon the Court to "put an end to the monstrous practices that seem about to overtake us." Chandler II, 398 U.S. at 141. On the other hand, Chief Justice Hughes, in commending to the Judicial Conference the formation of Circuit Councils, urged that they be given "power and authority to make the supervision all that is necessary to insure competence in the work of all the judges of the various districts within the circuit." Quoted Peter G. Fish, "The Circuit Councils: Rusty Hinges of Federal Judicial Administration," 37 U. Chi. L. Rev. 203, 205 (1970).

In the First Congress Theodore Sedgwick asked incredulously, suppose a man "acquires vicious habits, an incurable indolence, or total neglect of the duties of his office, which forbode mischief to the public welfare, is there no way to arrest the threatened danger? . . . Must the tardy, tedious, desultory road, by way of impeachment be travelled to overtake" this man? 1 Ann. Cong. 460.

48. See supra, Chapter IV, text accompanying n. 174.

49. Professor Bailyn has shown that the Colonists feared that liberty was the necessary victim of the aggressiveness of power, with "its endlessly propulsive tendency to expand itself beyond legitimate boundaries." Bailyn 56–57; Berger, Congress v. Court 8–14.

50. Edward Rutledge remarked in the South Carolina Convention: "The very idea of power included a possibility of doing harm," and arguments resting on abuse of power "tend to destruction of all confidence—the withholding of all power—the annihilation of all government." 4 Elliot 276. In the Massachusetts Convention, James Bowdoin said, "A possibility of

having little or no experiential footing must not serve as an excuse for doing nothing.

The argument that judges are protected for the protection of the public [51] must not be pressed so far as to absolve them of responsibility, to the public detriment.[52] Absolutes are out of favor in every realm of human endeavor. Nor were the Founders absolutists: on the very issue of the independence of each department James Wilson said, "this position, like every other, has its limitations." [53] We should be slow to attribute to the Founders an intention to create an impenetrable shield for judges, under the guise of "absolute independence," which they never conceived.

---

abuse . . . is by itself no sufficient reason for withholding the delegation. If it were a sufficient one, no power could be delegated." 2 Elliot 85. To the same effect, Samuel Stillman, ibid. 166. In North Carolina, James Iredell said, "No power of any kind or degree, can be given but what may be abused; we have, therefore, only to consider whether any particular power is absolutely necessary. If it be, the power must be given, and we must run the risk of abuse." 4 Elliot 95.

51. Kurland, supra, n. 41 at 698.

52. Lord Eldon stated that "He knew as well as any man, the importance of preserving the independence of the judges; but there was something equally dangerous with a condition of dependence, and that was, that they should be placed above all law and all control." 7 *Parl. Deb.* 766 (1806). Lord Chancellor Erskine "joined with peculiar fervor with the noble and learned lord [Eldon], in the sentiment, that judges should not be placed above the law, and be permitted to trample on the right of the subject." Ibid. 768. In this country St. George Tucker stressed that "absolute independence of the judiciary . . . is not . . . incompatible with the strictest responsibility." 1 Tucker, App. 359. If impeachment is indeed a delusive guarantee of that "strictest responsibility," as noted jurists, statesmen, and scholars have declared (Justice Miller and Judge Biggs, supra, Chapter IV, 205 and 204; Woodrow Wilson, ibid., n. 204; Hatton Sumners and Senator McAdoo, ibid., text accompanying nn. 199–200) we are amply justified in embracing the alternative, judicial removal of judges, particularly if Congress, the Constitutional arbiter of impeachment, presses it upon us.

53. 1 Wilson 299. Despite their devotion to the separation of powers, the Framers recognized that a certain amount of "blending" was inescapable. In *Federalist* No. 48 at 321, Madison stated that "unless these departments be so far connected and blended as to give each a constitutional control over the others, the degree of separation which the maxim requires, as essential to a free government, can never in practice be duly maintained." To the same effect, 1 Wilson 299; William Davie, 4 Elliot 121. See also Felix Frankfurter & James M. Landis, "Power of Congress over Procedure in Criminal Contempts in 'Inferior' Federal Courts—A Study in Separation of Powers," 37 *Harv. L. Rev.* 1010, 1012–1014 (1924).

Chapter VI

IS REMOVAL LIMITED
TO MISCONDUCT
IN OFFICE?

IMPEACHMENT

It is generally said, though a few voices to the contrary are not wanting, that impeachment is limited to acts performed in an official capacity.[1] For example, William Rawle stated in 1825 that except for treason and bribery "all offenses not immediately connected with office," such as "murder, burglary, robbery," "are left to the ordinary course of judicial proceedings." [2] Rawle cited no authority for his exclusion, and history speaks against him; for impeachment, it will be recalled, originated in the need to reach nobles, ministers, and Crown officials who could not be brought to book by ordinary criminal process.[3] And there are practical considerations which militate against the Rawle view. He himself observed that courts "can neither remove

---

1. For citations to the general view, see John Feerick, "Impeaching Federal Judges: A Study of the Constitutional Provisions," 39 *Fordham L. Rev.* 1, 55 n. 286 (1970). For broader views: 2 George T. Curtis, *History of the Formation of the Constitution of the United States of America* 260 (New York, 1861) ("where the individual has, from immorality or imbecility . . . become unfit to exercise the office."); 1 Roger Foster, *Commentaries on the Constitution of the United States of America* 597–598 (Boston, 1895) ("a public speech when off duty which encourages insurrection"); 2 David Watson, *The Constitution of the United States* 1026 (Chicago, 1910) ("public behavior which brings disgrace upon himself and shame upon his country"); 1 Thomas Cooley, *The General Principles of Constitutional Law in the United States of America* (Boston, 4th ed. 1931) ("any act of wilful official misconduct or any act which tends to put the office in disrepute").
2. Rawle 215. Story noted Rawle's statement but said that the matter had not been judicially settled by the Senate. Story §§ 801, 802.
3. See supra, Chapter II, text accompanying nn. 22–26, 41.

nor disqualify the person convicted, and therefore the obnoxious officer might be continued in office." [4] Imprisonment after conviction does not vacate the office for installation of a successor. As Lemuel Shaw, afterwards the celebrated Chief Justice of Massachusetts, arguing for the prosecution in the impeachment of Judge Prescott in Massachusetts (1821) said: "It would certainly be a great defect in the Constitution if a man could be brought to the bar one day, convicted of an infamous offense, and sent to the pillory, and the next, could assume the robes of office, and sit in judgment and denounce . . . a fellow criminal not more infamous than himself." [5]

Shaw's view that to shield a perjurer or forger from removal "would be a great defect in the Constitution" has much to commend it. Retention in office of one who has betrayed his utter untrustworthiness can only discredit the conduct of public affairs. The gravamen of "official" misconduct such as bribery or corruption resides in the fact that it is "destructive of confidence in the integrity of the courts." [6] For this reason, presumably, Coke stated that "Though the bribe be small, yet the fault is great." [7] To conclude that the Founders would have impeached a judge who accepted a bribe of $100, but would shield one who forged a note for

---

4. Rawle 217–218. For a statute that expressly provided for disqualification by a criminal court to hold office, see supra, Chapter IV, text accompanying n. 128. If impeachment be the exclusive means of removal and disqualification, such a statute is barred. If it is not exclusive, there is the formidable difficulty of selecting from the myriad State and federal crimes and codifying those that shall serve as a basis for disqualification in a criminal proceeding.

5. *Trial by Impeachment of James Prescott, Probate Judge* 181 (Boston, 1821). Having been at pains to demark "political" from "private" offenses in tracing the very different origins of "high misdemeanors" and "misdemeanors," I do not now propose to blur the distinction but rather to suggest that when a "private" offense also results in injury to the State it may overlap and constitute a "political" offense as well, just as tortious conduct may also be criminal.

6. When Judge G. G. Barnard was impeached by the New York Assembly in 1872, Judge Charles Rapallo of the New York Court of Appeals declared in the course of the trial that Barnard's use of appointments of receivers, guardians, etc., "as instruments of patronage" was "destructive of confidence in the integrity" of the courts and brought "scandal and reproach upon the court." Quoted in Foster, supra, n. 1 at 596 n. Compare the charge lodged against Chief Justice Scroggs by the House of Commons. Infra, text accompanying n. 50. Nicholas Moore, the first Chief Justice of the provincial court, was impeached by the Pennsylvania Assembly (1684) because some of his official action respecting justices of the country court resulted in "drawing the Magistrates into Contempt of ye people, and weakening their hands in the administration of justice." William Loyd, *The Early Courts of Pennsylvania* 61 (Boston, 1910). Compare infra, text accompanying n. 44.

7. 3 Coke *Institutes* 147.

$10,000 or who filed a perjured affidavit in a private transaction, would attribute to them a thralldom to concepts from which they were far removed.[8] Does history compel us to depart from common sense? Let us begin by inquiring whether English impeachments embraced nonofficial conduct, postponing the harder question: what should be the scope of impeachable nonofficial misconduct.

That English impeachments comprehend nonofficial conduct seems tolerably clear. Impeachments were brought against the Duke of Buckingham because he procured titles of honor for his poor kindred and paid for the office of Great Admiral;[9] against Viscount Mordaunt because he made uncivil addresses to Tayleur's daughter and because he prevented Tayleur from standing for Parliament;[10] against the Earl of Arlington because he lodged a popish priest in his family;[11] against Chief Justice North because he assisted in drafting a "proclamation against tumultuous petitions";[12] against Chief Justice Scroggs for notorious excesses and debaucheries;[13] against Lord Treasurer Middlesex because he purchased claims due to the King at an inadequate price.[14] Then there were charges against the Duke of Buckingham and the Earls of Oxford, Arlington, and Danby for procuring great gifts

---

8. Compare their rejection of the separation of powers as an absolute. Supra, Chapter V, text accompanying n. 54, and the intensely practical approach of Elias Boudinot in the First Congress to removal of a paralyzed minister, supra, Chapter V, text accompanying n. 32; and of Theodore Sedgwick to removal for ignorance, incapacity or incurable indolence. Supra, Chapter V, nn. 45 and 48.

9. Art. 2 and 11, 2 Howell 1307, 1308–1309, 1316 (1626) (London, 1809). In this and the following examples, the charges are selected from a group of charges. And as in the case of the examples cited in Chapter II, text accompanying nn. 62–91, these charges did not for one reason or another eventuate in convictions. My reason for employing the latter to give content to "high crimes and misdemeanors" are set forth supra, Chapter II, text accompanying nn. 100–105a. Among them were the fact that both Wooddeson and Story cite such examples, and more important, that one such example, the giving of "bad advice" was cited in the Virginia Ratification Convention by both Francis Corbin and Edmund Pendleton as impeachable conduct. Supra, Chapter II, n. 169; see also Chapter II, n. 105. In the seventeenth-century struggle of the English to throw off absolutist shackles, the sympathy of the Founders lay with the Commons rather than with the Lords.

10. 6 Howell 785, 789–790 (1666), Art. 1 and 3.

11. 6 Howell 1053, 1055 (1674), Art. 1 (5). The intense anti-Catholic feeling of the time is exemplified by Charles II's forced acceptance in 1673 of the "Test Act that excluded Roman Catholics from office under the Crown." Trevelyan 459.

12. 4 Hatsell 115–116.

13. 8 Howell 197, 200 (1680), Art. 8.

14. 2 Howell 1183, 1233–1234 (1624).

from the King.[15] Hatsell stated of the early impeachments that they included "maladministration of justice
and extra-judicial conduct in the judges of the
realm." [16] And Wooddeson was careful to state that
"the abuse of high office . . . have been the *most
usual* grounds for impeachment"; among other examples, he cited that of "a confidential adviser of his
sovereign" who "obtained exorbitant grants or incompatible employments," [17] thus recognizing that the
practice, as the foregoing examples illustrate, embraced charges that pretty clearly fell outside the ambit
of purely "official" acts. Some of the charges may perhaps be regarded as more or less distantly *related* to
the office, although the charges against Scroggs and
Mordaunt, and Arlington's private lodgement of a
"popish priest," cannot be so explained.

Before 1787 some state constitutions had expressly
restricted removal, whether by impeachment or otherwise, to "misconduct in office"; [18] others proceeded for
maladministration,[19] which implicated improper management of official affairs.[20] Presumably the Framers
were at least familiar with the provisions of their own
state constitutions.[21] Charles Pinckney introduced a
plan in the Convention which provided for the trial
of federal officers for "all crimes . . . in their offices." [22]
On August 20, Gouverneur Morris, seconded by
Pinckney, proposed impeachment for "neglect of duty
malversation, corruption." [23] Like maladministration,

---

15. Buckingham, 2 Howell 1307, 1316–18 (1626), Art. 12; Orford, 14
Howell 241 (1701), Art. 1; Arlington, 6 Howell 1053, 1055 (1674), Art. 2;
Danby, 11 Howell 599, 626 (1678), Art. 6.
16. 4 Hatsell 63.
17. 2 Wooddeson 601–602.
18. Massachusetts Constitution (1780), Art. 8, 1 Poore 963; New Hampshire Constitution (1784), 2 Poore 1286; New York Constitution (1776),
Art. 33, 2 Poore 1337; South Carolina Constitution (1778), Art. 23, 2
Poore 1624.
19. Delaware Constitution (1776), Art. 23, 1 Poore 276 (maladministration, corruption or other means, by which the safety of the Commonwealth
be endangered); Virginia Constitution (1776), 2 Poore 1912 (same as Delaware); North Carolina Constitution (1776), Art. 23 (violation of the Constitution, maladministration or corruption), 2 Poore 1413; Vermont Constitution (1777), Art. 27, 2 Poore 1864.
20. Nicholas Bailey, *English Dictionary* (London, 6th ed. 1733); 2 Samuel
Johnson, *Dictionary of the English Language* (London, 3d ed. 1765).
21. In the Virginia Convention, Madison referred to the variations in the
State constitutions. 3 Elliot 376.
22. 1 Farrand 24; 3 Farrand 595, 604, 608.
23. 2 Farrand 342, 344.

malversation has reference to conduct in office.[24] But
with these precedents and suggestions before them, the
Framers did not adopt "misconduct in office" or "maladministration." "Maladministration" was in fact rejected on Madison's suggestion, and "high crimes and
misdemeanors" was adopted in its place. True, the
rejection was grounded on Madison's protest that
"maladministration" would place tenure at "the pleasure of the Senate," as well it might if all petty misconduct in office were impeachable. But this interchange,
it will be recalled, had reference to removal of the
President, which poses quite different problems from
removal of judges. Why should the Framers have
sought to shield officers who committed perjury or
forgery outside of office, bearing in mind that ministers,
high Crown officers, and Justices were historically
reached by impeachment, not indictment? If the
Framers were minded to shield misconduct outside of
office, they knew well enough how to limit undesirable
facets of "high crimes and misdemeanors," as they
had done in the case of treason and pardons.[25] It was
no more difficult to limit the state formula "misconduct in office" to "corrupt, oppressive and other grave
misconduct in office" than to substitute "and other
high crimes and misdemeanors." Here again we should
not be too quick to carry over to judges and other
"civil officers" [26] the "great offenses" which the
Founders conceived were required by impeachment
of the President.

Let us now examine how the issue has been treated
in federal impeachments. The problem was raised in
the very first case, the impeachment of Senator William Blount in 1797. Charged with conspiracy to seize

---

24. Bailey's *Dictionary*, supra, n. 20, defines "malversation" as "mis-
demeanor in an office," and "misdemeanor" as "a behaving one's self ill."
For early examples of "malversation" and "maladministration" see 6
Oxford English Dictionary (Oxford, 1933).

25. Infra, Chapter VII, text accompanying nn. 23–25. Compare Hatsell's
statement that the early impeachments included "extra-judicial conduct." 4
Hatsell 63.

26. Removal of other officials was from the outset declared by the First
Congress to be within the Executive prerogative, Chapter IX, text accompanying nn. 170–171; and rarely indeed would the President insist, for example, upon retaining a Cabinet officer who brought disgrace upon his office
and therefore upon the administration. Practical politics would demand his
immediate resignation or dismissal.

English lands for delivery to England, while Spain and England were engaged in a war regarding which the United States was neutral, Blount's plea to the jurisdiction was in part that he was not accused of "malconduct in office." [27] It might have been difficult to convince Spain that a conspiracy to seize Spanish territory in which a Senator was implicated lacked official sanction; and his acts might well have embroiled the nation in a grave international incident.[28] Inferably, this is why the Senate expelled him on the ground that he was "guilty of a high misdemeanor entirely inconsistent with his public trust and duty as a Senator." [29] During the proceeding Jared Ingersoll, closing for Blount, noted that treason "is not necessarily a crime of 'office,' " though bribery is "a crime necessarily referring to the duties of an office." [30] Thus the words associated with "high crimes and misdemeanors" cut both ways and furnish no clue to the scope of the phrase. The argument for the defense, Story stated, was that the impeachment power "was strictly confined to civil officers . . . and this necessarily implied that it must be limited to malconduct in office,[31] a palpable nonsequitur. "Civil officers" describes the impeachable *person* and thereby excludes military officers and private citizens; but it does not purport to describe the *acts* which are offensive in a "civil officer." For the Managers of the impeachment,

---

27. Wharton 200, 260.
28. Compare the Act of June 5, 1794, ch. 50, § 1 (3d Cong. 1st Sess.), 1 Stat. 381–382 (1861), which made it a "high misdemeanor" for a citizen to accept a commission to serve a foreign state. And compare the Delaware and Virginia impeachment provisions for "offending against the State" by "other means by which the safety of the Commonwealth be endangered." Supra, n. 19.
29. Wharton 260. Since "high misdemeanor" was a term of art peculiar to impeachment, the expulsion is incompatible with the theory that dismissal of the impeachment for lack of jurisdiction was based on a judgment that "malconduct is office" was requisite to impeachment. Story correctly concluded that the decision "turned upon another ground, viz. that a senator was not an impeachable officer." Story § 802. The question was viewed as still open by Lewis Mayers, "Impeachment," *Encyclopaedia of the Social Sciences* 600, 601 (New York, 1937). Although Blount's counsel, Jared Ingersoll, addressed a few remarks to the "in office" point, he stated that "it is not necessary to the support of the defendant's plea." Wharton 290.
30. Wharton 290–291.
31. Story § 804. Story's summary of the arguments betrays partiality to impeachment for unofficial misconduct. Ibid. But conscious of the proprieties, for after all he was a Justice of the Supreme Court, he went on to say that he "Expressed no opinion" because these are "matters still *sub judice*," that is, questions to be decided by the Senate. Ibid. § 805.

Robert G. Harper called attention, among other things, to the state constitutions which antedated the federal Constitution; and he stated that the Framers knew of these restricted provisions but did not adopt them, thus indicating an intention to provide a power not so limited.[32] The point, however, was left open.[33]

Another facet of misconduct was considered in the 1912 impeachment of Judge Robert Archbald for entering into advantageous deals with persons who had cases pending before him.[34] Such deals can be regarded as a less obvious form of bribery,[35] but Chief Justice Taft viewed the conviction in broader terms. In an address before the American Bar Association, he stated that the conviction was "most useful in demonstrating to all incumbents of the federal bench that they must be careful in their conduct outside of court as well as in the court itself, and that they must not use the prestige of their official position, directly or indirectly, to secure personal benefit."[36] It is not so much the "personal benefit" as the fact that such deals shake confidence in the integrity of the courts which constitutes the core of the offense.[37]

That was made explicit in the 1936 impeachment of Judge Halsted Ritter, who was convicted because, among other things, his acceptance of large gifts from substantial property holders in his district brought his court "into scandal and disrepute."[38] Since no charge was made that the donors had cases pending before him, the Senate presumably inferred that the gifts were

---

32. Wharton 301.
33. Supra, n. 6.
34. The charges are abstracted in Simpson 207–213.
35. Feerick, supra, n. 1 at 53, suggests that the case "stands simply for the proposition that a judge who wilfully, corruptly and improperly uses the powers of his office for personal gain is subject to impeachment." But see supra, Chapter II, n. 15.
36. Simpson 59–60, quoting 36 Annual Rept. Amer. Bar Ass'n 431.
37. Cf. statement of Judge Rapallo, supra, n. 6.
38. Supra, Chapter II, text accompany n. 15. In one of the earliest American impeachments, that of Judge Francis Hopkinson in 1780, the Supreme Executive Council of Pennsylvania stated: "we conceive it to be indelicate for a Judge to accept presents from persons who frequently have business before him, though no cause be then depending." And it stated that it was of "highest importance . . . that the people should have a confidence in the integrity of the Judges." Edmund Hogan, *Pennsylvania State Trials* 58–59 Philadelphia, 1795. Hopkins was acquitted on factual grounds. "When there are complaints about the integrity of judges, suspicion turns into conviction that justice is not to be had in the courts." Robert B. McKay, "The Judiciary and Non-Judicial Activities," 35 *Law & Cont. Prob.* 3, 11 (1970).

designed to predispose the judge favorably to the donors in future cases. To this extent Ritter's acceptance was related to his official functions. The House, however, did not dwell on such subtleties, but stressed per Hatton Sumners that Ritter brought his court "into scandal and disrepute, to the prejudice of said court and public confidence in the administration of justice therein" and therefore was rendered "unfit to continue to serve as such judge." [39]

What should be the scope of impeachment for misconduct outside of office? If the smallest bribe is no less offensive than the largest because it destroys confidence in the integrity of the courts, forgery in a private transaction equally unfits a judge to sit in judgment, for it also destroys confidence in his fitness to administer justice. This, to borrow Hamilton's words, is an injury "done immediately to society itself." [40] The necessity of dealing with offenses such as perjury and forgery in private transactions precludes a wholesale bar to inclusion of nonofficial conduct in "high crimes and misdemeanors."

The difficulty, as is so often the case, lies in drawing the line. For example, in 1881 Judge E. St. J. Cox was impeached in Minnesota for frequenting bawdy houses and consorting with harlots.[41] Today such conduct might be viewed more indulgently, although the Supreme Court of Louisiana removed a judge in late 1970 for somewhat similar conduct.[42] One may not approve of the impeachment of a judge on the ground

---

39. Supra, Chapter II, n. 15. Serjeant Hawkins said, "the law abhors any the least tendency to corruption in those who are in any way concerned in its administration." 1 Hawkins, ch. 67 at 168.

40. *Federalist* No. 65 at 423–424.

41. Supra, Foster, n. 1 at 592. A demurrer to the charge was overruled. Twenty-five years later a somewhat similar scandal rocked New York. In 1906, Maxim Gorky came to raise funds for the Russian revolutionary movement in the wake of the Russo-Japanese war. Mark Twain and William Dean Howells sponsored a fund-raising rally. It became known that Gorky had brought his mistress, a Russian actress, with him. They were turned out of one hotel, after another; and the *New York Sun* thundered that "the purity of our inns is threatened." Twain and Howells hurriedly withdrew their sponsorship and the rally collapsed. Justin Kaplan, *Mr. Clemens and Mark Twain* 367–368 (New York, 1966).

42. In re Haggerty, 241 So. 2d 469 (La. 1970). Haggerty was charged with assisting in obtaining lewd films and procuring prostitutes to perform indecent acts at a stag party which he attended, and with associating with persons of known criminal reputation. The Louisiana Constitution provides for removal of a judge "for wilful misconduct relating to his official duties." Acts "relating to," the Court held, were acts "relevant or pertinent to the performance of his duties." Ibid. 478. "No doubt," it stated, the acts charged

that he frequents bawdy houses, but it is something else again to conclude that in the 1881 climate of opinion a Minnesota legislature was arbitrary in regarding such conduct as impeachable. The test cannot be that given misconduct viewed *in vacuo* seems petty, but rather whether it has a destructive impact upon confidence in public administration. Whether that test was properly applied by the Louisiana Court may be debatable, but the test itself as framed by that Court appears sound. Because the public has "a deep and vital interest" in the "office of judge," said the Court, "the official conduct of judges, as well as their private conduct, is closely observed. When a judge, either in his official capacity or as a private citizen, is guilty of such conduct as to cause others to question his character and morals, the people not only lose respect for him as a man but lose respect for the court over which he presides as well." When the Court concluded that the private conduct of the judge "cast dishonor upon the judicial office" and was therefore "prejudicial to the administration of justice" [43] it followed in the path of the House of Commons, which charged in 1680 that Chief Justice Scroggs "by his frequent and notorious excesses and debaucheries" brought "the highest scandal on the public justice of the kingdom." [44]

In this country judges enjoy a power denied to their English brethren, that of declaring legislation unconstitutional—in essence, the power to set the will of the majority aside.[45] This unique and essential role of the courts in our system rests largely on the confidence

---

were "related to the official duties of the respondent." Ibid. 479. The Chief Justice dissented on the ground that an array of character witnesses had testified that Haggerty's conduct had not affected his prestige.

43. Ibid. 478. "The public expects and is entitled to more than ordinary conduct on the part of a judge." Justice Tom C. Clark, "Judicial Self-Regulation and its Potential," 35 *Law & Cont. Prob.* 37, 40 (1970). A revision of the Canons of Judicial Ethics by a special committee of the American Bar Association under the chairmanship of former Chief Justice Roger F. Traynor of the California Supreme Court, and which included Justice Potter Stewart of the United States Supreme Court, stated that "public confidence in the judiciary is eroded by irresponsible or improper conduct by judges"; and that a judge "must expect to be the subject of constant public scrutiny. He must therefore accept restrictions on his conduct that might be viewed as burdensome by the ordinary citizen." *New York Times*, May 23, 1971, p. 1.

44. 8 Howell 197, 200, Art. 8.

45. Alexander Bickel, *The Least Dangerous Branch: The Supreme Court at the Bar of Politics* 16 (Indianapolis, 1962) ("counter-majoritarian" po-

of the people in their integrity. In the words of George Ticknor Curtis: "the position and functions of the judiciary . . . require absolute confidence." [46] A judge who by misconduct, in or out of court, brings "scandal and disrepute" on the bench undermines a pillar of our society.

To view "high crimes and misdemeanors" so broadly, some may object, is to invite the very "unlimited" senatorial discretion which, I was at pains earlier to show, was withheld. But a discretion confined to "high crimes and misdemeanors" is not really unlimited, for there are the common law precedents which give content to the phrase.[47] No formula can "limit" a headstrong Congress minded to exercise illimitable power, as the Andrew Johnson impeachment attests. Whatever the formula, we must look to the Senate for self-restraint in the exercise of power.[48] And if, on my analysis, impeachments are subject to judicial review, the Senate will not be left free to trivialize and pervert "high crimes and misdemeanors" into an instrument of petty political persecution. It will be for the Supreme Court finally to determine what are the limits of "high crimes and misdemeanors," in and outside of court.

REMOVAL FOR MISBEHAVIOR

In his *Institutes,* Coke states that "good behavior must be intended in matters concerning [the] office." [49]

tential of judicial review). De Tocqueville perceived that "the political power which the Americans have intrusted to their courts of justice is therefore immense." 1 Alexis de Tocqueville, *Democracy in America,* ch. VI at 100 (New York, 1899).

46. 2 Curtis, supra, n. 1 at 246 n. 1. See supra, n. 38; and Justice Frankfurter, infra, Chapter VIII, n. 126. Compare the words of Lord Chancellor Erskine in the proceedings respecting Justice Luke Fox (wherein articles of impeachment had been filed by the House of Commons with the House of Lords, and where the possibility of removal by Address to the King was under discussion): "The true question . . . had Mr. Justice Fox, by his misconduct, conduced to the degradation of our free government and constitution." 7 Parl. Deb. 768 (1806).

47. As James Wilson stated in the Pennsylvania Ratification Convention, "It is only in mathematical science that a line can be described with mathematical precision." 2 Elliot 425.

48. Compare Justice Stone in United States v. Butler, 297 U.S. 1, 79 (1936): "the only check upon our own exercise of power is our own sense of self-restraint" (dissenting opinion).

49. 4 Coke, *Institutes* 117. Compare the statute of 1 Wm. & Mary, c. 21,

Holdsworth regards this as the rule "except," citing Lord Mansfield, in "the case of a conviction upon an indictment for any infamous offense of such a nature as to render the person unfit to exercise the office." [50] If these be in fact the limits of forfeiture for "misbehavior" at a common law, removal for nonofficial conduct is narrowly confined.

Throughout I have relied on the postulate that when the Framers used a common law term in the Constitution they expected us to look to the common law for its content.[51] Whatever the differences that have agitated academicians,[52] it has been the long-standing practice of the Supreme Court to look to the common law for light. Now that practice has apparently been shelved, in *Williams v. Florida*.[53] Rejecting the tenet that references to "trial by jury" in the Constitution contemplate a jury of twelve, the majority of the Court asserts that "history" casts "considerable doubt on the easy assumption in our own past decisions that if a given feature existed in a jury at common law in 1789, then it was necessarily preserved in the Constitution." [54] For the majority, "the relevant inquiry . . .

---

§ VI (1688): "if any clerk of the peace . . . shall misdemean himself in the Execution of the said Office . . ." See also quotations from Bacon's *Abridgment* and Blackstone, supra, Chapter IV, n. 174.

50. Holdsworth states: "behavior means behavior in matters concerning the office except in the case of conviction upon an indictment for any infamous offense of such a nature as to render the person unfit to exercise the office." This appears in the chapter on "Constitutional Law," written by Holdsworth in 6 Halsbury, *Laws of England* 609 (London, 1932).

51. Supra, Chapter II, nn. 9 and 160; and text accompanying n. 160. The provisions of the Constitution "are framed in the language of the English common law and are to be read in the light of history." Smith v. Alabama, 124 U.S. 465, 478 (1888). The Constitution "must be interpreted in light of the common law, the principles and history of which were familiarly known to the Framers of the Constitution." United States vs. Wong Kim Ark, 169 U.S. 649, 654 (1898). "The language of the Constitution cannot be interpreted safely except by reference to the common law and to British institutions as they were when the instrument was framed and adopted. The statesmen and lawyers of the Convention who submitted it to the ratification of the Conventions of the Thirteen States, were born and brought up in the atmosphere of the common law and thought and spoke in its vocabulary . . . they expressed [their conclusions] in terms of the common law, confident that they could be shortly and easily understood." Ex Parte Grossman, 267 U.S. 87, 108 (1925); cf. United States v. Barnett, 376 U.S. 681, 688 (1964).

52. See Edmond Cahn, ed., *Supreme Court and Supreme Law* (Bloomington, Ind., 1954); John G. Wofford, "The Blinding Light: The Uses of History in Constitutional Interpretation," 31 *U. Chi. L. Rev.* 502 (1964); Raoul Berger, "Executive Privilege v. Congressional Inquiry," 12 *UCLA L. Rev.* 1044, 1046–1048 (1965); Charles A. Miller, *The Supreme Court and the Uses of History* (Cambridge, Mass., 1969).

53. 399 U.S. 78 (1970).

54. Ibid. 92. Dissenting, Justice Harlan justly stated that "before today

must be the function which the particular feature per-
forms and its relation to the purposes of the jury
trial." [55] Although this test would vastly simplify my
own task, I share the view of Justice Harlan that the
Court, under cover of a most dubious "doubt," has
"stripp[ed] the livery of history from the jury trial" and
preceeded "unburdened by the yoke of history." [56] The
consequences of the Court's new approach are so
far-ranging, the issue raised so fundamental, as to require an elaborate excursus best postponed to another
occasion. It must suffice to say, as Senator George
Wharton Pepper boldly stated at the bar of the Court,
that although we bow to the "law" declared by the
Court, "history remains history, in spite of judicial
utterances upon the subject." [57] And so I shall not
abandon the claims of history [58] in deference to changing fashions on the Court [59] but shall, as the Court itself was wont to do for upward of 150 years, look to
the common law for the meaning of a constitutional
term—"good behavior."

There is no square holding in the common law that
the power of a court to forfeit an office for "misbehavior" is limited to "misconduct in office," or that
a court is powerless to remove a public officer whose
nonofficial conduct injures confidence in the operation
of government. At most there is an early, sparse
enumeration of grounds for removal, which wears no
badge of preclusiveness. In the *Earl of Shrewsbury's
Case,* Coke made his oft-quoted statement, "there are
three causes of forfeiture or seizure for matter of fact,
as for abusing, not using, or refusing." [60] Although

---

it would have been unthinkable to suggest that the Sixth Amendment's
right to trial by jury is satisfied by a jury of six." Ibid. 122.
 55. Ibid. 99–100.
 56. Ibid. 122, Justice Harlan, dissenting.
 57. Myers v. United States, 272 U.S. 52, 70 (1926).
 58. Justice Frankfurter remarked, "legal history still has its claims."
Federal Power Commn. v. Natural Gas Pipeline Co., 315 U.S. 575, 609
(1942) (concurring opinion).
 59. As this is being written the public prints are full of comments about
how the "Warren Burger Court" has entered upon the task of revising some
of the doctrines of the "Earl Warren Court." Some earlier appointments to
the Court for the purpose of shifting the current of interpretation are instanced by Miller, supra, n. 57 at 35n.
 60. 9 Co. 46b, 50a, 77 E. R. 798, 805 (1611). Coke continued, "Abusing
or misusing, as if the marshal, or other gaoler suffer voluntary escapes, it is

Coke here engaged, more or less, in cataloguing prior cases,[61] there is no intimation that his "causes" exhausted the grounds of forfeiture, or were forever frozen. Four years later he affirmed in *James Bagg's Case* that a *corporation* which had no express power to remove could remove a burgess after conviction of an infamous crime, instancing perjury and forgery.[62] Coke hardly conceived that a *court* endowed with power to remove could do less; and the sweeping claim to power he made on behalf of the King's Bench in *Bagg's Case* itself [63] repels an inference that he would have felt barred, in a forfeiture case, from examining into charges that the officer had been guilty of forgery or perjury because there was no prior conviction.[64] To deny to a corporation power *itself* to remove on criminal charges preferred by it is to withhold from an accuser uncontrolled power to stamp the brand of infamy on the accused. But that consideration has no

a forfeiture of their offices . . . So if a forester or parker fell and cut wood, unless for necessary brush, it is a forfeiture of their offices, for destruction of vert is destruction of venison . . . As to non-user (which concerns the case at bar) there is a difference when the office concerns the administration of justice or the commonwealth, and the officer, *ex officio*, or of necessity ought to attend without any demand or request; there the non-user or non-attendance in Court is a forfeiture."

61. For example, his reference to a forester's abuse of office summarized Earl of Pembrook v. Sir Henry Barkley, Popham 116, 79 E. R. 1223 (1597), where the Earl had granted the lieutenantship of a forest to Barkley, who cut costly timber beyond his needs. Trees, the court held, were needed to shelter and succour the game, and "it was a cause of forfeiture of an office at common law to cut the trees, as well in the case of a forester, as in the case of a park-keeper." "Every voluntary act," said the court, "done by an officer contrary to that which belongs to his office is a forfeiture of the office." Popham 117–118, 79 E. R. 1224.

62. 11 Co. 93b, 77 E. R. 1271 (1615).

63. "[T]o this Court of King's Bench belongs authority, not only to correct errors in judicial proceedings, but other errors and misdemeanors extrajudicial, tending to breach of the peace, or oppression of the subjects, or to raising of faction, controversy, debate, or to any manner of misgovernment; so that no wrong or injury, either public or private, can be done but that it shall be (here) reformed or published by due course of law." 11 Co. 98a, 77 E. R. 1277–1278. Even when insulating judges from private suits in Floyd v. Baker, and asserting by way of dictum that "for any surmise of corruption" they should be answerable only "before the King himself," he put to one side the case of a judge who had conspired "out of court" as "extrajudicial." Supra, Chapter II, text accompanying nn. 45–46.

64. This reading is confirmed by Bacon's *Abridgment:* "Extortion is punishable at common law by fine and imprisonment, and also by removal from office in the execution whereof it is committed." Bribery is "punishable not only with forfeiture of the offender's office of justice, but also with fine and imprisonment. Also it is said in general, that all willful breaches of the duty of an office are forfeitures of it." 3 Bacon, "Offices and Officers" (N) pp. 744, 745. No mention here of prior conviction as a condition of forfeiture; rather Bacon assumes that forfeitures of office and criminal sanctions are independent and cumulative processes.

relevance to removal by an impartial court in a forfeiture proceeding. In sum, Coke, generalizing several grounds of forfeiture, did not purport to set forth the exclusive grounds of forfeiture, if only because it is unreasonable to infer that he meant to withhold from his own court power to remove for forgery or perjury, which he shortly afterward conferred upon a *corporation* that had no removal power whatsoever. And these offenses could involve nonofficial conduct, for perjury and forgery may be committed in private transactions. In this light, Mansfield carved no "exception" for such nonofficial misconduct in *forfeitures* for "misbehavior" because no such exception was needed.

Although the Mansfield dictum is of questionable relevance, the manner in which he dealt with several issues is instructive. His "exception" did not emerge in a judicial forfeiture proceeding but in a case, *Rex v. Richardson*,[65] involving the power of the corporation of Ipswich to remove a portman of the borough [66] charged with nonattendance. Mansfield held that there was no cause for removal; he then proceeded to set some dicta afloat. First, on the score of nonattendance, he dismissed *Bagg* because "there is no authority since Bagg's Case, which says that the power of trial as well as of amotion [removal] . . . is not incident to every corporation," [67] preferring a 1728 dictum in *Lord Bruce's Case* that "the modern opinion has been that a power of amotion is incident to the corporation." [68] Mansfield said, "this modern opinion is right. It is necessary to the good order and government of corporate bodies, that there should be such a power." [69] In short, Mansfield thrust Coke's restrictive dictum

---

65. 1 Burr. 517, 538, 97 E. R. 426, 438–439 (1758).
66. A "portman" was "one of a selected number of citizens, chosen to administer the affairs of a borough." *Oxford English Dictionary* (Oxford, 1933).
67. 1 Burr. 538, 97 E. R. 438–439.
68. 2 Strange 819, 820, 93 E. R. 870. Bruce too was pure dictum. After holding that quo warranto would not lie for forfeiture, Bruce stated without citation of authority, "Besides the modern opinion has been that a power of amotion is incident to the corporation, though *Bagg's Case* seems contrary." Thus Mansfield disposed of Coke's dictum by way of dictum and in reliance on yet a third dictum.
69. 1 Burr. 538, 97 E. R. 438.

aside [70] and evoked a broader incidental power of removal, with respect to misconduct in office, because
it was "necessary to good order and good government."
He noted acutely in passing that Coke himself had
fashioned one incidental power: after conviction of an
infamous crime "the power of amotion is incident to
every corporation." [71] Second, with respect to offenses
having "no immediate relation" to office but "of so
infamous a nature, as to render the offender unfit to
execute any public franchise" Mansfield stated, "it is
now established 'that though a corporation has express
power of amotion, yet there must be previous indictment and conviction.' " [72] Neither Mansfield, nor the
editors of the *English Reports* (usually so generous
with confirming citations) cite the cases that "established" the gratuitous (by way of dictum) curtailment
of an *express* removal power. In *Bagg's Case,* Coke
conferred an *incidental* power upon a corporation to
remove after conviction in the absence of an express
power to remove.

From Mansfield we learn that dicta are of no
moment when opposed to considerations of "good
order and government"; and we may also deduce an
underlying principle from his statement respecting
removal by a corporation of an officer convicted of
an infamous crime. It was not the conviction, which
was only conclusive evidence of the misconduct, but,
I suggest, the fact that the offense was of so "infamous
a nature, as to render the offender *unfit to execute* any
public franchise" that constitutes the ground of removal.[73] If the foregoing analysis is sound, there is
little reason to regard removal for infractions of "good
behavior" as restricted to misbehavior immediately
related to the office. The test, rather, is whether the

---

70. He stated with respect to Bagg's Case, "previous conviction was not a
circumstance at all necessary to the judgment in that case: for there was
no sufficient cause of amotion at all." Ibid.

71. Ibid.

72. Ibid. Coke had required conviction for all offenses, in or out of office;
Mansfield would permit removal by a corporation without conviction for all
misconduct in office, an expansion of Coke's dictum.

73. Mansfield, "like Coke, had a deep impatience of the unintelligent and
mechanical use of precedent merely for its own sake and without any true
relevance to the underlying principles involved in a legal issue." Sir C. K.
Allen, *Law in the Making* 207 (Oxford, 6th ed. 1958).

misconduct renders the offender unfit to execute public office. Nevertheless, one who would maintain that the power to forfeit for nonofficial behavior exists must take into account Coke's association in his *Institutes* of "good behavior" with behavior "in office," [74] of the fact that he is echoed by Hawkins and by Bacon's *Abridgment*,[75] of the fact that the reported cases deal only with misbehavior "in office," and the view of Coke and others that the absence of cases in support of a given claim argues against it.[76]

All of which poses the larger question: to what did eighteenth-century English and American judges look for evidence of the common law? Did they feel themselves bound by dicta, or only by the point actually decided? Did they regard extrajudicial statements, even by the judges themselves or in the *Abridgments,* as "law" by which they were bound? What was the relation between decided cases and governing principles? Where existence of constitutional power turns on the scope of common law terms employed in the Consti-

---

74. Coke himself said, however, that the law is to be sought in cases "and not in any private opinion," a view repeated by Hale. Infra, text accompanying nn. 86 and 87. In his 1792 *Dissertation*, Chief Justice Nathaniel Chipman of Vermont cautioned that "the opinions contained in the following Dissertation, are [not] to be considered precedents; they are only private opinions." N. Chipman, *A Dissertation on the Act Adopting the Common and Statute Laws of England*, preface, Chipman Reports (Vt. 1792) (Rutland, 1871).

75. Supra, Chapter IV, n. 174.

76. "And as usage is a good interpreter of laws, so non-usage when there is no example is a great intendment that the law will not bear it." Coke on Littleton 81b. "By 1237," states Sir C. K. Allen, "that very British (and very human) argument 'I never heard of such a thing!' has commended itself to judicial dialectic." Allen, supra, n. 73 at 185. But it did not become an immutable rule. In 1469 Justice Yelverton stated that when a novel case arises upon which there is no previous decision, that he looked to the Canonist and Civilians, and like them resorted "to the law of nature, which is the ground of all laws," the first principle of which was that it should be as beneficial as possible to the "common weal." Anonymous, Y. B. 8 Ed. IV 9, quoted by Allen, supra, at 193–194. Not long before Coke, counsel protested before Sir Edward Anderson that he had vainly "searched all the books" for "one case" in support of the claim. "What of that?" asked Anderson; "shall we not give judgment because it is not adjudged in the books before? we will give judgment according to reason." Resceit, Goldsborough 96, 75 E. R. 1019 (1518).

So too, when Justice Powys stated in Ashby v. White, 2 Ld. Raym. 938, 944, 92 E. R. 126, 130 (1703), "This action is not maintainable . . . never the like action was brought before," Justice Powell retorted, "As to the novelty of the action, I think it is no argument against the action, for there have been actions on the case brought, that had never been brought before." 2 Ld. Raym. 943, 92 E. R. 132. Chief Justice Holt agreed with Powell, saying that novelty "is an argument, when it is founded on reason, but it is none when it is against reason." 2 Ld. Raym. 957, 92 E. R. 138.

See also infra, Rust v. Cooper, n. 97; Rex v. Bembridge, n. 97; and Chief Justice Parker, infra, n. 88.

tution, it is essential to go behind the black-letter
rubrics, to view the materials as might an eighteenth-
century English judge when faced with an issue not
theretofore decided—to consider, in short, the weight
to be given to dicta, to extrajudicial statements, and
to cases versus principles distilled from them, before
the door to the power is slammed shut in the name
of the common law.

When Lord Mansfield vigorously brushed dicta
aside—"I care not for the supposed dicta of judges,
however eminent, if they be contrary to all principle," [77]—he was no innovator. Chief Justice Hobart
had early dismissed a Coke dictum,[78] and he was followed by Chief Justice Vaughan [79] and in 1699 by
Chief Justice Holt. Rejecting some dicta of Coke in
Bonham's Case as "obiter and not pertinent to the
case there," Holt stated: "as the opinion was not
judicial, so it has no authority in law for its foundation." [80] If dicta played a small role in the determination of an as yet undecided point, it follows that out-
of-court statements by judges carried no greater weight;
and their repetition in *Digests* and *Abridgments* could
add little to their conclusiveness.

From Coke onward, the authentic evidence of the
law was to be sought in decided cases. "Book cases,"
said Coke, "are principally to be cited for deciding of
cases in question, and not any private opinion." [81] He
was followed by Hale, who said that decisions of
judges "are a greater evidence thereof [the law] than
the opinion of any private persons, as such, whatsoever." [82] For Blackstone, too, the judicial utterances

---

77. Quoted 4 Campbell, Justices 317.
78. In Lord Sheffeild v. Ratcliffe, Hobart 334, 345, 80 E. R. 475, 486
(1615), Chief Justice Hobart, speaking of an earlier case, stated, "I hold
that opinion that is called a resolution, to be but a matter of discourse, and
no point of judgment, nor pertinent to the judgment of that case, and to be
erroneous."
79. "An opinion given in court, if not necessary to the judgment given of
record . . . is no judicial opinion, nor more than a gratis dictum." Bole v.
Horton, Vaughan 366, 382, 124 E. R. 1113, 1114 (1670).
80. Groenvelt v. Burwell, 1 Ld. Raym. 454, 468, 91 E. R. 1202, 1212
(1699). Chief Justice Marshall unabashedly dismissed some of *his own* dicta
when they were pressed upon him in Cohens v. Virginia. See supra, Chapter
IV, n. 130.
81. Coke on Littleton 254a.
82. Sir Matthew Hale, *History of the Common Law of England* 67 (London, 3d ed. 1739). So too, Chief Justice Vaughan said that "An extra-

were the "most authoritative evidence" of the common law,[83]—the "sure foundation," said Edmund Burke, to be found in the "decisions contained in the notes taken and from time to time published . . . called Reports." [84] This was known to post-Revolutionary America. Writing in 1786, James Kent stated that the common law "can only be discovered & known by searching into the decisions of the English courts which are the *only evidence* of the Common Law and these decisions are regarded with us as authentic evidence of the common law and therefore cited with us as precedents." [85]

The "fundamental principle . . . stated by Coke, Hale, and Blackstone" was "that these cases do not make law, but are only the best evidence of what the law is." [86] Holdsworth adds, "if the cases are only evidence of what the law is the Courts must decide what weight is to be attached to this evidence in different sets of circumstances." [87] One such circumstance was the "inconvenient" operation of a rule, given great weight, though not articulated, by Coke in *Bagg's Case.* Although the corporation was without express power to remove, Coke drew the power out of thin air because irremovability of a convict would be "inconvenience," which, in Holdsworth's translation, "would be contrary to public policy." [88] When Mansfield desired to broaden the removal power of a corporation, he put the "incidental power" on grounds of "good order and government," a reformulation of "inconvenience" in positive terms. To anticipate the imputation that this is to read back into the seventeenth and eighteenth cen-

---

judicial opinion given in or out of court is no more than the prolatum or saying of him who gives it." Bole v. Horton, Vaughan 366, 382, 124 E. R. 1113, 1124 (1670).

83. 1 Blackstone 69.
84. Quoted by Sir William Holdsworth, *Some Lessons from Our Legal History* 18–19 (New York, 1928).
85. Letter of July 8, 1786, to Simeon Baldwin, quoted 1 Julius Goebel, *The Law Practice of Alexander Hamilton* 50n (New York, 1964), emphasis added.
86. Sir William S. Holdsworth, "Case Law," 50 *L. Q. R.* 180, 184 (1934).
87. Ibid. 185.
88. Ibid. When it was argued in Omichund v. Barker, 2 Eq. Ca. Abr. 397, 401, 22 E. R. 339, 342 (1748), that the admission of infidels as witnesses was a novelty, the argument was rejected by Chief Baron Parker (see infra, text accompanying n. 91), who stated, "the rejecting of these witnesses would be destructive of trade, and, I think, subversive of justice, and attended with infinite other inconveniences."

turies modern notions of judicial adaptation, let me emphasize, in Holdsworth's words, that "Coke is never tired of insisting that the fact that a rule would lead to inconvenient results—inconvenient either technically or substantially—is a good argument to prove that the rule is not law." [89] Later Chief Justice Vaughan stated that "the premises must be clear out of the established law, and the conclusion well deduced before great inconvenience be admitted for law." [90] In terms of removal by judicial forfeiture for misconduct outside of office which discredits the administration of government, Vaughan would have insisted upon "clear," "established law"—that is, decisions on the point, not dicta—before concluding that such an officer was insulated from removal. And Coke presumably would have held that the "inconvenience" of retaining such an officer argues against a rule that he is irremovable.

Finally, there was the doctrine that the cases merely illustrate a principle; in the words of Chief Baron Parker (1748), "the law of England is not confined to particular precedents and cases but consists in the reason of them." [91] This view was restated by Mansfield in 1762: "The reason and spirit of cases make law; not the letter of particular precedents." [92] Translated into terms of misconduct outside of office, the underlying principle for removal, I have suggested, was that the misconduct had rendered the offender "unfit to execute any public franchise"; that is to say, a perjurer or forger simply could not command the public respect indispensable to the administration of justice. Suppose for example that a town treasurer had been brought before Mansfield, charged with cheating and unfair dealing (what is now called fraudulent misrepresentations) in private transactions,[93] which were not

---

89. Holdsworth, supra, n. 86 at 185, quoting Coke on Littleton 379a, "an argument *ab inconvenienti* is strong to prove it is against law."
90. Craw v. Ramsey, Vaughan 274, 285, 124 E. R. 1072, 1077 (1670).
91. Omichund v. Barker, 2 Eq. Ca. Abr. 397, 401, 22 E. R. 339, 342. This was on the argument that the admission of infidels as witnesses "has not been done [and] cannot be done." Francis Bacon had stated earlier, "The rule, like the magnetic needles, points to the law, but does not settle it." Quoted Holdsworth, supra, n. 86 at 189.
92. Fisher v. Prince, 3 Burr. 1363, 1364, 97 E. R. 876 (1762); and see supra, n. 73 and infra, n. 97.
93. Compare with Serjeant Hawkins statement, supra, n. 39.

then indictable offenses; [94] is it likely that Mansfield would have held that he was not "unfit to execute any public franchise"? [95] Doubtless Mansfield knew that the Commons had impeached Chief Justice Scroggs because, among other things, Scroggs's out-of-court conduct had brought "the highest scandal on the public justice of the kingdom." It may be doubted that Mansfield would have determined that a judge may bring his court into "scandal and disrepute" provided only that his misconduct outside of court skirted criminality. [96]

If we are to attribute to the Framers an intention by employment of "good behavior" to send us to the "common law" for the content of the words, we must allow them awareness that a good part of the iceberg was beneath the surface, that the "law" was not confined to rubrics in the *Abridgments,* that it was not sought in dicta but in cases squarely decided, that principles deduced from the cases played an overriding role, and that problems of "inconvenience" were influential in guiding determination of as yet undecided cases.

For this we have confirmatory evidence from two American jurists shortly after the Federal Convention. In a *Dissertation* published in 1792, Chief Justice Nathaniel Chipman of Vermont first quoted Lord Mansfield: "The law of England would be an absurd science indeed, were it decided upon precedents only. Precedents serve to illustrate principles . . . the law of England depends upon principles." [97] And Chipman

---

94. 2 Sir William Russell, *Crimes and Misdemeanors,* 1374–80 (London, 1819).
95. In Jones v. Randall, Lofft 384, 385, 98 E. R. 706, 707 (1774), Mansfield said, "There is no positive law nor any case in the books but Mr. Dunning argues rightly . . . that if it is bad in principle, this is sufficient."
96. R. M. Jackson, *The Machinery of Justice in England* 289 n. 1 (London, 5th ed. 1967), said of the modern substitute for scire facias, that the "ground for cancellation would be 'misbehavior' which means (a) in the execution of office, or (b) scandalous behavior in his private capacity."
97. Chipman, supra, n. 74 at 68. Mansfield said, "The law would be a strange science if it rested solely on cases; and if after so large an increase of commerce, arts, and circumstances accruing, we must go to the time of Richard I to find a case and see what is law. Precedent indeed may serve to fix principles . . . But precedent, though it be evidence of law, is not law itself; much less the whole of the law." Jones v. Randall, Lofft 384, 385, 98 E. R. 706 (1774). Observing in Rust v. Cooper, 2 Cowp. 629, 632, 98 E. R. 1277, 1279 (1777), that there was "no case exactly similar" to the case at bar, Mansfield said, "But the law does not consist in particular cases; but in

concluded that the Vermont Act which adopted the common law "gives to the citizens of the State the rules, maxims and precedents of the common law, so far as they serve to illustrate principles—principles only." [98] In 1795 Zepheniah Smith, soon to be Chief Justice of Connecticut, wrote in a pioneer treatise that "A judge, therefore, in forming his opinion, with respect to any particular case, must take into view the whole system of law, and make his decision conformable to the general principles on which it is founded. Nothing can be more improper than the practice of considering every case as standing on its own basis." [99]

Smith's summary of common law judicial practice anticipates in remarkable fashion that of Holdsworth in 1930; [100] it is this approach, I submit, that is to be attributed to the Framers when they employed the common law term "good behavior" in a document which they anticipated would serve untold generations. And in searching for the meaning of those words, it is well to remember that unlike "high crimes and misdemeanors," employed because the Framers considered that the phrase had a "limited" and "technical" meaning, there was no comparable expressed intention in the Convention to employ "good behavior" as a severely limited formula. The words, patterned after the phrase *quamdiu se bene gesserint* (so long as they behave themselves well) in the Act of Settlement, furnished no indication that the conduct was limited to

---

general principles, which run through the cases, and govern the decision of them." See also Rex v. Bembridge, 3 Doug. 327, 332, 99 E. R. 679, 681 (1783).

98. Chipman, supra, n. 74 at 68–69. Professor Goebel refers to the American "late eighteenth-century concept of the common law as a body of principles." 1 Goebel, supra, n. 85 at 33.

99. Zepheniah Smith, *A System of the Laws of the State of Connecticut* 39 (Windham, Conn., 1795). Holdsworth states: "it is important to remember that judges have always assumed the power to disregard cases which are plainly absurd and contrary to principle. Blackstone admits that they have this power." Holdsworth, supra, n. 86 at 186. In part this was due to the fact that the reports, made by private reporters, "possessed very different degrees of authority." Holdsworth, supra, n. 86 at 187. Professor Dawson considers that the modern theory as to the authority of decided cases had to await the appearance of adequate law reports. John P. Dawson, *The Oracles of the Law* 78–79 (Ann Arbor, Mich., 1968).

100. Holdsworth refers to the common law "principle that the authority of a decision is attached, not to the words used, not to all the reasons given, but to the principle or principles necessary for the decision of the case." Holdsworth, supra, n. 86 at 191. See also Theodore Plucknett, *Concise History of the Common Law* 349 (Boston, 5th ed. 1956).

official behavior. Sharper limits were necessary for impeachments, because they cut across the separation of powers and were subject to political cross-currents. But forfeitures of judicial office might more safely be left to a judiciary respected for its probity and impartiality.[101]

This is not to suggest that at the adoption of the Constitution the common law left judges with unlimited removal powers in forfeitures of office, but that "principled" removals were not foreclosed. What I would maintain is that we should not convert an absence of cases precisely in point,[102] nor dicta, into constitutional fetters; that a search be made for underlying principles exactly as English judges would have done had a case of misconduct outside of office been presented. And I would stress that removal should be for cause, for serious cause, and that the ultimate assurance against unprincipled removal for "misbehavior" lies in the availability of review by the Supreme Court. Finally, it is not my intention by the foregoing analysis to escape from the "meaning" the common law term "good behavior" had for the Founders, but only to indicate that the area of search for that meaning is not as restricted as may at first glance appear. For there is no surer way to defeat the Founders' intention to create a government of enumerated, "limited" powers than to interpret the common law terms they employed to fashion the "limits" in freewheeling fashion.

---

101. Supra, Chapter IV, n. 160.
102. Compare, supra, nn. 95, 97; and the remarks of Elias Boudinot in the First Congress "removal" debate: "It was asked, if we ever knew a person removed from office by reason of sickness or ignorance. If there never was such a case, it is perhaps, nevertheless proper that they should be removed for those reasons; and we shall do well to establish the principle." 1 *Ann. Cong.* 469. See also Thomas Hartley and Theodore Sedgwick, ibid. 480, 460. And see supra, Omichund v. Barker, n. 91; Jones v. Randall, n. 95; Rust v. Cooper, n. 97. In Selectmen of Bennington v. McGennes, 1 Chipman Rep. 44, 45 (Vt. 1790), Chief Justice Chipman charged the jury: "This is an action unsupported by precedent, and the question is, are there any principles of law or reason on which it can be supported."

Chapter VII

EXEMPTION
OF LEGISLATORS
FROM IMPEACHMENT

In the very first of its enigmatic verdicts, the Senate apparently held in 1797 that a Senator is exempt from impeachment. Senator William Blount, it was charged, had conspired to launch a military expedition that would wrest Florida and Louisiana from Spain and deliver it to England at a time when both were at war and the United States was neutral.[1] Immediately after the House advised of the impeachment, the Senate expelled Blount by a vote of 25 to 1 on the ground that he had "been guilty of a high misdemeanor, entirely inconsistent with his public trust and duty as a Senator."[2] Blount filed an answer to the impeachment which amounted to a plea to the jurisdiction, alleging that (1) a Senator is not a "civil officer" within the meaning of the impeachment provision, and (2) he was not charged with malconduct in office.[3] By a vote of 14 to 11 the Senate dismissed the charges on the ground that it "ought not to hold jurisdiction."[4] Forty years later Story justifiably construed the dismissal to mean that a Senator is not an impeachable "civil

---

1. Wharton 200, 253.
2. Ibid. 251–252. The power of the Senate to "expel" a member is conferred by Article I, § 5 (2). Unlike impeachment, expulsion does not require the filing of charges by the House but may be initiated by the Senate itself; the Senate is not required to sit as a tribunal to "try" the case as in the case of an impeachment, see supra, Chapter IV, n. 58; and expulsion is unaccompanied by a power to disqualify from office. Infra, text accompanying n. 8.
3. Wharton 260. A third plea, that Blount was entitled to jury trial, was not argued by his counsel. Supra, Chapter II, text accompanying nn. 147–149.
4. Wharton 316.

officer," and he concurred in that ruling.[5] Whether the ruling may with equal propriety be construed to hold that malconduct outside the duties of office is also not impeachable has been earlier discussed.[6]

Although it is late in the day to renew a challenge first made by Rawle in 1825 to the *Blount* ruling,[7] there are good reasons for doing so. Every claim to constitutional immunity, every exemption on constitutional grounds from ouster and disqualification of high officers charged with misconduct, needs to be closely scrutinized. There should be no room for suspicion that the Senate has improperly favored its own. And there exist good practical grounds for reconsideration. Meeting the argument in the *Blount* case that expulsion afforded the only remedy, Robert G. Harper pointed out that the expelled Senator cannot be "kept out in the future, for though the Senate may expel it cannot disqualify." [8] This deficiency found recent illustration when Congressman Adam Clayton Powell was excluded from the House for serious misconduct, only to be returned by his Harlem constituency at the next election.[9]

Much of the *Blount* proceedings was spent on a fine-tooth combing of the Constitution for the employment of "office" and "officer" in such a way as to show that a Senator was or was not a "civil officer"; one can only admire the tireless acuteness that produced such a plethora of examples cutting both ways. On the strength of a few such passages Story concluded later that a Senator is not a "civil officer." [10] Equally persuasive

5. Story § 793. In 1803 St. George Tucker stated: "It has been solemnly decided, that a senator is not a civil officer of the United States, and therefore not liable to impeachment," citing to Blount's impeachment. 1 Tucker, App. 335.

6. Supra, Chapter VI.

7. Rawle 214; infra, text accompanying n. 52.

8. Wharton 296, 314.

9. The charges were serious—"that he had wrongfully diverted House funds for the use of others and himself; and that he had made false reports on expenditures of foreign currency to the Committee on House Administration." Powell v. McCormack, 395 U.S. 486, 492, 494 (1969).

10. Story § 793, relies "particularly" on the Article II, § 3 clause that the President is to "commission all the officers," and members of Congress are not so commissioned. But by this reasoning many subordinate officers would be exempted from impeachment, for many are appointed by heads of departments and courts, whom the President does not commission, yet are "officers." James Bayard, Wharton 268. Story also invokes Article I, § 6, "no person holding any office under the United States shall be a member of

citations may be adduced to the contrary.[11] To set forth and examine all of the numerous examples cited by opposing counsel would be unproductive, for the counter-barrages of citations cancel each other out.

Let us begin, rather, with whether members of Parliament were exempt from impeachment. At once we encounter the fact that the vast bulk of impeachments were brought against Peers,[12] who were themselves members of the House of Lords, a tribunal that from early times asserted the exclusive right to try Peers.[13] Nor did membership in the House of Commons confer immunity from impeachment, as is testified by a number of cases: for example, that of Sir Giles Mompesson in 1620[14] and that of Sir Edward Seymour, Speaker

---

either house during his continuance in office." It would have been confusing to employ "office" to describe members of Congress; what was required was to draw a line which would bar members of other branches from membership in Congress. Again, Story cites Article I, § 6, "No senator or representative, or person holding an office of trust or profit under the United States shall be appointed an elector," apparently suggesting that a Senator does not hold an "office." But by this reasoning, a judge impeached, convicted, and disqualified "to hold any office" could yet be elected to the Congress, for a member of Congress would not be a "person holding an office." Wharton 269–270.

11. Article 1, § 9 (8) provides that "no person holding any office of profit or trust under" the United States shall accept a title from any foreign State. If a Senator holds no "office," it follows that he is exempt from this prohibition, so that we may have a Duke of Oklahoma serving in the Senate. The absurdity of this construction was pointed out by Bayard. Wharton 270. Again, Article II, § 1 (6) empowers Congress, on the death of both President and Vice President, to declare "what officer shall then act as President." By the Act of March 1, 1792, § 9, 1 Stat. 240 (2d Cong. 1st Sess.) (1850), Congress provided that in the case of such a vacancy, the Speaker of the House of Representatives shall exercise the office, Congressional recognition that a member of Congress is an "officer." Wharton 269. More closely in point, the North West Ordinance, enacted by the Continental Congress on July 13, 1787 (while the Convention was sitting), covered "the death of a representative, or removal from office." Ibid. 266. The foregoing citations and those in n. 10, supra, by no means exhaust the array mustered by both sides during the Blount trial, but they suffice to show that they cannot settle the issue whether a member of Congress is a "civil Officer" for impeachment purposes.

One citation, presumably not available to counsel in that trial, comes from the floor of the Convention itself. In the debate on the Resolution "requiring the Legis: Execut: & Judy. of the States to be bound by oath to support the articles of Union," Hugh Williamson suggested "that a reciprocal oath should be required from the Ntl. officers to support the Government of the States," a suggestion picked up and modified by Elbridge Gerry. 2 Farrand 87. Thus the Framers assumed that "officers" comprehends legislators. But with Congressman Bayard, I would not rely "in an argument upon so great a subject, upon nice distinctions or verbal criticism." Wharton 268.

12. Simpson 82–90.

13. Supra, Chapter I, text accompanying n. 22. Consider the impeachment of certain Lords for departing Parliament without leave and refusal to return. Proceedings against Nine Lords at York, 4 Howell 175, 181–182 (1642).

14. 2 Howell 1119 ("A member of parliament"). The Commons impeached "one of its own members, Mompesson." Chafee 106.

of the House, in 1680.[15] Rawle in an early commentary on the Constitution was therefore entirely correct in stating that "peers are necessarily impeached before peers, and members of the house of commons have been frequently the subject of impeachment." [16]

Presumably the Founders were aware of this practice. They had access to the records of English impeachments; [17] they made frequent references to impeachments of the King's ministers; [18] as assiduous students of English history and government [19] they cannot have been unaware of the fact that ministers were members of either the Lords or Commons and that such status did not insulate them from impeachment.[20] Story states, however, that "it is far from being certain, that the convention itself ever contemplated, that senators or representatives should be subjected to impeachment." [21] He puts the shoe on the wrong foot, for inferably he would place the burden of including members of Congress in the comprehensive provision for impeachment of "all civil officers" on proponents whereas, I suggest, the pervasive fear of congressional excesses [22] should require a showing that the Framers had a special reason for exempting them, particularly in light of the established English practice to the contrary.

---

15. 8 Howell 127, 136. Sir Francis Windebank, Secretary of State and then a member of the Commons, was impeached in 1640. 4 Howell 42. In 1647, eleven members of the Commons were impeached for high treason. 4 Howell 858, 914.

16. Rawle 214.

17. Supra, Chapter IV, n. 97. For references to English history, see James Wilson, 2 Elliot 470; George Nicholas, 3 Elliot 17. In Virginia, Patrick Henry commented, "The English history is frequently cited by gentlemen." 3 Elliot 316; and see 3 Elliot 398, 512. See also Madison, 3 Elliot 531; Governor Johnston, 4 Elliot 33; Archibald Maclaine, 4 Elliot 44; Henry Pendleton, 4 Elliot 263; and see supra, Chapter II, text accompanying nn. 5–9.

18. See George Nicholas, 3 Elliot 17; Patrick Henry, ibid. 512; Francis Corbin, ibid. 516; Henry Pendleton, 4 Elliot 263. Compare Gouverneur Morris' statement in the Convention that "certain great officers of State, a minister of finance, of war, of foreign affairs, etc., will be amenable by impeachment to public justice." 2 Farrand 53–54. Cf. supra, n. 17, and Chapter II, n. 228.

19. Supra, Chapter IV, nn. 4, 97.

20. Compare Gouverneur Morris' understanding of Parliamentary realities, his statement in the Convention that the Prime Minister was the real King. 2 Farrand 104.

21. Story § 793.

22. Berger, *Congress v. Court* 8–14. See also infra, text accompanying n. 48. Then too, one who maintains that "all" means less than all has the burden of proof. Supra, Chapter II, n. 141.

The Framers had fashioned impeachment after the English "model"; [23] they had taken pains to avoid some of its undesirable aspects, as when they tightly limited the scope of treason, blocked off pardons after impeachment, and separated impeachment and removal from subsequent indictment and punishment. [24] With impeachability of members of Parliament staring them in the face, the fact that the Framers did not also attempt to obviate the force of those precedents, that they expressed no desire to immunize members of Congress, that they did not fashion a plainly decipherable exemption, argues against the exemption. To establish the immunity it should require something more than inconclusive citations to the various uses of "office" and "officer" in the Constitution. These make good sense in their several contexts but they are of conflicting import when bent to a use for which they were not intended, namely, to throw light on the meaning of "civil officers" in the impeachment provisions. Judges, in whom the Founders had more confidence than in legislators, [25] were to be impeachable through their clumsy inclusion in the words "all civil officers," added at the last minute to the Executive Article II. Why not legislators? [26]

There are at least two statements on the floor of the Convention, not noticed by Story, which indicate that the Framers had in fact "contemplated that senators . . . should be subjected to impeachment." [27] Wilson said that "the Senators who are to hold their places during the same term with the Executive, ought to be subject to impeachment and removal." [28] And Hamilton proposed that "the Governor Senators and all officers of the United States" shall be liable to impeachment.[29]

23. Supra, Chapter IV, text accompanying nn. 209, 219.
24. Treason: Article III, § 3 (1); pardons: Article II, § 2 (1); the separation: Article I, § 3 (7).
25. Supra, Chapter II, n. 232.
26. Infra, text accompanying n. 52.
27. Supra, text accompanying n. 21. "In the consideration of the validity of Judge Story's interpretation, it might always be borne in mind that Story's *Commentaries* was published prior to the publication of Madison's *Notes of Debates*, and without any knowledge of the discussions in the Convention other than the records of the motions and votes contained in the Journal." Charles Warren, *The Making of the Constitution*, 479 (Cambridge, Mass. 1947).
28. 2 Farrand 68.
29. 1 Farrand 292.

When he came to explain the Constitution in the *Federalist,* he considered individual Senators impeachable.[30] What can better illustrate the inconclusiveness of a differentiation based upon a separate enumeration of "Senators and all officers" than Hamilton's casual assumption, after using those words, that "civil officers" comprehends both.

Certainly the Ratification Conventions did not regard the members of Congress as immune from impeachment; and it is to be borne in mind that for Jefferson and Madison the action of the Ratifiers carried even greater weight than the views expressed at the Convention, for it was the Constitution as explained to the Ratifiers that was adopted.[31] In those conventions, the chief objection to making the Senate the impeachment tribunal was that it could not be trusted to try its own members. This objection assumed that Senators were impeachable but criticized the provision for self-trial. Among such critics were James Wilson in Pennsylvania, George Mason and Patrick Henry in Virginia, and C. C. Pinckney in South Carolina.[32] Samuel Spencer's remark in North Carolina is illustrative; he adverted to the "impropriety" of the trial of guilty Senators "by their own body" because "they will always acquit their own members." [33]

The impeachability of members of Congress was firmly articulated by Samuel Stillman in Massachusetts: "the constitution provides for the impeachment . . . of every *officer in Congress,* who shall be guilty of malconduct. With such a prospect, who will dare to abuse the powers vested in him by the people?" [34] Stillman, parenthetically, reflected the widespread fear of congressional abuses in the very context of impeachment. In South Carolina, Edward Rutledge said: "If the

---

30. Infra, text accompanying n. 44.
31. Supra, Chapter III, n. 58.
32. Wilson said that because of the grant of the treaty and impeachment power to the "same body, it will not be so easy, as I think it ought to be, to call the senators to account in that business." 2 Elliot 477. Mason said in Virginia, "The Senators are to try themselves. If a majority of them were guilty of the crime, would they pronounce themselves guilty?" 3 Elliot 420. See also Henry, 3 Elliot 397. C. C. Pinckney said members of the Senate "might be tried by other Senators." 4 Elliot 265.
33. 4 Elliot 131.
34. 2 Elliot 168–169 (emphasis added).

President or the senators abused their trusts, they were liable to impeachment and punishment, and the fewer that were concerned in the abuse of the trust, the more certain would be their punishment." [35] Similar remarks were made by C. C. Pinckney, Henry, Mason, and Edmund Randolph.[36] That the Virginia Convention regarded Senators as impeachable is attested by proposed amendment number 18, which it attached to its ratification: "That some tribunal other than the Senate be provided for trying impeachments of senators." [37]

In scanning the records it must be borne in mind that legislators are not impeachable for their *legislative* acts—that is, where they vote collectively on bills and the like—assuming always that individual votes in consequence of bribery and corruption are distinguishable. It is in this light that statements such as that of Governor Samuel Johnston of North Carolina are to be read: "I never knew any instance of a man being impeached for a legislative act . . . no member of the House of Commons has ever been impeached, before the Lords, nor any Lord, for a legislative misdemeanor." [38] For the Commons were jealous to protect their privileges within the House.[39] When James Iredell stated that it is "very doubtful whether it would be proper to render the Senate impeachable at all," he may be understood to refer to it in a "collective capacity," as distinguished from misconduct by an in-

---

35. 4 Elliot 276.

36. C. C. Pinckney and Mason, supra, n. 32; Patrick Henry: "If you should see the Spanish ambassador bribing one of your senators with gold, can you punish him? Yes, you can impeach him before the Senate." 3 Elliot 355; Randolph: Senators "may also be impeached." 3 Elliot 202. In Massachusetts, General Brooks said if the conduct of the Senate "excites suspicion, they are to be impeached." 2 Elliot 45.

37. 3 Elliot 661. For a similar proposal by the North Carolina Convention, 4 Elliot 246.

38. It may be doubted that he was ignorant that members of Parliament had been impeached for non-legislative acts. Supra, text accompanying nn. 12–20. Richard Spaight said in North Carolina, "though the Senators are not impeachable, yet the President is." 4 Elliot 124. If this goes beyond acts in the "collective" capacity, it runs counter to the considered view of the North Carolina Convention. Supra, n. 37.

39. In its Protestation of December 18, 1621, the House of Commons declared that every member of the House "hath like freedom from all impeachment, imprisonment, molestation (other than by censure of the House itself) for or concerning any bill, speaking, reasoning, or declaring of any matter or matters touching the Parliament or Parliament's business." Quoted Chafee, 57, 58–59.

dividual Senator.[40] Collectively, the Senate must be exempt from impeachment for legislative action [41]— first because the Senate, no less than the judiciary, must be left free to exercise its discretion; and second because in the unlikely event that the entire Senate were corrupted it could not be expected to try itself, and the Constitution makes it the "sole" tribunal for the trial of impeachments. But the corrupt vote of an individual Senator as a result of bribery, for instance, is something else again.

Hamilton drew the distinction in the *Federalist* in speaking of treaties:

The Convention . . . might also have had in view the punishment of a few leading individuals in the Senate, who should have prostituted their influence in that body as the mercenary instruments of foreign corruption; but they could not, with more or equal propriety, have contemplated the impeachment and punishment of two thirds of the Senate, consenting to an improper treaty, than of a majority of the other branch of the national legislature, consenting to a pernicious or unconstitutional law . . . The truth is, that in all such cases it is essential to the freedom and to the necessary independence of the deliberations of the body, that the members of it should be exempt from punishment for acts done in a collective capacity.[42]

Thus Hamilton drew a clear line between "punishment of a few leading individuals in the Senate" for corruption and punishment for "acts done in a collective capacity." How Story could deduce that Hamilton's reasoning "does not lead to the conclusion that the learned author thought the senators liable to impeachment" [43] is beyond me. And Story also overlooks

---

40. Iredell said in the North Carolina Convention, "who ever heard of impeaching a member of the legislature for any legislative misconduct? It would be a great check on the public business, if a member of the assembly was liable to punishment for his conduct as such . . . [B]ut if a senator is impeachable, it could only be for corruption, or some other wicked motive, in which case, surely those senators who had acted from some upright motives would be competent to try him." 4 Elliot 127–128.

41. In *Federalist* No. 66 at 435, Hamilton said that members "should be exempt from punishment for acts done in a collective capacity."

42. Ibid. 434–435.

43. Story § 794.

Hamilton's purpose at this juncture. He had proposed in the Convention that Senators be impeachable; now he was engaged in countering an objection that "has been circulated with more earnestness and with greater show of reason than any other which has appeared against" the Senate function as a "court of impeachment," the objection that "it would constitute the Senators their own judge, in every case of a corrupt or perfidious execution of that trust." [44] That objection was not that Senators ought to be immune from impeachment for corruption; rather, as we have seen, the objectors posited that Senators were impeachable but could not be trusted to try their fellow members.

Story also remarked that "in some of the State conventions, the members of Congress were admitted by the friends of the Constitution not to be objects of the impeaching power." [45] These "admissions" by Archibald Maclaine and Governor Johnston in the North Carolina convention [46] were strange responses to Timothy Bloodworth's insistent question whether the "sole" power of impeachment "deprived the state of the power of impeaching any of its members." [47] Indeed, after Johnston's remark, Joseph Taylor replied that the power "now appeared to him in a still worse light than before." [48] In North Carolina fear of congressional power prevailed over all assurances and the Constitution was rejected. The remarks of Johnston and Maclaine, and of James Monroe, an opponent of the Constitution in Virginia,[49] are outweighed by the expressions of Wilson and Hamilton in the Federal Convention, of Samuel Stillman in Massachusetts, of George Mason, Patrick Henry, and Edmund Randolph in Virginia (confirmed by Virginia's proposed amend-

44. *Federalist* No. 66 at 434.
45. Story § 794. His citations will be found in 3 Elliot 43, 45, 56, 57, the first edition of 1827. The citations herein are to the 2d ed. of 1836, vol. 4.
46. 4 Elliot 33–34. Perhaps Richard Spaight may also be read for Senatorial immunity: "It is to be observed that though the Senators are not impeachable, yet the President is. He may be impeached and punished for giving his consent to a treaty, whereby the interest of the community is manifestly sacrificed." 4 Elliot 124. The treaty context, however, suggests that Spaight merely had the collective consent to a treaty in mind.
47. 4 Elliot 33–34. Timothy Bloodworth returned to this question, ibid. 34.
48. Ibid. 34.
49. 3 Elliot 219–220. Monroe was not cited by Story.

ment), and of C. C. Pinckney, Charles Pinckney, and Edward Rutledge in South Carolina.[50] The contrary view is strange: why should the Founders have discarded any instrument that might protect against congressional excesses and oppression when wrongfully initiated by its members?[51] As Rawle said in 1825, "a breach of duty is as reprehensible in a legislator as in an executive or judicial officer, and if this peculiar jurisdiction possesses so much value in respect to the two latter, it is difficult to conceive why the public should not have the benefit in regard to the former." [52]

Continuance of the immunity erroneously conferred upon Senator Blount merely confirms Spencer's early distrust that the Senate will ever favor its own. More than ever the Senate and House need to be beyond such suspicions; more and more there are protests that Congress may not insist upon high ethical standards for members of the judiciary and executive branches and countenance lesser standards for its own members. Equally high standards would be delusive without equally potent sanctions. General C. C. Pinckney, a Framer and Ratifier, may be understood to have expressed the general sentiment of the Founders when he stated in South Carolina: "No man, however great, is exempt from impeachment and trial." [53] The House would do well, in an appropriate case, to impeach one of its own members and thereby afford to the Senate the opportunity to overrule the implications of its judgment in the Blount case and to effectuate the intention of the Founders.

---

50. Supra, nn. 32, 36; text accompanying nn. 36 and 37. Story § 793 n. 3, noted that remarks in the South Carolina Convention ran counter to his views.

51. Joseph Taylor stated in North Carolina: "None can impeach but the representatives, and the impeachments are to be determined by the senators, who are one of the branches of power which we dread most under this Constitution." 4 Elliot 33. Compare his remarks supra, text accompanying n. 48.

52. Rawle 214; see also ibid. 218.

53. 4 Elliot 281.

Chapter VIII

THE IMPEACHMENT OF
JUSTICE SAMUEL CHASE

It has long been the accepted opinion that the acquittal of Justice Samuel Chase represents the triumph of justice over heated political partisanship.[1] Writing in 1899, Alexander Humphrey attributed the acquittal to the American bent for "giving the most ample protection to one who stands alone; of shielding weakness against power; of exacting fair play in every contest of life." [2] It is my purpose to show that these were the very standards flagrantly betrayed by Chase in his own conduct as a judge, that his removal would have served as a standing reminder that there is no room on our bench for an implacably prejudiced judge, and that his factional acquittal was a miscarriage of justice.

One who would exhume the mouldered bones of an old controversy owes a word of explanation. There is first the feeling engendered by a study of the impeachment record, so well described by Lord Chancellor Campbell with reference to the thwarted impeachment of Chief Justice Scroggs: "It would have been consolatory to us, in reading an account of the base action of Scroggs, if we could have looked forward

---

1. Looking back forty years at several impeachments, Story said, "Whatever may have been the opinions of zealous partisans at the time of their occurrence, the sober judgment of the nation sanctioned these [acquittals] . . . as soon as they became matters of history, removed from the immediate influence of the prosecutions." Story § 780. Justice Douglas stated: "Our tradition even bars political impeachment as evidenced by the highly partisan, but unsuccessful, effort to oust Justice Samuel Chase." Chandler II, 398 U.S. at 136. See also infra, n. 6; 1 Warren 293; 3 Albert J. Beveridge, *The Life of John Marshall* 185 et seq. (Boston, 1916–1919).

2. Humphrey, "The Impeachment of Samuel Chase," 33 *Am. L. Rev.* 827, 843 (1899).

to his suffering on a scaffold like Tresilian, or dying ignominiously in the Tower of London like Jeffreys. He escaped the full measure of retribution which he deserved." [3] Then there is the duty laid upon historians by Lord Acton, "to suffer no man and cause to escape the undying penalty which history has the power to inflict on wrong." [4] And there is the fact that the acquittal stands as a monument to the immunity of a judge guilty of demonstrably unfair and oppressive conduct on the bench. In following Acton's injunction, however, I shall not look to the exacting universal moral standard upon which he insisted,[5] but to standards extant in Chase's own time.

The disposition to dismiss the Chase impeachment as a manifestation of party spirit [6] overlooks that impeachment has almost always been associated with political partisanship.[7] But there is "partisanship" and "partisanship." When the House of Commons sought in the impeachment of the Earl of Strafford to break the back of Stuart absolutist claims, this was surely partisan, a struggle between nascent democratic forces and royalist adherents, yet none the less admirable for that.[8] So too, the "partisan" impeachment of Chase was a natural recoil from the gross partisanship of the judiciary, then little short of one hundred percent Federalist, which "amounted to an arm of that party." [9] Federalist judges were in the habit of launching intemperate attacks upon the opposition in harangues to the grand jury. In one such charge, Chief Justice Dana of Massachusetts had "denounced the Vice-President [Jefferson] and the minority in Congress as 'apostles

3. Campbell, *Justices* 268. For the trial of Scroggs, see supra, Chapter I, text accompanying nn. 224–240.

4. Quoted in Gertrude Himmelfarb, *Victorian Minds* 179 (New York, 1968). Indeed, Joseph Hopkinson, Chase's own counsel, reminded the Senate that it must pay attention to "another dread tribunal," to "posterity." After all the actors are laid to rest, he continued, "then comes the faithful, scrutinizing historian, who, without fear or favor, will record this transaction." 14 *Ann. Cong.* 355.

5. Himmelfarb, supra, n. 4 at 179.

6. "But party spirit ran high; politics rather than legal discrimination, moved Congress; and the general public seemed to accept the fact that the prosecution was a purely party move." 1 Warren 282. But see infra, n. 113.

7. Supra, Chapter II, text accompanying nn. 188–205.

8. Supra, Chapter I, text accompanying nn. 108–170.

9. 4 Malone 458. See supra, Chapter IV, n. 155.

of atheism and anarchy, bloodshed and plunder.' " [10]
Chase himself delivered a little less inflammatory ad-
dress to the grand jury in Maryland, attacking "certain
State and Federal legislation." Let Charles Warren, no
Jefferson sympathizer, describe it. Chase

delivered a long charge to the Federal grand jury in Baltimore, in which . . . he attacked the Act abolishing the
Circuit Judges [John Adams last-minute "midnight" ap-
pointees], saying that "the independence of the National
Judiciary is shaken to its foundation"; he also attacked the
new State Constitution of Maryland and universal suffrage,
which he said would "certainly and rapidly destroy all
protection to property and all security to personal liberty
and our Republican Constitution will sink into a mobacracy."

[It] is difficult to believe that he was not firing directly
at Jefferson when he used the following language: "The
modern doctrine by our late reformers, that all men in a
state of society are entitled to enjoy equal liberty and
equal rights [a 'doctrine' enshrined in the Declaration of
Independence!], have brought this mighty mischief among
us, and I fear it will rapidly destroy progress, until peace
and order, freedom and property shall be destroyed." [11]

Warren would extenuate by the fact that other judges
"had delivered political charges to the Federal Grand
Juries." But this only compounds the offense.[12] With
virtually one hundred percent control of the Judiciary,

---

10. 1 Warren 275.
11. Ibid. 276–277. Caesar Rodney, of counsel for the Managers of the
Chase impeachment, made a telling comment: "When a poor miserable
object like Callender [see infra, text accompanying n. 23], without character
and without influence, censures the measures of our administration, or rep-
robates an unconstitutional law, the respondent considers him guilty of
a crime . . . But a man elevated to the bench may declaim in the strongest
language against any measure or law of the United States, or of an
individual State with perfect immunity." 14 *Ann. Cong.* 640.
  Malone remarks that Chase "specifically condemned an Act of Congress
signed by the President and already upheld by the Supreme Court." 4
Malone 466; compare infra, n. 96. Stuart v. Laird, 1 Cranch (5 U.S.) 299,
309 (1803), tacitly sustained the Act of 1802 which repealed the Judiciary
Act of 1801 that provided for the "midnight judges."
12. 1 Warren 274–275. Speaking of charges by Jay, Cushing, Wilson,
and Iredell to grand juries, Frankfurter and Landis state: "These 'elegant'
and 'eloquent' speeches received wide publicity. Having a Federalist flair
with more or less pungency, they promptly aroused political opposition . . .
The judicial system was drawn into the vortex of politics." Understandably
"the emerging Jeffersonian Party came to regard the federal courts as a
political adjunct of the hated Federalists." Felix Frankfurter & James M.
Landis, *The Business of the Supreme Court* 20–21 (New York, 1927).

the Federalists were employing the bench as a political hustings. In lifting the Judiciary above every "gust of faction which might prevail in the two branches of our Government," [13] the Framers hardly intended to immunize political assaults from the bench on the other two branches, or on the opposition.[14] If it be partisanship to defend against such rank assaults, that goes at most to the motivation for the impeachment; it cannot diminish the force of charges fairly tried and proven. Attention must therefore focus, not on the justifiably "partisan" recoil, but on the *proof* of judicial misconduct.

Apologists for Chase, moreover, overlook that the acquittal was no less partisan than the impeachment. The Federalists "supported Chase completely in every test"; [15] and with the help of a cluster of disaffected Republicans whom John Randolph, leader of the impeachment, had alienated by his opposition to a judicious compromise of the Yazoo claims, blocked the two-thirds vote required for conviction.[16] In addition, the Federalists, according to Beveridge, were aided by the "mighty onslaughts of Martin and Hopkinson," counsel for Chase, and the "wretched performance" of

---

13. James Wilson, 2 Farrand 429.

14. Robert G. Harper, of counsel for Chase, though seeking shelter behind the custom of delivering political charges to grand juries, said it is "a practice which I am ready to admit is indiscreet." 14 *Ann. Cong.* 305. Judge James Winchester, who sat with Chase, said, "I regretted it [the charge] as imprudent." Ibid. 294. And John Purviance, an attorney who testified on Chase' behalf, said, "I thought these kind of charges ought not to be delivered from the bench." Ibid. 299.

Time has confirmed the judgment of the then "partisan" Charles Pinckney, a Framer, who wrote: "What think you, my friends, of our Supreme Court judges electioneering at town and county meetings, those grave and solemn characters who ought to be retired from the public eye, who ought never to be seen in numerous assemblies or mingle in their passions and prejudices, and who, with respect to all political questions and characters, ought to be deaf and blind to everything except what they hear in evidence?" Quoted 1 Warren 274.

15. 4 Malone 479.

16. Ibid. 479–480, 474. "Of the thirty-four Senators at this time twenty-five were Republicans and nine Federalists. It required twenty-three to convict and nineteen was the highest vote obtained against Chase." 1 Warren 291. See also, supra, Chapter II, n. 202. In the thirty days that elapsed between the presentation to the Senate of the articles of impeachment and the trial, "Jefferson's wise adjustment of the greatest financial scandal in American history" came before the House, and Randolph "attacked the Administration's compromise of the Yazoo fraud with a ferocity all but insane in its violence . . . he assailed Jefferson's Postmaster-General who was lobbying on the floor of the House for the passage of the President's Yazoo plan." 3 Beveridge, supra, n. 1 at 174. See also supra, Chapter II, n. 202.

the prosecution leader, Caesar Rodney.[17] Then too there were the quavering references by Chase's counsel to this "ancient and infirm man," "an aged patriot and statesman, bearing on his head the frost of seventy winters, and broken by the infirmities brought upon him by the labors and exertions of half a century."[18] And the issues were obscured by a protracted debate over whether impeachment required an indictable crime,[19] an issue with little merit and since settled against the Chase position.[20] Finally, there was the

---

17. 3 Beveridge, supra, n. 1 at 208, 212.

18. 14 *Ann. Cong.* 354, 503. Respecting his services as "patriot and statesman," it may be noted that in 1778, Chase, "utilizing information gained as a member of Congress . . . combined with others to attempt a corner in flour in view of the approach of the French Fleet." Hamilton was led to publish a letter stating that Chase had "the peculiar privilege of being universally despised." Edward S. Corwin, "Samuel Chase," *Dictionary Amer. Biog.* 34 (1930). "Oliver Wolcott of Connecticut, Washington's Secretary of the Treasury following the resignation of Hamilton, wrote that he had 'but an unworthy opinion' of Chase, while William Plumer, Speaker of the New Hampshire House of Representatives and another leading Federalist, expressed an equally unfavorable view . . . Justice James Iredell . . . wrote: 'I have no personal acquaintance with Mr. Chase, but am not impressed with a very favorable opinion of his moral character. . . .'" Irving Dilliard, "Samuel Chase," in 1 Leon Friedman and Fred Israel, eds., *The Justices of the United States Supreme Court* 185, 189 (New York, 1969). The Maryland Assembly narrowly failed to remove Chase from the office of chief judge of the general court of Maryland, Corwin, supra, at 34. District Judge Richard Peters wrote in 1804, "I never sat with him without pain, as he was forever getting into some intemperate and unnecessary squabble." Quoted 1 Warren 281. He himself lamented his lack of "self-command." Infra, text accompanying n. 99. Hardly an admirable character.

19. There were some remarkable shifts of advocacy on both sides. After Joseph Hopkinson and Luther Martin had insisted for the defense on the necessity of an indictable crime, 14 *Ann. Cong.* 357, 432, Robert G. Harper, closing for the defense, conceded that a judge who habitually omitted to hold court, not an indictable crime, could nevertheless be impeached. Ibid. 507. Despite this breach in the defense, Joseph Nicholson, to the amazement of the beholders, 3 Beveridge, supra, n. 1 at 207, disclaimed for the prosecution the argument that an impeachment was not a criminal prosecution. 14 *Ann. Cong.* 562.

Caesar Rodney of the prosecution then returned to the position that impeachment need not proceed for an indictable offense, but that if one were needed, it demonstrably had been perpetrated. 14 *Ann. Cong.* 591– 592, 599. Among other arguments, he relied on impeachment to enforce the requirement of "good behavior." See also supra, Chapter II, text accompanying nn. 42–43, and infra, Appendix B. In closing for the prosecution, John Randolph rejected the argument that impeachment was limited to indictable crimes. 14 *Ann. Cong.* 642–643. He made two points instinct with common sense. If an indictable crime was the prerequisite to impeachment, why could "it not have [been] said, at once, that any civil officer . . . convicted on an indictment, should (*ipso facto*) be removed from office? This would be coming at the thing by a short and obvious way," and it would have spared Congress the "cumbersome and expensive process, which has cost us so much labor." 14 *Ann. Cong.* 642. And he reduced the defense argument to the proposition that so long as officers "steer clear of your penal statutes" they may "abuse that power which they are bound to exercise with a sound discretion, and under a high responsibility for the general good." 14 *Ann. Cong.* 643.

20. Supra, Chapter II. As Macaulay said of the acquittal of Warren Hastings, "We do not blame the accused and his counsel for availing them

fact that the impeachment, which the inept John Randolph boasted had been "drawn by my own hand," [21] sought to bring down a lion with scattered fire. The result was to bog the trial in a morass of rulings on points of law in criminal cases that Chase had tried.[22]

Here I shall single out one issue: that in the trial of James Callender, charged with a libel against President John Adams,[23] Chase, in the words of Corwin, came to the case "with the evident disposition to play the 'hanging judge.'" [24] What may be forgiven to an impartial judge bent on rigorous enforcement of the law has a different complexion when it is allied to rabid partisanship and an implacable intention to convict the prisoner. An admirer tells us that Chase was "an ardent Federalist"; [25] he agitated for passage of "the odious Alien & Sedition Acts . . . and then threw himself into the forefront of the Federalist Judges who pushed hard for enforcement." [26] These acts, as is well known, split the nation.[27] Whatever its merits, says Samuel Eliot Morison, the Sedition Act "was foolishly enforced, so

selves of every legal advantage in order to obtain an acquittal. But it is clear that an acquittal so obtained can not be pleaded in bar of the judgment of history." 2 Thomas B. Macaulay, *Critical and Historical Essays* 515–516 (London, 1890).

21. 14 *Ann. Cong.* 642 Henry Adams said, "A worse champion for a difficult cause could not be imagined . . . Randolph was no lawyer; but this defect was a trifling objection compared with his greater unfitness in other respects. Ill-balanced, impatient of obstacles, incapable of sustained labor or of methodical arrangement, illogical to excess . . . the qualities which helped him in debate were fatal to him at the bar." 2 Henry Adams, *History of the United States of America* 151 (New York, 1962). McMaster states: "To such a trial there could be but one ending, and that ending was defeat." 3 John B. McMaster, *History of the People of the United States* 181 (New York, 1892).

22. 4 Malone 479.

23. The remarks were no worse than, if as bad as, those of Chief Justice Dana about Vice President Jefferson. Supra, text accompanying n. 10. Malone states: "Actually, the particular comments of Callender about Adams which led to his trial and conviction could have been matched in the writings of Peter Porcupine [a Federalist] and others, not to speak of a letter Alexander Hamilton was to write ere long." 3 Malone 471. Jefferson was "subjected to scurrilous attacks which went far beyond any that either of his predecessors had endured and which, in fact, would be difficult to match in the whole of American history." 4 Malone xx.

24. Corwin, supra, n. 18 at 36.

25. Humphrey, supra, n. 2 at 836.

26. Dilliard, supra, n. 18 at 194.

27. Philip B. Key, of counsel for Chase, said that the Sedition Law "strongly agitated the public feelings. In the State of Virginia it was peculiarly obnoxious; many of the most respectable characters considered it unconstitutional, and as a violation of the liberty of the press." 14 *Ann. Cong.* 394. Although it was never tested in the Supreme Court, the Court has declared that "the attack upon its validity has carried the day in the court of history." New York Times Co. v. Sullivan, 376 U.S. 254, 276 (1964).

as to confound political opposition with sedition." [28] "It became increasingly obvious," states Dumas Malone, that the sedition trials of 1800 "were in fact political trials in crucial election years. Their object, as Jefferson had perceived from the beginning, was the silencing of the opposition press." [29] Francis Wharton, an early and respected commentator, said that the Sedition Act "was pressed by Judge Chase with inquisitorial energy and executed with intolerant vigor." [30] Charles Warren refers to Chase's "prejudicial and passionate conduct of the trials of two Republicans, Thomas Cooper and James T. Callender"; [31] Henry Adams stated that Chase "had strained the law in order to convict for the government." [32] Chase's zeal had carried him so far in the trial of John Fries that President Adams felt constrained to pardon Fries and save him from the gallows. [33]

Charged as the issues were with partisanship, I would yet absolve Chase, had he conducted himself like a judge rather than a hangman. And so I turn to the charge made in Article 4, paragraph 4, of the articles of impeachment, that Chase's conduct was marked by "an indecent solicitude . . . for the conviction of the accused . . . highly disgraceful to the character of a judge, as it was subversive." [34] First I shall consider the facts, then the existing English precedents.

---

28. Morison 353.
29. 3 Malone 466; see also Morison, quoted supra, text accompanying n. 28. For the glaring political coloration of the Sedition prosecutions, see Frank Thompson & D. H. Pollitt, "Impeachment of Federal Judges: An Historical Overview," 49 *N. Car. L. Rev.* 87, 92–93 (1970).
30. Wharton 45.
31. 1 Warren 273.
32. 2 H. Adams, supra, n. 21 at 147–148.
33. Chase's "high-handed" conduct had driven "eminent counsel" from the case; prevented from arguing what they considered a crucial constitutional point, they "threw up their briefs." Ibid. See also Corwin, supra, n. 18 at 36. Warren remarks on Chase's "arbitrary and unusual rulings" in the Fries case. Warren 273. Fries declined other counsel and the trial shortly resulted in a death verdict. Thomas Adams, son of President John Adams, told William Lewis, counsel for Fries, that "his father wished to know the points which Mr. Dallas and he had intended to rely on, in favor of Fries, if they had defended him on the trial." Wharton 645. Counsel supplied the statement, and a pardon followed. Despite pointed criticism of the pardon by Hamilton, Wharton 643–645, John Adams wrote in 1809 that he recalled the Fries pardon "with infinite satisfaction, and which will console me in my last hour." Wharton 646.
34. 14 *Ann. Cong.* 86.

CHASE HAD PREJUDGED THE CASE BEFORE TRIAL AND DETERMINED TO CONVICT

Who would be willing to stake his life and his estate upon the verdict of a jury acting under the auspices of judges who had predetermined his guilt?

Alexander Hamilton [35]

Nothing, surely, can be more disgraceful in a judge than to come to a case with undisguised, overheated zeal to convict the accused. One hundred and forty years before the Callender trial, Sir Matthew Hale set forth what may be expected of a judge:

6. That I suffer not myself to be prepossessed with any judgment at all, till the whole business and both parties be heard.

7. That I never engage myself in the beginning of any cause, but reserve myself unprejudiced till the whole be heard. [36]

The Founders lifted this above the plane of pious aspiration by §8 of the Judiciary Act of 1789, which required of a Justice an oath to "administer justice without respect to persons, and to do equal right to the poor and to the rich, and that I will faithfully and impartially discharge and perform all the duties incumbent on me." [37] Thenceforth, at least, Justices were under a *duty* to act impartially.

---

35. *Federalist* No. 65 at 427. Jefferson wrote in 1782, "In truth, it is better to toss up cross and pile in a cause, than to refer it to a judge whose mind is warped by any motive whatever, in that particular case." 3 Thomas Jefferson, *Writings*, 236 (New York, G. P. Putnam, Ford ed. 1892–1899). Jefferson's great mentor, Chancellor George Wythe, stated in Virginia that "a judge should not be susceptible of national antipathy, more than malice towards individuals—whilst executing his office." Page v. Pendleton, Wythe's Va. Rep. 211n (1793). Such views found expression in the New Hampshire Constitution of 1784: "It is the right of every citizen to be tried by judges as impartial as the lot of humanity will admit." Art. I, § 35, 2 Poore 1283. It seems safe to say that this was an article of faith amongst the Founders.

36. 2 Campbell, *Justices* 207–208. These were rules Hale laid down for himself when he was appointed Chief Baron of the Exchequer in 1660. Compare the King's Bench practice of issuing attachments for contempt against judges of lesser courts "for acting unjustly, oppressively, or irregularly," "for any practice contrary to the plain rules of natural justice . . ." 2 Hawkins, ch. 22, §§ 25–26, pp. 149–150.

37. Act of Sept. 24, 1789, ch. 20, § 8 (1st Cong. 1st Sess.), 1 Stat. 76 (1850).

In the annals of Anglo-American justice there are happily few instances where a judge, before ever a case has been brought before him, has selected the victim, announced his determination to punish him for his "atrocious and profligate" libel,[38] procured his presentment by the grand jury, refused to excuse jurors who confessed their bias against the accused, at every step identified himself with the prosecution, and took every means to disconcert, discredit, and disable counsel for the defense. The House of Commons sought to hang such a man in the person of Chief Justice Scroggs.[39] Certainly he ought not to be suffered to sit in judgment any longer.

For the origin of Chase's intense prejudice against Callender we may call on Luther Martin, chief counsel for Chase, who nevertheless took the stand for Chase and testified that he had himself obtained *Prospect before Us* (written and published by Callender), read and underscored "a great portion of the book," "detested" it, and thought it a "book that ought to be prosecuted." When he learned that Chase, with whom he had a long-standing friendship, was going on circuit to Richmond, Virginia, he gave his copy to Chase, saying, "make what use of it you please." [40] He knew his man.

An unimpeachable witness, John T. Mason—according to Martin "a very worthy and respectable gentleman," a lawyer "of great legal knowledge" [41]—testified that he had met Chase in the circuit court at Annapolis in 1800, that Chase asked his opinion of *Prospect before Us,* told him that Martin had sent him a copy and "had scored the parts that were libellous," that he, Chase, "would carry it to Richmond as a proper subject for prosecution," that "before he left Richmond he would teach the people to distinguish between lib-

---

38. Infra, text accompanying n. 99. Proceeding to Richmond with "an unconstitutional prejudication," said Wharton, "With what tenacity he pursued the judgment thus formed, with what severity he executed it." Wharton 45.

39. Chapter I, text accompanying nn. 224–240. Malone remarks that Chase was "considerably less" than an "American Jeffries," 4 Malone 465, but I hazard that in those pioneer days a Jeffreys would have been hung from the nearest tree.

40. 14 *Ann. Cong.* 245–246.

41. Ibid. 487, 496.

erty and licentiousness of the press," and "that if the Commonwealth or its inhabitants were not too depraved to furnish a jury of good and respectable men, he would certainly punish Callender." [42] Instead of impeaching this testimony, Martin explained in part that Chase's remarks were "predicated upon the supposition, that Callender was, in reality the author," that "there was nothing personal as to Callender, but only an honest indignation expressed against a vile libeller, whomever he might be." [43] This puts matters in a worse light. To pin a "vile" criminal label on a presumptively innocent man upon the basis of mere "supposition" is the very excess of gross intemperateness.[44] Supposition or not, in a few days it led Chase unerringly to presentment and arrest of Callender.[45] Nor are the effect of prejudgment and deep-seated prejudice dissolved by "nothing personal." Regardless of their source they are injurious to the victim, and to the State which is vitally concerned in the integrity of the judicial process. In part, Martin dismissed the Mason testimony as "jocular," "sportive and facetious" conversation, a note frequently sounded by Chase's counsel.[46] Events proved that this was gallows humor, that Chase was in grim earnest.

---

42. Ibid. 216–217. Martin noted Mason's testimony respecting the "determination [Chase] expressed that he would bring Callender to punishment." Ibid. 488. Malone justly states, therefore, that Chase "had determined to punish the author before he got to Richmond." 3 Malone 471.

43. Ibid. 488. For Chase's own characterization of the libel, see infra, text accompanying n. 99. In fact, Chase was quite sure that Callender was the libeler, for Triplett and Winchester joined Mason in testimony that Chase had so identified Callender. For Mason, supra, text accompanying n. 42; for Triplett, infra, text accompanying n. 47. Judge Winchester, a bystander during the Chase-Mason conversation, said that the book "was spoken of as a book written by Callender." 14 *Ann. Cong.* 247. Compare Martin, supra, n. 42. Harper noted Triplett's testimony that Chase applied "harsh epithets" to "the reputed author" of the libel, and "to a person believed to be an atrocious offender." Infra, text accompanying n. 51.

44. See Judge Peters, supra, n. 18; and compare Marshall, C. J., infra, text accompanying n. 87.

45. Infra, text accompanying n. 47.

46. 14 *Ann. Cong.* 487; Harper, "mere jest," ibid. 238; Key, ibid. 411. Although Mason testified that the remarks were made in the course of a conversation "of a jocular complexion," he stated that it was "extremely unpleasant to relate the facts," ibid. 216; and Harper commented, "It must have been a most painful necessity, a cruel violence," which led him "to fulfil the detestable functions of informers." Ibid. 524. See also, Martin, ibid. 487. Why did not Chase's counsel attempt by cross-examination to establish that the conversation was all in "jest," taken seriously by none? Instead, Mason was under the "unpleasant duty" of relating the facts. It passes belief that a man who confessed that "his indignation was strongly excited, by the profligate and atrocious libel," ibid. 136, who broached

It fell to James Triplett to travel to Richmond on
the stagecoach with Chase. Chase handed him the book
and asked whether he had ever seen Callender. Thus
for the second time, first with Mason, now with Triplett, Chase himself brought up the Callender book,
evidence that the subject was boiling within him. Triplett replied with a rumored arrest of Callender under
the Virginia vagrant law, whereupon Chase commented that "it is a pity you have not hanged the
rascal," and that the federal government shows "too
much leniency towards such renegadoes." Several days
later Triplett met Chase in the Richmond court and
was told by him that the grand jury had made a presentment against Callender and that Triplett would have
"the pleasure of seeing Callender"—a pleasure presumably not a little shared by Chase—who would be
produced by the Marshal the next day.[47] From these
facts, and his statement to Mason that he "would carry
[the book] to Richmond as a proper subject of prosecution," [48] it may reasonably be inferred that Chase set
the presentment in motion. Instead of attempting to
impeach or rebut any part of this testimony, Martin
pooh-poohed it: a hundred gentlemen have used expressions like "it is a pity they have not hung the
rascal," but this is no "proof they would be guilty of
injustice towards them." [49] But a judge, like a juror,
"should be superior even to a suspicion of partiality." [50]
And if "proof" be needed, Chase himself supplied it;
his conduct of the trial demonstrated his intention to
"hang the rascal."

That the Triplett-Mason testimony was highly em-

---

the matter thereafter to a stranger on a stage coach, infra, text accompanying n. 43, was merely speaking "jocosely." Key maintained "That a man
of the intelligence of Judge Chase, had he conceived such a project, should
have thus jocosely . . . and in a public place have divulged it, is beyond all
belief." Ibid. 411. But as Henry Adams states, Chase's "temper knew no
laws of caution," 2 H. Adams, supra, n. 21 at 148, a fact that appears
from the statement of his own counsel, Harper. Infra, text accompanying
n. 51; see also ibid. at n. 83.

47. 14 *Ann. Cong.* 217–218. Triplett's testimony was not shaken on cross-
examination. Once more Martin dismisses the conversation as taking place
"in the moments of unsuspecting sociality and levity." Ibid. 489.

48. Bassett testified that "the book given to the jury" had "passages
scored," ibid. 223. Presumably this was the book "scored" by Martin (after
purchase in New York) and given to Chase.

49. Ibid. 489.

50. Infra, text accompanying n. 71. See also supra, n. 35.

barrassing to Chase counsel is revealed by Robert G. Harper, who stated that it

amounts to this . . . that respondent, in the course of some loose and thoughtless conversation, from which it would have been more prudent to abstain, applied some harsh epithets to "The Prospect Before Us," and its reputed author; and expressed an apprehension that he would escape punishment. But does it follow that because a judge remarkable for hasty and strong expressions, has applied some harsh and angry epithets to a person believed to be an atrocious offender, he will not do him justice, when he comes to trial." [51]

Twice Chase had gone out of his way to volunteer such remarks, once to an utter stranger, Triplett. He admitted, as will appear, that the "atrocious and profligate" libel had "excited" his "indignation"; he confessedly "expressed an apprehension that [an 'atrocious offender'] would escape punishment." Can it be concluded from the undisputed evidence that Chase had not prejudged the case?

Be it charitably assumed that Chase's pretrial statements were merely hasty ebullitions which did not express a considered determination to convict. The reproach of bias to which those remarks gave rise could now be dispelled by scrupulously fair conduct of the trial. For the standard that should have governed his conduct I turn to the words of his own counsel, Harper, who dwelt on the embarrassment a Senator must feel "of sitting on the trial of a person who, from political opposition, or any other cause, may have excited hostile or angry feelings in his mind . . . Hence he constantly leans toward the side of the accused: That his enemy is in his power, is always a reason for the utmost forbearance." [52] Instead of the "utmost forbearance",[53] of "constantly lean[ing] toward the side of the accused," Chase constantly leaned toward the

---

51. 14 *Ann. Cong.* 526.
52. Ibid. 502–503.
53. See Henry Adams' comment, supra, n. 46. Chase himself "lamented" his lack of "self-command." Infra, text accompanying n. 99.

prosecution. Harper conceded that "some parts of the honorable judge's conduct, though not criminal nor punishable by impeachment, may, if left without explanation, appear in an unfavorable light." [54] The unfavorable light proved to be beyond explanation.

Erroneous Rulings

Standing alone, erroneous rulings in the course of a trial merely constitute reversible error and of themselves furnish no ground for impeachment. But when these rulings consistently run against the accused, when all doubts are resolved against him,[55] when the rulings are illuminated by conduct that exhibits the judge's unflagging hostility to the accused, they go far to demonstrate that the judge, who before trial had announced his determination to "punish" the accused, has bent every ruling to his preconceived design. It would require much too extensive exposition and would be tedious besides to dissect all of the rulings that were alleged to be erroneous and prejudiced; so I must perforce content myself with two.[56]

EXCLUSION OF JOHN TAYLOR'S TESTIMONY

Immediately after John Taylor of Carolina was sworn, Chase called on defense counsel to state "what

---

54. 14 *Ann. Cong.* 237.

55. Marshall, who had been present at the Callender trial, was called as a witness for Chase and testified under evident embarrassment. He made answers "as to points of practice" which "were not favorable to his Associate Justice." 3 Beveridge, supra n. 1 at 194. See, e.g., infra, text accompanying n. 61.

56. Another much debated issue was Chase's denial of a continuance so that witnesses might be brought from New Hampshire, Pennsylvania, and remote parts of western Virginia. 14 *Ann. Cong.* 131. It must suffice to notice Chase's extraordinary statement, as related by the Clerk of court, William Marshall: "Judge Chase observed, that every person before he made a publication, if he meant to justify it, ought to know the names of his witnesses; and if he meant to justify it by documents, they ought to have been within his reach. It was not to be presumed, indeed, that he could calculate upon being able to procure his witnesses in a few days; that in this case, it was alleged that one witness resided in New Hampshire, which was a great way off. He said that the ordinary sittings of the court would be too short for him to obtain witnesses from so great a distance . . . he could not allow him to the next term." Ibid. 249. In other words, Chase put a publisher at the peril of having witnesses and out-of-state documents at hand before publication! His refusal to put the case over to the next term (at which Justice William Paterson presided, ibid. 254) suggests unwillingness to let his victim escape from his grasp.

they intended to prove by the witness." [57] The issue raised was whether the defense could prove part of a charge by one witness and the other part by another. "No evidence," said the judge, "is admissible that does not go to justify the whole charge." [58] Since it is the function of the prosecutor to object to proffered evidence and of the judge to rule on the objection, Chase, without waiting for the prosecutor to raise his voice, was taking over the prosecution—as he did throughout.[59] Not satisfied with exclusion of Taylor's testimony, Chase said, the "young gentlemen" were making "a popular argument, *calculated to deceive the people,* but very incorrect . . . [Y]ou have all along mistaken the law, and press your mistakes upon the court." [60] To accuse counsel of calculated deception and virtual incompetence is to vitiate confidence of the jury in the defense. In fact, Chase was himself "mistaken," as Chief Justice Marshall politely testified.

Marshall, who had been called as a witness for Chase, was asked by Randolph: "Did you ever, sir, in a criminal prosecution, know a witness deemed inadmis-

---

57. Wharton 706.

58. 14 *Ann. Cong.* 197. As if conscious that he had stepped out of character, Chase, when the prosecutor at last "objected to the introduction of such testimony, as being altogether inadmissible," said, "Being very much pressed, by the young gentlemen who defend the traverser, to admit this testimony, I was going to recommend to you to permit those questions [which but a moment earlier he had labelled deceptive and mistaken] to be put to the witness, though they certainly are irregular. I wish you would consent that they should be propounded. Mr. Nelson [the prosecutor] declared that he did not feel himself at liberty to consent to such a departure from legal principles." Wharton 708–709; 14 *Ann. Cong* 212. Thus prompted by the judge, how could he? By his failure to object the prosecutor had earlier "consented;" only when Chase ran off with the ball did the prosecutor belatedly refuse "consent."

59. For similar haste to rule before objection see Wharton 696, 703. Chase's "performance as judge was almost indistinguishable from that of the prosecution." Dilliard, supra, n. 18 at 194. The record shows that Chase all but conducted the prosecution. Compare the conduct of Lord Mansfield of the trial of John Horne for criminal libel. The Attorney General objected to Horne "calling witnesses except he had opened to what points he meant to call them." Mansfield said, "you had better not object, Mr. Attorney General; you had better hear his witnesses." 20 Howell 651, 740 (1777). When Horne Tooke, on trial for high treason, offered to admit that a document was in his own handwriting, Chief Justice Eyre stated, "In a case . . . so extremely penal to the prisoner, I do not think that the prisoner should be called on by counsel for the prosecution to look at a paper and say whether it is in his hand." 25 Howell 1, 73 (1794). In the same trial, Sir John Scott, Attorney General, later to be Lord Chancellor Eldon, said, to "a certain degree, at least, I ought to be counsel for those I prosecute, as well as counsel against them." Ibid. 555. This from a prosecutor!

60. Wharton 707–708 (emphasis added); 14 *Ann. Cong.* 198, 211–212.

sible because he . . . could only prove a part of a particular charge, and not the whole of it?" Marshall replied, "I never did hear that objection made by the court except in this particular case" [61]—evidence that Chase's exclusory ruling departed from the prevailing practice. The practice, so far as I could ascertain, had not found expression in case law at this time. But an 1833 case from Chase's own state of Maryland held that where the court does not clearly see that a fact offered in evidence is wholly irrelevant to the issue, "it is proper and usual in practice to admit the proof, on the assurance of counsel who tenders it, that it will turn out to be pertinent and material; otherwise material and important testimony might frequently and injuriously be excluded, which it is the province of the court to guard against." [62] The same view was expressed in 1836 by Justice Coleridge in England; [63] and both courts assumed that the proposition required no citation, which suggests that Marshall's statement reflected an established practice. An early text writer, Francis Wharton, labeled Chase's ruling as a "palpable and unprecedented violation of the law of evidence . . . a witness was rejected, who proved a material part of the defendant's case, simply because the particular witness was not able to prove the whole of it." [64]

INCLUSION OF BIASED JURORS

A more serious error was Chase's insistence, when jurors were challenged, upon an utterly unreasonable test of bias: "The only proper question is, 'Have you ever formed and delivered an opinion upon this charge.' He must have delivered as well as formed the opinion." If the juror "has neither read nor heard the charges, I am sure he cannot have formed or delivered an opinion on the subject." To slam the door on inquiry into bias

---

61. 14 *Ann. Cong.* 262.
62. Davis v. Calvert, 5 G. & J. (Md.) 269, 304 (1833).
63. Haigh v. Belcher, 7 C. & P. 389, 390, 173 E. R. 173, 174 (1836): "I think I must receive evidence of it, and trust to the statement of counsel . . . that by some further evidence it will be shown to be relevant." Compare Lord Mansfield, supra, n. 59.
64. Wharton 719.

he refused to let the indictment be read to the jurors.[65] Under these circumstances seven of the jurors had no alternative but to answer that they had not formed or delivered an "opinion on the charge." The eighth, John Bassett, had the hardihood to answer that "though he had never read nor heard the charges in the indictment . . . yet he had formed an unequivocal opinion that such a book as 'The Prospect Before Us' came within the sedition law. But no objection was made to him, and he was sworn like the rest." [66] Chase, so quick to interpose objections for the benefit of the prosecution, failed to follow in the footsteps of Justice Iredell, who had set aside the verdict on the earlier trial of John Fries when it appeared that one of the jurors was prejudiced.[67] Instead, Chase sought a loaded jury, as the testimony of another juror—Robert Gamble, a witness called by Chase—again shows. Gamble acknowledged in court that he thought Callender "to be a very unworthy character," but "the judge said, notwithstanding, I was a good juror." [68]

Luther Martin pitched the defense on some ancient learning.[69] Viner's *Abridgment,* citing some early au-

---

65. Ibid. 696–697.
66. Ibid. 697. Bassett was called as witness by Chase, and testified in the impeachment proceedings that he told Judge Chase that he "had read extracts of the book in the newspapers and had formed . . . an unequivocal opinion that the book was a seditious act." 14 *Ann. Cong.* 211–222, 224–225. The Clerk of the court, William Marshall, brother of the Chief Justice, and a witness called by Chase, testified that Bassett also said that "the author ought to be punished." 14 *Ann. Cong.* 253. Chase conceded that he had refused to excuse Bassett from service as a juror on his plea that "he had made up his mind, or had formed his opinion, that the publication, called 'The Prospect before Us,' from which the words charged in the indictment as libellous were said to be extracted, but which he had never seen, was, according to the representation of it, which he had received, within the Sedition Law." 14 *Ann. Cong.* 118–119.
67. Infra, text accompanying n. 78, and n. 79.
68. 14 *Ann. Cong.* 279. Chase acted in character. On the retrial of John Fries before Chase, "After he was sworn, Mr. Taggert, one of the jurors, expressed himself to the court to be very uneasy under his oath: he then meant that he had never made up his mind that the prisoner should be hung, but very often had spoken his opinion that he was very culpable . . . and wished to be excused. The court informed the juror that it was impossible to excuse him, now he was sworn." Wharton 610. Compare Justice Iredell's grant of a new trial to Fries when a juror's bias was belatedly disclosed. Wharton 606. A lowlier officer than Justice Chase, David Randolph, Marshal of the court, testified that one Samuel Myers, called for the Callender jury, said "he was prejudiced against Callender. I permitted him to go." 14 *Ann. Cong* 260. Compare the 1785 Pennsylvania statute, infra, text accompanying n. 74. The broad rule laid down two years later by Chief Justice Marshall, infra, text accompanying nn. 83, 90, indicates that this was the practice of the other judges.
69. 14 *Ann. Cong.* 457, 459.

thority, states that "If a juror says twenty times that he will pass for the one party; this is not a principal challenge; for it may be that he speaks it for the notice that he has of the thing in issue, and not for affection." [70] In other words, a juror who had witnessed a murder would be free from "bias" because he could speak from personal knowledge of the killing, possibly a survival from the time when jurors were witnesses. But how, one asks, could a juror be truly "impartial" who had an unshakable conviction because he had seen the murder with his own eyes?

By the time of the Chase trial, a more enlightened opinion had made its way. In 1764 Lord Mansfield stated: "A juror should be as white as paper, and know neither the plaintiff or defendant, but judge of the issue merely as an abstract proposition upon the evidence produced before him. He should be superior even to a suspicion of partiality." [71] And Blackstone had stated that the jury shall be "indifferently chosen and superior to all suspicion." [72] Whatever the ancient meaning of "stand indifferently," early American law had elected the path of Mansfield and Blackstone. Thùs the Vermont Constitution of 1777 recommended to the legislature to "provide against every corruption or partiality in the choice and return, or appointment, of jurors," [73] a recommendation repeated almost verbatim in a Pennsylvania law of March 19, 1785, which went on to require the Sheriff to swear that he will use "utmost

---

70. 21 Charles Viner's *Abridgment*, "Trial" (G) (d) at p. 266 (London, 1743). See also 2 Hawkins, supra, n. 36 at ch. 43, § 28. Chief Justice Marshall distinguished Hawkins in United States v. Burr, 25 Fed. Cas. No. 14,969g, pp. 49, 52 (C. Ct. Va. 1807): "The opinion which is there declared to constitute no cause for challenge is one formed by the juror on his own knowledge; in this case the opinion is formed on report and newspaper" publications. As will appear, Marshall adopted a far broader rule.

71. Mylock v. Saladine, I W. Bl. 480, 481, 96 E. R. 278 (1764). In the Trial of Peter Cook, 13 Howell 312 (1696), Cook said, "I am advised, that if any of the jury have said already that I am guilty . . . or the like, they are not fit or proper men to be of the jury." Chief Justice Treby replied, "You are right Sir, it is a good cause for challenge." Ibid. 333–334. And Treby stated, "if any man in this panel have any particular displeasure to the prisoner, or be unindifferent . . . I do admonish and desire him to discover so much in general; for it is not fit, nor for the honor of the king's justice, that such a man should serve on the jury." Ibid. 333. In 1798 a juror was set aside before Justice Buller because he exclaimed on looking at the prisoners, "damned rascals." Rex v. O'Coigly, 26 Howell 1191, 1226–29 (1798).

72. 4 Blackstone 95.

73. Ch. II, Sec. XXII, 2 Poore 1863.

diligence" to prevent the summoning or return of any man who in his judgment "will be influenced in determining the matters that come before him as a juror, by hatred, malice, ill-will, fear, favor, or affection, or by any partiality whatever." [74] The Massachusetts statute of June 26, 1784, required a juror to state whether he "hath directly or indirectly formed or given an opinion, or is sensible of any prejudice in the cause; and if it shall then appear to the Court that any juror does not stand indifferent in the cause, he shall be set aside." [75] Similarly, a New Hampshire law of June 17, 1785, declaring it "of the utmost importance, that impartial jurors should be appointed," directed that a juror who answered that he "is sensible of any prejudice in the cause" should be rejected as not "indifferent in said cause." [76] So important was the impartiality of jurors deemed by the Founders that it was incorporated in the Sixth Amendment provision for trial "by an impartial jury," and immediately reinforced by the requirement of §29 of the Judiciary Act of 1789 that a jury should be returned "so as shall *be most favorable* to an impartial trial." [77]

Of all this Chase was hardly ignorant. By Chase's own testimony his associate, Justice James Iredell, had ordered a new trial after John Fries had been found guilty, "solely on the ground . . . that one of the jurors . . . before he was sworn . . . had made some declaration unfavorable to the prisoner." [78] Since Chase then retried Fries, and reminded the jury of the prior conviction,[79] we may safely conclude that he knew Iredell had declared in the Fries proceedings that "if a juryman, not out of any particular malice against the individual, but from any *other* cause, appears to have

---

74. II Laws of Pennsylvania 262, Sections 1 and 2 (ed. A. J. Dallas) (Philadelphia, Hall & Sellers, 1793).

75. Mass. Laws of 1784.

76. Laws of New Hampshire 106, 109 (Portsmouth, John Melcher, 1792).

77. Act of September 24, 1789, ch. 20, § 29 (1st Cong. 1st Sess.) 1 Stat. 88 (1850) (emphasis added).

78. 14 *Ann. Cong.* 105. One year after the Chase impeachment, the New York court, on which sat Kent, sustained a challenge to a juror who had declared the toll in litigation "unlawful," on the ground that he "had previously given an opinion on the very question in controversy." Blake v. Millspaugh, 1 Johns. Rep. 316, 318 (1806).

79. Wharton 635.

formed a predetermined opinion, he was not fit to be a juryman" on the simple ground that "an improper bias is extremely difficult to get clear of." [80] Prior to the Callender trial Chase had participated in *Fowler v. Lindsey,* wherein Justice Paterson stated: "Jurymen, especially, should be above all prejudice, all passion, and all interest in the matter to be determined." [81] Chase knew or should have known that the impossible Procrustean rule he invoked—an opinion "formed and delivered upon this charge," which charge he barred a juror from reading—was contrary to the practice and to the 1789 federal mandate to select a jury "most favorable to an impartial trial."

Two years after the Chase impeachment, Chief Justice Marshall, in the trial of Aaron Burr, applied the broad Mansfeldian rule and held that the right to an impartial jury is secured by the Constitution. Because Marshall uncomfortably attempted to avoid flat repudiation of Chase's ruling—he had been reminded that in part Chase's impeachment rested on that ruling— [82] his statements require somewhat extended exposition. "The great value of the trial by jury," he said, "certainly consists in its fairness and impartiality." The "most distant relative of a party cannot serve upon his jury" because

the law suspects the relative of partiality; suspects his mind to be under a bias, which will prevent his fairly hearing and fairly deciding on the testimony which may be offered to him . . . It would be strange if the law would be so solicitous to secure a fair trial as to exclude a distant, unknown relative from the jury, and yet be totally regardless of those in whose minds feelings existed much more unfavorable to an impartial decision of the case . . . Is there less reason to suspect him who has prejudged the

---

80. Ibid. 606. From another report of the Fries case, United States v. Fries, 3 Dallas 515, 517–518 (C. Ct. Pa. 1799), we learn that the juror, Rhodes, denied making statements "pointed particularly at Fries, but admitted that he had made use of general expressions, indicating his disapprobation of the conduct of the insurgents," on which Iredell held that Rhodes had "manifested a bias, or predetermination, that ought never to be felt by a juror."
81. 3 Dallas 411 (1799).
82. United States v. Burr, 25 Fed. Cas. No. 14,692g at p. 49 (C. Ct. Va. 1807).

case . . . the law suspects him, and certainly not without reason.[83]

When the Chase ruling in *Callender* was pressed upon Marshall, he at first distinguished it because "Bassett had not read the book, and had only said that if it were such a book as it had been represented to him, he had no doubt of it being a libel"; later he added that "Bassett had formed no opinion about James T. Callender's being the author."[84] But where Chase, before ever he came to Richmond, believed Callender to be the author,[85] presumably the authorship was not hidden from Callender's fellow Virginians. Appearing in a court where Callender was on trial and where, it transpired, authorship was not once denied,[86] Bassett had no reason to volunteer an opinion whether Callender was the author, particularly since the question framed by Chase required no comment on authorship. That Marshall's attempt to distinguish the Chase ruling was merely designed to "save face" for an Associate Justice is attested, first, by the fact that in his summation of the "standard of impartiality" he stated, "if it be said that he has made up his mind, but has not heard the testimony [substitute 'read the book'], such an excuse only makes the matter worse";[87] and second, by his laying down that the first "proper question to be put to jurors" is "have you made up your mind on the case . . . from the statements you have seen in the papers or otherwise,"[88] followed by a row of rejections of jurors who had formed opinions based on rumors, reports, or newspaper accounts.[89] Chase, on the contrary, had held that if a juror "has neither read nor heard the *charges* [as expressed in the indictment], I am sure that he cannot have formed or delivered an opinion

---

83. Ibid. 50.
84. Ibid. 51–52, 77.
85. Supra, text accompanying nn. 42–47.
86. Cf. Wharton 700.
87. United States v. Burr, 25 Fed. Cas. No. 14, 693 at 77 (C. Ct. Va. 1807).
88. Ibid. 58.
89. Hezekiah Bucky (rumors) ibid. 77; James Compton (hearsay) ibid.; Yates Conwell (reports) ibid. 78; Jacob Beeson (newspapers) ibid.: David Creel, ibid.

on the subject," a ruling that is entirely incompatible with an opinion based on rumor or newspaper accounts.

Marshall left no doubt about the "standard of impartiality" for jurors; for he stated, "to save some altercation," that

it was certainly one of the clearest principles of natural justice, that a jury-man should come to a trial of a man for life with a *perfect freedom from previous impressions,* that it was clearly the *duty of the court* to obtain, if possible, men free from such bias . . . that the same right was *secured by the constitution . . .* which entitles every man under a criminal prosecution, to a fair trial by an "impartial jury." Can it be said, however, that any man is an impartial jury-man who has declared the prisoner to be guilty and to have deserved punishment? [90]

The Supreme Court read Marshall in broadest terms in *Reynolds v. United States:* "The theory of the law is that a juror who has formed an opinion cannot be impartial." [91]

Chase had ample reason to believe that this was the state of the law at the Callender trial. Before him were the sweeping utterances of Mansfield and Blackstone, of the English State Trials to which Iredell readily turned,[92] of Iredell's own ruling in the Fries case which Chase retried, of his associate, Justice Paterson, and the mandate of the Act of 1789 to return a jury "so as shall be most favorable to an impartial trial." The conclusion is irresistible that so acute and experienced a judge shut his eyes to these authorities, precisely because he *wanted* a jury loaded with jurors confessedly biased against the accused; that in execution of his own prejudgment he was hell-bent on conviction.

Other Prejudicial Misconduct

RIDICULE OF DEFENSE COUNSEL

Ridicule and derision are among the deadliest weapons employed by a judge bent on conviction. Ordinar-

---

90. Supra, n. 87 at 77.
91. 98 U.S. 145, 155 (1875).
92. Wharton 606; see supra, n. 71.

ily mute throughout the trial, the defendant is identified in the mind of the jury with his champion. Everything that discredits his counsel inflicts a wound on his cause, and to laugh counsel out of court is to persuade the jury that he has no defense.

Albert Beveridge, the Marshall biographer, notes the "sarcastic contempt" with which Chase treated defense counsel and agrees that "the interruptions of the sardonic old Justice were, as John Taylor of Caroline testified, in 'a very high degree imperative, satirical, and witty . . . [and] extremely well calculated to abash and disconcert counsel.' " [93] Luther Martin did not deny that Chase had "used unusual, rude and contemptuous expressions" towards the prisoner's counsel; he dismissed it as of no "legal consequence," [94] and explained that because Chase knew of Virginia's "violent" opposition to the Sedition Act, "he was anxious . . . to keep the bystanders in good humor, and to amuse them at the expense of the very persons who were endeavoring to excite the irascibility of the audience against him. Hence the mirth, the humor, the facetiousness, by which his conduct was marked during the trial . . . for it is admitted that he kept the bystanders in great good humor, and excited peals of laughter at the expense of counsel." [95] His co-counsel, Charles Lee, said that when Chase found defense counsel "had a tendency to mislead and influence the public against a statute of Congress . . . he endeavored to turn sentiments and reasoning into ridicule, and he produced by his wit a

---

93. 3 Beveridge 190; 14 *Ann. Cong.* 207.
94. 14 *Ann. Cong.* 475. In his Answer, Chase denied that he was "intentionally rude or contemptuous in his conduct." Ibid. 134. But he himself confessed to his "naturally quick" temper and "lamented" his "lack of self-command." Ibid. 135. See accompanying n. 99, *infra.* A judge who because of temperamental defects "unintentionally" prejudices the fair trial of an accused is no less unfit to sit than one who prejudices the trial intentionally. In fact, Chase's prejudgment and conduct show that he was intentionally "rude and contemptuous."
95. Ibid. 478–479. Luther Martin's successful defense of Chase had a sequel that beggars fiction. In 1810, Martin, a heavy drinker, appeared as counsel before Chase on circuit in Baltimore, somewhat more inebriated than usual. Chase said to him, "I am surprised that you can so prostitute your talents." Martin replied, "Sir, I never prostituted my talents except when I defended you and Col. Burr"; and turning to the jury, he added confidentially, "a couple of the greatest rascals in the world." P. S. Clarkson, & R. S. Jett, *Luther Martin of Maryland* 280 (Baltimore, 1970). *In vino veritas.* I am indebted to Alfred Konefsky, Esq., for this citation.

considerable degree of merriment at their expense." [96]
All this "mirth and humor" was at the "expense" of
defense counsel. No evidence was adduced by Chase
that he at any time derided the prosecution. The influence of defense counsel upon public opinion had, of
course, no place in the trial, and even less could Chase
sacrifice the rights of the accused to a fair trial for the
benefit of that opinion.

In contrast to his co-counsel, Martin, Harper had to
allow that "wit . . . has nothing to do on the bench. If
a judge should happen to possess it, attempts to dis-
play it in the discharge of his official functions, would,
perhaps, be unbecoming, or even improper, but certainly not criminal." [97] But impeachment, as we have
seen, is not "criminal"; its purpose is merely to remove
an unfit person from office. Nor was it "wit" in the
abstract that was at issue, but wit confessedly employed
"to turn [defense] sentiments and reasoning into ridicule" with the manifest object of destroying the jury's
confidence in them and therefore in the cause which
they were representing.

Not content with "ridicule," Chase plainly exhibited
his "disgust," as Chief Justice Marshall testified, with
the way defense counsel were conducting the defense.[98]
Chase conceded in his Answer that he found the attitude
of defense counsel "irritating and highly incorrect," that
it "might have produced some irritation in a temper
naturally quick and warm, and that this irritation might,
notwithstanding his endeavor to suppress it, have appeared in his manner and in his expressions; for he had
occasions of feeling and lamenting the want of a sufficient caution and self-command in things of this
nature." And he had "no hesitation to acknowledge,
that his indignation was strongly excited by the atrocious
and profligate libel." But "he denies that it any manner
influenced his conduct towards" the defendant.[99]

---

96. 14 *Cong. Rec.* 428. See also the testimony of William Marshall and
Nicholas, ibid. 255, 214. Chase's anxiety to protect the public from being
influenced "against a statute of Congress," did not extend to protection
against his own abuse of a federal statute. Supra, text accompanying n.
11, and n. 11.
97. 14 *Ann. Cong.* 537.
98. Ibid. 264.
99. Ibid. 135, 136.

Against this juxtapose his remark that the "young gentlemen" were making "a popular argument, calculated to deceive the people, but very incorrect," [100] a charge that they were wilfully seeking to mislead court and jury. The jury could only conclude from such remarks by an "aged" Justice of the Supreme Court that counsel were unworthy of credence.

CONSTANT INTERRUPTIONS OF DEFENSE COUNSEL

Another device calculated to prejudice an advocate's presentation of his case is to keep him off balance by constant interruptions. It is as if the umpire at a football game were constantly to trip the players on one side. Hay testified that "I was more frequently interrupted by Judge Chase on that trial, than I have ever been interrupted during the sixteen years I have practiced at the bar." [101] Said Nicholas: "Not many sentences were uttered by counsel at a time without interruption." [102] The Clerk of the court, William Marshall, testified, "I have rarely seen a trial where the interruptions were so frequent." [103] Today such judicial conduct is deemed a denial of due process because it deprives an accused of a fair trial.[104] Here it is set forth as another piece in the mosaic of Chase's design to convict Callender.

The cumulative effect of Chase's hostility and derision was, as both Henry Adams and Corwin noted, to drive defense counsel out of court.[105] Unable to endure fur-

---

100. Supra, text accompanying n. 60; 14 *Ann. Cong.* 255.
101. 14 *Ann. Cong.* 200.
102. Ibid. 215.
103. Ibid. 255.
104. The "judge's persistent and repeated interruptions of defense counsel during the trial and during counsel's summation with sharp critical comments, undoubtedly tended to prejudice defendant before the jury and to deprive her of a fair trial." United States v. Cassagniol, 420 F. 2d 868, 879 (4th Cir. 1970). The Supreme Court condemned "numerous comments to defense counsel, indicating at times hostility, though under provocation," because it "demonstrated a bias and lack of impartiality" which "may well have influenced the jury." Offut v. United States, 348 U.S. 11, 16 (1954) (contempt case).
105. Referring to Chase's "high-handed conduct" during the trials of both Fries and Callender, Corwin states, "On both of these occasions Chase's evident disposition to play the 'hanging judge' brought him into serious collision with counsel who threw up their briefs." Edward S. Corwin, "Samuel Chase," 4 *Dictionary Amer. Biog.* 34, 36 (1930). Henry Adams states that Chase's "over-bearing manners had twice driven from his court the most eminent counsel of the circuit." 2 H. Adams, supra, n. 21 at 147–148.

ther humiliation and harrassment they withdrew in the midst of the trial.[106] One cannot improve on the mordant comment of Caesar Rodney, of counsel for the House, later Attorney General of the United States. A prisoner can as effectually be deprived of the benefit of counsel, he said, "by preventing their speaking on the points which they consider material to the defence, or by a rude course of over-bearing, insulting conduct toward them, which will totally disqualify them for the task, as if you were to nail their lips or clap a padlock on their mouths." [107] Chase's conduct throughout the trial, to my mind, was prejudiced, oppressive, and well calculated to effectuate his prejudgment of guilt.

Was it oppressive by the standards of his own time? Blackstone had stated that "tyrannical partiality of judges" was a "crime of deep malignity"; [108] and Hamilton had roundly condemned prejudgment. Writing of Chief Justice Holt, Plucknett states that "it was an old theory that prisoners tried for felony needed no counsel, for the judge was their defender; Holt lived up to the letter of the rule." And he quotes Sir Richard Steele to the effect that a prisoner who stood before Holt knew that "all would be gathered from him which could

---

106. Hay explained that he could not continue when to do so was to be "subjected to more humiliation than any man vindicating another in a court of justice was bound on any principle to encounter." 14 *Ann. Cong.* 203. For Nicholas' testimony, ibid. 213.

107. Ibid. 623. Francis Wharton, editor of the early State Trials, commented, "the slap [Chase] gave Mr. Nicholas and Mr. Hay at the outset . . . completely deprived those two eminent lawyers of their self-possession." Wharton 718–719n. For an illustration of the perfervid partisanship that led to the Chase acquittal, consider John Quincy Adams' (at this stage "in a highly partisan phase" of his career, 4 Malone 478 n. 37) summary of the evidence: "Not only the casual expressions dropped in private conversations among friends and intimates, as well as strangers and adversaries . . . as well at public taverns and in stage coaches, had been carefully and malignantly laid up and preserved for testimony in this prosecution . . . hours of interrogation and answer were consumed . . . to prove the insufferable grievance that Mr. Chase had more than once raised a laugh at the expense of Callender's counsel, and to ascertain the tremendous fact that he had accosted the ATTORNEY GENERAL of *Virginia* by the appellation of Young Gentleman!!" Quoted 3 Beveridge, supra, n. 1 at 190–191 n. 4. Disclosure of prejudgment in "casual conversation" with a "stranger" in a stage coach betrays deep emotional commitment. As the German proverb has it, "When the heart is full, the mouth spills over." Presumably young Adams, most of whose career had been spent in the diplomatic service, had never been laughed out of court by the ridicule of a judge "at his expense." When "Young Gentleman" comes from the mouth of a venerable Justice in the midst of a trial, not once but three times in as many minutes, Wharton 707–709, it is patently belittling, designed to suggest to the jury that defense counsel is still immature, in judgment as well as in years.

108. Infra, text accompanying n. 112.

conduce to his safety; and that his judge would wrest no law to destroy him, nor conceal any that would save him." [109] In 1792 the great Erskine referred on the trial of Thomas Paine to "the accused, in whose favor the benevolent principle of English law makes all presumptions, and which commands the very judge to be his counsel." [110] Contemporary opinion surely expected that a judge could not undertake the role of counsel *against* the prisoner. And as we shall now see, oppressive judicial conduct was punishable by one means or another.

IMPEACHABILITY OF OPPRESSIVE JUDICIAL CONDUCT

The corollary of Hamilton's statement that no man "would be willing to stake his life and his estate" before a judge "who had predetermined the case" [111] is that such a judge is unfit to sit in judgment. Earlier Blackstone had stated: "There is yet another . . . crime of deep malignity . . . This is the *oppression* and tyrannical partiality of judges, justices, and other *magistrates* . . . in the administration and under the colour of their office. However, when prosecuted, either by impeachment in parliament, or by information in the court of king's bench (according to the rank of the offenders), it is sure to be severely punished with forfeiture of their offices [and] . . . imprisonment." [112] By "according to the rank of the offenders," Blackstone presumably referred to the fact that lesser judges were indictable whereas justices were subject to impeachment.[113] The

---

109. Plucknett, *Concise History* 247. Chase was aware of the English practice, as his comment during the treason trial of John Fries shows. Fries' counsel had withdrawn from the case because of Chase's high-handed conduct, Wharton 612; and Fries declined other counsel. So Chase said to Fries, "The court will be watchful of you; they will check anything that may injure yourself; they will be your counsel, and give you every assistance and indulgence in their power." Wharton 629. For an index of his "assistance and indulgence" we need no more than his statement to the jury that "Fries was convicted by the jury" on the prior trial of the case, Wharton 635, an outrageously prejudicial statement.
110. Quoted 6 Campbell, *Chancellors* 438. Mark how Mansfield and Eyre interposed as counsel *for* the accused, supra, n. 59.
111. Supra, text accompanying n. 35.
112. 4 Blackstone 141. See Lord Erskine, supra, Chapter V, n. 52.
113. Supra, Chapter II, text accompanying nn. 45–61.

line so drawn had reference to the *mode* of prosecution; it did not constitute a dispensation to Justices for conduct reprehensible in a lesser judge.

At common law lesser judges could be punished by attachment for contempt because of "oppressive, unjust or irregular practice contrary to the obvious rules of natural justice." Thus a judge was "laid by the heels for sitting in judgment in a cause where he himself was lessor of the plaintiff in ejectment." [114] And Bacon's *Abridgment* states that he could be attached "for denying a defendant a copy of the declaration . . . time to make his Defense." [115] The common denominator of these offenses is that they deny a fair trial; and it can hardly be doubted that evidence of prejudgment accompanied by prejudicial rulings and unrelenting harrassment of counsel for one side would have been similarly penalized. Such misconduct, as Blackstone noted, was also indictable in the case of lesser judges and impeachable in Justices. Indeed, conduct that was punishable in a lesser judge could hardly be condoned in a Justice. Among the charges against Justice Berkley was that on the trial of an indictment "he did much discourage counsel," [116] an understatement when applied to Chase's conduct of the Callender trial. Chief Justice Scroggs was charged with "browbeating" witnesses and prejudicing the jury against them by disparaging remarks.[117] Such charges may be generalized under "abuse of power," a misuse of power illustrated by a number of English impeachments.[118] Relying on

---

114. Ibid. at n. 61. See also, Anonymous, 1 Salk. 396, 91 E. R. 343 (1699): Anonymous, 1 Salk. 201, 91 E. R. 180 (1702) (per Holt, C. J.).
115. 1 Bacon, "Attachment" (A) p. 182.
116. Supra, Chapter II, text accompanying n. 67.
117. 8 Howell 163, 171, Articles 2 and 9. These were in the charges of "high misdemeanors" originally lodged by the Commons. An interesting reflection of these standards is to be found in a Colonial case of about the same time: "The grand jury of Philadelphia County in 1686 presented Justice James Claypoole 'for endeavoring by an indirect way to prepossess Judge Moore in a case it was to be tried before him in the provincial court, being by us looked upon to be of a dangerous consequence,' and for 'menacing and abusing the jurors in the trial of John Moon which was an infringement of the rights and properties of the people.' " William Loyd, *The Early Courts of Pennsylvania* 54 (Boston 1910). Cf. the impeachment of Justice Moore, ibid. 59–61.
118. Supra, Chapter II, text accompanying n. 81. The Duke of Suffolk was charged with delaying justice by stopping writs of appeal (private criminal prosecutions) for the deaths of complainants' husbands. 4 Hatsell 60n. Viscount Mordaunt was charged with causing the illegal arrest and detention of Tayleur, 6 Howell 785, 789, 790–791, Art. 5.

Wooddeson's statement of English law, Story said that judges have been impeached for "acting grossly contrary to the duties of their office." [119] Against the background of Blackstone's, Hamilton's and Jefferson's statements, it hardly seems likely that unbiased judges of Chase's own time would have concluded that Chase did not act "grossly contrary" to the duties of his office.

Chase's conduct was not merely an oppressive misuse of power, but in two respects it was illegal as well. The Act of 1789 required of him an oath to administer justice impartially,[120] and that oath imposed upon him a statutory duty to do so.[121] When he sat in judgment on a case that he had prejudged and acted in a clearly prejudiced manner, he acted contrary to that oath and therefore contrary to law. Similarly, the Act required that a jury should be returned "so as shall be most favorable to an impartial trial." [122] Chase's insistence that confessedly biased jurors must serve plainly violated the statutory mandate. Finally, a criminal defendant, said Marshall, had a "right . . . secured by the constitution" to have jurymen who came with "a perfect freedom for previous impressions," and it was clearly the duty of the court to obtain, if possible, men "free from such bias." In seating confessedly biased jurors, Chase violated both his duty and Callender's constitutional right to an "impartial jury." Impeachment, stated Blackstone, was provided so that "no man shall dare to assist the crown in contradiction to the laws of the land." [123] No one, Governor Johnston assured the North Carolina Ratification Convention, "need be afraid that officers who commit oppression will pass with immunity." [124]

The evidence shows that before ever Chase was called

119. Story § 800.
120. Supra, text accompanying n. 37.
121. Compare Marbury v. Madison, 1 Cranch (5 U.S.) 137, 180 (1803): when "a judge swear[s] to discharge his duties agreeably to the constitution," the constitution forms the "rule for his government." Berger, *Congress v. Court* 238.
122. Supra, text accompanying n. 77.
123. 1 Blackstone 244. Speaking for the managers of the Chase impeachment, G. W. Campbell was therefore altogether correct in stating that England employed impeachment "to check the abuses of power in the highest officers" and to punish them "for such acts as were unauthorized, illegal, or oppressive." 14 *Ann Cong.* 330.
124. 4 Elliot 48.

on to preside, he had selected the victim, announced his determination to punish him for his "atrocious" libel, procured his presentment by the grand jury, refused to exclude admittedly biased jurors, identified himself at every step with the prosecution, and employed every means to discredit and disable defense counsel.[125] By the standards of his own day, this was an oppressive misuse of power; and it furnished grounds for impeachment under English law, to which the Founders looked for guidance.

"The sure foundation upon which alone [the judiciary] can rest," said a Chase apologist, "is the confidence of all the people without respect to party or faction in its integrity, its calm reason and its impartial judgment." [126] Chase himself charged a jury that a man who "attempts to destroy the confidence of the people in their officers . . . effectually saps the foundation of the government." [127] By his conduct Chase destroyed confidence in the impartial administration of justice.[128] For he brought flaming prejudice, not "calm reason and impartial judgment," to the trial of Callender. That is the lesson that needs to be drawn from the richly justified attempt to bring him to justice, not that his acquittal represents a triumph over gross partisanship.

---

125. If this has been proved, Warren's statement that Chase was "not prompted by a spirit of persecution and injustice as charged," 1 Warren 282, does not square with the facts, particularly when it is recalled that Chase was an uncurbed Federalist partisan.

126. Humphrey, supra, n. 2 at 846. Justice Frankfurter stated: "Our judicial system is absolutely dependent upon a popular belief that it is as untainted in its workings as the finite limitations of disciplined minds and feelings makes possible." Quoted Philip Kurland, "The Judicial Process," *New York Times*, December 12, 1970, p. 31. In the impeachment of Judge Francis Hopkinson in 1780, the Supreme Executive Council of Pennsylvania stated that it was of "highest importance . . . that the people should have a confidence in the integrity of the Judges." Edmund Hogan, *Pennsylvania State Trials* 58–59 (Philadelphia, 1795). Eighty years later George Ticknor Curtis said, "The position and functions of the judiciary . . . require absolute confidence." 2 G. T. Curtis, *History of the Formation of the Constitution of the United States of America* 246n (New York, 1861).

127. This was Chase's charge in the trial of Thomas Cooper. 3 Beveridge, supra, n. 1 at 35.

128. The "manners and methods" of the "National judges" in "the enforcement of the Sedition Act aroused against them an ever increasing hostility . . . until finally the very name and sight of National judges became obnoxious to most Americans. In short, assaults upon the National Judiciary were made possible chiefly by the conduct of the National judges themselves." Ibid. 29–30.

Chapter IX

THE IMPEACHMENT OF
PRESIDENT ANDREW JOHNSON

HISTORICAL BACKGROUND

More than one hundred years have passed since President Andrew Johnson escaped conviction by one vote, yet the record remains immediately relevant. His impeachment poses an issue which may again confront us: is the President impeachable for violating a statute —for example, an act that prohibits the use of appropriated funds for maintenance of ground troops in Cambodia [1]—if in his judgment it invades his constitutional prerogatives? And Johnson's trial serves as a frightening reminder that in the hands of a passion-driven Congress the process may bring down the very pillars of our constitutional system. To one who considers that impeachment may yet have an important role to play, the record is a sobering admonition against lighthearted resort to such removal of the President.

Some knowledge of the historical background is essential to understanding of the forces that erupted into impeachment. The history of Reconstruction, however, is a "controversial subject;" [2] and an untutored lawyer ventures into its shoals at his peril. At the risk of oversimplification I must nevertheless attempt a brief

---

1. Special Foreign Assistance Act of 1971, Pub. Law 91–652, § 7a, 84 Stat. 1942 (91st Cong. 2d Sess.).
2. Morison 709, which contains an excellent summary of the Reconstruction period. I have relied largely on Eric L. McKitrick, *Andrew Johnson and Reconstruction* (Chicago, 1960); W. R. Brock, *An American Crisis: Congress and Reconstruction 1865–1867* (London, 1963).

sketch of the path that led to the impeachment and trial.

Historians have dispelled the view that either Johnson or the Reconstruction radicals were villains; rather it was their deep commitment to opposing, honestly-held views which set them on a collision course. At the outbreak of the Civil War Johnson was a Democratic Senator from a border state, Tennessee, the only southern Senator to oppose secession.[3] After Lincoln's inauguration and the opening gun at Fort Sumter, he introduced and the Senate adopted a Resolution which was to be the leitmotiv of his subsequent conduct. It stated that the North was not fighting a war of conquest and had no desire to interfere with slavery where it already existed, and that the only aim of the North was to preserve the Union.[4] Tennessee was in great part overrun by the Confederate forces, and when Grant's victories opened western Tennessee, Lincoln made Johnson military governor of Tennessee.[5] His remarkable performance led Lincoln to pick him as Vice President in 1864.[6] Came the assassination of Lincoln, and Johnson was catapulted into the presidency, translated from an actor on a provincial stage to leader of victorious national forces whose goals he did not really comprehend or share.[7]

In its inception a war to "preserve the Union," the protracted conflict had become a struggle to free the slaves. The appalling cost in bloodshed led the North to seek some larger justification than preservation of the Union,[8] just as the Wilsonian generation had to believe that World War I was fought to make the world safe for democracy. Varying as were the shades of opinion in the North as to the desirability of Negro

---

3. Brock 30.
4. Milton Lomask, *Andrew Johnson: President on Trial* 20 (New York, 1960).
5. Ibid. 22.
6. McKitrick 90. Probably the politically sensitive Lincoln was not averse to strengthening the ticket by inclusion of a War Democrat.
7. Brock 29, 160; Lomask 184.
8. The "most profound emotion was conviction that the sacrifice should not be in vain"; the war had "become a war to create a more perfect Union." Brock 168, 2.

suffrage,[9] there was yet a deep commitment to Negro freedom.[10] Lincoln's policy of conciliation leaned towards gradualism; and Johnson's policy, says Samuel Eliot Morison, "was identical with Lincoln's." [11] But where Lincoln had a genius for timing, for compromise and leadership, Johnson altogether lacked Lincoln's sensitive political antennae,[12] was without roots in the Republican party which had elected him, and, as will appear, was indeed temperamentally flawed.[13]

Acting under the Executive power in the period between Lincoln's assassination and the meeting of Congress in December 1865, Johnson had set up provisional civil governments in all of the Confederate states save Texas.[14] A Johnson critic, W. R. Brock, states that "no man could deny that these States were now controlled by men who had undertaken to be loyal to the United States, who had abolished slavery." [15] The new state governments, however, proceeded to enact Black Codes, designed to "keep the Negro 'in his place.' " [16] In the eyes of the North, this was to render its bloody sacrifices vain.[17] Johnson, says a Johnson apologist, "trusted the Southern whites and assumed that left alone they would deal fairly with the Negroes"; he "never fully grasped the impact of the Black Codes on the Northern mind," [18] the feeling that "lives had not been sacrificed to restore the world of 1860." [19] Although Johnson's approach was more humane, Brock considers that "fundamentally, he

9. As late as 1869, Senator Henry Wilson, who voted for Johnson's conviction, stated: "There is not today a square mile in the United States where the advocacy of the equal rights and privileges of those colored men has not been in the past and is not now unpopular." C. G. 40. III. 672 (1869). Negro suffrage "was unacceptable to the bulk of the [Republican] party." Brock 97, 285; McKitrick 55–58. See infra, n. 21.
10. Brock 3–4.
11. Morison 707, 715; Lomask 54, 56; C. Vann Woodward, *Reunion and Reaction* 14 (Boston, 1951). Seeking to soften the effect of Johnson's bitter White House speech of February 22, 1866, Senator John Sherman said on February 26th, "Johnson's plan has met the approval of the Cabinet of Abraham Lincoln . . . he adopted the policy of President Lincoln *in haec verba.*" Cong. Globe 39, I, App. 126.
12. McKitrick 135.
13. Brock 31; McKitrick 90.
14. Morison 711–12.
15. Brock 96.
16. Morison 712–13, 707, 709; Lomask 134; McKitrick 169.
17. Brock 2, 160.
18. Lomask 145.
19. Brock 160; Lomask 184.

agreed with [the Southerners] about the place of the negro in society." [20] Certainly he expressed fear of a war between the races if Negroes were too quickly enfranchised; [21] and he vetoed the establishment of Negro suffrage in the District of Columbia, which did not invade his cherished doctrine of states rights.[22]

When the Congress assembled in December 1865, they found Southern representatives knocking at the door—among them Alexander Stephens, the Vice President, and other high officials of the Confederate states —who seemed to epitomize in Northern eyes "the unchastened spirit of rebellion." [23] The emancipation of the Negro had rendered inoperative the constitutional provision that limited the count of slaves to three-fifths in apportioning representation, thus increasing Southern strength in Congress.[24] To admit the Southerners would enable Northern and Southern Democrats to block all moves for effective enfranchisement of the blacks.[25] At the same time it would break the grip of the Republican party on the administration, as Thaddeus Stevens frankly recognized.[26] With equal candor he said that the Southern states "ought never to be recognized as valid States, until the Constitution shall be amended . . . as to secure perpetual ascendancy" with the aid of Negro suffrage

---

20. Brock 38; McKitrick 204.
21. Lomask 219. On February 22, 1866, Senator Sherman stated: "I say with the President, that to ask of him to extend to four millions of these people the right of suffrage when we have not the courage to extend it to those within our control, when our States . . . have refused to do it, is to make of him an unreasonable demand." C. G. 39. I. App. 128.
22. Lomask 219. Brock 254, mistakenly considers that the veto "had been provided to prevent clear infractions of the Constitution, not to decide points on which honest men might differ and the majority had spoken." One of the Framers, James McHenry, explained to the Maryland legislature that the veto was given "its present form, in the hope that a revision of the subject and the objections offered against it might contribute in some instances to perfect those regulations that inattention, or other motives had at first rendered imperfect." 3 Farrand 144, 148. See also the statements of George Mason and James Wilson, 2 Farrand 78, 73. For vetoes on nonconstitutional grounds prior to the Civil War, see Edward S. Corwin, *The President: Office and Powers* 338–39 (New York, 3d ed. 1948).
23. Brock 36; "they expected to be welcomed back into Congress as though nothing had happened." McKitrick 178.
24. Brock 21; Article I, § 2 (3).
25. Brock 6, 114.
26. "With the basis unchanged, the eighty-three southern members, with the Democrats that will in the best times be elected from the North, will always give them a majority in Congress and in the Electoral College. They will at the very first election take possession of the White House and the halls of Congress." C. G. 39. I. 74.

to the Republican party.[27] The Republican North had not fought and conquered rebellion in order to surrender the fruits of victory to the unrepentant rebels. So, as "sole judge" of the "qualifications" of its members, Congress refused to admit the Southern applicants.[28] It embarked on a series of measures to assure protection of the Negroes, a Freedmen's Bureau Bill to aid in the relief of ex-slaves and to protect civil rights, and a Civil Rights Bill to effectuate the principles implicit in both the Freedmen's Bill and in the Thirteenth Amendment.[29] These bills were not the handiwork of radicals but were sponsored by the moderate chairman of the Senate Judiciary Committee, Lyman Trumbull of Illinois [30]—whose attempts, joined by other influential moderate Republicans, Senators William P. Fessenden, J. W. Grimes, and John Sherman, to achieve an accommodation with Johnson proved unavailing.[31] Johnson's vetoes threw the moderate Republicans, who occupied a "swing" position, into the arms of the Radicals.[32]

Johnson stood on high ground. He took at face value the earlier slogan that no state could secede from the indissoluble Union. Hence despite attempted secession it remained a state, with all its rights and privileges; from which it necessarily followed that in the absence of the "unrepresented" eleven Southern states no action by Congress that impaired State Rights could

---

27. Morison 714; Brock 100.
28. In our own time Powell v. McCormack, 395 U.S. 486 (1969), decided that the power of exclusion is confined to the three standards contained in Article I, § 3 (3), residence, age and citizenship. That decision is solidly anchored in the records of the Convention. James Wilson stated, "this particular power would constructively exclude any other power of regulating qualifications." 2 Farrand 251; see also Dickinson, ibid. 123. Charles Warren, *The Making of the Constitution* 423–34 n. 1 (Cambridge, Mass. 1937), quotes Hamilton to the effect that "The qualifications . . . are defined and fixed in the Constitution; and are unalterable by the Legislature." See also Warren, ibid. at 422.
29. McKitrick 278–79.
30. Ibid.; Brock 105.
31. McKitrick 76, 274; Brock 110. See Trumbull's speech after the vetoes. McKitrick 291–92.
32. McKitrick 11–12, 291–92. Some time later Representatives Godlove S. Orth of Indiana and Shelby Cullom of Illinois sought to explore the possibility of a general reconciliation with Johnson. Cullom later wrote that Johnson gave them to understand that they "were on a fool's errand and that he would not yield. We went away, and naturally joined the extreme radicals in the House, always voting with them afterwards." McKitrick 324.

have constitutional validity.[33] On the other hand Congress, by Article I, §8(15), was empowered to "suppress insurrections"; and by Article IV, §4, the United States was directed "to guarantee to every State in this Union a republican form of government." Under this guarantee, the Supreme Court had held in 1849, "it rests with Congress to decide what government is the established one in a State," and it concluded that Congress' decision "is binding on every other department of the government." [34] Inferentially the Court differentiated between a state and its government; [35] it was therefore for Congress to determine whether the "government" of a rebellious state was entitled to recognition. Thus although the question what was a "republican form of government" was tricky,[36] the Congress too had a constitutional position. When Congress sought to advance the Fourteenth Amendment, this also was opposed by Johnson on the same ground that no valid action could be taken in the absence of the eleven unrepresented states. He ignored the fact that their presence would render such measures altogether impossible,[37] and that he himself had "violated" State Rights by insistence upon ratification of the Thirteenth Amendment by the rebel states before the military

---

33. In his message to Congress of December 1865, Johnson stated: "The true theory is that all pretended acts of secession were, from the beginning, null and void . . . The States attempting to secede placed themselves in a condition where . . . their functions [were] suspended but not destroyed." David M. Dewitt, *The Impeachment and Trial of Andrew Johnson* 29 (New York, 1903). See also McKitrick 289; Brock 113, 148. In his veto message Johnson stated: "As eleven states are not at this time represented in either branch of Congress, it would seem to be [the President's] duty . . . to present their just claims to Congress," Brock 120, thus in substance representing himself as the champion of the South against Congressional assaults.

34. Luther v. Borden, 7 How. (48 U.S.) 1, 42.

35. Chief Justice Chase stated in Texas v. White, 7 Wall. (74 U.S.) 700, 725 (1868), that a state entered into an "indissoluble union"; that attempts at secession were "absolutely null"; but he drew a distinction between the state and the wrongful acts of its government. Ibid. 730. For an earlier statement; in 1865, of this view of Chase, see McKitrick 115.

36. "It was argued that a State which disenfranchised large numbers of citizens was not republican, and that the national government had therefore the right to insist that it should become 'republican' before it was recognized as loyal." Brock 269. In terms of suffrage, that applied no less to the North. And the Framers indicated that the existence of slavery within a State was not incompatible with a "republican form of government" for they provided for the count of non-free persons on a three-fifths basis and foreclosed the prohibition of the importation of slaves before 1808. Article I § 2 (3) and § 9 (1).

37. McKitrick 357; Brock 148, 6. There was an "overwhelming majority, in every Southern legislature, against the Fourteenth Amendment." Brock 182, 183.

would turn over administration to elected state officials.[38]

There is no doubt about Johnson's uprightness and honesty;[39] he had an "extreme reverence for the Constitution," an "almost hypnotic determination to follow what he conceived as its spirit and letter."[40] But there was no give in the man; he never appreciated that the other side could also have a tenable, respectable position; and as Eric McKitrick remarks, he "never understood that he was expected to bargain with leading senators at all."[41] He was impervious to counsel, whether by moderate Republicans who sought to build a bridge to the party or by his own Cabinet.[42] Chief Justice Chase recorded that he vainly counseled Johnson against removal of Secretary of War Stanton in order to avoid exciting the nation; Johnson, said Chase, was in fact unaware of the depth of "the feeling against him."[43] When the break came with the Republican party because of his vetoes of the Freedmen's Bureau and Civil Rights Bills,[44] he was cut off from the party that elected him; and in the election of November 1866 his policy suffered a stunning defeat.[45] Well could Congress conclude that the overwhelming victory gave it a clear mandate to go forward with its policy.[46]

Meanwhile stories of atrocities suffered by Negroes at the hands of Southern whites, of the failure of white justice to Blacks, continued to flow North.[47] It seemed as if the ringing endorsement of congressional policy at the polls made no difference in Southern behavior;[48] and before long even the moderate Republicans came

38. Dewitt 29–30; McKitrick 92; Lomask 86, 98.
39. McKitrick 4; Brock 30.
40. McKitrick 93.
41. Ibid. 318.
42. Ibid. 137, 312; Brock 31, 108–09; Lomask 157.
43. McKitrick 498–99, n. 20.
44. Ibid. 274–325.
45. Ibid. 447; Brock 168. Lomask 236, remarks, "Here was a President cut off from organized political support, repudiated by the people and opposed by at least sixty per cent of the press."
46. McKitrick 448; Brock 168.
47. McKitrick 449, 457–59; Brock 135. A *cause célèbre* was that of the Virginian, Dr. James L. Watson, who killed a Negro for having accidentally inflicted about fifty cents worth of damage on his carriage while passing it on a narrow road, an insult to the doctor's wife. Five justices of the peace, sitting as an "examining court" acquitted him. Thereupon he was tried and found guilty of murder by a military commission. Johnson ordered Watson released; the preceding trial was "final." McKitrick 458–59.
48. McKitrick 457.

to "accept the necessity of some form of military rule for the South." [49] The upshot was a Reconstruction Bill which divided the South into military districts, empowering the commanders to protect civil rights and to set up military courts if the state courts were inadequate.[50] Ignoring the "existing violence and terrorism," Johnson vetoed this Bill also, in part on the ground that State Rights were being invaded because the Bill forced upon the Southern states Negro suffrage which they would not adopt of their own free will.[51] Since administration of the act fell to the President, before long, fortified by an interpretive opinion of the Attorney General,[52] "he began interfering with the efforts of the federal commanders" to put the act into effect.[53] Johnson also continued in his opposition to the Fourteenth Amendment, and indeed virtually advised Alabama against ratification.[54] Not unjustifiably the Radicals accused Johnson of inciting the South to resistance.[55]

The key to enforcement of military reconstruction was in the hands of the Secretary of War and in the concomitant control of military commanders.[56] The Secretary, Edwin M. Stanton, was a holdover from

---

49. Ibid. 476.
50. McKitrick 448–85; Brock 190–91; Lomask 208–209; Dewitt 199–201.
51. Brock 199–200; cf. Lomask 207. In Georgia v. Stanton, 6 Wall. (73 U.S.) 50, 76–77 (1867), the Supreme Court held that whether Congress may by the Reconstruction Acts "totally abolish the existing State government" of a defeated Confederate state and supplant it by military occupation is a matter of "political jurisdiction."
52. Dewitt 224.
53. McKitrick 493. In the words of his apologist, Lomask 240, Johnson believed that military domination "should be tempered as much as possible in practice by instructions emanating from [the army's] constitutional head."
54. McKitrick 471–472, 449; Brock 148, 173.
55. At the trial Manager Williams charged that Johnson "fostered disaffection and discontent throughout the lately revolted States." *The Trial of Andrew Johnson, President of the United States, Cong. Globe* (40th Cong. 2d Sess., 1868) Supplement 334 (hereafter cited as "Trial"). See also Senator Frederick T. Frelinghuysen, ibid. 522; Manager George S. Boutwell, ibid. 285; cf. McKitrick 168–212, 449.
56. Boutwell said, "there was no possibility of his obtaining the control of the War Department and of the Army unless he could disregard . . . the act of regulating the tenure . . . passed March 2, 1867." Trial 284. Senator Orris S. Ferry, who voted Johnson "guilty," stated that "possession of the Department of War would confer vast influence either in favor of or against the whole system of reconstruction adopted by Congress, according to the views of the possessor." Trial 452. In a word, the Cabinet minister had to be responsible to Congress, not to the President. But, stated the Supreme Court, the "secretary of war is the regular constitutional organ of the president, for the administration of the military establishment of the nation." United States v. Eliason, 16 Peters (41 U.S.) 291, 302 (1842).

Lincoln's first term.[57] By the Radicals' own testimony, he had close ties with them; [58] he "sneaked out cabinet secrets to the Radicals," [59] at a time when Radicals and the President were pursuing divergent policies and relations were badly strained. Critics of Johnson notice Stanton's "reputation for duplicity" and his "defective loyalty"; [60] and that he "conferred with various Republican leaders to draft yet one more Reconstruction Act," [61] designed to put an end to Johnson's obstructive interpretations of the earlier acts. He also had covertly framed that section of the Army Appropriation Act of March 2, 1867, which would oblige the President to transmit all orders through the General in Chief, who could not be removed without Senate consent.[62] Further to tie Johnson's hands, a provision of the Tenure of Office Act of March 2, 1867, aimed to make removal of the Secretary of War dependent upon the Senate's consent.[63] But Stanton had become a thorn in Johnson's side, and finally Johnson removed him, statute or no. At last Congress had a nail on which to hang an impeachment.[64]

Up to this point, one finds it hard, but for the removal of Stanton, to sympathize with Johnson. He might well have followed the line suggested by his Secretary of the Navy, Gideon Welles (whom McKitrick terms "one of the narrowest and most rigid minds of the entire period"),[65] to loyalist Governor

---

57. For extended discussion of Stanton, see Dewitt 241–284.
58. Ibid. 243. According to Senator Henry Wilson, Stanton "put himself into communication with the Republicans in Congress, and kept them well informed of what was going on in the councils of the administration." Ibid. 255, and see ibid. 270.
59. Morison 715; Lomask 80, 244.
60. Brock 208–209; McKitrick 495.
61. Brock 209; McKitrick 495.
62. Dewitt 202n.; Lomask 239; see generally Brock 208; McKitrick 482n.
63. Act of March 2, 1867, ch. 154, 14 Stat. 430 (39th Cong. 2d Sess.). Brock 208 states: "Before the Thirty-Ninth Congress dissolved it had done its best to tie the hands of the President so that he had no option but to execute the will of Congress."
McKitrick 495 states: "The act had grown directly out of the wholesale removals from rank-and-file federal offices made by Johnson both during and after the election campaign of 1866. It was designed primarily to protect Republican office holders from executive retaliation." Section 1 was devoted to this purpose. For the history of the Act and of the proviso dealing with members of the Cabinet, see Dewitt 180–199.
64. For three prior, abortive attempts to bring impeachment proceedings, see McKitrick 491–504; Dewitt 358–388; for the fourth and final impeachment development, see McKitrick 504–506.
65. McKitrick 517.

Pease of Texas. Pease had complained about the hostility of Texans to Unionist men and principles, and Welles counseled: " 'Let the people decide.' And if the people chose a government, which Pease disliked, then he must be 'patient, forbearing, submit to the majority. Do not organize against them and keep up antagonism.' " [66]

Yet there were extenuating circumstances. As military governor of Tennessee, Johnson had learned at first hand "the terrible difficulty of coercing a hostile state," and he feared "the great dangers of indefinite military government." [67] If, as Brock concludes, the "restoration of the Southern States was not enough without a reconstruction of Southern minds," the Radicals had taken on an all but impossible task. [68] Bayonets can produce sullen subservience but they cannot change minds. The North was to learn that "social revolution such as Congress intended the reconstruction of the South to be, cannot be accomplished except by overwhelming force applied mercilessly over a long period of time." [69] For merciless force the North had no stomach, and so "the South succeeded in wearing down Northern willingness to apply even limited force." [70] McKitrick, who lays bare Johnson's short-

66. Brock 187–188.
67. McKitrick 138, 255. Johnson saw Federal troops in the South "as the ultimate sanction behind the authority of the United States, not as agents for the day to day work of police and justice. There was thus a good deal of practical common-sense behind his State rights view. The enforcement of the law must depend on the will of the local community." Brock 160. "Moderate Republicans had insisted that the existing governments in the South must be allowed to initiate the process of Reconstruction . . . because they knew instinctively that the stability of Reconstruction would be enhanced if they did not assume responsibility for it." Brock 199. In the midst of the trial, Chief Justice Chase wrote: "I do not believe in military domination any more than I do in the slaveholding oligarchy; nor do I believe that anything has been accomplished by military supremacy in the rebel states that could not have been, as well, if not better accomplished by civil supremacy, authorized and regulated by Congress, with military subordination." But he still preferred "military domination for a time . . . to any such plan as that proposed by the President." Letter to Dr. J. E. Snodgrass, March 16, 1868, Robert B. Warden, *Life of Salmon Portland Chase* 682 (Cincinnati, 1874).
68. Brock 14.
69. Morison 722. Speaking to the Fugitive Slave Act in 1852, Senator Charles Sumner said, "it lacks that essential support in the public conscience of the States, where it is to be enforced . . . without which any law must become a dead letter . . . a law which could be enforced only by bayonets, was no law." *Cong. Globe* 32. I. App. 1111.
70. Morison 722. Writing of the postwar occupation of Japan, Dean Acheson, *Present at the Creation* 428 (New York, 1969), stated that a "free society cannot long steel itself to dominate another people by sheer force."

comings, acknowledges that of the two policies, "it was Johnson's which contained the greatest long-range wisdom," and that "few American scholars . . . will ever find very much to praise in Radical Reconstruction." [71]

It was high tragedy that by an accident of history a man whose will ran counter to that of the party which had elected him, and ultimately to that of the great majority in the North, became President at a time of tremendous national crisis. But once President, he was by the Constitution entitled to exercise his own judgment, which in the event proved to be wiser than that of the majority. More than once President and Congress have had conflicting policies. But though "other Presidents have felt that their constitutional duty compelled them to resist the will of Congress . . . a wiser and more flexible man might have discovered a course of action aimed at reconciliation rather than at emphasizing the unfortunate divisions in the nation." [72] A President, however, is not to be removed merely for differing with Congress. Such differences were contemplated as part of the checks and balances of the Constitution, "designed to blunt the impact of majority rule." [73] In the oft-quoted words of Justice Brandeis, "The doctrine of the separation of powers was adopted by the Convention of 1787, not to promote efficiency but to preclude the exercise of arbitrary power. The purpose was, not to avoid friction, but, by means of inevitable friction incident to the distribution of the governmental powers among three departments, to save the people from autocracy." [74]

Nothing is clearer than the intention of the Founders to repudiate and reject "legislative omnipotence." [75] Notwithstanding, the Radical leaders, Morison justly

71. McKitrick 6, 328; Brock 304. Morison 720, regrets "that the magnanimous policy of Lincoln was not long followed"; see ibid. 725, 705.
72. Brock 175.
73. Ibid. 249. James Iredell, leader of the struggle for adoption in North Carolina, and later a Justice of the Supreme Court, rejected impeachment of the President "for want of judgment," even if there was a "difference of opinion" between him and his constituents, and a fortiori between him and Congress. 4 El iot 126. As George Nicholas stated in the Virginia Convention, "We do not trust our liberty to a particular branch: one branch is a check on the other." 3 Elliot 242.
74. Myers v. United States, 272 U.S. 52, 293 (1926), dissenting opinion.
75. Supra, Chapter II, n. 2; Berger, Congress v. Court 10-12.

states, "by a series of unsurpations . . . intended to make the majority in Congress the ultimate judge of its own powers, and the President a mere chairman of a cabinet responsible to Congress." [76] Impeachment would not merely clear the road of an obstructive President, making possible the succession of a dyed-in-the-wool Radical, Ben Wade,[77] but it would set a precedential seal on Radical aims.[78] "When impeachment finally arrived," Brock states, "every one accepted the fact that the breach of the Tenure of Office Act was not the real cause of the impeachment; it was necessary to prove a specific breach of the law but the reason was the need to demonstrate that a President could not pursue a policy rejected by the legislature." [79] Let the inimitable Ben Butler, leading Manager for the prosecution, tell us in his own words: the "momentous question, here and now, is raised whether the *presidential office itself (if it has the prerogatives and power claimed for it) ought, in fact, to exist as a part of the constitutional government of a free people.*" [80] This invitation to rewrite the Constitution was not merely the unguarded remark of a prosecutor; it expressed a view shared by Stevens, and it was reiterated by Frederick T. Frelinghuysen, who voted "guilty": "The issue joined now to be settled

---

76. Morison 720. "The establishment of senatorial control over dismissals . . . might be used to extend the control of Congress over policy. It might be extended further and establish some degree of Cabinet responsibility to the legislature." Brock 258–61. Compare Stevens, infra, nn. 79, 216.

77. In the House Ebon C. Ingersoll had prophesied, "I shall for one be grievously disappointed if, within ten days from this time, honest old Ben Wade is not President of the United States." Dewitt 360. After passage of the Tenure-of-Office Act, said Morison 720, "The next move was to dispose of Johnson by impeachment, so that Radical Ben Wade, president pro tem of the Senate, would succeed to his office and title." See also Brock 75; Lomask 236–237.

78. Senator Richard Yates, who voted "guilty," stated: "constructions of our Constitution and laws here given and precedents established by these proceedings will be quoted as standard authorities in all similar trials hereafter." Trial 484.

79. Brock 260. In his argument for the prosecution, Thaddeus Stevens stated, "To obey the commands of the sovereign power of the nation [Congress], and to see that others should obey them, was [Johnson's] whole duty." Trial 321. Earlier Stevens stated in the House, "Andrew Johnson must learn he is your servant and that as Congress shall order he must obey." Corwin, supra, n. 22 at 28. Manager John A. Bingham said of Johnson's claim of right "to construe the Constitution for himself, to determine the validity of your laws for himself . . . That is the whole case; it is all there is to it." Trial 393. It was seen, states Brock 261, "that a denial to the President of a right to use his own interpretation of the Constitution as an instrument of policy would mean legislative supremacy."

80. Trial 32.

is, where is lodged the *ultimate* power of the nation— in one man or in the representatives of the people." [81] The Radicals were playing for high stakes.

THE TRIAL

Introductory

The current revulsion against Johnson may lead some to reject Morison's judgment that the Johnson impeachment "was one of the most disgraceful episodes in our history." [82] "No valid ground," he states, "legal or otherwise, existed for impeachment." [83] McKitrick views it as a "great act of ill-directed passion . . . supported by little else." [84] Yet the legal issues are not so easily dispatched. What made the trial "disgraceful" was not that the charges were altogether without color of law but that the proceeding reeked with unfairness, with palpable prejudgment of guilt. The filing of impeachment charges against a President, however unjustified his differences with Congress, does not place him outside the pale.

The tone of the proceedings was set by the bold claims asserted in his opening statement by Benjamin F. Butler. The Senate, he stated, does not sit "as a court" and "has none of the attributes of a judicial court"; "you are bound by no law," he told the Senate, "you are a law unto yourselves." [85] Now it is true that Parliament was a law unto itself, even in cases of treason. But the narrow definition of treason by the Framers made it impossible for Congress to follow

---

81. Trial 522. Stevens' biographer stated: "Caught in the meshes of the check-and-balance system of the American constitutional government, he now [January 1867] showed not the slightest hesitation in tossing the whole thing overboard. He would redefine the power relationship in the government in his own terms; and these terms were: first, that Congress was to be the sole sovereign power, and second, that none of this power was to be shared with the President or the Court." Fawn M. Brodie, *Thaddeus Stevens: Scourge of the South* 292 (New York, 1959).

82. Morison 720. The classic account of the trial is David M. Dewitt, *The Impeachment and Trial of Andrew Johnson* (New York, 1903). Although it is charged with sympathy for Johnson, I found it to be scrupulously accurate in citation and reasonable in inferences.

83. Morison 721; Arthur M. Schlesinger, Sr., *Political and Social History of the United States* 242 (New York, 1929).

84. McKitrick 506; see also Brock 277.

85. Trial 30.

in the path of Parliament. And "high crimes and misdemeanors" had been adopted because the words were thought to have a technical, limited meaning, and precisely so that the President would not be left at the "pleasure of the Senate." [86] The door to illimitable power was barred.

So too, the text of the Constitution refutes the claim that the Senate does not sit as a court. Article 1, §3(6), provides that the Senate "shall have the sole power to try all impeachments"; Article II, §4, provides for a removal upon "conviction"; both imply judicial trial. Then too, the Article I, §3(3), provision limiting "judgment in cases of impeachment," and the Article III, §2(3), provision that "the trial of all crimes, except in the cases of impeachment, shall be by jury," again imports judicial trial. The implications of these provisions were summed up in Hamilton's reference to the Senate in "their judicial character as a court for the trial of impeachments." [87] In the very first impeachment, that of Senator William Blount in 1797, the Senate stated that it was "directed by the Constitution" to sit as "a High Court"; and the Senate sat as a court in the impeachment of Justice Samuel Chase in 1805.[88]

The importance of the fact that the Senate sits as a "court for the trial" of impeachment was recognized by Butler: if "this body here is a court in any manner . . . then we agree that many, if not all, the analogies of the procedures of courts must obtain; that the common law incidents of a trial in court must have place; that you may be bound in your proceedings and adjudications by the rules and precedents of the common . . . law, that the interest, bias, or preconceived opinions or affinities to the party of the judges may be open to inquiry." Jefferson, when Vice President, had embodied this view in the manual of practice he drew up for the Senate.[89]

It is the essence of unfairness that a trial, to borrow from Hamilton, takes place "under the auspices of judges who had predetermined" the guilt of the ac-

86. Supra, Chapter I; Chapter II, text accompanying nn. 5, 106–108, 158.
87. *Federalist* No. 65 at 423.
88. Blount: Wharton 257; Chase: 14 *Ann. Cong.* 92–98.
89. Trial 30. For Jefferson, supra, Chapter IV, text accompanying n. 219.

cused.[90] Patrick Henry proudly boasted in the Virginia Ratification Convention that "elsewhere," not here, people "may be tried by the most partial powers, by their most implacable enemies, and be sentenced . . . with all the forms of a fair trial." [91] Judge Edmund Pendleton said in that Convention, "it is unconstitutional to condemn any man without a fair trial. Such a condemnation is repugnant to the principles of justice." [92] That principle was expressed in the Sixth Amendment provision for trial "by an impartial jury." And in one of its first acts, §8 of the Judiciary Act of 1789, the First Congress required of a Justice an oath "impartially" to perform his duties.[93]

What, it may be asked, has all this to do with impeachment? Were not the Peers, as the Managers insisted, immune from inquiry into their bias or partiality? That immunity derived from the proposition that "a peer of the realm might not be challenged." [94] But that ancient practice can hardly be reconciled with the spirit of our constitutional guarantees. It was given to the Senate to sit in judgment, Hamilton explained, because "what other body would be likely . . . to preserve, unawed and uninfluenced, the necessary impartiality between an *individual* accused, and the *representatives of the people,* his accuser." [95] The Senate was made judge, not in order to lessen the guarantees, but to insure that the accused would not be crushed by the oppressive weight of the House of Representatives. The President, no less than the lowliest citizen, is entitled to the protection of due process, and the essence of due process is fair play.[95a] To conclude that the President on trial is without guarantees that shield the meanest offender would be to render the Constitution contemptible.

---

90. *Federalist* No. 65 at 427; quoted supra, Chapter VIII, text accompanying n. 35.
91. 3 Elliot 516.
92. Ibid. 236.
93. Quoted supra, text accompanying n. 37.
94. Butler: Trial 30; Bingham, ibid. 392. The "peer" quotation appears ibid. 30, and is taken from Trial of the Duke of Somerset, 1 Howell 521 (1551).
95. *Federalist* No. 65 at 425.
95a. Supra, Chapter III, text accompanying nn. 86–88; Galvan v. Press, 347 U.S. 522, 530 (1954).

"It is impossible," said a Framer, William Davie, in the North Carolina Convention, that "there should be impartiality when a party affected is to be the judge." [96] The Senators, as they well knew, were sitting in judgment on their own cause. Before the trial, Thaddeus Stevens had recalled to his hearers in the House debate on the articles of impeachment that the Senate had voted four times in favor of the Act; he had said, "Let me see the recreant who will now dare to tread back upon his steps and vote upon the other side." [97] Gracelessly he pressed the point home in his closing argument before the Senate: "Wretched man [this offspring of assassination], standing at bay, surrounded by a cordon of living men, each with the ax of an executioner uplifted for his just punishment. Every Senator now trying him . . . voted for this same resolution, pronouncing his solemn doom. Will any of them vote for his acquittal on the ground of its unconstitutionality?" No Senator, he menacingly added, would "suffer himself to be tortured on the gibbet of everlasting obloquy. How long and dark would be the track of infamy which must mark his name, and that of his posterity!" [98] Suppose that a Negro charged with rape were to be tried by a jury composed of men who outside of court had already declared him guilty: would it not be a lynching bee though garbed in "all the forms of a fair trial"? Could anything more starkly reveal prejudgment than Stevens' audacious reminder to the Senate that they stood as a cordon, "each with the ax of an executioner uplifted"? Minimally, such patent disqualification should have led the Senate to welcome submission of the key issue—the meaning and constitutionality of the Tenure Act—to the courts; but judicial "interference" was roundly rejected. For Senator George H. Williams and others the issue was "res adjudicata." [99] Since each Senator who quarreled with

---

96. 4 Elliot. See supra, Chapter VIII, n. 35.
97. *Cong. Globe* 40. II. 1612.
98. Trial 323. For Logan the issue was "res adjudicata." Ibid. 261.
99. Ibid. 458. "Now," continued Williams, "after these proceedings which go upon the express ground that Mr. Stanton is within the provisions of the tenure-of-office act, we are asked to eat up our own words and resolutions and stultify ourselves by holding that the act did not apply to

Johnson had voted repeatedly that the Tenure Act was constitutional, he was sitting in judgment on his own cause, a situation which earlier had led the exquisitely sensitive Senator Charles Sumner to condemn Senator John Stockton for voting against his own malodorous unseating.[100]

Although an effort to compress into a chapter a tale which sprawls across three volumes of a printed record [101] cannot linger on cumulative evidence, a few added details must flesh out the charge of unfairness. Consider the indecent haste with which defense counsel were forced to trial. The House agreed to the articles of impeachment on March 3, 1868, presented them to the Senate on March 5, and the court was convened on March 13. Defense counsel requested forty days to prepare an answer to the articles but were allowed ten, to March 23.[102] A replication was filed by the Managers on March 24; [103] the defense requested thirty days from the filing for preparation of their case, but the Senate set the opening of the trial for March 30.[104] This was extraordinary short shrift. Preparation for the trial had long been under way in the House; Judge William Lawrence, a member of the Judiciary Committee, had published a comprehensive article in 1867 to show that impeachment did not require a criminal offense; [105] a brief prepared by Lawrence was filed by Butler at the close of his opening statement, and Butler acknowledged his indebtedness "to the exhaustive and

---

Mr. Stanton." Ibid. 459. Senator Alexander C. Cattell's opinion said of the "constitutionality" of the act, "I cannot consent to even consider this a debatable point. The Senate has solemnly adjudicated this question for itself on four distinct occasions." Ibid. 526. To the same effect, Senators Charles Sumner and James W. Patterson. Ibid. 468, 509. Plainly, these Senators, though sitting as judges, could not rise above the commitments they made as legislators, underscoring the wisdom of the rule that precludes one from sitting in judgment on his own cause.

100. Dewitt 75. Ben Wade suffered from an additional disqualification: as potential successor to Johnson if he were removed, Wade was precisely under the same disability as led the Framers to displace the Vice President as presiding officer upon a trial of the President—his interest in the succession. Supra, Chapter III, n. 56. For details of the "not very creditable" Stockton incident, see Brock 114n; McKitrick 319, 323; Dewitt 66–79.

101. *Trial of Andrew Johnson,* 3 vols. (Washington, D.C., U.S. Government Printing Office, 1868).

102. Trial 3, 6, 8.

103. Ibid. 28.

104. Ibid. 23, 29.

105. Lawrence, "The Law of Impeachment," 6 *Am. L. Reg.* (N. S.) 641 (1867).

learned labors" of Lawrence.[106] Thus, as Thomas A. R. Nelson of defense counsel said, the Managers "were armed at all points and ready to contest the cause," whereas defense counsel (gathered from all points of the compass) "were suddenly summoned from [their] professional pursuits," [107] which were far removed from the complex, highly specialized learning involved in impeachment.

Again, in the midst of the trial, Henry Stanbery of defense counsel was taken ill, and William M. Evarts asked for an adjournment of from 24 to 48 hours, or at least for the balance of the day, on the plea that Stanbery was responsible for that portion of the proof which was then in process of presentation.[108] Butler's response to a request ordinarily honored without demur was a tirade akin to his waving of the "bloody shirt": "while we are waiting for the Attorney General to get well . . . numbers of our fellow-citizens are being murdered day by day. There is not a man here who does not know that the moment justice is done on this great criminal these murders will cease." The Senate adjourned until noon of the next day.[109]

Prejudicial rulings by the Senate on admissibility of evidence stud the record, overruling those of Chief Justice Chase. For example, Johnson had stated in a communication to the Senate on December 12, 1867, introduced in evidence by the Managers, that "every member of my Cabinet advised me that the proposed [Tenure Act] was unconstitutional. All spoke without doubt or reservation; but Mr. Stanton's condemnation of the law was the most elaborate and emphatic." After detailing Stanton's citation of authorities—he had served as Buchanan's Attorney General—Stanton, Johnson continued, "advised me that it was my duty to defend the power of the President from usurpation,

106. Trial 29, 41.
107. Ibid. 286.
108. Ibid. 174.
109. Ibid. 208, 209. Manager Williams embellished this bloody theme, referring to "the loyal men whose carcasses were piled in carts like those of swine, with the gore dripping from the wheels, in that holocaust of blood, that carnival of murder which was enacted in New Orleans." Remember, he intoned, "that while your loyal brethren are falling from day to day in southern cities by the assassin's knife" etc., etc. Ibid. 335.

and to veto the law." [110] Evarts offered to prove the truth of this statement by the other Cabinet members who were present at the meeting.[111] The offer tended to show that Johnson's reliance on the advice of his Cabinet negated a wrongful intention in disobeying the act; it placed the Senate in the awkward position of attacking Johnson's "unlawful" disobedience of a statute, which Stanton, the object of congressional solicitude, had himself declared unconstitutional. The Chief Justice held the evidence admissible but was overruled by the Senate.[112] In a letter written the next day, April 19, 1868, to Gerrit Smith, Chase said, "I was greatly disappointed and pained [by this exclusion] . . . The vote, I fear, indicated a purpose which, if carried into effect, will not satisfy the American people, unless they are prepared to admit that Congress is above the Constitution." [113]

With Stevens, Sumner was one of the great actors in the spectacle, utterly unfitted by his fanatical commitment to sit in judgment on Johnson. At about the time the impeachment proceedings were pending in the House, Sumner called Johnson "the enemy of his country" and charged that he "has become the successor of Jefferson Davis." "What sort of a trial," chided Senator Reverdy Johnson, would Johnson have at Sumner's hands "should he be impeached for being an enemy of his country?" [114] In his opinion on the case, Sumner poured scorn on the "technicalities, which are so proverbial in the courts," dismissed "the quibbles of lawyers on mere questions of form," and refused "to shut out from view that long list of transgressions explaining and coloring the final acts of defiance." [115]

---

110. Ibid. 51–52.
111. Ibid. 225, 231.
112. Ibid. 231, 232. Compare the attempt to exclude the testimony of General W. T. Sherman, infra, text accompanying nn. 230–231. While the Managers were pressing the defense to get on with the case they themselves consumed "hour after hour," reported in "long columns," with captious objections to evidence. Evarts, ibid. 209. Compare the conduct of Lord Mansfield, supra, Chapter VIII, n. 59.
113. Warden, supra, n. 67 at 685.
114. *Cong. Globe* 39. II. 525, 542; ibid. 544. On another occasion Sumner declared, "Because the President may be impeached the Senate is not obliged to be silent with regard to him." Senator Sherman replied, "shall we, the judges . . . decide beforehand that the President ought to be removed before the House of Representatives have laid any indictment?" Ibid. I. 733.
115. Trial 463, 474. Sumner was not alone in going outside the issues.

And following Stevens' lead, he reminded the Senate of the "execration" heaped upon the Supreme Court in consequence of the *Dred Scott* decision, and asserted that "the present trial, like that in the Supreme Court, is a battle with slavery. *Acquittal is another Dred Scott decision,* and another chapter in the Barbarism of Slavery." Sitting in judgment on a case laced with perplexing issues and doubts of guilt, Sumner, obsessed with his own righteousness and infallibility, could say, "To my vision the path is clear as day." [116] The implacable ruthlessness of Sumner and Stevens recalls the Grand Inquisitor who burned deviants from the "truth" at the stake.

Before we enter further into the trial, we should glance at Butler and his fellow Manager, George S. Boutwell, who, with James M. Ashley, are described by McKitrick "as baleful a trio of buzzards as ever perched in the House." Boutwell had preferred the "monstrous charge . . . that Johnson was accessory to the murder of Lincoln." [117] Butler had "illustrated an oration on the horrors of presidential reconstruction

---

Manager John S. Logan said, "when the blood of Lincoln was warm on the floor of Ford's theater, Andrew Johnson was contemplating treason." Ibid. 268. Manager Stevens stressed that "Johnson did usurp the legislative power." Ibid. 323. Manager Williams argued that "the great crime of Andrew Johnson" was that he "set up his own will against that of the law-making power, with a view to forcing the rebel States into Congress on his own terms." Ibid. 326. Boutwell argued that Johnson's "crime is one—the subversion of the Government. From the nature of the case we are compelled to deal with minor acts of criminality by which he hoped to consummate the greatest of crimes." Ibid. 281. Among the offenses Senator Sherman found was that Johnson "abandoned the party which trusted him with power." Ibid. 450. For similar utterances see the opinions of Senators Frelinghuysen, Yates ("the aider and abettor of treason"), Jacob M. Howard ("none but a traitor"). Ibid. 522, 484, 506. The issues "involved in the article of impeachment," stated the opinion of Senator Justin S. Morrill, "only thinly cover . . . graver questions raised by the recent rebellion." Ibid. 477.

As Senator Fessenden remarked, "To go outside the charges preferred, and to convict him because, in our belief, he committed offenses for which he is not on trial, would be to disregard every principle which regulates judicial proceedings." Ibid. 457. One cannot be convicted of rape on proof of larceny.

Sumner's scandalous reflections on counsel for the defense cannot be passed over: "The lawyers have made a painful record. Nothing ever occurred so much calculated to bring the profession in disrepute . . . Next to an outright mercenary, give me a lawyer to betray a great cause." Ibid. 473. Since he was hardly vilifying the Managers who had joined him in full cry, we may take these shafts to be aimed at Curtis, Evarts et al. The great betrayal was by Sumner, who sought to reduce a fair trial to an empty charade.

116. Ibid. 474; Brock 76, 78.

117. McKitrick 492; Morison 720. The "same dark suspicion . . . as to his complicity in the assassination plot" was voiced by Ashley in the House. *Cong. Globe* 40. I. 19.

by waving a bloody shirt which allegedly belonged to
an Ohio carpet bagger flogged by Klansmen in Mississippi." [118] The "composite personality" of the Managers, said McKitrick, "was a curious blend of dem-
agogue and rascal," and as Morison justly states, "they
appealed to every prejudice and passion." [119] In their
zeal to convict they were contemptuous, as we shall
see, of constitutional restrictions; indeed, Stevens
had allegedly called the Constitution a "worthless bit of
old parchment." [120]

But I would concur with Butler, on the basis of the
materials earlier set forth in Chapter II, that a common
law crime is not prerequisite to impeachment. For
present purposes it suffices to accept his inclusion within impeachable offenses of a "violation of the Constitution, or law." [121] So impeachment was epitomized
by Blackstone and restated by Kent.[122]

Freedom of Speech and Article 10

It seems safe to say with Morison that ten of the
eleven articles of impeachment "rang changes on the
removal of Stanton." [123] The one exception, article 10,

---

118. Morison 721.
119. McKitrick 507; Morison 721. Consider Boutwell's incendiary closing
argument that Johnson "has brought disorder, confusion and bloodshed
to the homes of twelve millions of people." Trial 285; see supra, n. 115.
120. Lomask 238; supra, n. 81.
121. Trial 29. Benjamin B. Curtis argued for the defense that a federal
statutory crime was indispensable to impeachment. Ibid. 134. It is not true,
as claimed by Senator George F. Edmunds, that the Constitution did not
intend to "cramp" administration of impeachment "by any specific definition of high crimes and misdemeanors, but to leave each . . . to be decided
. . . in the patriotic and judicial good sense of the Representatives of the
States." Ibid. 428. Not only did the Framers regard "high crimes and misdemeanors" as having a technical, limited meaning, supra, Chapter II, text
accompanying n. 159, but they contemplated that the President would be
impeached for "great offenses," some of which they enumerated. Supra,
Chapter II, text accompanying nn. 163–171.
122. Blackstone: infra, text accompanying n. 197. 1 James Kent, Commentaries on American Law 289, 2d ed. (New York, 1832): "if the President will use the authority of his station to violate the Constitution or law
of the land, the House of Representatives will arrest him in his career
by resorting to the power of impeachment." See also 2 George T. Curtis,
History of the Formation of the Constitution of the United States 260
(New York, 1860). Compare supra, Chapter II, text accompanying nn.
62, 73.
123. Morison 720–721. Boutwell stated that "The removal of Mr. Stanton,
contrary to the Constitution and the laws, is the particular crime of the
President for which we now demand his conviction." Trial 273. Compare
the opinions filed by Senators Orris S. Ferry, ibid. 451 (who dismissed out
of hand the related "conspiracy" charges of articles 4, 5, 6, and 7); Sherman, ibid. 446; Grimes, ibid. 420; John B. Henderson, ibid. 516. Article 11,
a lumbering catch-all, was insisted upon by Stevens because if "without

was Butler's brainchild, originally rejected by the House of Representatives in the Thirty-Ninth Congress, later again turned down by the House Committee, but finally bulled through the House by Butler.[124] In brief, article 10 charged that Johnson, in speeches (made on his "Swing Around the Circle" before the November, 1866, elections) had attempted to bring Congress into disgrace, ridicule, and contempt. Doubtless Johnson's remarks were intemperate but, as Senator Sherman had pointed out, members of Congress had all too often resorted to grossly abusive epithets, and Johnson was not to be blamed for responding to bitter invective in kind.[125] The fact is, as Senator Henderson said, the speeches injured Johnson rather than Congress;[126] they were disastrous to his own cause and contributed not a little to the overwhelming victory of the Republicans at the polls.[127]

Johnson's criticism of Congress was no less within "the usual latitude of debate" than was Sumner's "enemy of his country," which the presiding officer of the Senate sustained on that very ground.[128] Sumner insisted for himself "upon complete freedom of debate" and invoked John Milton's "glorious . . . Give me the liberty . . . to argue freely above all liberties."[129] That is not a liberty reserved for Senators alone. But Manager Thomas Williams claimed that

---

this article [cavilling judges] do not acquit him, they are greener than I was in any case I ever undertook before the quarter sessions." *Cong. Globe* 40. II. 1612; Trial 320.

124. Dewitt 384–86. Senator Sherman reminded the Senate that "The House of Representatives of the Thirty-Ninth Congress refused to rest an accusation upon these speeches." Trial 450.

125. For example, Sumner had called Johnson "the enemy of his country," the "successor of Jefferson Davis," *Cong. Globe* 39. II. 525, 542. Ashley asserted that Johnson had turned the White House "into a den of thieves and pardon brokers," and asserted that he was a "loathing [sic] incubus." *Cong. Globe* 40. I. 19. Stevens read an extract from the *New York World*, wherein Johnson was described as "an insolent drunken brute, in comparison with whom even Caligula's horse was respectable," and ironically denounced it as a "vile slander." Dewitt 63. The outrageous epithets hurled at Johnson during the trial were collected by Nelson. Trial 286.

Senator Sherman said, "regarding [the President] as he is; a man who never turned his back upon a foe . . . a man whose great virtue has been his combative propensity; as a man who repelled insults here on the very spot where I now stand, when they came from traitors arming themselves for the fight; can you ask him because he is President, to submit to insult?" *Cong. Globe* 39. I. App. 129.

126. Trial 519.

127. Ibid.; McKitrick 428–438.

128. *Cong. Globe* 39. II. 525, 526.

129. Ibid. 541.

the Constitution gives Congress "the right freely to criticize the public conduct of the President ... by making him amenable to them for all his errors, as they are not to him." [130] The Senate burst into laughter when Evarts reminded them of the article 10 charge that Johnson had been "unmindful ... of the harmony and courtesies which ought to exist and be maintained between the executive and legislative branches" and commented that under Williams' view this was "a rule that does not work both ways," and that it enabled one clad in mail to draw a dagger against the unarmed.[131]

The right to criticize official actions, said Madison, was essential to good government; and "it is the duty, as well as the right, of intelligent and faithful citizens" to control governmental action "by the censorship of public opinion," [132] a right further secured by the First Amendment guarantee of free speech. It was not left to Congress to try its critics, even when the criticism was uttered by the President. Although he voted "guilty," Senator James A. Patterson rejected article 10 because "in view of the liberty of speech which our laws authorize, in view of the culpable license of speech which is practiced and allowed in other branches of the Government, I doubt if we can at present make low and scurrilous speeches a ground of impeachment." [133] Senator Sherman, who also voted "guilty," shared this opinion: "we must guard against making crimes out of mere political differences, or the abuse of the freedom of speech." [134] We shall never know whether the fury which possessed the Republicans would have led them to convict on this article, because after conviction on articles 11, 2, and 3 failed by one vote, they beat a retreat.[135] Like the Alien

---

130. Trial 335.
131. Trial 357, 4.
132. 6 Madison, *Writings* 394. See Curtis's superb analysis, Trial 135. Senator Fessenden justly held that "To deny the President a right to comment freely upon the conduct of coordinate branches of the Government would not only be denying him a right secured to every other citizen of the Republic, but might deprive the people of the benefit of his opinion of public affairs, and of his watchfulness of their interests and welfare." Trial 456. See also opinions of Senator George E. Vickers, Trial 462, and Senator Thomas A. Hendricks, Trial 490.
133. Trial 509.
134. Trial 450.
135. Trial 412, 414–415.

and Sedition Acts, article 10 may be regarded as a brazen assault on the right freely to criticize the government, not least the Congress.[136]

WAS STANTON WITHIN THE ACT?

"It is now forgotten," said McKitrick, "that the gaping absurdities of that law [Tenure of Office Act] were hardly so obvious then as they came to seem later; the questionable part of the proceeding could only emerge by demonstration."[137] That view seems to me wholly mistaken. From the beginning defense counsel impaled the prosecution arguments with deadly accuracy; and in what concerns the trial, virtually every point here made is drawn from the arguments of defense counsel, buttressed at every point by their faithful citations to the record and the authorities.

Here I must pause to pay tribute to as valiant a group of advocates as can be found in the annals of the American bar: Benjamin B. Curtis of Massachusetts, who had written one of the two dissents in the *Dred Scott* case and had resigned from the Supreme Court; William M. Evarts of New York, destined to be Secretary of State; Henry Stanbery of Kentucky, who had resigned his post as Attorney General in order to participate in the defense; Thomas A. R. Nelson of Tennessee, and William S. Groesbeck of Ohio, who appeared at the last minute when Jeremiah S. Black withdrew from the case under circumstances that did him little credit.[138] To appear for Johnson in the inflamed state of public opinion itself required courage of a high order: he had been rejected at the polls; he was excoriated by the great majority of the Northern press; and he was hated as an apostate by the Republicans, who controlled both Houses.[139] Nelson did not exaggerate when he said that the "Manager treats him as if he were a political leper, and as if his very touch

---

136. Bingham himself described article 10 as proceeding for "seditious words tending to incite the people to revolt against the Thirty-Ninth Congress." Trial 402.
137. McKitrick 490.
138. Trial 295–296, 335–337, 342, 350; Dewitt 397–400.
139. Supra, n. 45; cf. McKitrick 490, 505 n. 32.

would communicate contagion." [140] The Managers indulged in vituperation without restraint by the Senate; yet defense counsel, who must have felt themselves in the midst of a pack of wolves, never lost their composure, never departed from measured, reasoned advocacy. If Thomas Erskine's defense of Tom Paine was more eloquent, it was not more noble. Great advocacy like great music must be heard to be appreciated. But enough emerges from the musty record to shed luster on the defense and to convince that it constitutes a high-water mark in the history of American advocacy.

Republican resentment against Johnson's use of patronage during the 1866 elections, the feeling that offices were "consecrated to the party," and the desire to "protect Republican officeholders from executive retaliation" gave rise to the Tenure of Office Act.[141] Sections 1 and 6 of the Act purported to make removal of civil officers (appointed with consent of the Senate) unlawful without Senate consent. The subject of controversy was the *proviso*

that the Secretaries of State . . . of War . . . shall hold their offices respectively for and during the term of the President by whom they may have been appointed and for one month thereafter, subject to removal by and with consent of the Senate.[142]

Was Stanton frozen into office by this proviso? He had been appointed by Lincoln during his first term and held over into the second term and the Johnson succession. Since he had not been appointed by Johnson, the question presented was whether Stanton came within "the term of the President by whom they have been appointed."

A preliminary glance at the legislative history will be illuminating. It was well summarized in the opinion filed by Senator Sherman. The bill was introduced in the

---

140. Trial 295; compare Sumner's remarks, supra, n. 115.
141. Dewitt 88; McKitrick 495; Brock 258, 61; Senator Sherman, Trial 448; but cf. Lomask 182.
142. Supra, n. 63.

Senate and "excepted from its operation the heads of departments" because "it was deemed unwise to take from the presidential office the power to remove such heads of departments as did not possess his confidence." The House struck the exception; the Senate debated the omission and refused to concur, so the matter went to a Conference Committee of both Houses, and the proviso emerged. Sherman stated that the Senate conferees (of whom he was one) "certainly would not have been justified in agreeing to a proposition thrice defeated by the vote of the Senate"; [143] that is, to removal conditioned on Senate consent. A few details will confirm Sherman's summary. Senator George F. Edmunds had charge of the bill and explained the first appearance of the exception to the Senate: it seemed "just" that the President "in selecting these named Secretaries, who . . . are the confidential advisers of the Executive . . . should be persons . . . in whom he could place entire confidence and reliance, and that whenever it should seem to him that the . . . relations between . . . them had become . . . inharmonious, he should be allowed to dispense with the services of that officer." [144]

When the compromise fashioned by the Conference was presented to the Senate, Senator George Williams explained that "the effect of this [immaterial] provision will amount to very little one way or the other; for I presume that whenever the President sees proper to rid himself of an offensive and disagreeable Cabinet minister, he will only have to signify that desire and the minister will retire." [145] Although this was evasive, Johnson could hardly be guilty of a serious offense in removing an "offensive" minister in the face of an "immaterial" provision. Sherman was more forthright. Senator James R. Doolittle recalled assertions in the debate that the object was to keep Stanton in office; and Sherman replied, "That this provision does not apply to the present case is shown by the fact that its language is so

143. Trial 448.
144. *Cong. Globe* 39. II. 382, 383.
145. Ibid. 1515. Earlier Williams had said, "we ought not to strip him of this power, which is one that it seems to me it is necessary and reasonable that he should exercise." Ibid. 384.

framed as not to apply to the present President." [146] Earlier he explained that "the proposition now submitted by the conference committee is that a Cabinet minister shall hold his office during the life or term of the President who appointed him. If the President dies the Cabinet goes out." [147] Manifestly Sherman meant that Stanton, "appointed" during the "life or term" of Lincoln, could not after Lincoln's death invoke the protection of the proviso. In the House, Robert C. Schenck, a member of the Conference Committee who submitted the Conference report, stated that the terms of Cabinet office "expire with the term of service of the President who appoints them." [148] Thus "term" was identified with "service," with "life," not with a four-year span—an identification which undercuts the Managers' argument that Johnson had no "term" of his own but was merely filling out Lincoln's term.

Let Senator Timothy O. Howe, who voted "guilty," sum up: "This section was explained to the Senate by members of the [conference] committee at the time it was reported as not designed to affect the power of the President to remove the Secretary of War. Upon examining the provisions then it was my opinion that it did not affect his authority in that regard. And after all the debate I have heard upon the point since, I have not been able to change that opinion." [149] Sherman also could not bring himself to repudiate that history: Stanton "was not appointed by this President nor during the presidential term . . . I stated explicitly [to the Senate] that the act as reported did not protect from removal the members of the cabinet appointed by Mr. Lincoln, that President Johnson might remove them at his pleasure; and I named the Secretary of War as one that might be removed." [150] Sumner, so scornful of "technicalities of the law" and "quibbles of lawyers" when they stood in the way of conviction, was ready

---

146. Ibid. 1516.
147. Ibid. 1515. No Senator questioned Sherman's statements. See Senators Thomas A. Hendricks, Charles B. Buckalew, Reverdy Johnson, Trial 491, 511, 431. Senator Fessenden said the explanation "was received with unanimous acquiescence." Trial 454.
148. *Cong. Globe* 39. II. 1340.
149. Trial 496.
150. Trial 449.

enough to resort to them when they would promote a blood-letting. Legislative history, he learnedly quoted, is inadmissible in construing a statute,[151] a view which enabled Senator Edmunds to ignore his own prior affirmations.[152] Whatever the merits of the "technical" rule of interpretation, in this particular situation it would enable the Senators who sat in judgment to repudiate their own representations upon enactment of the law. And it would be a sorry act, as Senator John B. Henderson stated, to convict Johnson "for taking the same view that we ourselves took on the passage of the act," [153] and this under a statute that was at best ambiguous.[154]

Independent of the legislative history, the language of the statute itself shows that the Act was not designed to cover Stanton. It provides that the Secretaries shall hold their offices "during the term of the President by whom they may have been appointed." The Managers maintained that Johnson was serving out Lincoln's four-year term, pinning their case to the Article II, §1(1), provision that the President "shall hold his office during the term of four years." Stanton had been appointed by Lincoln during his first term; he had not been reappointed (that is, nominated, and confirmed by the Senate, the constitutional indicia of "appointment") [155]

---

151. Trial 468.
152. Trial 426. For history of the Act see opinion of Senator Sherman, one of its architects. Trial 448–49.
153. Trial 518; see also Senator Trumbull, Trial 418.
154. Senator Trumbull said that the Act "must be admitted to be a doubtful statute," Trial 418. Senator Henderson stated that "this difficulty of construction is the result of the effort made on the passage of the bill to reconcile a radical difference between the two Houses of Congress on this very question of Cabinet officers. It has sprung out of a most reprehensible and vicious practice—that to save important measures from defeat these differences between the two Houses are to be healed and covered up in conference committees with ambiguous or unmeaning phrases. The truth is . . . we often purposely obscure the controverted point and devolve its solution upon the courts, or the President." Trial 517–518. Manager Boutwell conceded that "if a law passed by Congress be equivocal or ambiguous in its terms, the Executive . . . may apply his own best judgment." Trial 279. It may be added that courts construe a statute to avoid constitutional doubts; to avoid holding the statute an encroachment on the President's constitutional province, the statute would be construed not to cover Stanton. Kovacs v. Cooper, 336 U.S. 77, 85 (1949).
155. As Senator Trumbull concluded, the word "appointed" in the act "must be construed to mean a legal appointment which could only be made by and with the advice and consent of the Senate." Trial 418. This was conceded by Manager Williams if "appointment" be read in "the constitutional way." Trial 326. See also Senator Fessenden, Trial 454. The Managers looked to the Constitution for the meaning of the statutory word "term," infra, nn. 159, 160. The statutory "appointment" stands no differently.

either by Lincoln in his second term or by Johnson, but merely held over under Lincoln's original appointment "during the pleasure of the President of the United States for the time being," [156] very much as a tenant may continue to occupy real property after expiration of a lease at "the pleasure" of the landlord. John A. Logan, one of the Managers, let slip that "Stanton was *appointed* by Mr. Lincoln in his first term . . . and *continued* by Mr. Lincoln in his second term." [157] Manager John A. Bingham was driven to maintain that the Secretaries were to hold their offices "during the entire term, if it should be eight years or twelve years or sixteen years, of the President by whom they were appointed." [158] Yet he himself asserted that "the presidential term named . . . in the act of 1867 is the constitutional term of four years. It must be so . . . there is no other term." [159] That view was shared by his fellow Managers and affirmed by Senator Williams: "When the Constitution speaks of the term of the President, it means a definite period of four years." [160] Inescapably, as Senator William P. Fessenden held, "the two terms of Mr. Lincoln were as distinct as if held by different persons." [161] True, that construction involves an absurdity: Stanton's appointment on this reading expired one month after Lincoln's first term, and two years before the passage of the law.[162] From the legislative history we know that the proviso was not intended to apply to Stanton at all. Equally absurd results attend the contrary reading by the Managers,[163] the consequence of a conference compromise intended to paper over irreconcilable differences by resort to "equivocal" language.

---

156. Trial 54.
157. Trial 262, emphasis supplied.
158. Trial 400.
159. Ibid.
160. John A. Logan, Trial 262; Boutwell, Trial 277; Bingham, Trial 400; Senator George H. Williams, Trial 458.
161. Trial 454. Senator Trumbull held, "The fact that Mr. Lincoln was his own successor in 1865 did not make the two terms one," Trial 418. We are accustomed to speak of the first term and second term of a President. See also Groesbeck, Trial 312.
162. Manager Williams, Trial 326; Senator Edmunds, Trial 426. For other absurdities, see Sumner, Trial 468.
163. For example, in case of Johnson's impeachment, his successor, Wade, could not remove the Secretaries appointed by Johnson. Senator Henderson, Trial 518; and see Stanbery, Trial 371–72.

Still another difficulty is presented by the Managers' argument that Johnson was merely rounding out Lincoln's second four-year term.[164] In providing that the President "shall hold his office during the term of four years," the Constitution implies that he must be alive to "hold" it—dead men cannot hold office.[165] Consequently Lincoln's second term expired with his death. The Managers' insistence that Johnson had no term of his own, that he was serving out Lincoln's term, fails to take account of the fact that the Vice President, under Article II, §1(1), is "chosen for the same term" as the President. When the President dies, "the powers and duties of the said office," *not* the term of the President, "shall devolve on the Vice President" (Article II, §1(6)); and the latter exercises those powers during the term for which *he* was elected, that is, his own term.[166] On the reasoning of the Managers, Johnson was suspended in limbo without a term of office,[167] contrary to the popular understanding that the presidential term is "called the term of the person who happened for the time being to be in the office."[168] In my judgment, Stanton, appointed during Lincoln's first term, fell outside the statutory protection for Secretaries "during the term of the President by whom they may have been appointed." It follows that the discharge of Stanton did not contravene the statute.

Was the Tenure Act Constitutional?

In curtailing the President's power to remove a member of his Cabinet, the Tenure of Office Act unconstitutionally invaded his exclusive prerogative. That

164. Boutwell, Trial 277; Butler, Trial 34.
165. Curtis, Trial 124; Groesbeck, Trial 312; Senator Garrett Davis, Trial 443; Senator Fessenden, Trial 454.
166. Curtis, Trial 124; Senator Buckalew, Trial 511. The difficulty Senator Williams experienced that on the defense view there would be "two presidential terms, between the 4th of March, 1865, and the 4th of March, 1869." Trial 458, vanishes when we accept that the presidential term of Lincoln expired on his death and another presidential term began with Johnson's succession. Although a constitutional term has a temporal span of four years, the Constitution itself recognizes that it may be divided by death. Senator Buckalew, Trial 511.
167. According to the Managers' theory that Johnson "never had a term we have the anomaly of a person on whom the office of President is devolved, and who is impeached as President . . . who has no term of office." Senator Trumbull, Trial 418; see also Senator Fessenden, Trial 454.
168. Senator Trumbull, Trial 418.

was settled in our time by *Myers v. United States;* [169] but there is no need to import hindsight of what was hidden in the future, for the materials on which *Myers* was based were spread before the Senate by defense counsel. A resume of those materials will light up the arrogant contempt with which prosecution and "judges" treated constitutional restrictions.

When establishment of a Department of Foreign Affairs was under consideration in the First Congress, a great debate was provoked by a clause which purported to *grant* to the President the right to remove the Secretary of Foreign Affairs. A number of conflicting theories were aired, but the argument that the House lacked power to make the grant carried the day, and the words "to be removable by the President" were replaced by a declaration of "sentiment" or "sense" of the House "upon the meaning of a constitutional grant of power to the President." Madison concurred on the ground that the Legislature is "not in possession of this power." [170] In 1807 John Marshall admirably summed up the "removal" debate; in the last stage Egbert Benson moved to amend the bill

so as clearly to imply the power of removal to be solely in the President. He gave notice, that, if he should succeed in this, he would move to strike out the words which had been the subject of debate. If those words continued, he said, the power of removal by the President might hereafter appear to be exercised by virtue of a legislative grant only, and consequently to be subjected to legislative instability; when he was well satisfied in his own mind, that it was, by fair construction, fixed in the constitution. The motion was seconded by Mr. Madison, and both amendments were adopted. As the bill passed into a law it has ever been considered as a full expression of the sense of the legislative on this important part of the American constitution.[171]

---

169. 272 U.S. 52 (1926).
170. Berger, *Congress v. Court* 146.
171. 5 John Marshall, *Life of George Washington* 231–232 (London, 1807); Trial 127. The Act of September 2, 1789, §7, provided, "That *whenever* the Secretary shall be removed from office by the President . . . the assistant shall act" (emphasis added).

The fact that the First Congress recognized a *constitutional grant of removal* power to the President alone was so strenuously controverted during the Johnson trial that it seems worthwhile to set forth additional recognition of the effect of the 1789 action, stretching right up to the time when the Tenure of Office Act made a breach in the settled practice. John Adams, then Vice President, had cast the deciding vote as presiding officer of the Senate in the 1789 debate; and in 1800, as President, he summarily "discharged" Timothy Pickering "from any further service as Secretary of State." [172] In 1826 James Kent stated in his *Commentaries* that the legislative construction of 1789 "has ever since been acquiesced in and acted upon, as of decisive authority in the case." [173] Joseph Story said in 1833 that "in the debate in 1789 . . . the final vote seems to have expressed the sense of the legislature that the power of removal by the executive could not be abridged by the legislature." [174] In 1839 Justice Thompson stated, "it was very early adopted as the practical construction of the Constitution, that this power was vested in the President alone." [175] Years after serving in both the Congress and the executive branch, Madison summed up: "The claim [of the Senate] on *constitutional* grounds, to a share in the removal as well as the appointment of officers, is in direct opposition to the uniform practice by the Government from its commencement. It is clear that the innovation would . . . vary essentially the existing balance of power." [176]

There were in addition a row of opinions by divers Attorneys General, which carry great weight because they issue from the chief law officer of the United States. In 1818, William Wirt said of an appointee

---

172. Trial 119; 1 Adams 448.
173. 1 Kent, supra, n. 122 at 310; Trial 299. In 1825 William Rawle wrote, "Neither should the fear of giving offence to the public . . . deter him from the immediate exercise of his power of removal on proof of incapacity or infidelity in the subordinate officer." Rawle 164.
174. 2 Story, § 1538, p. 364 n. 2; Trial 299.
175. Ex parte Hennen, 13 Pet. (38 U.S.) 230, 259; Trial 314.
176. Letter to Edward Coles, October 15, 1834, 4 James Madison, *Letters and Other Writings of James Madison* 368 (Philadelphia, 1867); and see letter to John M. Patton, March 24, 1834, 9 Madison, *Writings* 534 (New York, 1910).

"during the pleasure of the President," that the President has "the power of removal." [177] In 1851, J. J. Crittenden, quoting Madison in the 1789 debate, "it is absolutely necessary that the President should have the power or removing from office," concluded that "the determination of Congress was in accordance with his views, and has been since invariably followed," the power of removal being "vested by the Constitution in the President." [178] Caleb Cushing described it in 1856 as "established constitutional doctrine"; [179] and Jeremiah S. Black advised the President in 1860 that "Congress could not . . . take away from the President, or in anywise diminish the authority conferred upon him by the Constitution." [180]

Republican members of the Reconstruction Congress recognized the practice. When Senator Williams explained the Tenure of Office Bill, he stated that "this bill undertakes to reverse what has heretofore been the admitted practice of the Government . . . it was due to the exalted office of the President . . . that he should be left to choose his own Cabinet." [181] In his opinion on the case, Senator Sherman stated that "the power to remove Cabinet officers since the passage of [the 1789] act was repeatedly recognized by all who took part in the debate on the tenure-of-office bill." [182] Sumner also recognized that the act "reversed the practice of eighty years." [183] That practice was expressed in an unvarying formula employed down the years in all commissions issued—to hold office "during the pleasure of the President of the United States for the time being"—the very formula in which Stanton's own appointment was couched.[184] One who did not shut his eyes to the evidence must have concluded as did Senator Thomas A. Hendricks: "The judgment of the

177. 1 Ops. Att'y Gen. 212 (June 15, 1818).
178. 5 ibid. 288, 290 (January 23, 1851).
179. 8 ibid. 223, 232 (December 10, 1856).
180. 9 ibid. 462, 468 (July 31, 1860).
181. Cong. Globe 39. II. 384.
182. Trial 448.
183. Trial 470. Sumner comments in topsy-turvy fashion that this reversal, which "overcame the disposition to stand on ancient ways, would seem to increase rather than diminish" the "weight" of the passion-inspired 1867 "construction."
184. Trial 115, 54.

First Congress was that the President has the right under the Constitution to remove the Secretaries, and that judgment is supported by the uniform practice of the Government from that day till the meeting of the Thirty-Ninth Congress." [185]

How did the Radicals meet this mass of evidence? For Manager Thomas Williams "The old law was— not the Constitution—but a vicious practice that had grown out of a precedent involving an early and erroneous construction of that instrument," the act of "that small and inexperienced Congress," not to be taken as an "oracular outgiving upon the meaning of the Constitution." [186] Butler asked why a matter decided by an early, divided Congress could not be "settled more authoritatively by the greater unanimity of another Congress," [187] a view adopted by Senator Sumner: the 1789 debate represented at best "but a congressional construction of the Constitution, and as such subject to be set aside by another voice from the same quarter." [188]

But the First Congress was not just another Congress, still less an "inexperienced" body in matters of constitutional meaning. It was in the words of Charles Warren an "almost adjourned session" of the Federal Convention.[189] As Madison wrote in 1832, it "contained sixteen members . . . fresh from the Convention which framed the Constitution, and a considerable number who had been members of the State Conventions which had adopted it" [190] and where it had been the subject of lively debate. Madison presciently observed in the 1789 debate,

it is proper that this interpretation should now take place rather than at a time when the exigency of the case may require the exercise of the power of removal. At present, the disposition of every gentleman is to seek the truth, and abide by its guidance when it is discovered.

---

185. Trial 492.
186. Trial 326, 329.
187. Trial 32.
188. Trial 470.
189. Warren, *Congress, the Constitution, and the Supreme Court* 99 (Boston, 1925).
190. 3 Farrand 518.

If we wait, he continued, until the President shall

exercise the right of removal, if he supposes he has it; then the Senate may be induced to set up their pretensions. And will they decide so calmly as at this time, when no important officer in any of the great departments is appointed to influence their judgments? The imagination of no member here, or of the Senate, or of the President himself, is heated or disturbed by faction. If ever a proper moment for decision should offer, it must be one like the present.[191]

From time to time there were, of course, critics of the practice in the Senate, on which the Managers leaned heavily, but the practice itself was never disturbed. And the reason in large part was what Justice William Johnson referred to in 1827 as the "presumption, that the contemporaries of the constitution have claims to our deference . . . because they had the best opportunities of informing themselves of the understanding of the framers of the constitution, and the sense put upon it by the people, when it was adopted by them." [192] That rule of construction harks back at least as far as Chief Justice Prisot in the fifteenth century,[193] and it was restated by Coke: "Great regard ought in construing a law, to be paid to the construction which the sages who lived about the time or soon after it was made put upon it, because they were the best able to judge of the intention of the makers at the time when the law was made." [194] It is because of this that a construction put upon the Constitution by the First Congress has ever been regarded as authoritative;

---

191. 1 *Ann. Cong.* 547.

192. Ogden v. Saunders, 12 Wheat. (25 U.S.) 213, 290. See also Stuart v. Laird, 1 Cranch (5 U.S.) 299, 309 (1803) (practice for several years after 1789 "fixed the construction"); Cohens v. Virginia, 6 Wheat. (19 U.S.) 264, 418 (1821). What Congressman William Vans Murray said in the House in 1796, "We have all seen the Constitution from its cradle, we know it from its infancy, and have the most perfect knowledge of it and more light than ever a body of men . . . ever had of ascertaining any other Constitution," 5 *Ann. Cong.* 701 (4th Cong. 1st Sess.), was even more true of the First Congress.

193. The "judges who gave these decisions in ancient times were nearer to the making of the statute than we now are, and had more acquaintance with it." Windham v. Felbridge, Y. B. 33 Hen. VI 38, 41 (Mich. pl. 17), quoted C. K. Allen, *Law in the Making* 193 (Oxford, 6th ed. 1958).

194. Quoted by Curtis, Trial 127.

and Republican dismissal of that construction, the better to dispatch Johnson, is but another index of their contempt for constitutional restrictions.

PRESIDENTIAL DISREGARD OF AN UNCONSTITUTIONAL STATUTE

If the Tenure of Office Act constituted an unconstitutional invasion of the President's exclusive prerogative of removal, did he have a right to disobey it? On this issue Corwin concluded,

it seems clear that the impeachers had the better of the argument for all but the most urgent situations. No one doubts that the President possesses prerogatives which Congress may not constitutionally invade; but neither does any one doubt that he is under obligation "to take care that the laws be faithfully executed." And, he was endowed by the Constitution with a qualified veto upon acts of Congress with the idea among others that he might thus protect his prerogatives from legislative curtailment. But this power being exercised, this power of self-defense is at an end; and once a statute has been duly enacted, whether over his protest or with his approval, he must promote its enforcement.[195]

That view won my concurrence in an earlier study of a conflict between Congress and the Executive in the domain of "executive privilege"; [196] but the argument to the contrary by Johnson's counsel and further study have persuaded me that Corwin's view is mistaken.

Here, however, Congress had a respectable legal argument. Impeachment, stated Blackstone, is provided so "that no man shall dare assist the crown in contradiction to the laws of the land." [197] There were early cases and presidential utterances which indicated

---

195. Corwin, supra, n. 22 at 79. For earlier expression see 3 W. W. Willoughby, *The Constitutional Law of the United States* 1503–1504 (New York, 2d ed. 1929).

196. Berger, "Executive Privilege" 1114–1117.

197. 1 Blackstone 244; supra, Chapter I, text accompanying nn. 130–131 (Strafford: subverting the Constitution); Chapter II, text accompanying n. 73 (Seymour: employing appropriated funds for purpose other than that specified).

that the President was under a duty to execute a law.[198] Even the stiff-necked Jackson, according to Roger Taney, a member of his Cabinet, "never expressed a doubt as to the duty and obligation upon him in his Executive character to carry into execution any act of Congress regularly passed, whatever his own opinion might be of the constitutional question." [199] In 1854 Attorney General Caleb Cushing advised the President that repassage of an act "after a veto, gives constitutionality to what would otherwise be the usurpation of executive power on the part of Congress," but he contemplated "a law constitutional in its nature." [200] And on two occassions Johnson himself had expressed readiness to execute what he regarded as an unconstitutional law. In his veto of the Second Freedmen's Bureau Bill, Johnson, who had earlier condemned the Civil Rights Act as unconstitutional, said that it was "now the law of the land" and "will be faithfully executed" until "declared unconstitutional by courts." [201] So too, in *Mississippi v. Johnson,* wherein it was sought to prevent the President from carrying out the military occupation for which the Reconstruction Act provided, Attorney General Stanbery told the Court that though the President had vetoed the act as unconstitutional, he felt after repassage that he was under a duty "faithfully to carry out and execute these laws." [202] And there was the Court's question in that case: if the President "refuses to execute the Acts of Congress . . . may not the House of Representatives impeach the President for such refusal?" [203] Nevertheless, the issue

---

198. Kendall v. United States, 12 Pet. (37 U.S.) 524, 613 (1838): "To contend that the obligation imposed upon the president to see the laws faithfully executed implies a power to forbid their execution, is . . . entirely inadmissible." See also United States v. Smith, 27 Fed. Cas. 1192, 1230 (No. 16,342) (C. Ct. N.Y. 1806). In 1790, Jefferson, then Secretary of State, said, "The Executive, possessing the rights of self-government from nature, cannot be controlled in the exercise of them but by a law, passed in the forms of the Constitution." Quoted Edward S. Corwin, "The Steel Seizure Case: A Judicial Brick without Straw," 53 *Colum. L. Rev.* 53, 54 (1953). See Berger, "Executive Privilege" 1115. Did Jefferson mean conformity with constitutional formalities or within constitutional bounds?
199. Quoted 1 Charles Warren, *The Supreme Court in United States History* 763–764 (1922).
200. 6 Ops. Att'y Gen. 680, 682–683 (August 23, 1854). But see the opinion of Attorney General Jeremiah S. Black, supra, text accompanying n. 180.
201. Dewitt 96–97.
202. 4 Wall. (71 U.S.) 475, 492 (December 1866).
203. Ibid. 501.

whether the President was bound to execute a law which *encroached on his presidential prerogatives* had never been squarely presented; and there was solid ground for Johnson's view that he was privileged to disobey the law in self-defense.

The Managers in large part built their case on the proposition that the veto exhausted the power of the President; after that, Butler asserted, "he must execute the law, whether in fact constitutional or not." [204] For, said Bingham, the Constitution then said "expressly IT SHALL BE A LAW." [205] But they overlooked the view of the Founders that a law beyond the powers conferred was void; it was no law at all. That view was summed up by Hamilton in the "clear" principle that "every act of a delegated authority, contrary to the tenor of the commission, under which it is exercised, is void." [206] In the Massachusetts Convention Theophilus Parsons stated that "an act of usurpation is not obligatory; it is not law; and any man may be justified in his resistance." [207] Justice James Wilson, one of the leading Framers, stated in his Philadelphia Lectures in 1791 that "whoever would be obliged to obey a constitutional law, is justified in refusing to obey an unconstitutional act of the legislature." [208] This was

---

204. Butler, Trial 36; Bingham, Trial 384.
205. Trial 384.
206. *Federalist* No. 78 at 505. In Marbury v. Madison, 1 Cranch (5 U.S.) 137, 177–178 (1803), Chief Justice Marshall declared that a law "repugnant to the constitution, is void," and is "not law," that it cannot be "void, yet, in practice, completely obligatory." Trial 355.
207. 2 Elliot 94; see Groesbeck, Trial 314. The North Carolina Convention proposed the inclusion in a Declaration of Rights (No. 3) the statement "that the doctrine of non-resistance to arbitrary power and oppression is . . . destructive of the good and happiness of mankind." 4 Elliot 243. For comparable citations, see Berger, *Congress v. Court* 178.
208. 1 Wilson, *Works* 186; and he stated that an unconstitutional law is "void and has no operation." Ibid. 330. This was the view Chief Justice Chase expressed during the trial in a letter to Gerrit Smith, April 19, 1868: "Nothing is clearer to my mind than that acts of Congress, not warranted by the Constitution, are not laws." Warden, supra, n. 67 at 685. It was repeated in Norton v. Shelby County, 118 U.S. 425, 442 (1886): "An unconstitutional law is not a law . . . it imposes no duties . . . it is in legal contemplation as inoperative as though it had never been passed." See also Chicago, Ind. & Louisville Ry. v. Hackett, 288 U.S. 559, 566, 567 (1913). See Henderson, Trial 518.
Since then courts have qualified the statement to protect one who relied on a court's earlier determination that a statute was valid, and have therefore refused to impair such rights by a new retroactive declaration of invalidity. Chicot County Dist. v. Bank, 308 U.S. 371, 374 (1940). But here Congress was repudiating, not relying upon, the prior construction. And since we view the case in the frame of 1868, the yet unborn Chicot qualification has no relevance. Our guide must be the materials available in 1868,

a response to a deep-rooted fear of legislative tyranny and despotism,[209] and it found expression in the Supremacy Clause. It was not every law which was made "binding" by Article VI, §2, but only those "which shall be made in pursuance" of the Constitution. A law that was not "in pursuance" of the Constitution, that is, which was inconsistent therewith, said Hamilton, "would not be the supreme law" and therefore not binding.[210] Manager Bingham agreed that "an unconstitutional law . . . is no law at all" but maintained that it is for the courts, not the President, to determine that.[211] His qualified concession is not to be taken seriously in light of his repeated assertion that the Senate is "the exclusive judge of the law . . . no matter what any court may have said touching any question involved in the issue." [212] That was also the view of Boutwell.[213] And Sumner held in his opinion that "the Supreme Court is not the arbiter of the acts of Congress," its decision "can not bind Congress." [214]

Curtis did not press the argument beyond the needs of the case: "if a law is passed over his veto which he believes to be unconstitutional, and that law affects the interest of third persons, those whose interests are affected must take care of them." But when "a question arises whether a particular law has cut off a power confided to him by . . . the Constitution, and he alone can raise that question, and he alone can cause a judicial decision to come between the two branches of the Government to say which of them is right," then he is

---

that is, the affirmations of the Founders, of Marshall, C. J., which led Chief Justice Chase to declare in the very context of the trial that an unconstitutional act was "not law."

209. Berger, *Congress v. Court* 8–14.

210. *Federalist* No. 33 at 202; Berger, *Congress v. Court* 223–244. Governor Edmund Randolph stated in the Virginia Ratification Convention with respect to the oath to support the Constitution, "this only binds them to support it in the exercise of powers constitutionally given." 3 Elliot 204.

211. Trial 384.

212. Ibid.; see also ibid. 380 and 404. See also infra, 294.

213. Boutwell said, "it would be no relief to [Johnson] for his willful violation of the law . . . if the court itself had pronounced the same to be unconstitutional." Ibid. 271. Butler apparently questioned whether the Court ever had declared a federal act unconstitutional where it did not touch on its own prerogatives. Ibid. 36–37.

214. Ibid. 471. Senator Grimes, on the other hand, concluded, "The Constitution has provided a common arbiter in such cases of controversy—the Supreme Court." Ibid. 423; see Berger, "Executive Privilege" 1354.

guilty of no violation of law by raising that question.[215] Sumner recognized that some laws might be disobeyed; for example, the "impossible" case, an act that "the President should not be Commander in Chief," on the ground that such an act "would be *on its face unconstitutional*. It would be an act of unreasoning madness . . . a self-evident monstrosity, and therefore must be disobeyed." [216] But he distinguished the cases in which constitutionality is a matter of "opinion," [217] and this on an issue that confessedly had been regarded as settled for eighty years. In fact, Sumner was distin-

---

215. Trial 126–27; see also Groesbeck, ibid. 314. The compatibility of that view with Johnson's position in Mississippi v. Johnson is pointed up by Kutler's comment on the statement of Attorney General Stanbery to the Court in that case: "Whatever his opinion of the Reconstruction Acts, he was not in the least prepared to condone an assault upon the independence, integrity and obligations of his President in order to secure a desirable end. And this, of course, reflects most interestingly upon Andrew Johnson, who certainly had fixed ideas on executive power and independence—ideas which transcended his views of the Reconstruction Acts." Stanley I. Kutler, *Judicial Power and Reconstruction Politics* 97 (Chicago, 1968). A President who would sooner accept a setback to a cherished goal than suffer a diminution of the Executive power could hardly be expected to consent to impairment of that power for accomplishment of a *Congressional* goal.

216. Trial 471. Boutwell also stamped this as an "extreme case and not within the range of possibility," and said "that it would be the duty of the President to disregard such legislation." Ibid. 277. Yet Congress was guilty of precisely this "unreasoning madness." By a section added to the Army Appropriation Act of March 2, 1867, it "severely limit[ed]" the President's function as commander-in-chief: military orders were to be issued only through the General of the Army." McKitrick 13; Brock 208. This section, framed by Stanton himself, Dewitt 202n, Lomask 239, deprived the Commander-in-Chief of the right to communicate directly with a subordinate. Without subscribing to present-day inflated executive claims built on the Commander-in-Chief clause, one may yet conclude that if the Commander-in-Chief does not even have the power to issue a direct order to a subordinate, this grant is an empty shell.

Thad Stevens grotesquely misconceived the role when he told the House that "though the President is Commander in Chief, Congress is his commander, and God willing, he shall obey!" Lomask 238. George Mason, one of the Framers, stated in the Virginia Ratification Convention that Congress is to raise an army, "and then the President is to command without any control." 3 Elliot 498, and see ibid. 496. Another Framer, James Wilson, cited to the Pennsylvania Convention as evidence that the President will *not* be "the *tool* of the Senate" that he "shall be commander in chief." 2 Elliot 512. George Nicholas, comparing the powers of the president to those of a governor, reminded the Virginia Convention that the militia, "when actually embodied, were under the sole command of the governor." 3 Elliot 497. Madison's statement in the Convention that the "president is to have command, and in conjunction with the Senate, to appoint the officers," implies that Senate "consent" has no application to "command." 3 Elliot 394. See also the explanation to the Maryland Legislature by Luther Martin, one of the Framers. 3 Farrand 172, 218; and Story § 1492. Commenting on Hamilton's explanation in *Federalist* No. 69 at 448, that the "Commander in Chief" clause grants the President "supreme command and direction of the military and naval forces, as first General and admiral," Corwin states that this means that "no one can be put over him or authorized to give him orders in the direction of the said forces." Corwin, supra, n. 22 at 276. On the historical evidence, I submit, the Congressional curb on President Johnson's right directly to communicate with military subordinates constituted a clear infringement on his prerogative as Commander-in-Chief.

217. Trial 472.

guishing between express and implied grants of power. But what, asked Curtis, "is the difference between a power conferred upon the President by the express words of the Constitution and a power conferred upon the President by a clear and sufficient implication in the Constitution?" [218] For eighty years the existence of an "implied" exclusive presidential power of removal had been recognized constitutional doctrine. "With the Constitution," said the Supreme Court, "what is reasonably implied is as much a part of it as what is expressed." [219]

To this Evarts added an argument which proceeded from the oath that the Constitution requires from the President alone: "I . . . will, to the best of my ability, preserve, protect, and defend the Constitution of the United States" Article II, § 1 (8).[220] Central to the constitutional scheme is the separation of powers, the principle that each of the three branches is confined within its own boundaries and will exercise no powers not confided to it. Hamilton stated in *Federalist* Number 51 that to maintain the separation of powers each department is given the "necessary constitutional means and personal motives to resist encroachments of the others." [221] Only the veto power, it may be replied, was "given" to the President. I would agree that a veto exhausts Presidential power when the issue is the *wisdom* of the legislation. But the object of the Framers was to prevent *"encroachments,"* and they were too practical to limit the President's power to "defend" the Constitution against a breach of its very essence—the separation of powers. Preservation of that separation goes to the very existence and functioning of the constitutional scheme. Repassage over a veto was not designed to free Congress from constitutional limitations. Congressional action beyond those limits may still be

---

218. Ibid. 127.
219. Dillon v. Gloss, 256 U.S. 368, 373 (1921).
220. Trial 339. His view was accepted by Senators Grimes and Reverdy Johnson, ibid. 423, 431.
221. *Federalist* at 337. Most feared were the encroachments of Congress. The reassurance by Governor Johnston in the North Carolina Convention is typical: "The Congress cannot assume any other powers than those expressly given them without a palpable violation of the Constitution." 4 Elliot 142. For similar statements, see Berger, *Congress v. Court* 8–14.

challenged by private individuals whose rights are impaired; and Curtis pointed out that the President must be equally privileged to invoke judicial aid, since no one but he can complain of an unconstitutional invasion of *his* prerogatives.[222] The President is no more punishable for disobedience of an unconstitutional statute than is a citizen who challenges the constitutionality of congressional action. Indeed, the oath to "protect and defend the Constitution" posits both a right and a duty to do so, which minimally must extend to a right to protect the President's own constitutional functions from congressional impairment.[223]

Since the issue involved conflicting claims to constitutional power, it was not left to Congress finally to determine the boundaries of its own power. In *Federalist* Number 78, Hamilton rejected the view that the legislative body "are themselves the constitutional judges of their own powers, and that the construction they put upon them is conclusive." [224] Still less may Congress unilaterally decide a boundary dispute with the Executive, for neither branch, in Madison's words, has "an exclusive or superior right of settling the boundaries between their respective powers." [225] That function, said Madison after a lifetime in government, must fall to the courts.[226] There is not the slightest inkling in the records of the several Conventions that in the event of a boundary dispute between Congress and the President, Congress was empowered to settle

---

222. Trial 126–127; Evarts, ibid. 346. His view was adopted by Senator Buckalew, ibid. 514; cf. Senator Vickers, ibid. 461.

223. Senator Reverdy Johnson, a noted lawyer, stated in his opinion, "If by the Constitution the power of removal was vested in him, he was bound by the very terms of his official oath to maintain it. Not to have done so would have been to violate the obligation of that oath." Ibid. 431; and see supra, n. 220.

224. *Federalist* at 506; Trial 374; Berger, *Congress v. Court* 186–87.

225. *Federalist* No. 49 at 328; see Evarts, Trial 348.

226. Madison affirmed the right of each department to interpret its own powers and to act upon that interpretation "without involving the functions of any other" department. But, he went on, "it may always be expected that the judicial branch . . . will . . . most engage the respect and reliance of the public as the surest expositor of the Constitution, as well in questions . . . concerning the boundaries between the several departments of the Government as in those between the Union and its members." 4 James Madison, *Letters and Other Writings of James Madison* 349 (Philadelphia, 1867). Justice Jackson stated that "Some arbiter is almost indispensable when power . . . is also balanced between different branches, as the legislative and the executive. Each unit cannot be left to judge of the limits of its own power." Robert H. Jackson, *The Struggle for Judicial Supremacy* 9 (New York, 1941).

the matter by impeachment.[227] The Hamilton-Madison pronouncements alone would preclude such an inference. And that inference would stand the separation of powers, the painstaking precautions against legislative usurpations, on their head.

A much discussed collateral issue was whether Johnson's removal of Stanton rested on a bona fide intention to present the issue to the courts.[228] It would take us far afield to sift out all the facts that bear on this issue; let a few details suffice. Johnson had offered Stanton's post to General Grant on the condition either that he would hold the office and drive Stanton to the courts or, if he preferred to avoid controversy, to resign in time for appointment of another. Grant replied that Stanton "would have to appeal to the courts to reinstate him," and that if Grant would change his mind, he would inform the President. The offer on this understanding was corroborated by Grant at a Cabinet meeting. For whatever reason, he did not carry through but suddenly vacated the office, which Stanton promptly occupied. Johnson's reproachful letter to Grant of February 10, 1868, stated: "You knew the President was unwilling to trust the office with any one who would not, by holding it, compel Mr. Stanton to resort to the courts." This statement was confirmed by the five Secretaries who heard Grant's admission at the Cabinet meeting.[229]

Meanwhile Johnson had offered the post to General William T. Sherman, and Sherman testified that on January 30, 1868, Johnson "referred to the constitutionality of . . . the civil tenure-of-office bill . . . and it was the constitutionality of that bill which he seemed desirous of having tested, and which, he said, if it

227. There is at least one indication to the contrary. To the extent that the removal issue would become involved in controversy between the President and Senate, said Elbridge Gerry in the 1789 debate, "let it go before the proper tribunal; the judges are the Constitutional umpires on such questions." 1 *Ann. Cong.* 473. For other recognition in that debate of the over-riding judicial role, see Berger, *Congress v. Court* 147–148.

228. For example, Stanbery referred to the testimony to show "throughout the purpose of the President declared at all times, from first to last, to bring this question to judicial arbitrament." Trial 378.

229. Trial 81; Dewitt 284–285, 318–320, 323–324. For exclusion of the Cabinet members corroborative testimony, see *supra*, text accompanying nn. 111–113.

could be brought before the Supreme Court properly, would not stand half an hour." [230] Here was unimpeachable testimony which disposed of the issue, but the prosecution met it with a barrage of objections which even the majority of the Senate could not stomach, testifying to the prosecution's thirst for vengeance, not justice. [231] Then there was Johnson's remark that he was pleased to have the matter in Court when Stanton caused his successor, General Lorenzo Thomas, to be arrested and charged with a "high misdemeanor" for accepting the office in violation of the Tenure of Office Act. The arrest took place on February 22, 1868, the House resolved on impeachment on February 24, and the charges were abandoned on February 26. [232] Thus it was Congress rather than the President which avoided submission of the controversy to the courts.

Why did not Johnson institute a quo warranto action, the Managers queried. [233] Traditionally the executive branch does not seek a preliminary judicial dec-

---

230. Trial 173.
231. Trial 150–173. Compare Manager Williams concession that "estoppels are odious, because they exclude the truth." Trial 334. This was not a trial before a lay jury, against whose credulity the exclusory rules were fashioned, but before a court, composed in good part of lawyers, accustomed to discount old wives' tales.
232. Trial 174, 168–169. The incident is detailed in Dewitt 351–353. When Johnson was informed he said, "Very well—that is the place I want it in—the courts." Ibid. 352.
The following facts are set forth to show that the dismissal of the case, though in form by Thomas, in fact was engineered by Stanton et al. Richard T. Merrick, an attorney employed by General Thomas, testified that the arrest took place on February 22, Trial 204 (for docket entries, Trial 174), that counsel appeared before Chief Justice Cartter (said to be a close friend of Stanton, Lomask 276) on February 26, announced that Thomas' bail had surrendered him to the Court and handed the Court a petition for habeas corpus. The Chief Justice "ruled that [Thomas] was not in custody at all, and that he did not purpose to put him in custody," Trial 205–206, Dewitt 376–377, thereby blocking action on the habeas corpus.
Walter S. Cox, an attorney, testified he was employed by the President in the presence of Thomas to institute necessary legal proceedings "without delay to test General Thomas' right to the office." Trial 200. After conferring with the Attorney General, he decided that Thomas should be surrendered so that he could bring habeas corpus. When Cox surrendered Thomas to the court, Stanton's counsel objected that they did not desire that Thomas "should be detained in custody"; thereupon the Chief Justice would not "allow him to be held in custody." Cox then moved for Thomas' discharge, "not supposing that the counsel on the other side would consent to it . . . They made no objection, however, . . . and accordingly the chief justice did discharge him." Trial 202.
The explanation of this readiness to abandon the Cartter action lies in the fact that the House had voted the articles of impeachment on February 24, Trial 3, two days after the arrest of Thomas instigated by Stanton, hence the unwillingness of Stanton to facilitate a trial of the issue on habeas corpus.
233. Boutwell, Trial 271; Thomas Williams, ibid. 332; Bingham, ibid. 395.

laration whether it has power to act; rather, it acts and leaves it to the affected party to challenge the action, as did Stanton himself until he and his Radical allies chose to rely on the impeachment. But quo warranto, the Managers argued, can only be instituted by the government.[234] The practice, however, is for the affected individual to request the Attorney General to institute the suit on his behalf. To assume that Johnson would have blocked the Attorney General's consent to a court suit when the alternative was trial of the issue by an infuriated Congress borders on the grotesque. And the speed with which the impeachment was instituted—three days after the order of removal issued— the repeated assertions during the trial that no judicial decision could be binding on the Senate,[235] demonstrate that the congressional charge of lack of diligence in seeking judicial relief was spurious.[236] The House wanted to submit the issue to a "cordon" of "executioners," not to a dispassionate tribunal.

Finally, whether Johnson was sufficiently diligent seems to me beside the point. The issue of "intent" was germane only to the defense theory that impeachment must be based on a common law or statutory crime. When the Managers and Senate rejected that theory the subsidiary issue of "intent" went with it. "Intent" is further irrelevant (1) if Stanton was not

---

234. Boutwell, ibid. 271; Bingham, ibid. 395.
235. Removal: February 21, 1868, ibid. 53; impeachment: February 24, 1868 (House resolved on). Trial 3. For comments on judicial decisions, supra, text accompanying nn. 212–213.
236. Stevens' "Radical ally, James M. Ashley of Ohio, made it quite clear [in January 1867] that Congress need not allow any court decision to impair or abridge its authority. Ashley reminded his audience that if the Court again issued a 'political decision,' Congress could take advantage of the constitutional mode of getting rid of the Court, as well as the President." Kutler, supra, n. 215 at 66; see also, ibid. 79.

For bare-faced hypocrisy Butler's statement is surely unsurpassed: "If the President had really desired solely to test the unconstitutionality of the law . . . instead of his defiant message to the Senate of the 21st of February, informing them of the removal, but not suggesting that purpose . . . he would have said, in substance: 'Gentlemen of the Senate, in order to test the constitutionality of the law . . . which I verily believe to be unconstitutional and void, I have issued an order of removal . . .' Had the Senate received such a message the Representatives . . . might never have deemed it necessary to impeach the President for such an act." Trial 37. So the impeachment turned on a breach of punctilio! Compare with this Bingham's flat assertion in his closing argument for the Managers, that Johnson "had no power . . . to raise the question at all." Trial 395. Bingham was "a prominent and responsible party spokesman on constitutional and legal questions." Kutler, supra, n. 215 at 15.

protected by the statute, and (2) if Johnson was justified in resisting an unconstitutional encroachment on
executive prerogatives. Given lawful action, "motive"
is of no moment. When Congress, for example, legis-
lates "within the reach of its lawful power," the courts
will not inquire into the motives which induced it to
enact the statute.[237] That principle is equally applicable to executive action within statutory or constitutional
limits.

Let Chief Justice Chase summarize the issues:

Nothing is clearer to my mind than that acts of Congress,
not warranted by the Constitution, are not laws. In case
a law, believed by the President to be unwarranted by the
Constitution, is passed, notwithstanding his veto, it seems
to me that it is his duty to execute it precisely as if he held
it to be constitutional, except in the case where it directly
attacks and impairs the executive power confided to him
by that instrument. In that case it appears to me to be
the clear duty of the President to disregard the law, so
far at least as it may be necessary to bring the question
of its constitutionality before the judicial tribunals ... How
can the President fulfill his oath to preserve, protect and
defend the Constitution, if he has no *right to defend* it
against an act of Congress, sincerely believed by him to
have been passed in violation of it? [238]

The impeachment and trial of Andrew Johnson, to
my mind, represent a gross abuse of the impeachment
process, an attempt to punish the President for differing with and obstructing the policy of Congress. It
was the culmination of a sustained effort to make him
subservient to Congress, to alter the place of a coordinate branch in the constitutional scheme. It undermined the separation of powers and constituted a long
stride toward the very "legislative tyranny" feared and

---

237. Magnano Co. v. Hamilton, 292 U.S. 40, 44 (1934); Fletcher v. Peck,
6 Cranch (10 U.S.) 87, 130 (1810).
238. Warden, supra, n. 67 at 685. Johnson's term had not long to run,
and as Chief Justice Chase asked in a letter to Clark Williams, May 16,
1868, "What possible harm can result to the country from continuance of
Andrew Johnson months longer in the presidential chair, compared with
that which must arise if impeachment becomes a mere mode of getting rid
of an obnoxious President?" Warden, ibid. at 694–695.

fenced in by the Founders. Had it succeeded, no President, in the words of Senator Trumbull, would "be safe who happens to differ" with the Congress "on any measure deemed by them important." [239]

That this "towering act of abandoned wrath" [240] failed is due, to quote Morison, to "seven courageous Republican senators who sacrificed their political future by voting for acquittal." [241] In the midst of the storm that beat upon them they stood upright.[242] Their calm, reasoned opinions, looking into the future, seeking to preserve the constitutional structure, stand in sharp contrast to the fierce invective of Butler, Bingham, Boutwell, Stevens, and Sumner. To the seven recusant Senators we owe it that American justice was not indelibly stained, and for this they deserve to be enshrined in the American Pantheon.

---

239. Trial 420. James G. Blaine, who had voted for impeachment, said later, "The sober reflection of after years has persuaded many who favored Impeachment that it was not justifiable on the charges made, and that its success would have resulted in greater injury to free institutions than Andrew Johnson in his utmost endeavor was able to inflict." McKitrick 487 n. 2. Many analysts "have concluded that had impeachment proved successful as a weapon to remove a politically inacceptable President, the precedent would have been established for the removal of any President refusing persistently to cooperate with Congress, an eventuality implying the establishment of a parliamentary form of government with legislative ascendancy." Alfred H. Kelly & Winfred A. Harbison, *The American Constitution: Its Origin and Development* 477 (New York, 1948).

240. McKitrick 489.

241. Morison 721. But see McKitrick 508 n. 38.

242. In explaining his vote of "guilty," Senator Edmunds noticed that "the appeals and remonstrances of the press of the country, touching our disposition of the case, have been urgent." Trial 424. In more florid rhetoric, Senator Yates stated: "We are not alone in trying this cause. Out on the Pacific shore a deep murmur is heard from thousands of patriot voices; it swells over the western plains . . . with ever increasing volume it advances on by the lakes and through the busy marts of the North, and reechoed by other millions on the Atlantic strand, it thunders upon us a mighty nation's verdict, *guilty.*" Trial 488; see also McKitrick 505 n. 32. The arm-twisting of crucial Senators in response to this thundering horde is set forth by Dewitt 524–549.

CONCLUSION

Scholarly studies are more apt to provoke fresh polemics than to still incessant debate. Even so, I would maintain that history furnishes a plain answer to at least one question that has long cluttered analysis: the test of an impeachable offense in England was not an indictable, common law crime. And when the Framers withheld from Congress the power to inflict criminal punishment which had been exercised by Parliament under "the course of Parliament" as distinguished from the general criminal law, when they limited congressional sanctions on impeachment to removal and disqualification and left criminal punishment to subsequent indictment and conviction, they plainly separated impeachment from criminal process. To insist despite that separation that impeachment is criminal is to raise grave constitutional doubts: does a subsequent prosecution by indictment constitute "double jeopardy"; is "trial by jury" required on impeachment?

By far the lion's share of the debate about impeachment in the last forty years has revolved about the question whether the constitutional provisions for impeachment impliedly bar removal of judges for infractions of "good behavior" by way of a judicial forfeiture proceeding. The arguments for an implied exclusion of removal by judges seem to me insubstantial, and to impose a needless burden upon Congress, which has far more important tasks to perform than to rid us of unsavory judges. The congressional power to impeach is better held in reserve against the failure or neglect of either the Executive or Judiciary to rid the government of servants who have demonstrated their unfitness to hold public office.

Congressman Gerald Ford's proposal to impeach Justice William O. Douglas raises anew the question posed in the Johnson impeachment: is the power to impeach illimitable? Parliament, it is true, asserted virtually unlimited power; but the Framers had no intention of conferring such power upon Congress. Untrammeled declarations of treason in any form were made impossible by a tight definition of treason. And the Framers adopted "high crimes and misdemeanors" because they thought the words had a "limited," "technical" meaning. Whether they misconceived the actual scope of the words is of no moment if they acted upon that view,[1] as the records of the Convention show they did.

For special reasons the Founders conceived that the President would be impeachable for "great offenses" such as corruption, perfidy. Does it follow that they meant equally to limit the broader content of "high crimes and misdemeanors" when applied to judges who, unlike the President, cannot be turned out of office by the electorate but have life tenure conditioned on "good behavior"? And if "high crimes and misdemeanors" should be construed more broadly when applied to judges, do they comprehend disgraceful misconduct outside of office? These are important and difficult questions which deserve more attention than they have received. Having wrestled with them I felt constrained to propose solutions; but I regard my proposals merely as stepping-stones to further analysis.

What lessons are to be drawn from the impeachment of Andrew Johnson? To deduce from its failure that impeachment of the President has proven its unfitness as an instrument of government is to disregard the Founders' knowledge that possible abuse of a power is no argument against its grant.[2] Much less does abuse

---

1. As Charles Evans Hughes said of the Colonists' reliance on Magna Charta: "They had a notion of rights that were fundamental, immutable, and they intended to make those rights secure. It matters not whether they were accurate in their understanding of the Great Charter, for the point is not what it meant when granted by King John, but what the Colonists thought it meant, and what the framers and ratifiers of our constitutional provisions intended by 'law of the land' or 'due process of law.' " C. E. Hughes, *The Supreme Court of the United States* 186 (New York, 1928). For other citations, Berger, *Congress v. Court* 26–27.

2. Supra, pp. 191–192.

spell abandonment of a granted power. The Framers foresaw that impeachment might be subject to super-heated partisanship, that it might threaten presidential independence; but recalling Stuart oppression they chose what seemed the lesser of evils.[3] In our own time the impeachment of President Truman, apparently for his conduct of the Korean War, was suggested by its staff to the Republican high command.[4] There have been reiterated demands for the impeachment of President Nixon, arising out of dissatisfaction with his program for disengagement from the war in Vietnam. President Kennedy concurred with Attorney General Robert Kennedy that if he had not moved to expel Soviet nuclear missiles from Cuba at the time of the confrontation with Khrushchev, he "would have been impeached."[5] Those who are unwilling to concede that the President, without a congressional declaration of war, may commit us to a full-scale war with all its ghastly consequences may yet turn to impeachment as a curb on such presidential adventures.

The chief lesson which emerges from the Johnson trial is that impeachment of the President should be a *last resort.* Inevitably it becomes colored by party spleen, however justified in purpose; an attempt should first be made to accomplish that purpose by less explosive means. Some consider that by exercise of its power over appropriations Congress can bring the President to terms. But should Congress, for example, bring a several-billion foreign aid program to a jarring halt because the executive branch declines to furnish information about the planned disposition of the appropriated funds? Should it delete an appropriation for a vital agency because it refuses to disclose information required by statute about its operations?[6] To my mind this seems to bring a meat-ax to solution of the problem. A happier approach is to submit a controversy

---

3. Supra, Chapter II, text accompanying nn. 213–219. For Edmund Burke, impeachment remained the "great guardian of the purity of the Constitution." E. Burke, *The Works of Edmund Burke* 397 (Boston, 1839).
4. Acheson, supra, Chapter IX, n. 70 at 485, 521.
5. Robert F. Kennedy, *Thirteen Days: A Memoir of the Cuban Missile Crisis* 67 (New York, 1969). Senators Richard Russell and J. W. Fulbright had urged stronger action. Ibid. 53–54.
6. Cf. Berger, "Executive Privilege" 1112–1114.

between Congress and the President, arising out of conflicting claims to power, to the courts, as Andrew Johnson wished to do. That approach met with the approval of Chief Justice Chase; unaware of that history I sought in 1965 to demonstrate that there are no legal obstacles to submission of such controversies to the courts.[7] Conflicting boundary claims are preeminently suited to judicial arbitrament, the least disruptive of solutions. Such arbitrament calls for a realization by both Congress and the President that neither can unilaterally decide the scope of the other's powers. Congress apparently is readier than the President for such a course;[8] and the President would be well advised to ponder on the Johnson trial as an unhappy alternative.

If impeachment of the President there must be, it is, as Senator Fessenden stated, a power "to be exercised with extreme caution" and in "extreme cases." Because it has proven itself infected with the taint of party, it needs to be limited to a cause that would win the assent of "all right-thinking men,"[9] not merely of an exasperated majority such as whipped on the Johnson impeachment.

Finally, a decent regard for the design of the Founders, a resolve to avoid the excesses which forever stigmatized the Johnson trial, should constrain the Congress to disclaim unlimited power and to act within constitutional confines.[10] If there are indeed "limits" to the impeachment power, the Senate may no more act in excess of those limits when it acts "judicially" than when it acts "legislatively." Every branch of government is confined to the "limits" drawn in the Constitution, and the chief purpose of those "limits" was to fence in the much-feared legislative branch. It was not left to the unlimited discretion of that branch to disrupt the other branches through

---

7. Ibid. 1333–1360.
8. Ibid. 1044, 1362.
9. Trial 457.
10. Edmund Burke admonished the House of Commons with respect to a mooted impeachment, "We stand in a position very honorable to ourselves and very useful to our country, if we do not abuse the trust that is placed in us." Quoted 1 Todd 194.

resort to the impeachment power.[11] The tremendous consequences of such disruption were disclosed by the Johnson impeachment; and the narrow escape from "legislative omnipotence" in that trial should lead us to say as Voltaire said of God: if judicial review did not exist, it would have to be invented.[12]

---

11. Bingham's denial of the Court's right to "decide all questions arising under the Constitution and laws" was illustrated by a *reductio ad absurdum:* "according to this logic the Supreme Court would come to sit in judgment at last upon the power given exclusively to each House to judge of the elections and qualifications of our own members." Trial 381. Exactly that "extreme" supposition with respect to "qualifications" has come to pass. Powell v. McCormack, supra, Chapter III, text accompanying nn. 6–14.

12. Evarts, to be sure, premised that the proceedings of the Senate "are incapable of review" in order to press upon the Senate its duty to consider the evidence it had excluded. Trial 344. Standing in the eye of the conflagration, cognizant that at the very time of the impeachment, Congress had enacted, over Johnson's veto, a bill depriving the Supreme Court of jurisdiction to decide the then pending appeal of W. H. McCardle on habeas corpus to release him from imprisonment by the military under the Reconstruction Act, Dewitt 403n, Lomask 240–242, Evarts wisely avoided adding fuel to the flames.

EPILOGUE

MUST IMPEACHMENT PRECEDE INDICTMENT?

A great debate has been raging about whether the President or Vice President must be impeached before he can be indicted. It turns on the provisions of Article I, §3 of the Constitution:

> Judgment in Cases of Impeachment shall not extend further than to removal from Office, and disqualification ... but the Party convicted shall nevertheless be liable and subject to Indictment, Trial ...[1]

Let us begin with the words themselves; "nevertheless" is defined as "notwithstanding or in spite of." Consequently §3 must be understood to mean that an indictment may be filed "in spite of" a prior removal or impeachment. It does violence to language to twist this into a requirement that an impeachment must precede indictment. The implication of "shall nevertheless be liable" to indictment is that the given party is

---

1. Constitution, Article I, §3. It is reported that Special Prosecutor Leon Jaworski advised the grand jury not to indict President Nixon: "It was researched at the time and the conclusion was that legal doubt on the question was so substantial that a move to indict a sitting President would touch off a legal battle of gigantic proportions." *N.Y. Times*, March 12, 1974, p. 24.

When I first studied Article I, §3, I was engrossed in the *separation* of the removal on impeachment from the indictment and unwittingly wrote that "[r]emoval would enable the government to replace an unfit person with a proper person, leaving 'punishment' to a later and separate proceeding . . ." Supra, Chapter II, text before n. 131. At that time the problem whether impeachment *must* precede indictment had never crossed my mind; since then my incautious words have been read to endorse that view. Nixon v. Sirica, 487 F. 2d 700, 757 (D.C. Cir. 1973) (MacKinnon, J., dissenting); Brief for Appellant at 20, Nixon v. Sirica, supra. I hereby repudiate such endorsement, for study of the problem has convinced me that §3 has no such requirement.

315

already liable, that the words are merely designed to preserve existing criminal liability rather than to qualify it.[2] It would be unreasonable to attribute to the Framers an intention to insulate officers from criminal liability by mere appointment to office; like all men they are responsible under the law.[3] Thus Solicitor General Robert H. Bork concluded in a brief designed to demonstrate that Vice President Spiro Agnew could be indicted before he was impeached: "[A] civil officer could be both impeached and criminally punished even absent the Article I, Section 3 proviso."[4]

Since Article II, §4 provides without discrimination for the impeachment of the "President, Vice President and all civil officers," Mr. Bork's statement should be equally applicable to the President. Furthermore, after impeachment and removal the President is returned to the body of the citizenry.[5] No special dispensation is required to allow prosecution of a citizen; nor is there a scrap of evidence that the Framers were minded to clothe an ex-President in any immunity whatsoever. On the contrary, immunity was denied to him as President. It follows that the President is criminally triable while in office, because no special provision is required for trial of an ex-President. An interpretation of the saving clause that makes the President triable only *after* removal from office would therefore reduce the clause to "mere surplusage,"[6] unless we adopt an alternative—that it was designed solely to foreclose the argument of double jeopardy.

Solicitor General Bork justly concluded, as did

---

2. See discussion of double jeopardy at text accompanying nn. 7–10 infra.

3. "[N]o officer of the law may set that law at defiance with impunity. All the officers of government, from the highest to the lowest . . . are bound to obey it." United States v. Lee, 106 U.S. 196, 220 (1882). See n. 17 infra.

4. Memorandum for the United States at 10 n.**, Application of Spiro T. Agnew, Civil No. 73-965 (D. Md.) (memorandum filed Oct. 5, 1973, concerning the Vice President's claim of constitutional immunity, prepared by Solicitor General Robert H. Bork).

5. As Chief Justice Marshall stated, he "is elected from the mass of the people" and "returns to the mass of the people." 1 D. Robertson, *Trial of Aaron Burr* 181 (1808). See note 17 infra.

6. Cohens v. Virginia, 19 U.S. (6 Wheat.) 264, 394 (1821). Chief Justice Marshall added, "This cannot, therefore, be the true construction of the article."

Justice Story 140 years ago,[7] that the "sole purpose" of the Article I, §3 "indictment" proviso "is to preclude the argument that the doctrine of double jeopardy saves the offender from the second trial." [8] That danger arose from the English practice, wherein criminal punishment and removal were wedded in one proceeding; hence it was the part of caution to ward off an inference that a prior impeachment would constitute a bar to indictment. With Solicitor General Bork, I would conclude that the "nevertheless . . . subject to indictment" clause was not designed "to establish the sequence of the two processes, but solely to establish [that a prior conviction upon impeachment] does not raise a double jeopardy defense in a criminal trial." [9] So viewed, the "nevertheless" clause seeks to *preserve* the right to a subsequent criminal prosecution, not to prescribe that it must be preceded by impeachment. Justice Miller's statement in *Langford v. United States* that "the ministers personally, like our President, may be impeached; or if the wrong amounts to a crime, they may be indicted" [10] likewise rebuts insistence that indictment must follow after impeachment.

This conclusion is further buttressed by other factors. "The only explicit immunity in the Constitution," said

7. 1 Story, §782.
8. Bork, supra, n. 4 at 8.
9. Ibid. at 10. Mr. Bork properly points out that "impeachment and the criminal process serve different ends so that the outcome of one has no legal effect upon the outcome of the other," a conclusion justly rested on James Wilson:
Impeachments . . . come not . . . within the sphere of ordinary jurisprudence. They are founded on different principles; are governed by different maxims, and are directed to different objects; for this reason, the trial and punishment of an offense in the impeachment, is no bar to a trial of the same offense at common [criminal] law.
Bork, supra, n. 4 at 8–9, citing 1 Wilson 324.
Bork, at 11, also cites cases in state courts that reached a similar conclusion under constitutional provisions modeled on Article 1, §3, such as Commonwealth v. Rowe, 112 Ky. 482, 66 S.W. 29 (1902); State v. Jefferson, 90 N.J.L. 507, 101 A. 569 (Ct. Err. & App. 1917). In addition, Bork, at 16n, points to United States v. Kerner (involving an indictment and conviction of Circuit Judge Otto Kerner prior to impeachment) then pending in the 7th Circuit and since decided in favor of the Department of Justice position that such a judge is a subject of indictment and conviction prior to impeachment and removal. N.Y. Times, Feb. 21, 1974, p. 6. To this may be added that Justice William Rehnquist, then Assistant Attorney General, Office of Legal Counsel, advised Attorney General John Mitchell that the United States could prosecute Justice Abe Fortas without waiting on impeachment. Keeffe, "Explorations in the Wonderland of Impeachment," 59 A.B.A.J. 885, 886 (1973).
10. 101 U.S. 341, 343 (1879).

Solicitor General Bork, "is the limited immunity granted Congressmen" [11] in Article I, §6, which provides:

> The Senators and Representatives . . . shall in all cases, except treason, felony or breach of the peace, be privileged from arrest during their attendance at the session of their respective Houses, and in going to and returning from the same.

In the words of Mr. Bork:

> Since the Framers knew how to, and did, spell out immunity, the natural inference is that no immunity exists where none is mentioned.[12]

The Supreme Court has employed that principle of construction.[13] Not only is this the "natural inference," but we have the testimony of Charles Pinckney, one of the most active participants in the Constitutional Convention, who, in explaining the Constitution to the South Carolina Ratification Convention, stated that no immunity for the President was intended. Speaking in the Senate in 1800, Pinckney said that "it never was intended to give Congress . . . any but specified [privileges], and those very limited privileges indeed." [14] And addressing himself to certain privileges under discussion, he stated, "No privilege of this kind was intended for your Executive, nor any except which I have mentioned for your Legislature. The Convention . . . well knew that . . . no subject had been more abused than privilege. They therefore determined to set the example, in merely limiting privilege to what was necessary, and no more." [15] James Wilson, considered by Washington

---

11. Bork, supra, n. 4 at 4.
12. Ibid. at 5.
13. See, e.g., T.I.M.E., Inc. v. United States, 359 U.S. 464, 471 (1959): "We find it impossible to impute to Congress an intention to give such a right to shippers under the Motor Carriers Act when the very sections which established that right in Part I [for railroads] were wholly omitted in the Motor Carriers Act."
14. 10 Annals of Cong. 72 (1800).
15. Ibid. 74. In the course of his remarks, Pinckney addressed himself to the questions "why the Constitution should have been so attentive to each branch of Congress . . . and have shown so little to the President . . . in this respect. Why should the individual members of either branch . . .

"to be one of the strongest men in the Convention," [16] assured the Pennsylvania Ratification Convention that "not a *single privilege* is annexed to his [the President's] character." [17] Remarks such as these were a response to the pervasive distrust of executive power.[18] Nothing in the prior English practice, with which the Framers were familiar,[19] suggests a requirement that impeachment had to precede indictment. On several occasions the Parliament preferred to refer the case to the courts; and one of the most learned lawyers in Parliament, Sir John Maynard, said of the charges against Sir Adam Blair: "I would not go before the Lords, when the law is clear, and may be tried by juries." [20] Constitutional history therefore confirms the inference properly drawn from the face of the Constitution that no immunity was given to the President.

By a feat of legerdemain Mr. Bork would read the President out of this history. He recognizes that the impeachment debate "related almost exclusively to the Presidency" and that "the impeachment clause was expanded to cover the Vice President and other civil officers only toward the very end of the Convention." [21] Mr. Bork's view presents the anomaly that the history of the impeachment provision, framed entirely in the context of the President, refers only to the "Vice President and all civil officers," who were virtually unmentioned and were added as a last-minute afterthought. Thus a provision the "sole purpose" of which was to forfend the double jeopardy argument, which was not designed "to establish the sequence" of impeachment or

---

have more privileges than him [*sic*]." Ibid. Thus the withholding of presidential immunity was no oversight; it was intentional. The explanation lies in history cited by the Supreme Court. See text accompanying n. 39 infra.

16. M. Farrand, *The Framing of the Constitution* 21 (1913).

17. 2 Elliot 480 (1836). In his Lectures of 1791, James Wilson, a Justice of the Supreme Court, rephrased this as follows: "[T]he most powerful magistrates should be amenable to the law . . . No one should be secure while he violates the constitution and the laws." 1 Wilson 425.

18. Berger, Executive Privilege 49–50, 52–53 (1974). Hamilton was constrained to rebut attacks upon grants to the President by those who, "[c]alculating upon the aversion of the people to monarchy," portrayed the President "as the full-grown progeny of that detested parent." *Federalist* No. 68 at 448.

19. Infra, General Index, pages cited under heading "Founders." Compare supra, Chapter II, text accompanying nn. 81 ff., with supra, Chapter II, text before n. 167; and see supra, Chapter IV, n. 217.

20. 12 Howell 1211, 1212.

21. Bork supra, n. 4 at 6–7.

indictment, and which is accompanied by an "immunity" provision limited to Congress (without immunity for felonies) so that "the natural inference is that no immunity exists where none is intended," suddenly is found to establish precisely that "sequence" and to confer exactly that un-"natural" immunity on the President. When we emerge from Bork's elaborate argument that the President must be impeached before he is indicted, it adds up to a claim of immunity from criminal prosecution that was denied him. On what grounds is this analytical somersault justified?

Mr. Bork first states that the Framers' "remarks strongly suggest an understanding that the President, as Chief Executive, would not be subject to the ordinary criminal process . . . For example . . . Gouverneur Morris observed that the Supreme Court would 'try the President after the trial of the impeachment.' " [22] That this is ill-considered shorthand emerges from the reference to a trial by the Supreme Court, which can only hear an appeal. Bork also cites Hamilton for the assertion that "the Framers' discussion assumed that impeachment would precede criminal trial." [23] Hamilton's participation in the Convention was sporadic and had little, if any, influence.[24] At the close of the Convention he handed Madison a plan in which he proposed that the President be impeached and removed and "be afterwards tried and punished." [25] So far as the records show, it was not considered by the Convention. The Framers were fastidious draftsmen, keenly alive to the weight of every word.[26] They employed neither "after" nor "afterward"; [27] and it is not for us to supply

---

22. Bork, supra, n. 4 at 6, citing 2 Farrand 500 (1911).
23. Bork, supra, n. 4 at 17. Another citation by Bork, at 6, is to 2 Farrand 64–69, 626. Nothing relevant to the impeachment-indictment sequence is contained in those pages.
24. J. Miller, *Alexander Hamilton: Portrait in Paradox* 174–176, 178 (1959).
25. 3 Farrand 617, 625.
26. Compare their rejection of "high misdemeanor" because it has a "technical meaning too limited" and the substitution of "high crimes and misdemeanors" for "maladministration." Supra, Chapter II, text accompanying nn. 107–108. As was said by Chief Justice Taney: "[N]o word was unnecessarily used, or needlessly added . . . Every word appears to have been weighed with the utmost deliberation, and its force and effect to have been fully understood." Holmes v. Jennison, 39 U.S. (14 Pet.) 540, 571 (1840).
27. Compare Hamilton's suggestion that on impeachment the President

a word thus omitted, to convert "nevertheless" (in spite of) into "afterward," that is, to transform a nonsequential provision into a prescribed sequence. Nor can the mistaken Morris-Hamilton versions of the provision be read to create the very immunity that the Framers intentionally withheld from the President when they squarely faced the issue. The §3 proviso must be read together with the immunity provision; if possible both should be given effect.[28] Above all, we "cannot rightly prefer" a meaning "which will defeat rather than effectuate the Constitutional purpose." [29]

If, however, the remarks of Morris and Hamilton are to override this withholding of immunity, they no less demand that the "Vice President and all civil officers" likewise first be impeached and then indicted. Mr. Bork's anticipatory answer was that "[i]t is, of course, significant that such remarks referred only to the President, not to the Vice President and other civil officers." [30] How could it be otherwise when the President was the sole object of discussion? There was no allusion to impeachment of the others until the end when the "Vice President and all civil officers" were casually added to the impeachment provision without discussion.[31] As Bork himself has stated, "[N]one of the general debates addressed or considered the particular nature of the powers [or immunities] of the Vice President or other civil officers." [32] How then could the Framers consider the denial to them of an immunity allegedly granted to the President? The fact is that all the history cited by Mr. Bork to establish the prior indictability of the Vice President had reference to the President alone and establishes *his* prior indictability.

After his bow to history, Mr. Bork turns to the struc-

---

be suspended until judgment, 3 Farrand 617, 625, with the rejection of such a motion made by Morris and Rutledge. 2 Farrand 612. When Hamilton stated in *Federalist* No. 69 at 446 that "[t]he President would be liable [in impeachment] and would afterwards be liable to [criminal] prosecution," he was referring to his own plan rather than a faithful rendition of Article I, §3.
  28. For the appropriate rule of construction, see, e.g., United States v. Menasche, 348 U.S. 528, 538–539 (1955); cf. Fisher v. District of Columbia, 164 F. 2d 707, 708–709 (D.C. Cir. 1948).
  29. United States v. Classic, 313 U.S. 299, 316 (1941).
  30. Bork, supra, n. 4 at 6.
  31. Supra, Chapter IV, text accompanying nn. 112–116.
  32. Bork, supra, n. 4 at 7.

ture of the Constitution, wherein he finds "embedded" reasons for drawing the distinction between the President and the others.[33] No such distinction was, of course, drawn by the Founders; it is the product of presidential counsel 185 years after the event. In a nutshell, Bork rings the changes on "the singular importance of the President." [34] The crucial nature of the President's executive responsibilities, on which Mr. Bork lays such great store, played no role in the impeachment debate. Instead, opponents of impeachment urged that it would invade the President's "independence" and violate the separation of powers,[35] a central principle from which the Framers proceeded. The felt necessity for a curb on presidential transgressions, however, overcame this "independence" argument; despite the "crucial nature" of his powers, the Framers gave Congress power to oust him for various noncriminal offenses.[36] They made no move to interfere with the normal criminal process that applied to every person; on the contrary, they withheld from him an immunity from criminal prosecution that, but for felonies, they expressly conferred upon Congress.

"This limited grant of immunity" to Congress, Bork explains, "demonstrates a recognition that, although the functions of the legislature are not lightly to be interfered with, the public interest in the expeditious and even-handed administration of the criminal law outweighs the cost imposed by the incapacity of a single legislator. Such incapacity does not seriously impair the functioning of Congress." [37] A very different conclusion needs to be drawn from the fact that "a limited

---

33. Ibid.
34. Ibid. at 18.
35. Rufus King referred "to the primitive axiom that the three great departments of Govts. should be separate & independent," and asked, "Would this be the case if the Executive should be impeachable?" 2 Farrand 66. Charles Pinckney stated that impeachment by the Legislature would give it "a rod over the Executive and by that means effectually destroy his independence." Ibid.
36. George Mason, expressing the view that prevailed, stated, "No point is of more importance than that the right of impeachment should be continued." Ibid. 65. Edmund Randolph stated. "The Executive will have great opportunity for abusing his power." Ibid. 67. See also the remarks of James Madison and Elbridge Gerry. Ibid. 66. The vote was 8 to 2 in favor of retaining the impeachment power. Ibid. 69. For a discussion of noncriminal offenses, see supra, Chapter II, text accompanying nn. 1–187.
37. Bork, supra, n. 4 at 16.

grant of immunity" was conferred upon members of Congress, whereas none whatever was given to the President: The President was not nearly as "important" in the eyes of the Framers as he is in those of Bork. "There is little doubt," said the Supreme Court, "that the instigation of criminal charges against the critical or disfavored legislators by the executive in a judicial forum ['the judges were often lackeys of the Stuart monarchs'[38]] was the chief fear prompting the long struggle for parliamentary privilege in England."[39] Both the "speech and debate" clause and the "immunity from arrest" clause were "consciously" drawn by the Framers "from this common historical background,"[40] which bespeaks fear of rather than special solicitude for executive power. Moreover, the Founders had observed that the most powerful ministers could be condemned to death without endangering the continuity of government, indeed, in the case of the Earl of Strafford, conducing to the preservation of liberty.[41] It is no answer to point to the invulnerability of the King because first, as Gouverneur Morris pointed out, "[the first Magistrate] is not the King but the prime-Minister,"[42] and second, as James Iredell emphasized, the President, unlike the King, was made triable.[43]

A kindred speculation is that "[t]he Framers could not have contemplated prosecution of an incumbent President because they vested in him complete power over execution of the laws, which includes, of course, the power to control prosecutions."[44] When President Nixon acted on this premise and discharged Special Prosecutor Archibald Cox, who was engaged, among other things, in investigating whether the President was implicated in the Watergate coverup and other criminal acts, a storm of outrage swept over the White House.[45] It is reasonable to infer that the Framers

38. United States v. Johnson, 383 U.S. 169, 181 (1966).
39. Ibid. 182; see also ibid. 178.
40. K. Bradshaw & D. Pring, *Parliament and Congress* 95 (1972).
41. Supra, Chapter I, text accompanying nn. 106–129, 167–168.
42. 2 Farrand 69.
43. 4 Elliot 109.
44. Bork, supra, n. 4 at 20.
45. The discharge was held illegal by District Judge Gerhard Gesell. Nader v. Bork, 366 F. Supp. 104 (D.D.C. 1973).

never intended to permit the President to shield himself from criminal indictment by the control given him over such prosecutions. Next Mr. Bork argues that the presidential pardoning power extends to a pardon for himself, thus rendering criminal conviction ineffectual.[46] Such a pardon after conviction would be an even greater affront to the nation than Nixon's discharge of Cox to impede his own prosecution. The "pardon" provision must be read in harmony with the "immunity" provision; it was not designed to confer an immunity intentionally withheld.[47] Constitutional construction should not depart from common sense; [48] it should not proceed from horribles that the nation would reject and that would have even more greatly affronted the Founders.

Like Solicitor General Bork, Professor Alexander Bickel declares that the Article I, §3 provision "does not remotely say that impeachment must precede indictment" and like him he considers that the "case of the President . . . is unique." He does not base this on the "original intention" but on the premise that "[i]n the presidency is embodied the continuity and indestructibility of the state." [49] He would thereby import into our system the monarchical notion that the continuity of the state was embodied in the crown: "*L'Etat c'est moi*." [50] But by the eighteenth century,

---

46. Bork, supra, n. 4 at 20.
47. In Ex parte Grossman, 267 U.S. 87, 121 (1925), the Court said that the pardoning power "is a check entrusted to the executive for special cases. To exercise it to the extent of destroying the deterrent effect of judicial punishment would be to pervert it; but whoever is to make it useful must have full discretion to exercise it. Our Constitution confers this discretion on the highest officer in the nation in confidence that he will not abuse it." An abuse "would suggest a resort to impeachment . . ."
48. A respected scholar and judge, Herbert F. Goodrich, stated that "[i]f a legal rule fails to satisfy the untechnical requirements of ordinary common sense the premises behind the rule had better be carefully examined." Gavin v. Hudson & Manhattan Co., 185 F. 2d 104, 105–106 (3d Cir. 1950).
49. Bickel, "The Constitutional Tangle," *The New Republic*, Oct. 6, 1973, pp. 14, 15.
50. Gibbon says of Rome that "the obsequious civilians unanimously pronunced that the republic is contained in the person of its chief." 4 E. Gibbon, *The History of the Decline and Fall of the Roman Empire* 509 (Nottingham Soc'y ed. undated). A current illustration is furnished by the statement of Emperior Haile Selassie of Ethiopia on March 11, 1974, aibet with recognition of the winds of change: "[W]hile the monarchy was a durable institutiop needed to hold Ethiopia togetheir, its once overwhelming political power was not 'eternal' and could be varied according to the requirements and exigencies of the times." *N.Y. Times*, March 12, 1974, p. 13.

Parliament had prevailed in its struggle with the King; and the downfalls of Charles I and James II had shown that the indestructibility of a King was not synonymous with the "indestructibility of the state." For Blackstone the "sovereign power" meant "the making of the laws"; it had come to rest in Parliament, "this being the place where that absolute despotic power, which must in all governments reside somewhere, is entrusted by the constitution of these kingdoms." [51] Therefore, if we are to look to the history the Founders had before them, the Parliament rather than the King was the repository of sovereignty, the symbol of "continuity." Among the revolutionary changes made by the Founders was to establish that sovereignty resided in the people and that the officers of government were merely their servants and agents.[52] In the words of Gouverneur Morris, "[T]he people are the King." [53] Presidents come and go but the people remain. The consensus of the Founders was that the President's main function was to execute the laws, that as commander in chief he was merely the "first General." [54] Such functionaries are expendable rather than indispensable; thus the view of the President taken by the Framers is incompatible with the proposition that in him the Framers "embodied the continuity and indestructibility of the state." The fact that they made him removable from office alone suggests that a hiatus in his office was not thought to threaten that "indestructibility." This also emerges from Hamilton's statement about the King: There is "no punishment to which he can be subjected without involving the crisis of a national revolution," [55] implying thereby that removal or indictment of the President could have no calamitous effect.

The nation has also survived a number of presidential deaths and assassinations without impairment of the presidency or the "indestructibility of the state." It is a mistake, I suggest, to identify the "continuity"

51. 1 Blackstone 49, 160–161 (1765).
52. Berger, *Congress v. Court* 174–175 (1969). See also G. Wood, *The Creation of the American Republic, 1776–1787* 362, 377, 382, 530 (1969).
53. 2 Farrand 69.
54. Berger, Executive Privilege 51–52, 61–63.
55. *Federalist* No. 69 at 446.

of the presidency with that of a given President. Whatever befalls a President, the state and the presidency are "indestructible." [56] The fact is that a Vice President is immediately available to assume executive functions without skipping a beat; and if he is unavailable there is a row of statutory successors. William Henry Harrison died and was succeeded by John Tyler, Zachary Taylor by Millard Fillmore, Warren G. Harding by Calvin Coolidge, and Franklin D. Roosevelt by Harry Truman. Upon assassination, Lincoln was succeeded by Andrew Johnson, James A. Garfield by Chester A. Arthur, William McKinley by Theodore Roosevelt, and John F. Kennedy by Lyndon B. Johnson. One may hazard that Tyler was an improvement on Harrison; certainly Theodore Roosevelt was an improvement on McKinley, as was Coolidge on Harding; Truman was at least an adequate substitute for an ailing and sinking Franklin Roosevelt. That is not a bad list to pit against the unfortunate succession of Andrew Johnson to the chair of Abraham Lincoln. A senseless assassination creates a shock for which the nation is utterly unprepared, in contrast to a removal on impeachment or conviction on indictment of a President in whom the nation has lost confidence.

Obviously, Professor Bickel states, "the presidency cannot be conducted from jail, nor can it be effectively carried on while an incumbent is defending himself in a criminal trial." [57] The second proposition is by no means obvious; Andrew Johnson did not personally participate in his impeachment and he continued to perform the duties of his office.[58] A President equally may entrust his defense in a criminal trial to his counsel. If he feels constrained to be present, that is no more disturbing to the performance of his duties than his parallel presence at an impeachment trial; in either case the effect on his functioning is the same. While

---

56. In the words of Arthur Schlesinger, Jr.: "The Presidency, though its wings could be clipped for a time, was an exceedingly tough institution. . . . It had endured many challenges and survived many vicissitudes. It was nonsense to suppose that its fate as an institution was bound up with the fate of the particular man who happened to be President at any given time." A. Schlesinger, Jr., *The Imperial Presidency* 405 (1973).
57. See Bickel, supra, n. 49 at 15.
58. The Framers rejected suspension prior to conviction. See n. 27 supra.

it is true that the presidency "cannot be conducted
from jail," it is unrealistic to postulate that a convicted President could not be released on bail pending
appeal. Moreover, the attempt of a convicted President
to hang on to his office would present a spectacle that
the nation would find intolerable. A storm of public
outrage such as would make the "firestorm" after the
Cox discharge seem like a sputtering candle could
sweep him from office. If the President lacked the
sensitivity to resign,[59] an impeachment could speedily
follow; the most partisan congressman would hardly
summon the hardihood to reject the verdict of the
people. The test of the availability of criminal process,
I suggest, should not turn on hypotheticals that strain
credulity. "[O]f what value," said Macaulay, "is a
theory which is true only on a supposition in the
highest degree extravagant?" [60]

There is a last practical consideration, which Solicitor General Bork summarized in the context of "civil
officers":

[I]f Article I, Section 3, clause 7, were read to mean that
no one not convicted upon impeachment could be tried
criminally, the failure of the House to vote an impeachment, or the failure of the impeachment in the Senate,
would confer upon the civil officer accused complete and
—were the statute of limitations permitted to run—permanent immunity from criminal prosecution however plain
his guilt.[61]

That would be no less true of the President. No great
stretch of the imagination is required to conceive that
partisanship in Congress may defeat an impeachment
of the President in the House or conviction by two-
thirds of the Senate. Suppose that Special Prosecutor
Leon Jaworski were convinced that he had evidence
that would establish the President's guilt. Although a
partisan one-third of the Senate might differ, can it be

---

59. Vice President Spiro Agnew resigned after indictment and before
trial, explaining in part that the welfare of the nation would thereby be
served. *N.Y. Times*, Oct. 11, 1973, p. 35.
60. 2 T. Macaulay, *Critical and Historical Essays* 128 (1890).
61. Bork, supra, note 4 at 9–10.

reasonable that he should be barred from prosecution because an impeachment fell prey to partisanship?

A mistake against which we must be ever vigilant is to read our own predilections back into the minds of the Framers.[62] One of the most eminent of the Founders, James Iredell, later a Justice of the Supreme Court, cautioned:

We are too apt, in estimating a law passed at a remote period, to combine, in our consideration, all the subsequent events which have had an influence upon it, instead of confining ourselves (which we ought to do) to the existing circumstances at the time of its passing.[63]

These are not merely the yearnings of a legalistic "strict constructionist"; they are a canon of historiography. The task of the historian, Ranke taught, is to establish the facts of history *wie es eigentlich gewesen war;* the search must be for what actually happened and, if we find it, not to substitute for it what should have happened. As in the task of construing any document, the primary function is to ascertain the intention of the draftsmen. When that intention is discovered, what Iredell said becomes of prime importance: "The people have chosen to be governed under such and such principles. They have not chosen to be governed, or promised to submit upon any other." [64]

It is easier, however, to preach such vigilance than to practice it, as I can testify from personal experience in the very context of the distinction here under discussion. Influenced by the difficulty of giving the words "high crimes and misdemeanors" a narrow construction in the case of the President and a broad one for judges, I initially concluded that they must be given a single meaning. But I was led to alter my view upon consideration of the fact that judges were added to the

---

62. Compare Justice Sutherland on "sovereignty" in United States v. Curtiss-Wright Export Corp., 299 U.S. 304 (1936), discussed in Berger, "The Presidental Monopoly of Foreign Relations," 71 *Mich. L. Rev.* 1, 26–33 (1972).

63. Ware v. Hylton, 3 U.S. (3 Dall.) 199, 267 (1796). See Berger, *Congress v. Court* 22–23.

64. 2 G. McRee, *Life and Correspondence of James Iredell* 146 (1857–1858).

impeachment provision at the last minute with no reference either to judges or to governing standards. From this and other data I reasoned that stricter standards of conduct might be required of a judge, that is, that the range of impeachable offenses might be broader.[65] Whatever the validity of that reasoning, it cannot be invoked for the President who was the subject of the debates and the constitutional restrictions; a broader application of those restrictions to judges does not warrant a total immunity from criminal prosecution for the President. Sensible, however, of the "difficulties involved in adoption of the view that impeachment of judges requires a less restricted reading of those words [high crimes and misdemeanors] than does that of the President," I suggested that "[p]erhaps a better solution is to take a more hospitable approach to removal of judges *by judges* for infractions of good behavior . . . ,"[66] indicating thereby that I entertained some doubts about my change of position.

The problem of giving two meanings to the same words in the very same context has continued to trouble me, the more so as I examined the difficulties which Mr. Bork's analysis engendered, his attempt to render utterances exclusively directed at the President applicable solely to "the Vice President and all civil officers," who were not mentioned. My thinking has reverted to my initial view, additionally influenced by the statement of the Supreme Court in *Atlantic Cleaners & Dyers v. United States:* "[T]here is a natural presumption that identical words used in different parts of the same act are intended to have the same meaning . . ."[67] Here the presumption is fortified by the fact that the words are used not in different parts of the Constitution but in one place, in the very same context; and Mr. Bork seeks to give them a different meaning with respect to whom they apply. No trace of an intention to give them that dual meaning is to be found in the history of the provision. This is not to say that the presumption

65. Supra, Chapter II, text accompanying nn. 180–187.
66. Supra, Chapter II, text following n. 187.
67. 286 U.S. 427, 433 (1932).

is irrebuttable,[68] but that the rebuttal cannot rest on factors that were not before the Framers, on an image of the presidency which is a product of our times and which they emphatically did not share.

Such distinctions represent but another attempt to revise the Constitution under the guise of euphemisms, derived from an exalted notion of the presidency which is far removed from the egalitarian sentiments of the Founders.[69] When the subpoena to Jefferson issued, Albert Beveridge, who had scoured the newspapers of the time, comments, "For the first time, most Republicans approved of the opinion of John Marshall. In the fanatical politics of the time there was enough honest adherence to the American ideal, that all men are equal in the eyes of the law, to justify the calling of a President, even Thomas Jefferson, before a court of justice." [70] It is we who have surrounded the President with a mystique that has contributed heavily to an "imperial presidency." [71] When we forget that the President is "but a man . . . but a citizen" [72] we are on the road that has unfailingly led to Caesarism. It was because the Founders had learned this lesson from history that presidential powers were enumerated and limited, and that immunity from arrest was altogether withheld.

IMPEACHMENT: MR. ST. CLAIR'S "INSTANT HISTORY"

If the House "be found incompetent to one of the greatest [causes] . . . it is impossible that this form of trial

---

68. The Court stated,
> Where the subject matter [impeachment] to which the words refer is not the same in the several places where they are used, or the conditions are different, or the scope of the legislative power exercised in one case is broader than that exercised in another, the meaning may well vary to meet the purposes of the law, to be arrived at by a consideration of the language in which those purposes are expressed, and of the circumstances under which the language was employed.

Ibid.
69. See Raoul Berger, "The President, Congress, and the Courts," 83 *Yale L. J.* 1111 (1974), n. 1. Herbert Butterfield, who has considered the problems of historiography in his penetrating study, *George III and the Historians* (rev. ed. 1969), remarked that "it is often necessary to know a great deal of history before one is equipped for the interpreting of historical documents." Ibid. 18. This is more essential with respect to a constitution. See text accompanying n. 64 supra.
70. 3 A. Beveridge, *The Life of John Marshall* 450 (1919).
71. See A. Schlesinger, Jr., supra, n. 56 at ix.
72. 1 T. Carpenter, *The Trial of Colonel Aaron Burr* 90 (1807).

should not, in the end, vanish out of the constitution. For we must not deceive ourselves: whatever does not stand with credit cannot stand long. And if the constitution should be deprived ... of this resource, it is virtually deprived of everything else, that is valuable in it. For this process is the cement which binds the whole together ... here it is that we provide for that, which is the substantial excellence of our constitution ... by which ... no man in no circumstance, can escape the account, which he owes to the laws of his country." [73]

When a client proclaims that he will "fight like hell" to balk impeachment it may be expected that his lawyer will follow suit. Not surprisingly, therefore, James St. Clair, chief defense counsel for President Nixon, has favored the House Judiciary Committee with a lengthy memorandum that purports to prove by recourse to history that the President may only be impeached for an indictable crime.[74] That standard would virtually nullify impeachment for the nonindictable offenses which were the chief concern of the Founders and which the evidence plainly shows they considered impeachable. Despite its issuance from the august precincts of the White House, the memorandum is but "lawyer's history," a pastiche of selected snippets and half-truths, exhibiting a resolute disregard of adverse facts, and simply designed to serve the best interests of a client rather than faithfully to represent history as it actually was.

Although defense lawyers are notoriously not the best source of constitutional history,[75] such pseudo-history cannot be ignored because, as J. R. Wiggins

73. 7 E. Burke, *Works* 14 (1839) (Burke's opening statement at the trial of Warren Hastings).

74. J. St. Clair, "An Analysis of the Constitutional Standard for Presidential Impeachment," issued in late February 1974. The memorandum consists of six pages of summary and a body of sixty-one pages.

75. The value of such "history" is illuminated by the citation, ibid. at 42–43, of the argument of Luther Martin on behalf of Justice Samuel Chase in 1805. Martin, a heavy drinker, appeared in 1810 before Justice Chase on circuit in Baltimore, somewhat more inebriated than usual. Chase complained, "I am surprised that you can so prostitute your talents." Martin replied, "Sir, I never prostituted my talents except when I defended you and Col. Burr"; and turning to the jury he added confidentially, "[A]

said of a similar submission by the then Deputy Attorney General William P. Rogers on the issue of executive privilege, "Unless historians bestir themselves . . . the lawyers' summary that has placed 170 years of history squarely behind the assertion of unlimited executive power to withhold information threatens to get incorporated into that collection of fixed beliefs and settled opinions that governs the conduct of affairs. History thereafter may become what lawyers mistakenly said it was theretofore." [76] "Legal history," said Justice Frankfurter, "still has its claims." [77]

In the present controversial atmosphere it is all too easy to say "a plague on both your houses" and even-handedly to attribute partisan readings of history to one and all. My study, however, of the meaning of "high crimes and misdemeanors," the central issue of impeachment, was undertaken in 1968–1970, submitted to the *Southern California Law Review* in midsummer of 1970, and published in 1971,[78] long before Watergate surfaced and before there was any thought that President Nixon might be impeachable. Composed in the quiet of a university, uninfluenced by fees or hopes of preferment, my study may or may not be mistaken, but it can hardly be dismissed as biased, simply because there then was no occasion whatsoever for partisan bias.

Indictable Offenses

Let us begin in midstream with the Nixon-St. Clair thesis that impeachment is available only for an indictable crime. Former Attorney General Elliot L. Richardson recently stated, "It seems clear to me as a matter of common sense that impeachable offenses cannot be limited to matters defined in the U.S. Penal

couple of the greatest rascals in the world." P. Clarkson & R. Jett, *Luther Martin of Maryland* 280 (1970). *In vino veritas*.
76. Wiggins, "Lawyers as Judges of History," 75 *Proceedings Mass. Hist. Soc'y* 84, 104 (1963).
77. FPC v. Natural Gas Pipeline Co., 315 U.S. 575, 609 (1942) (concurring opinion).
78. Berger, "Impeachment for 'High Crimes and Misdemeanors,'" 44 *S. Cal. L. Rev.* 395 (1971).

Code." [79] Common sense is buttressed by this historical record. Mr. St. Clair, quoting the Supreme Court, recognizes that under federal law there are no crimes except as declared by statute: "The legislature authority of the Union must first make an act a crime, affix a punishment to it. . . ." [80] That is what the Act of 1790 did for treason and bribery; [81] but with the exception of a handful of statutes, such as those that make "high misdemeanors" of privateering against friendly nations, [82] launching military expeditions against them from American soil, [83] practicing law by a federal judge, [84] conspiring or counseling to insurrection or riot, [85] there are no indictable "high misdemeanors." Consequently, the offenses the Founders particularly had in mind would be unimpeachable. Consider "subversion of the Constitution"—usurpation of power, the very offense that prompted the addition of the words "high crimes and misdemeanors." George Mason said in the Federal Convention:

Treason as defined in the Constitution will not reach many great and dangerous offenses. Hastings is not guilty of Treason. Attempts to subvert the Constitution may not be

---

79. *Harv. L. Record,* March 15, 1974, p. 9.
80. St. Clair, supra, n. 74 at 17, quoting United States v. Hudson & Goodwin, 11 U.S. (7 Cranch) 32 (1812).
81. Act of April 30, 1790, ch. 9, §§1, 21, 1 Stat. 112, 117.
Professor Jefferson Fordham states that "treason is defined as a crime by the Constitution in the judicial article with the element of sanction left to the Congress." Fordham, Book Review, 47 *S. Cal. L. Rev.* 673, 676 (1974). The Supreme Court held that, to constitute a crime, it is necessary to "affix a punishment to proscribed conduct." United States v. Hudson & Goodwin, 11 U.S. (7 Cranch) 32 (1812). Had Congress elected not to "affix a punishment," treason would not have constituted a "crime"; no one could have been prosecuted for treason. By the Act of 1790, treason was made a crime; it will hardly be maintained that prior thereto treasonable acts were indictable. An unpunishable "crime" is like "a grin without a cat."
Since, as Fordham recognized, "the definition appears to be intended for all purposes, including impeachment," 47 *S. Cal. L. Rev.* at 676, it cannot be *assumed* that impeachment for treason was criminal in nature. The fact that George Mason emphasized that "treason" as defined would not reach "subversion of the Constitution" and suggested "maladministration" which, to say the least, comprehended *some* acts of noncriminal nature, alone argues against such an assumption. See 2 Farrand 550. The substitution of "high crimes and misdemeanors" for Mason's "maladministration" indicates that the association of "high crimes and misdemeanors" with "treason" was not thought to render "high crimes and misdemeanors" criminal for impeachment purposes.
82. Act of June 14, 1797, ch. 1, §1, 1 Stat. 520.
83. Act of June 5, 1794, ch. 50, §5, 1 Stat. 384.
84. 28 U.S.C. §454 (1970).
85. Act of June 5, 1794, ch. 50, § 1, 1 Stat. 381–382.

Treason as above defined. . . . It is the more necessary to extend the power of impeachments.[86]

Under Mr. St. Clair's interpretation the manifest intention of the Framers to reach such subversion would be frustrated by the lack of an indictable crime, for no federal statute has made it a crime. So too, other categories of "high crimes and misdemeanors," under the English practice upon which our impeachment provisions were modeled and which were mentioned by the Founders, such as "abuse of power," "betrayal of trust," and "neglect of duty," would also fall by the wayside. Yet Madison stated that protection against presidential "negligence" was indispensable, that perversion of the office "into a scheme of . . . oppression," that is, "abuse of power," should be impeachable.[87] Madison, C. C. Pinckney, and Gouverneur Morris referred to "betrayal of trust"; [88] Edward Rutledge spoke of "abuse of trust," as did Hamilton in *The Federalist*.[89]

Madison, the leading architect of the Constitution, furnished three illustrations of impeachable offenses that have never been made indictable crimes: (1) In the Virginia Ratification Convention he stated that "if the President be connected, in any suspicious manner with any person, and there be grounds to believe that he will shelter him," he may be impeached.[90] (2) In the First Congress—that "almost adjourned session of the Convention"—he said that the President would be impeachable if he "neglects to superintend [his subordinates'] conduct, so as to check their excesses." [91] (3) There too he stated that "the wanton removal of meritorious officers" would be impeachable.[92] To this day all of these categories of "high crimes and misdemeanors" have not been made indictable crimes, reflecting a continuing judgment by Congress, which

---

86. 2 Farrand 550. Chapter II, supra, incorporates the article cited in note 78 supra.
87. Supra, Chapter II, text accompanying n. 167.
88. Ibid.
89. *Federalist* No. 65 at 423.
90. Supra, Chapter II, text accompanying n. 168.
91. 1 *Annals of Cong.* 372–373 (1789) (page running head "History of Congress").
92. 1 *Annals of Cong.* 498 (1789) (page running head "History of Congress").

has the "sole" jurisdiction of impeachment, that indictable crimes are not a prerequisite to impeachment, as four convictions by the Senate for nonindictable offenses confirm.[93]

One hundred and forty years ago Justice Story pointed out that only treason and bribery were made indictable offenses by statute and that insistence on indictable crimes would enable impeachable offenders to escape scot-free and render the impeachment provisions "a complete nullity." [94] The absurdity of Mr. St. Clair's analysis is pointed up by his incongruous juxtaposition of the 1790 treason and bribery statutes. "Any person" could be indicted under the "treason" Act whereas the "bribery" Act was specifically directed against judges who had accepted bribes.[95] Even today it is open to question whether the bribery statute embraces the President.[96] Judicial bribery was not mentioned in the Convention, but Gouverneur Morris emphasized that the President "may be bribed," and he instanced that "Charles II was bribed by Louis XIV" [97] and that therefore the President ought to be impeachable. Notwithstanding that the President was the only mentioned object of constitutional impeachment for "bribery," he would be unimpeachable on Mr. St. Clair's reasoning because the penal "bribery" statute was confined to judges. Nor can we take seriously Mr. St. Clair's argument that "high crimes and misdemeanors" must involve criminal "offenses of such a serious nature [as] to be akin to treason and bribery." [98] Treason and bribery are rank unequals. Treason is the arch offense—betrayal of the state to the enemy—

---

93. Supra, Chapter II, n. 15.
94. Supra, Chapter II, text accompanying n. 125. See 1 Story §§796, 798. An earlier work, Rawle 273, had come to the same conclusion.
95. See n. 81 supra.
96. Members of Congress and officers of the United States were added by the Act of Feb. 26, 1853, ch. 81, §6, 10 Stat. 171. Today, 18 U.S.C. §201 (1970) covers "public official[s]," defined as "member[s] of Congress . . . or an officer or employee or person acting for or on behalf of the United States, or any department." Under the prior Act, an "officer of the United States" was deemed one "appointed by the President . . . or the head of some executive department." United States v. Van Wert, 195 F. 974, 976 (N.D. Iowa 1912); cf. United States v. Germaine, 99 U.S. 508, 510 (1878); and under the maxim *noscitur et sociis* the words "employee or person" might similarly exclude the President.
97. Supra, Chapter II, text accompanying n. 167.
98. St. Clair, supra, n. 74 at 34.

whereas acceptance of so much as $50 as a bribe for favorable official action suffices to constitute bribery. Who would maintain that acceptance of such a petty bribe is more heinous than presidential usurpation or abuse of power?

It remains to add two Founders' statements that repel the equation of an impeachable offense with an indictable crime. After adverting to impeachment in the North Carolina Ratification Convention, James Iredell stated that "the person convicted is *further liable* to a trial at common law, and may receive such common-law [criminal] punishment as belongs to a description of such offenses, *if it be punishable by that law.*" [99] In other words, an offense may be impeachable although it is not criminally punishable. Similar recognition is evidenced by George Nicholas' distinction in the Virginia Ratification Convention between disqualification from office and "further punishment if [the President] has committed such high crimes as are punishable at common law." [100] This clearly implies that some "high crimes" are not thus punishable and nevertheless impeachable. Finally, there is Hamilton's statement in *The Federalist* Number 65 that an impeachment proceeding "can never be tied down by such strict rules ... as in common [criminal] cases [which] serve to limit the discretion of the courts in favor of personal security," [101] an analysis which Department of Justice lawyers concede "cuts against the argument that 'high crimes and misdemeanors' should be limited to criminal offenses." [102] We can hardly prefer Mr. St. Clair to Hamilton, Madison, et al. as an expounder of the Framers' intention. That Mr. St. Clair can maintain against this background that we should "*uphold the intent of the drafters* of the Constitution that impeachable offenses be limited to criminal violations" [103] only illustrates to what lengths advocacy will go.

---

99. Supra, Chapter II, n. 111 (emphasis added).
100. Supra, Chapter II, text accompanying n. 131. See n. 117 infra for Hamilton's similar statement.
101. *Federalist* No. 65 at 425–426.
102. Office of Legal Counsel, Dep't of Justice, Legal Aspects of Impeachment: An Overview, February 14, 1974 [hereinafter cited as Justice Dep't Memorandum], p. 14.
103. St. Clair, supra, n. 74 at 38–39 (emphasis in original).

High Crimes and Misdemeanors

Mr. St. Clair belabors the fact that in England, where removal from office and criminal punishment were united in one and the same proceeding, impeachment was criminal in nature,[104] a fact no one would dispute, albeit the crime, as we shall see, was of a peculiar sort. He totally ignores the impact of a momentous departure from the prior English practice, embodied in Article I, §3(7), the separation between removal and criminal proceedings:

> Judgment in Cases of Impeachment shall not extend further than to removal ... and disqualification to hold and enjoy any Office ... but the Party convicted shall nevertheless be liable ... to Indictment ... and Punishment, according to Law.[105]

In other words, if criminal law covered the offense, it would be indictable. Thus removal was to be a prophylactic measure, to remove an unfit man from office; criminal punishment was left to a separate proceeding. As Justice Story stated in 1830, impeachment "is not so much designed to punish an offender as to secure the state against gross official misdemeanors.... [I]t simply divests him of his political capacity," [106] it removes and disqualifies him from office. Thus, in place of the combined English removal and criminal proceedings the Framers divorced the two, with consequences that James Wilson immediately perceived:

> Impeachments ... come not ... within the sphere of ordinary [i.e., criminal] jurisprudence. They are founded on different principles; are governed by different maxims, and are directed to different objects; for this reason, the trial

---

104. Ibid. at 7, 10, 12, 13, 20, 26, 38. "To further reinforce the criminal nature of the process," says St. Clair, ibid. at 26–27, "an early draft provided that an impeachment was to be tried before the Supreme Court," as if the Court was to hear no civil cases. By the same reasoning, the subsequent transfer of the trial to the Senate should mark the offense as noncriminal.
105. Constitution, Article I, §3.
106. Supra, Chapter II, text accompanying n. 132. See n. 117 infra.

and punishment of an offense on impeachment, is no bar to a trial of the same offense at common law.[107]

When Mr. St. Clair emphasizes the criminal nature of impeachment in England, he overlooks that there it was part and parcel of a criminal proceeding. The separation of the two in our Constitution demands a construction of impeachment in noncriminal terms lest it fall afoul of other constitutional provisions.

First there is double jeopardy. Were impeachment criminal in nature, as Mr. St. Clair repeatedly stresses, a conviction or acquittal on impeachment would bar a criminal indictment and a prior conviction or acquittal on indictment would bar an impeachment, for no man can be tried twice for the same offense.[108] Both Wilson and Story were aware of the play of double jeopardy in the constitutional provision.[109] The Framers meant to have both impeachment and indictment available, not to put Congress to a choice between either one or the other. Mr. St. Clair says not a word of the impact on double jeopardy of the separation of removal from indictment, a matter set forth for Mr. St. Clair in my book, *Impeachment: The Constitutional Problems,* which he quotes when it fits his needs.[110] Another example of selective history in this same focus is his citation of the Article III, §3(3) provision that "trial of all crimes except . . . impeachment shall be by jury" in order to demonstrate that impeachment was limited to "criminal matters." [111] He ignores the fact, which I had also pointed out, that, with this exception before them, the draftsmen of the Sixth Amendment omitted it and extended trial by jury to "all criminal proceedings." Presumably they felt no need to exempt impeachment from the Sixth Amendment because they did not consider it a criminal prosecution. If impeachment be indeed criminal in nature, as Mr. St. Clair maintains, it must be tried by jury, not by the Senate, because "all criminal proceedings" means *all,* particu-

107. 1 Wilson 324.
108. Supra, Chapter II, text accompanying nn. 133–139a.
109. Ibid. Story §782; for Wilson, see supra.
110. St. Clair, supra, note 74 at 3.
111. Ibid. at 37–38.

larly after the omission of the prior exception, and second, because the Bill of Rights modifies all prior provisions of the Constitution that are in conflict with it.[112]

Constitutional analysis need not depart from common sense;[113] the fact that the criteria of what were impeachable crimes in England were employed by the Framers to identify causes for removal from office does not serve to make removal criminal, as a familiar example will make clear. Suppose that Jones runs a red light at eighty miles an hour and crashes into Smith, severely injuring Smith and destroying his car. Such reckless driving constitutes a criminal offense, but that does not convert a civil suit to recover damages on those facts into a criminal proceeding. The difference was appreciated by Solicitor General Bork, who pointed out that "just as an individual may be both criminally prosecuted and deported for the same offense . . . a civil officer could be both impeached and criminally punished. . . ."[114] Deportation, the Supreme Court held, "is not punishment for a crime. . . . It is but a method of enforcing the return to his country of an alien who has not complied with the conditions" laid down for his residence,[115] exactly as impeachment is designed solely to remove an unfit officer for the good of the state. That criminal prosecution may also be had on the same grounds does not render either deportation or removal by impeachment criminal. Solicitor General Bork justly concluded that "conviction of impeachment under our Constitution has no criminal consequences," whereas "impeachment in England was designed to accomplish punishment as well as removal."[116] Without criminal penalties such as fine or imprisonment, and limited to removal of an unfit officer, impeachment cannot be criminal in nature.[117]

But, Mr. St. Clair argues, such terms as "convicted"

---

112. Supra, Chapter II, text accompanying nn. 140–142.
113. See n. 48 supra.
114. Bork, supra, note 4 at 10 n.**.
115. Fong Yue Ting v. United States, 149 U.S. 698, 730 (1893).
116. Bork, supra, n. 74 at 10 n.**.
117. Hamilton distinguished between "their removal from office" and *"their actual punishment* in cases which would admit of it." *Federalist* No. 70 at 461 (emphasis added). He thus recognized, as did Iredell and Nicholas, that *some* impeachable offenses could not be punished criminally. See text accompanying nn. 99–100 supra.

and the like "are all terms limited in context to criminal matters." [118] This terminology was taken into account by me in 1970, and I suggested that the Framers, engaged in an immense task—the drafting of a written Constitution for a new nation in the short space of fourteen weeks—could not at each step undertake "to coin a fresh and different vocabulary." That would have involved an insuperable labor.[119] As the Department of Justice lawyers recognize, quoting Professor John Pomeroy's mid-nineteenth-century treatise, "The word is borrowed, the procedure is imitated, and no more; the object and end of the process are far different." [120] To give this borrowed terminology conclusive effect on the issue of criminality is to invite the application of double jeopardy and trial by jury rather than by the Senate, as well as to disregard all of the statements by the Founders that clearly demonstrate their intention to make nonindictable offenses impeachable, an intention that courts normally strive to effectuate. Were these conflicting pulls between terminology and "original intention" and the like to be posed to a court, it would attempt to balance them not, like Mr. St. Clair's selective history, to avoid the inescapable task of weighing heavily countervailing factors.

More than a little confusion has resulted from the fact that the Constitution employs the words "high crimes and misdemeanors." The starting point is that "high crimes and misdemeanors" and ordinary "crimes and misdemeanors" are altogether different in meaning and origin. "High crimes and misdemeanors," which the historical evidence shows meant "high crimes and *high* misdemeanors," referred to offenses against the state, as the companion words "treason, bribery" indicate. Such offenses were triable by Parliament under the *Lex Parliamentaria* or law of Parliament. When the words were first employed in 1386 there was no such ordinary crime as "misdemeanor"; lesser crimes were then punishable as "trespasses." "Misdemeanors"

---

118. St. Clair, supra, n. 74 at 38.
119. Supra, Chapter II, text following n. 155.
120. Justice Dep't Memorandum, supra, n. 102, Appendix 1 at 24. Compare text accompanying nn. 113–114 supra.

supplanted "trespasses" early in the sixteenth century, and, as Fitzjames Stephen pointed out, they were proceedings for wrongs against the individual and were triable in the courts rather than in Parliament.[121] It is safe to say that "high crimes and misdemeanors" were words of art peculiar to parliamentary impeachment[122] and had no relation to ordinary "crimes and misdemeanors" that were triable by the courts. "High misdemeanors," it may be added, never entered the criminal law administered by the English courts, nor were ordinary "misdemeanors" a criterion for impeachments.[123]

In the main, Mr. St. Clair accepts this analysis: He states that "high crimes and misdemeanors" "was *the standard phrase*" used in "*parliamentary impeachments,*" "a unitary phrase *meaning crimes against the state,* as *opposed to those against individuals.*"[124] He agrees that the word "high" modifies both "crimes and misdemeanors," and "refers to official conduct, conduct relating to one's function with respect to the State."[125] But he repeatedly skitters from "high misdemeanor" to "misdemeanor"; he cites, for example, Blackstone's distinction between "crimes" and "smaller faults and omissions . . . termed misdemeanors," notwithstanding that Blackstone, as Mr. St. Clair notices, differentiated "high misdemeanors" as "high offenses against the King and government."[126] The Framers

---

121. Stephen 60.
122. Justice Frankfurter stated, "Words of art bring their art with them. They bear the meaning of their habitat . . . whether it be loaded with recondite connotations of feudalism." Frankfurter, "Some Reflections on the Reading of Statutes," 47 *Colum. L. Rev.* 527, 537 (1947). For the meaning of "high crimes and misdemeanors," see text accompanying nn. 86–93 supra.
123. Supra, Chapter II, text accompanying nn. 27–37.
124. St. Clair, supra, n. 74 at 19 (emphasis in original).
125. Ibid. at 25, 33. His explanation of "high" is rested on "modern usage," citing to the House Judiciary Comm., 93d Cong., 1st Sess., *Impeachment: Selected Materials* 622 (Comm. Print 1973). The citation to p. 622 is to a reprint of my 1971 article, at which point I was tracing the centuries-long development, culminating in Blackstone!
126. St. Clair, supra, n. 74 at 23, 21–22. He neglected to notice Blackstone's statement in his discussion of "Misprisions . . . generally denominated *contempts* or *high misdemeanors;* of which 1. The first and principal is the *mal-administration* of such high officers, as are in public trust and employment. This is usually punished by the method of parliamentary impeachment . . ." 4 Blackstone 121 (emphasis in original). Contempts were punished by the respective tribunals against whom contemptuous conduct was proven, the courts or the Parliament. I recall no case in which Parliament turned to a court for punishment of a contempt against itself.

well understood that "high misdemeanors" had a "technical meaning too limited"; [127] and intellectual honesty demands an end to such verbal play on "misdemeanor," an end to shifts from historical meaning to "its present day context," whereunder "the purpose of inclusion of the *word 'misdemeanor' is to include* lesser *criminal* offenses that are not felonies." [128] For the Framers undeniably borrowed "high misdemeanor" from the law of Parliament; they did not borrow "misdemeanor" from the "criminal" law of the courts. To glide from *their* meaning to the "modern context" and to a view that "misdemeanor" "include[s] lesser *criminal* offenses" is to revise the Constitution, the very thing Mr. St. Clair should most fear, lest it lead to the unbridled discretion not long since attributed to Congress by Vice President Gerald Ford and former Attorney General Kleindienst.[129]

Mr. St. Clair's Theories

Mr. St. Clair does not attempt to deal with the constitutional separation between impeachment and indictment, the consequent problems of double jeopardy, trial by jury of "all criminal prosecutions," or the long-standing dichotomy between parliamentary trials of

---

127. Supra, Chapter II, text accompanying n. 159.
128. St. Clair, supra, n. 74 at 34 (emphasis in original). It is beside the point to say that "in *common parlance* a misdemeanor is considered a crime by lawyers, judges, defendants, and the general public," ibid. at 33, first, because a "high misdemeanor" is quite different from a "misdemeanor," and second, because the test of such a "technical" common law term is not present "common parlance" but what it meant to the Framers. The language of the Constitution cannot be interpreted safely except by reference to the common law and British institutions as they were when the instrument was framed and adopted. The statesmen and lawyers of the Convention who submitted it to the ratification of the Conventions of the Thirteen States, were born and brought up in the atmosphere of the common law and thought and spoke in its vocabulary . . . [T]hey expressed [their conclusions] in terms of the common law, confident that they could be shortly and easily understood.
Ex parte Grossman, 267 U.S. 87, 108 (1925); cf. United States v. Barnett, 376 U.S. 681, 688 (1964).
To import "high" by resort to history as a special species of crime and then to argue that the words " 'high crimes and misdemeanors' . . . are so clear and unequivocal in and of themselves" that it is not "necessary to look beyond the words," St. Clair, supra, n. 74 at 32, 38, indicates that the right hand knew not what the left was doing. This maneuver was designed to invoke the "plain meaning" rule, which once shut off extrinsic evidence, but which has been badly battered in the last fifty years. Wirtz v. Bottle Blowers Ass'n, 389 U.S. 463, 468 (1968); United States v. American Trucking Ass'ns, 310 U.S. 534, 543–544 (1940); Boston Sand & Gravel Co. v. United States, 278 U.S. 41, 48 (1928) (Holmes, J.).
129. Supra, Chapter II, text accompanying n. 1; *Wash. Star-News*, April 11, 1973, p. A2.

political "high misdemeanors" and court trials of
criminal "misdemeanors"; instead he spins out some
far-fetched theories. He begins with the American
"commitment to two central and interrelated ideas.
The first is the theory of limited government and the
second is the mechanism of separation of powers." [130]

Both President Nixon and Mr. St. Clair disregard
the fact that the Framers adopted impeachment as *a
breach* in the separation of powers. In the Federal
Convention Rufus King dwelt on the "primitive axiom
that the three great departments of Govts. should be
separate & independent. . . . Would this be the case
if the Executive should be impeachable? . . . [I]t would
be destructive of his independence and of the principles
of the Constitution." [131] Charles Pinckney likewise
urged that it would "effectually destroy his independence." [132] But such views were decisively rejected by
a vote of 8 to 2, because, as George Mason stressed,
"[N]o point is of more importance than that the right
of impeachment should be continued." Madison
"thought it indispensable that some provision should
be made for defending the Community against the
incapacity, negligence or perfidy of the chief Magistrate." Impeachment was favored by Edmund Randolph because the "Executive will have great opportunity of abusing his power." [133] It was precisely to
effectuate the limits on executive power embodied in
the Constitution that impeachment was adopted. As
Elias Boudinot, for years President of the Continental
Congress, said in the First Congress, impeachment is
an "exception to a principle," the separation of
powers.[134] Commenting on Hamilton's statement that
impeachments were regarded "as a bridle in the hands

---

130. St. Clair, supra, n. 74 at 2.
131. Ibid. 2 Farrand 66–67.
132. Particularly disconcerting is St. Clair's non sequitur that the President "was, while President, unindictable by ordinary criminal process.
This, of course, is why some members of the Constitutional Convention,
Mr. Pinckney, for example, thought impeachment was wholly unnecessary."
St. Clair, supra, n. 74 at 10. Pinckney explained to the Senate in 1800 that
congressmen were given specific and very limited privileges (immunity
from arrest) and none were given to the President. 10 *Annals of Cong.* 72,
74 (1800). This ill comports with an attribution to him of presidential
unindictability.
133. 2 Farrand 69, 65, 67; supra, Chapter II, text accompanying n. 167.
134. 1 *Ann. Cong.* 527.

of the legislative body upon the executive servants . . ." [135] Department of Justice lawyers state that Hamilton was "justifying the exceptions to the separation of powers found in the American provisions relating to impeachment." [136] The extraordinary spectacle now presented by presidential attempts to define the jurisdiction of the House Judiciary Committee and to limit its access to White House documents based on an invocation of the separation of powers stands history on its head. This invasion of the House's "sole" power to impeach, expressed in the Constitution, is more grotesque when it is compared to Mr. Nixon's strenuous claims of inviolable "confidentiality" of which the Constitution contains not a trace.

Mr. St. Clair muddies the waters when he cites James Iredell's 1786 statement that the North Carolina Constitution was not designed to fashion a legislative "despotism" but to "guard against the abuse of unlimited power." [137] First, in 1788 the Framers accomplished that purpose by a careful grant to Congress of enumerated and limited powers. And second, that Iredell himself believed that impeachment for nonindictable offenses was not identifiable with legislative "despotism" is evident in his reference to "impeachment for concealing important intelligence from the Senate" respecting foreign relations.[138] Mr. St. Clair himself quotes Madison's statement that "the executive magistracy is carefully limited," whereas the "legislative department derives a superiority . . . , its constitutional powers being at once more extensive, and less susceptible of precise limits." [139] "In republican government," said Madison, "the legislative authority necessarily predominates." [140] What we are witnessing is a presidential effort to abort the accountability to Congress that the Founders designed in the impeachment process. This process does not endow Congress with unlimited power, for it must act within the confines of

---

135. *Federalist* No. 65 at 425.
136. Justice Dep't Memorandum, supra, n. 102, Appendix 1 at 23.
137. St. Clair, supra, n. 74 at 4.
138. Supra, Chapter II, n. 131.
139. St. Clair, supra, n. 74 at 5.
140. *Federalist* No. 51 at 338.

"high crimes and misdemeanors." [141] It is St. Clair who would confer illimitable power on the President by making him unaccountable in an impeachment proceeding except on terms that the President lays down. As well may a banker under suspicion dictate the terms of investigation to a bank examiner.

One of Mr. St. Clair's mistakes is to postulate two unpalatable alternatives: at one pole indictable crimes, at the other unlimited congressional discretion.[142] But there is a median possibility which in fact was the choice of the Framers: Impeachment would be both limited and noncriminal. In noticing that "high crimes and misdemeanors" had a "technical meaning too limited," the Framers exhibited awareness that the words had a "limited" content defined by the English practice at the adoption of the Constitution. As we have seen, they repeatedly referred to the established categories, namely, subversion of the Constitution, abuse of power, neglect of duty—all nonindictable and *limited* offenses.[143] To be sure, these are broad categories, but no more so than many standards employed by the law, such as restraint of trade, the care of an ordinary prudent man, or due process itself.

The English categories expressed the evils at which the Framers squarely aimed; Mr. St. Clair's attempts to explain them away are a grasping at straws. Consider his argument based on the rejection of "maladministration" as an impeachable offense in favor of "high crimes and misdemeanors" in an effort to show that "impeachment was designed to deal exclusively with indictable criminal conduct." "Thus," he states, the Framers "manifested their intention to narrow the scope of impeachable offenses." [144] Without doubt the phrase "high crimes and misdemeanors" is narrower

---

141. Supra, Chapter II, text accompanying nn. 156–173.
142. St. Clair, supra, n. 74 at 14.
143. Supra, Chapter II, text accompanying nn. 81ff., 167–171.
144. St. Clair, supra, n. 74 at 30–31, 32. He argues that Gouverneur Morris' argument for retention of Mason's proposed "maladministration" on the ground that "it will not be put in force & can do no harm—an election of every four years will prevent maladministration," 2 Farrand 550, "expressed the will of the Convention," St. Clair, supra, n. 74 at 31, notwithstanding that the Convention then proceeded to reject Morris' plea for "maladministration" and substituted "high crimes and misdemeanors." Such analysis is sloppy.

than "maladministration," which might include minor examples of mismanagement. But rejection of "maladministration" does not spell a "narrowing" of "high crimes and misdemeanors"; we need to look to "high crimes and misdemeanors" itself for the content the phrase had in both parliamentary practice and the eyes of the Framers. Each of the categories recognized by the Founders, such as "abuse of power" and "neglect of duty," was a category at English law of "high crimes and misdemeanors" and each represents a form of maladministration, that is, "improper management of public affairs." Thus "maladministration" within the parameters of "high crimes and misdemeanors" undoubtedly was to be impeachable. For this we have Madison's testimony. Referring to displacement "from office [of] a man whose merits require that he should be continued in it" (wanton discharge), Madison stated that the President "will be impeachable by this House, before the Senate, for such an act of maladministration." [145]

Equally without merit is Mr. St. Clair's assertion that "[t]he Convention rejected all noncriminal definitions of impeachable offenses. . . . Terms like 'malpractice,' 'neglect of duty' . . . and 'misconduct' were all considered and discarded." [146] In fact, however, "malpractice" and "neglect of duty" were considered and "agreed to" at an early stage; [147] later, when the issue was whether the President should be impeachable, Franklin urged that impeachment was needed when the President's "misconduct should deserve it." [148] This was not put to a vote and it was not "rejected." Instead, the Framers adopted "high crimes and misdemeanors," which *included* "neglect of duty" and serious "misconduct" in office, as the Framers were well aware. Since the generic "high crimes and misdemeanors" embraced those particulars, there was no need to spell them out; an omission to do so cannot

---

145. 1 *Annals of Cong.* 517 (1789) (page running head "History of Congress").
146. St. Clair, supra, n. 74 at 31.
147. 1 Farrand 88.
148. 2 Farrand 65.

therefore be twisted into a "rejection" of the particulars.

Next Mr. St. Clair scoffs at the Framers' comments on impeachable categories because they antedated the Convention's decision on the "nature of the executive branch." Hence there was "no clear concept of who would be impeached." [149] But by July 20, the date of the early remarks, it had been settled, in Madison's words, that "the Executive Magistracy . . . was to be administered by a single man." [150] The later discussions avouched by St. Clair merely have reference to the several methods of electing the President; they did not alter impeachability of that "single man." [151] By his own admission, the last discussion of the subject on September 8 was Mason's admonition that provision must be made for "great and dangerous offenses," such as the nonindictable subversion of the Constitution, which led directly to the adoption of the phrase "high crimes and misdemeanors." [152] Moreover, when the Founders referred to the earlier categories in the several Ratification Conventions, they clearly demonstrated their satisfaction with the noncriminal content of "high crimes and misdemeanors"; and, as we have seen, Madison listed still other nonindictable offenses in the First Congress.

To illustrate "the opposition of the Framers to the abuse in the English tradition," Mr. St. Clair points to their proscription of bills of attainder, corruption of blood, and narrow definition of treason.[153] These examples demonstrate, however, that the Framers well knew how to reject undesirable practices. The fact that they defined treason narrowly and left "high crimes and misdemeanors" untouched indicates that they were content to follow English practice in "high crimes and misdemeanors," [154] as their references to the several

---

149. St. Clair, supra, n. 74 at 27–30.
150. 2 Farrand 66.
151. St. Clair, supra, n. 74 at 28–29.
152. Ibid. at 30–31.
153. Ibid. at 14, 16–17, 40.
154. A striking example of the Founders' assumption that English law would be applicable unless barred is exhibited by the First Congress' prohibition of resort to "benefit of clergy" as an exemption from capital punishment, an exemption first afforded by the common law to the clergy and

categories confirm. Mr. St. Clair further argues that the treason and attainder examples "express the deep commitment to due process which permeates the Constitution. This due process would be emasculated if the impeachment process were not limited to indictable offenses." [155] Since it is the intention of the Framers that Mr. St. Clair purports to seek, we must view due process as they did. For them due process merely demanded conformity with the procedure required by the law of the land. Hamilton gave, as an example, "due process of law, that is by indictment or presentment of good and lawful men, and trial and conviction in consequence." [156] Charges filed by the House and trial by the Senate under the ascertainable law were all that due process required in the eyes of the Framers.

Still another of Mr. St. Clair's contributions to history is his dismissal of the "impeachments between 1621 and 1715 [which] had as their main purpose the achievement of parliamentary supremacy." Indeed, "some individuals were impeached merely because they . . . were favorites of the King and hence rivals of the Parliament in settling State policy." [157] Shades of the dissolute Duke of Buckingham! His "boundless influence over both James I and Charles I," said Professor Chafee, "was one of the greatest calamities which ever hit the English throne," and he, Macaulay

---

then to such of the laity as could read. Supra, Chapter II, text accompanying n. 120.

St. Clair also argues that because the "pardon power is explicitly excluded for impeachment convictions" it "can only be understood as a reaction to and rejection of the English political impeachments." The exclusion proves exactly the contrary: The fact that a pardon *cannot* save one convicted on impeachment shows an intention to *preserve* impeachments of whatever nature. The exception for pardons derived from English history and practice, when the pardon of the Earl of Danby by Charles II, after his impeachment, blew up a storm. As a result, the Act of Settlement fashioned a partial bar to such pardons; and a remark by George Nicholas in the Virginia Ratification Convention shows that the Founders were aware of this history: "Few ministers will ever run the risk of being impeached, when they know the King cannot protect them by a pardon." Supra, Chapter I, text accompanying n. 213; Chapter II, n. 7 and text accompanying n. 229.

155. St. Clair, supra, n. 74 at 17.

156. 4 A. Hamilton, *Works* 237 (Lodge ed. 1904). The "due process" of the Fifth Amendment, said Charles Curtis, incontrovertibly "meant a procedural due process, which could be easily ascertained from almost any law book." Curtis, "Review and Majority Rule," in *Supreme Court & Supreme Law* 177 (E. Cahn ed. 1954). The shift to "substantive" due process began in the late nineteenth century. R. McCloskey, *The American Supreme Court* 128–132 (1960); Hamilton, "The Path of Due Process of Law," in *The Constitution Reconsidered* 167 (C. Read ed. 1938).

157. St. Clair, supra, n. 74 at 12–13, 15.

stated, illustrates why "favorites have always been highly odious." [158] Such impeachments, according to Mr. St. Clair, "distorted" the process in order to achieve "parliamentary supremacy," which he labels an "abuse." [159] This is a hair-raising description of a process that halted the tide of monarchical absolutism which was sweeping over Europe. Mr. St. Clair's conclusion that this aspect of impeachment was opposed by the Framers as "an abuse in the English tradition" [160] reveals unfamiliarity with the fact that for them that parliamentary struggle was the cradle of liberty.[161] In truth, their expressions of distrust of "favorites," their hatred of Stuart absolutism [162] which had engendered the great English impeachments, their abiding faith in the legislature [163] which led the Framers to give it a "bridle" on the executive, their repeated references to impeachable offenses such as subversion of the Constitution, abuse of power, and even to the giving of "bad advice" by Ministers to the Crown [164] that emerged from this struggle for parliamentary supremacy, demonstrate that the Framers, far from regarding these as "abuses" and "distortions" to be repudiated, adopted them en bloc in order to save the nascent democracy from executive usurpations and excesses. Mr. St. Clair's reading of history underlines anew the wisdom of Pope's injunction—"Drink deep, or taste not the Pierian spring."

Selectivity: Other Examples

Let me close with a few additional examples of discriminatory selectivity which a lawyer employs to acquit a client but which hardly comport with the duty

---

158. Supra, Chapter II, text accompanying nn. 95–99.
159. St. Clair, supra, n. 74 at 13, 16.
160. Ibid. at 16.
161. "The privileges of the House of Commons, for which the people had fought in the seventeenth century . . . [they] held to be synonymous with their liberty . . ." J. Clive, Macaulay 124–125 (1973).
162. Supra, Introduction, text accompanying notes 29 and 31; Chapter II, nn. 215, 228.
163. Justice Brandeis referred to the deep-seated conviction of the English and American people that they "must look to representative assemblies for the protection of their liberties." Myers v. United States, 272 U.S. 52, 294–295 (1926) (dissenting opinion). The constitutional provision for impeachment is one piece of evidence for that view.
164. Supra, Chapter II, text accompanying nn. 91, 94a–99, 169.

of one who professes to give a faithful historical account. After alluding to treason and bribery, Mr. St. Clair states, "Other crimes for which impeachments were brought included the misappropriation of government funds, participation in various plots against the government . . . and voicing religious beliefs prohibited by the laws." By the First Amendment, he continues, the Constitution "specifically rejected the English precedents of impeaching individuals for their religious beliefs." [165] From this one might conclude that he had exhausted the roster of impeachable offenses. Where is mention of subversion of the Constitution, abuse of power, betrayal of trust, and neglect of duty, which were impeachable offenses in England, and to which the Founders adverted?

Again, Mr. St. Clair quotes Erskine May for the proposition that "impeachments are reserved for extraordinary crimes and extraordinary offenders," [166] but he neglects to add May's statement that "[i]mpeachments by the Commons, for high crimes and misdemeanors beyond the reach of the [criminal] law . . . might still be regarded as an ultimate safeguard of public liberty." [167] Throughout, Mr. St. Clair plays a tattoo on the fact that impeachment was a proceeding "for great men and great causes." [168] Would he read out of the Constitution the express provision for impeachment of "all civil officers" who are not "great men"? Is not the President a "great man" by any standard? Then too, "great offenses" for the Founders were the impeachable offenses that they enumerated, for which we cannot now substitute a new version supplied by defense counsel.

Consider finally Mr. Clair's selection from Edmund Burke at the trial of Warren Hastings:

We say, then, not only that he governed arbitrarily, but corruptly . . . that is to say, that he was a giver and receiver

---

165. St. Clair, supra, n. 74 at 12.
166. Ibid. at 9.
167. T. E. May, *Parliamentary Practice* 39 (17th ed. 1964).
168. See, e.g., St. Clair, supra, n. 74 at 9.

of bribes. . . . In short, money is the beginning, the middle, and the end of every kind of act done by Mr. Hastings.[169]

The emphasis on "money" is apt to overshadow that Hastings was charged with governing "arbitrarily," the classic impeachable offense, and that Burke's accusations reached far deeper than "bribery." In his opening statement before the Lords he stated,

It is by this tribunal that statesmen who *abuse their power* . . . are tried . . . not upon the niceties of a narrow [criminal] jurisprudence, but upon the enlarged and solid principles of morality.[170]

Observe that Burke, the hero of the Founders for his defense of the American revolt, emphasized that "abuse of power" was not to be tried by the narrow principles of criminal law. And he concluded, "I impeach Warren Hastings of high crimes and misdemeanors, I impeach him in the name of the Commons . . . whose parliamentary *trust* he has betrayed . . ." [171] To ignore these statements while concentrating attention on "bribery" is to deal in halftruths and to stray from candor.

Enough has been set out to expose Mr. St. Clair's cavalier treatment of history; and though it is tempting to invoke the Latin maxim, so often applied by the courts—false in one thing, false in everything—I prefer rather to forego analysis of the rest of the sixty-one-page St. Clair memorandum in order to spare the reader a needlessly wearisome and tedious journey. Against this background it is sheer effrontery to say, as does St. Clair,

[a]ny analysis that broadly construes the power to impeach and convict can be reached only by reading Constitutional authorities selectively, by lifting specific historical precedents out of their precise historical context, by disregarding the plain meaning and accepted definition of technical, legal terms—in short, by placing a subjective gloss

---

169. Ibid. at 14.
170. Burke, supra, n. 73 at 11, 14.
171. Ibid. at 267.

on the history of impeachment that results in permitting the Congress to do whatever it deems most politic.[172]

In conclusion, Mr. St. Clair has resolutely closed his eyes to adverse facts throughout, to the impact of the American separation of removal on impeachment from criminal trial by jury of "all criminal prosecutions" if, as he argues, the removal proceeding must be regarded as criminal in nature. "Historical reconstruction," said a distinguished English historian, Sir Herbert Butterfield, "must at least account for the evidence that is discrepant, and must explain how the rejected testimony came to exist." [173] Judges too require lawyers to meet the arguments of opposing counsel. When Mr. St. Clair neglects to do so and wraps himself in the cloak of pseudo-history, he lays himself open to the suspicion that he is not so much engaged in honest reconstruction of history as in propaganda whose sole purpose is to influence public opinion in favor of a client who is under grave suspicion. An "acquittal so obtained," said Macaulay, "cannot be pleaded in bar of the judgment of history." [174]

* * *

Newsweek of May 27, 1974, p. 74, reports:
Confronted with the blast from Berger, White House sources rejoined that while the memorandum did bear St. Clair's signature, it had in fact been prepared under the "guidance" of University Professor Charles Alan Wright, who is Mr. Nixon's constitutional law specialist. At this, Berger's hackles rose. "That's even worse," he snapped. "St. Clair is a courtroom lawyer. Wright is supposed to be a scholar. What was merely venal from St. Clair is heinous coming from Wright." In response, Wright was quick to point out that he had not done the primary research on the paper. His role, he said, was that of reviewer and critic. But he found himself siding with Berger on at least one point: "You borrow trouble," he said, "if you indulge in a selective presentation . . . you hurt yourself if you leave out relevant information."

---

172. St. Clair, supra, n. 74 at 60.
173. Butterfield, supra, n. 69 at 225.
174. 2 Macaulay, supra, n. 60 at 516.

THEODORE DWIGHT'S INDICTABILITY CITATIONS

For his assertion that impeachment requires an indictable crime, Theodore Dwight, Trial by Impeachment, 6 Am. L. Reg. (N.S.) 257, 266–267 (1867), also invoked two English cases which proceeded for "high crimes and misdemeanors." In the first, Lord Chancellor Macclesfield was charged in 1725 with the sale of offices of Master in Chancery against the "laws and statutes of this realm," 16 Howell 770–775. But it no more follows that impeachment lies only for violations of statute than it would follow that "high misdemeanors" are not impeachable because one case had proceeded for high treason. Nevertheless, though Lord Campbell later commented that "there can be no doubt that the sale of all offices touching the administration of justice (with a strange exception in favor of Common Law Judges) was forbidden by the statute of Edward VI," 4 Campbell, *Chancellors* 536–537, the issue was strenuously argued, and in my judgment remains subject to considerable doubt, which would require an extensive excursus to set forth.

Let it suffice that Serjeant Pengelly, arguing for the Commons and sensible of the weight of the argument for Macclesfield, stated in rebuttal:

if the misdemeanors of which the Earl impeached stands accused, were not crimes by the ordinary rules of law in inferior courts, as they have been made out to be; yet they would be offenses of a public nature, against the welfare of the subject, and the common good of the kingdom, committed by the highest officer of justice, and ... would demand the exercise of the extraordinary jurisdiction vested in your judicature for the public safety, by virtue whereof your lordships can inflict that degree and kind of punishment which no other Court can impose (16 Howell 1360).

That the Lords proceeded under their own broad power rather than either statute or common law is again inferable from their rejection of "a friendly motion . . . that the opinion of the Judges be asked, 'whether the sale of an office that hath relation to the administration of justice be an offence against the common law," 4 Campbell, *Chancellors* 534, a question that suggests doubt whether the statute applied.

The second Dwight citation, the impeachment of Lord Melville in 1805 (seventeen years after adoption of our Constitution), involved the charge that as Treasurer of the Navy Melville permitted the use of navy moneys for other purposes. The Lords sought the opinion of the judges upon three questions, the nature of which adequately appears from the answers. First, the judges stated that the lodging of navy moneys in a private bank pending payment of assigned bills "upon the Treasurer" was not a crime. Second, they stated that money may not be withdrawn by the Treasurer for the purpose of deposit in a private bank, but if such "intermediate deposit . . . is made, bona fide, as the means . . . of more conveniently applying the money to navy services" such withdrawal was lawful. Third, they stated that the Treasurer might lawfully apply navy funds to any other use whatsoever, public or private, without express authority to do so. 29 Howell 1468–1471. Melville was acquitted, ibid. 1482. In light of what Hallam called an "undisputed principle," that "supplies granted by Parliament, are only to be expanded for particular objects specified by itself," 2 Hallam 357, the third answer is inexplicable, particularly in its blessing for use of Navy money for "private" purposes. Perhaps the explanation lies in the practicalities: at the time of the trial the alleged offense was 24 years old; the Commons itself had been badly split—"his impeachment was only carried in the House of Commons by the deciding voice of the Speaker; the Members voting 216 for and 216 against, the younger Pitt, then Prime Minister, doing all in his power to defeat the impeachment." Simpson 39–40. Then too, Melville had resigned his post as First Lord of the Admiralty, as soon as his conduct had been arraigned in the Commons, 29 Howell 555, so that the proceeding smacked of beating a dead horse. At best, the Melville acquittal is but one against a number of convictions for "high crimes and misdemeanors" which plainly fell short of indictable offenses.

Appendix B

LUTHER MARTIN'S INDICTABILITY CITATIONS

In order to sustain his argument in the impeachment of Justice Samuel Chase, Luther Martin, his leading counsel, maintained that judges were indictable for violation of their official duties. He dismissed *Floyd v. Barker,* supra, Chapter II, text accompanying n. 46, out of hand because "the reasons there assigned, however correct they might be as to the judges in England, can have no possible application to the judges of the United States." 14 Ann. Cong. 434. Nevertheless American courts accepted Coke. Five years after Martin spoke, in 1810, Chancellor Kent held that the Coke doctrine "has a deep root in the common law," and took note of Coke's statement that no judge was to be questioned for judgment given, "either at the suit of a party, or of the king." *Yates v. Lansing,* 5 Johns. 282, 291, 293. In 1867, William Lawrence, who sought to lay a predicate for the impending impeachment of Andrew Johnson, wrote, "It is a rule of the common law that judges of record are freed from all presentations whatever except in Parliament, where they may be punished for anything done by them in such courts as judges." William Lawrence, "The Law of Impeachment," 6 Am. L. Reg. (N.S.) 641, 664 (1867). Compare *Bradley v. Fisher,* 12 Wall. (80 U.S.) 335, 350 (1871). It became accepted doctrine that judges enjoyed immunity from *private* suits for actions in their judicial capacity, the issue really decided in *Floyd v. Barker.*

Martin leaned more heavily on Viner's statement that "A justice cannot rase a record, nor imbecile [embezzle?]

356

it." 14 Ann. Cong. 435. Viner cited Brooke's Corone, which in turn cited 2 Rich. 3, 9, 10. No such statute appears in the Statutes at Large nor Statutes of the Realm; but a cognate statute which responds in part to the Viner quotation is 8 Rich. II, cap. 4: "if any Judge is convicted of the false entering of pleas, rasing [erasure] of Rolls and changing of Verdicts . . . before the King and his Council . . . he shall be punished by Fine and Ransom [a treble fine, Jenkins 162, 145 E. R. 104 (undated)]." This was a statute of 1385, at a time when great ministers and the Justices were tried before the "King and his Council." Supra, Chapter I, text accompanying nn. 22, 50–53; Chapter II, text accompanying nn. 22–26, and impeachment is older than indictment of a peer, supra Chapter II, n. 36.

Martin's quotation of Viner made two further points: (1) a judge cannot "file an indictment which is not found." Apparently this refers to *Rex v. Marsh*, 3 Mod. 66, 87 E. R. 42 (1603), wherein a Mayor who also served as Coroner and seemingly acted in a quasi-judicial capacity, had inserted additional names in an indictment after it had been found, and was therefore himself held guilty upon a subsequent "information." If the information be assimilated to an indictment, the case at most illustrates "indictment" of a lesser judge, who was treated differently from a Justice of the higher courts. Supra, Chapter II, text accompanying nn. 55–59. (2) Martin also quoted Viner's statement that a judge cannot "give sentence of death where the law does not give it." 14 Ann. Cong. 435. Jenkins relates that this happened in a manor court, again a lesser court, and that the Star Chamber decided that the judge should "be fined and imprisoned and lose his office." Jenkins 162, 145, E. R. 104 (undated). Indictments were not employed by the Star Chamber. Edward Jenks, *A Short History of English Law* (147 London, 2d ed. 1920).

Martin (14 Ann. Cong. 435) also quoted 1 Hawkins, ch. 69 [actually ch. 67], sec. 6, to the effect that bribery in a judge is "punishable, not only with forfeiture of the offender's office of justice, but also with fine and imprisonment." Hawkins' marginal citation to 1 Rushworth's *Collections*, fol. 31, which deals with the impeachment and conviction of Lord Chancellor Bacon for bribery, show that he had no thought of indictment. Indeed, Hawkins himself states that the law "frees the Judges of all Courts of Record from all Prosecutions whatsoever, except in the Parliament, for anything done by them openly in such courts as judges." 1 Hawkins, ch. 72, sec. 6. Luther Martin, in sum, fell decidedly short of establishing that Justices were indictable in England, and it follows that their indictability was not the test of impeachment.

EARLY ENGLISH
BRIBERY STATUTES

Whether bribery was indictable by statute turns on whether there were effective bribery statutes.

20 Edw. III (1346), 1 Statutes at Large 111 (London, 1706), provides that the Justices

shall not from thenceforth, so long as they shall be in Office of Justice, take fee nor robe of any Man, but of ourself, and that they shall take no gift nor reward by themselves, nor by other, privily or apertly, of any man that hath to do before them by any way, except meat and drink, and that of small value . . . upon pain to be at our will, body, lands, and goods, to do thereof, as shall please us."

Coke refers to it as the "supposed act of 20 E. 3" and states: "we were desirous to see the record of the act of 20 E. 3. cap. 1, but there is no record of any such act in the parliament roll." 3 Coke *Institutes* 146. On the other hand, the compilers of the Statutes at Large recite on the title page (in 1706) that the Statutes were "carefully examined by the Rolls of Parliament."

A successor statute compounds confusion. 8 Rich. II, cap. III (1384) provides that Justices

should not take Fee nor Robe of any except the King, and that they should not take Gift nor Reward, by them nor yet by other, privily or apertly, of any Man which should have anything to do afore them in any wise, except Meat and Drink, of small value . . . Upon pain of loss of their Office, and making to the King Fine and Ransom.

359

But for the reduced penalties, the language of 8 Rich. II follows that of the earlier statute closely. Does this indicate that the draftsmen, for some reason, thought the earlier statute either non-existent or ineffective? Assume an effective 20 Edw. III, the question then arises whether it was superseded by 8 Rich. II, which provided more limited penalties.

9 Rich. II (1385) provides:

First, it is accorded and assented, That all the statutes made by the Parliament in the time of the king's noble progenitors, and in his own time ... shall be firmly holden and kept, and due execution thereof done, according to the effect of the same; except the statute of the Justices and Barons of the Exchequer made at the last Parliament [8 Rich. II, c. 3], which, because it is very hard, and needeth declaration, the King will that it be of no force till it be declared by Parliament.

Since the precedent 8 Rich. II was thus to be "of no force," does 9 Rich. II confirm that the still earlier 20 Edw. III was nonexistent or ineffective, or was the latter revived?

Confusion is increased by still another statute, 11 Hen. IV (1410), which declares that judges, among others, shall not take any gift or reward for doing of their services and provides penalties; which led Coke to comment, "if that which is imprinted as the first chapter of 20 E. 3. had been an act of parliament, then this statute of 11 H. 4. would never have inflicted this kinde of punishment, which is other and far lesse, than that which is mentioned in 20 E. 3." 3 Coke *Institutes* 146. In short, Parliament acted as if there were no earlier statutory provision. But the validity of 11 Hen. IV is itself questionable. Coke states that it "never yet was printed, and the cause thereof was, for that in the margin of the parliament roll of this act, it is written *respectuatur per dominum principem et concilium;* a strange presumption without warrant of the king his father, and of the parliament, to cause such a respectuatur to be made to an act of parliament." 3 Coke *Institutes* 225. Stephen conjectures that "respectuatur" means "it is respited or adjourned," i.e., held in abeyance. 3 Stephen 250 n. 3. Coke reads "principem" as the son rather than the father and King, but *principem* was often used in the sense of ruler, and the conjunction of "principem et concilium" might be understood to mean the "ruler and his council." It may be added that 11 Hen. IV does not appear in the Statutes of the Realm, so that the "respectuatur" has been respected. In the 14th and 15th centuries, Holdsworth states, the crown possessed an "undoubted power . . . of suspending the operation of statutes." 2 Holdsworth 443 (London, 4th ed. 1936).

The effect of 9 Rich. II and 11 Hen. IV upon earlier statutes is further clouded by the fact that 8 Rich. II, c. 3 "was repealed in 1881 by the Statute Law Revision Act," 44 & 45 Vic. c. 59, though Stephen adds, citing to Coke, "why, I cannot say." He concludes that there is "no statute against" bribery, "though there can be no doubt that such conduct was an offense at common law." 3 Stephen 250.

Appendix D

CONGRESSMAN DAVID STONE
ON "GOOD BEHAVIOR"
AND IMPEACHMENT (1802)

What escaped Judge Otis (supra, Chapter IV, n. 249) was discerned by Congressman David Stone of North Carolina, who, in the course of the debate on the repeal of the Act for a New Organization of the Judiciary System (January 13, 1802), stated that Judges "doubtless shall, (as against the President's power to retain them in office,) . . . be removed from office by impeachment and conviction; but it does not follow that they may not be removed by other means. They shall hold their offices during good behavior, and they shall be removed from office upon impeachment and conviction of treason, bribery, and other high crimes and misdemeanors. If the words impeachment of high crimes and misdemeanors, be understood according to any construction of them hitherto received as established, it will be found, that although a judge guilty of high crimes and misdemeanors, is always guilty of misbehavior in office, yet that of the various species of misbehavior in office, which may render it exceedingly improper that a judge should continue in office, many of them are neither treason nor bribery; nor can they be properly dignified by the appellation of high crimes and misdemeanors; and for the impeachment of which no precedent can be found; nor would the words of the Constitution justify such impeachment.

"To what source, then, shall we resort for a knowledge of what constitutes this thing called misbehavior in office? The Constitution, surely, did not intend that a circumstance, as a tenure by which the judges hold their offices,

362

should be incapable of being ascertained. Their misbehavior certainly is not an impeachable offence; still it is the ground by which the judges are to be removed from office. The process of impeachment, therefore, cannot be the only one by which the judges may be removed from office, under, and according to the Constitution. I take it, therefore, to be a thing undeniable, that there resides somewhere in the government a power to declare what amounts to misbehavior in office by the judges, and to remove them from office for the same without impeachment." 11 *Ann. Cong.* 72 (7th Cong.) (Washington, D.C., Gales & Seaton, 1851). Stone mistakenly concluded that "the Constitution does not prohibit their removal by the legislature," which is true enough if one seeks for an express prohibition; but in other respects his analysis is sound and in accord with history.

BIBLIOGRAPHY

BOOKS

Acheson, Dean. *Present at the Creation* (New York, W. W. Norton, 1969).

Adams, Henry. *History of the United States of America.* 9 vols. (New York, Antiquarian Society, 1962).

Adams, John. *Works.* C. F. Adams ed. 10 vols. (Boston, Little, Brown, 1850).

Alexander, James. *A Brief Narrative of the Case and Trial of John Peter Zenger,* S. N. Katz ed. (Cambridge, Mass., Harvard University Press, 1963).

Allen, Sir C. K. *Law in the Making,* 6th ed. (Oxford, Clarendon Press, 1958).

Anson, Sir William. *Law and Custom of the Constitution,* 4th ed. 2 vols. (Oxford, Clarendon Press, 1935).

Archives of the State of New Jersey (New Jersey, 1st Ser. 1885).

Bacon, Matthew. *A New Abridgment of the Laws of England,* 3d ed. (London, 1768).

Bailyn, Bernard. *Ideological Origins of the American Revolution* (Cambridge, Mass., Harvard University Press, 1967).

Bancroft, George. *History of the Formation of the Constitution of the United States of America.* 2 vols. (New York, D. Appleton, 1882).

Bellamy, J. G. *The Law of Treason in England* (Cambridge, Cambridge University Press, 1970).

Berger, Raoul, *Congress v. The Supreme Court* (Cambridge, Mass., Harvard University Press, 1969).

Beveridge, Albert J. *The Life of John Marshall,* 4 vols. (Boston, Houghton Mifflin, 1916–1919).

Bickel, Alexander. *The Least Dangerous Branch: The Supreme Court at the Bar of Politics* (Indianapolis, Bobbs-Merrill, 1962).

Blackstone, Sir William. *Commentaries on the Law of England.* 4 vols. (Oxford, 1765–1769).

Bodet, Gerald P., ed. *Early English Parliaments: Hight Courts, Royal Councils and Representative Assemblies* (Boston, D. C. Heath, 1968).

Borkin, Joseph. *The Corrupt Judge* (New York, C. N. Potter, 1962).

Bradshaw, K., and P. Pringle. *Parliament and Congress* (London, Constable, 1972).

Brock, W. R. *An American Crisis: Congress and Reconstruction* (London, Macmillan, 1963).

Brodie, Fawn M. *Thaddeus Stevens: Scourge of the South* (New York, W. W. Norton, 1959).

Broom, Herbert. *Constitutional Law Viewed in Relation to the Common Law* (London, W. Maxwell, 1866).

Bryce, Viscount James. *American Commonwealth* (New York, Macmillan, 1908).

Burke, Edmund. *Works.* 9 vols. (Boston, Little, Brown, 1839).

Butterfield, Sir Herbert. *George III and the Historians,* rev. ed. (London, Macmillan, 1969).

Cahn, Edmond, ed. *Supreme Court and Supreme Law* (Bloomington, University of Indiana Press, 1954).

Campbell, Lord John. *Lives of the Chancellors.* 7 vols. (London, John Murray, 1848–1850).

———. *Lives of the Chief Justices* (New York, James Cockcrofts, 1874).

Carpenter, David. *The Trial of Colonel Aaron Burr.* 3 vols. (Philadelphia, Hopkins and Searle, 1808).

Chafee, Zechariah, Jr., ed. *Documents on Fundamental Human Rights* (Cambridge, Mass., Harvard University Press, 1952).

———. *Three Human Rights in the Constitution* (Lawrence, University of Kansas Press, 1956).

Chalmers, George, ed. *Opinions of Eminent Lawyers* (Burlington, Vt., C. Goodrich, 1858).

Chipman, Chief Justice Nathaniel. *A Dissertation on the Act Adopting the Common and Statute Laws of England,* Chipman Reports, Vermont, 1792 (Rutland, Tuttle, 1871).

Chitty, Joseph. *Criminal Law,* 5th Amer. ed. 3 vols. (New York, Banks & Gould, 1847).

Churchill, Sir Winston. *Marlborough: His Life and Times,* Abridged ed. (New York, Scribner, 1968).

Clarke, Mary P. *Parliamentary Privilege in the American Colonies* (New Haven, Conn., Yale University Press, 1943).

Clarkson, P. S., and R. S. Jett. *Luther Martin of Maryland* (Baltimore, Johns Hopkins Press, 1970).

Clive, John M. *Macaulay* (New York, Knopf, 1973).

Coke, Sir Edward. *Institutes of the Laws of England.* 4 vols. (London, 1628–1645).

Colbourn, H. Trevor. *The Lamp of Experience* (Chapel Hill, University of North Carolina Press, 1965).

Comyns, Baron John. *A Digest of the Laws of England* (London, 1766).

Cooley, Thomas. *The General Principles of Constitutional Law in the United States of America.* 4th ed. (Boston, Little, Brown, 1931).

Corwin, Edward S. *Court over Constitution: A Study of Judicial Review as an Instrument of Popular Government* (New York, P. Smith, 1938).

―――. *The President: Office and Powers,* 3d ed. (New York, New York University Press, 1948).

Crosskey, William W. *Politics and the Constitution in the History of the United States.* 2 vols. (Chicago, University of Chicago Press, 1953).

Curtis, George T. *History of the Formation of the Constitution of the United States.* 2 vols. (New York, Harper, 1861).

Dane, Nathan. *Digest of American Law* (Boston, Hilliard, 1824).

Dawson, John P. *The Oracles of the Law* (Ann Arbor, University of Michigan Press, 1968).

d'Ewes, Sir Simonds. *Journal,* Notestein ed. (New Haven, Conn., Yale University Press, 1923).

Dewitt, David M. *The Impeachment and Trial of Andrew Johnson* (New York, Macmillan, 1903).

Edwards, Sir J. G. *Historians and the Medieval Parliament* (Glasgow, Glasgow University Press, 1960).

Elliott, Jonathan. *Debates in the Several State Conventions on the Adoption of the Federal Constitution,* 2d ed. 4 vols. (Washington, J. Elliot, 1836).

Elton, G. B. *England under the Tudors* (London, Methuen, 1955).

―――. *The Tudor Constitution* (Cambridge, Cambridge University Press, 1960).

Farrand, Max. *The Records of the Federal Convention of 1787.* 4 vols. (New Haven, Conn., Yale University Press, 1911).

Federalist, The (New York, Modern Library, 1937).

Fitzherbert, Sir Anthony. *Nature Brevium,* Eng. trans. (London, 1652).

Foss, Edward. *The Judges of England.* 7 vols. (London, Longmans, Green, 1848–1864).

Foster, Roger. *Commentaries on the Constitution of the United States.* 2 vols. (Boston, Boston Book, 1895).

Frankfurter, Felix, and J. M. Landis. *The Business of the Supreme Court* (New York, Macmillan, 1927).

Gibbon, Edward. *The History of the Decline and Fall of the Roman Empire.* 6 vols. (New York, Nottingham).

Goebel, Jr., Julius. *The Law Practice of Alexander Hamilton.* 2 vols. (New York, Columbia University Press, 1964–1969).

Gunther, Gerald. *John Marshall's Defense of McCulloch v. Maryland* (Palo Alto, Calif., Stanford University Press, 1968).

Hale, Sir Matthew. *The History of the Pleas of the Crown,* 1st Amer. ed. 2 vols. (Philadelphia, R. H. Small, 1847).

Hallam, Henry. *The Constitutional History of England.* 2 vols. (London, John Murray, 1884).

Hamilton, Alexander. *Works,* Henry Cabot Lodge ed. 12 vols. (New York, Putnam, 1904).

Hamlin, Paul A. *Legal Education in Colonial New York* (New York, New York University Press, 1939).

Handlin, Oscar, and Mary Handlin eds. *The Popular Sources of Political Authority: Documents on the Massachusetts Constitution of 1780* (Cambridge, Mass., Harvard University Press, 1966).

Haskins, G. L. *The Statute of York and the Interests of the Commons* (Cambridge, Mass., Harvard University Press, 1935).

Hatsell, John. *Precedents of Proceedings in the House of Commons.* 11 vols. (London, 1796).

Hawkins, William. *History of Pleas of the Crown.* 2 vols. (London, 1716).

Haynes, Evan. *Selection and Tenure of Judges* (National Conference of Judicial Councils, 1944).

Hill, Christopher. *The Century of Revolution* (New York, W. W. Norton, 1961).

———. *Puritanism and Revolution* (London, Secker & Warburg, 1958).

Himmelfarb, Gertrude. *Victorian Minds* (New York, Knopf, 1968).

Hogan, Edmund. *Pennsylvania State Trials* (Philadelphia, E. Hogan, 1795).

Holdsworth, Sir William S. *A History of English Law.* 12 vols. (London, Methuen, 1903–1938).

———. *Some Lessons from Our Legal History* (New York, Macmillan, 1928).

Howell's State Trials (Cobbett's Collection). 35 vols. (London, R. Bagshaw, 1809–1826).

Hughes, Charles Evans. *The Supreme Court* (New York, Columbia University Press, 1928).

Hurst, James Willard. *The Legitimacy of the Business Corporation in the Law of the United States* (Charlottesville, University of Virginia Press, 1970).

Jackson, Justice Robert H. *The Struggle for Judicial Supremacy* (New York, Knopf, 1941).

Jackson, R. N. *The Machinery of Justice in England.* 5th ed. (London, Macmillan, 1967).

Jefferson, Thomas. *The Manual of Parliamentary Practice* (1801) in Senate Manual (55th Cong., 1899) 67–153.

――――. *Writings,* P. L. Ford ed. 10 vols. (New York, Putnam, 1892–1899).

Jenks, Edward. *A Short History of English Law,* 2d ed. (London, Macmillan, 1920).

Jennings, Sir Ivor. *Parliament,* 2d ed. (Cambridge, Cambridge University Press, 1957).

Jolliffe, J. E. A. *The Constitutional History of Medieval England,* 2d ed. (London, A. & C. Black, 1947).

Journals of the Council of the State of Virginia, W. Hall ed. (Richmond, Virginia State Library, 1952).

Kaplan, Justin. *Mr. Clemens and Mark Twain* (New York, Simon & Schuster, 1966).

Keasbey, Edward. *The Courts and Lawyers of New Jersey* (New York, Lewis Historical Pub. Co. 1912).

Kelley, Alfred H., and W. A. Harbison. *The American Constitution: Its Origins and Development* (New York, W. W. Norton, 1948).

Kennedy, John F. *Profiles in Courage* (New York, Harper, 1961).

Kennedy, Robert F. *Thirteen Days: A Memoir of the Cuban Missile Crisis* (New York, New American Library, 1969).

Kent, James. *Commentaries on American Law,* 2d ed. 4 vols. (New York, Halsted, 1832).

Kenyon, John P. *The Stuart Constitution 1623–1688* (Cambridge, Cambridge University Press, 1966).

Kutler, Stanley I. *Judicial Power and Reconstruction Politics* (Chicago, University of Chicago Press, 1968).

Lapsley, G. T. *Crown, Community and Parliament in the Later Middle Ages* (Oxford, Blackwell, 1951).

Levy, Leonard. *Legacy of Suppression* (Cambridge, Mass., Harvard University Press, 1960).

――――. *Origins of the Fifth Amendment: The Right Against Self-Incrimination* (New York, Oxford Press, 1968).

Lomask, Milton. *Andrew Johnson: President on Trial* (New York, Farrar, Straus, 1960).

Lovell, C. R. *English Constitutional History* (Oxford, Oxford Press, 1962).

Loyd, William. *The Early Courts of Pennsylvania* (Boston, Boston Book, 1910).

Macaulay, Thomas B. *Critical and Historical Essays.* 2 vols. (London, Longmans, Green, 1890).

May, Thomas E. *Parliamentary Practice.* 17th ed. (London, Butterworth, 1964).

McCloskey, Robert G. *The Modern Supreme Court.* (Cambridge, Mass., Harvard University Press, 1972).

McIlwain, Charles H. *The High Court of Parliament and Its Supremacy* (Hamden, Conn., Archon Press, 1962).

McKitrick, Eric. *Andrew Johnson and Reconstruction* (Chicago, University of Chicago Press, 1960).

Maclay, Senator William. *Sketches of Debates in the First Senate of the United States, 1789–1791* (Harrisburg, Pa., L. S. Hart, 1880).

McMaster, John B. *History of the People of the United States.* 8 vols. (New York, D. Appleton, 1892).

McRee, Griffith L. *Life and Correspondence of James Iredell.* 2 vols. (New York, D. Appleton, 1857–1858).

Madison, James. *Letters and Other Writings of James Madison.* 4 vols. (Philadelphia, Lippincott, 1867).

———. *Writings of James Madison,* G. Hunt ed. 9 vols. (New York, Putnam, 1900–1910).

Maitland, Frederic W. *Constitutional History of England* (London, Cambridge University Press, 1913).

———. *Memoranda de Parliamenti* (London, Rolls Series, 1893).

Malone, Dumas. *Jefferson and His Times,* 4 vols. (Boston, Little, Brown, 1948–1970).

Marke, Julius. *Vignettes of Legal History* (South Hackensack, N. J., F. B. Rothman, 1965).

Marshall, Chief Justice John. *Life of George Washington.* 5 vols. (London, Phillips, 1804–1807).

Miller, Charles A. *The Supreme Court and the Uses of History* (Cambridge, Mass., Harvard University Press, 1969).

Miller, John C. *Alexander Hamilton: A Portrait in Parodox* (New York, Harper and Row, 1959).

Morison, Samuel Eliot. *Oxford History of the American People* (New York, Oxford Press, 1965).

Pasquet, Desire. *Essays on the Origin of the House of Commons* (Cambridge, Cambridge University Press, 1925).

Plucknett, Theodore, *Concise History of the Common Law,* 5th ed. (Boston, Little, Brown, 1956).

———. *Statutes and Their Interpretation* (Cambridge, Cambridge University Press, 1922).

Pocock, J. G. A. *The Ancient Constitution and the Feudal Law* (Cambridge, Cambridge University Press, 1957).

Poore, Ben P. *Federal and State Constitutions, Colonial Charters*, 2 vols. (Washington, D. C., U. S. Government Printing Office, 1877).

Powicke, Sir Maurice. *King Henry III and the Lord Edward* (Oxford, Clarendon Press, 1947).

Pusey, Merlo. *Charles Evans Hughes* (New York, Macmillan, 1951).

Radin, Max. *Anglo-American History* (St. Paul, Minn., West, 1936).

Rawle, William. *A View of the Constitution*, 2d ed. (Philadelphia, P. H. Nicklin, 1829).

Roberts, Clayton. *The Growth of Responsible Government in Stuart England* (Cambridge, Cambridge University Press, 1966).

Robertson, David. *Trial of Aaron Burr*. 2 vols. (Philadelphia, 1808).

Rushworth, John. *Historical Collections*, 8 vols. (London, 1721).

Russell, Sir William. *Crimes and Misdemeanors*. 2 vols. (London, Butterworth, 1819).

Schlesinger, Arthur, Jr. *The Imperial Presidency* (Boston, Houghton Mifflin, 1973).

Schlesinger, Arthur M., Sr. *Political and Social History of the United States* (New York, Macmillan, 1929).

Simpson, Alexander. *A Treatise on Federal Impeachment* (Philadelphia, Law Association of Philadelphia, 1916).

Smith, Joseph. *Cases and Materials on Development of Legal Institutions* (St. Paul, Minn., West, 1965).

Smith, Zepheniah. *A System of the Laws of the State of Connecticut* (Windham, Conn., Z. Smith, 1795).

Stephen, Sir James F. *Criminal Law of England* (London, Macmillan, 1863).

——. *History of Criminal Law*. 3 vols. (London, Macmillan, 1883).

Story, Joseph. *Commentaries on the Constitution of the United States*, 5th ed. 2 vols. (Boston, Little, Brown, 1905).

Swisher, Carl B. *Collected Papers of Homer Cummings* (New York, Scribner, 1939).

Tanner, J. R. *English Constitutional Conflicts of the Seventeeth Century, 1603–1688* (Cambridge, Cambridge University Press, 1928).

——. *Tudor Constitutional Documents 1485–1603* (Cambridge, Cambridge University Press, 1928).

Taswell-Langmaid, T. P. *English Constitutional History*, 9th ed. (London, Sweet & Maxwell, 1929).

Thorne, Samuel E. *Introduction to a Discourse upon the Exposition and Understanding of Statutes* (San Marino, Calif., Huntington Library, 1942).

Tocqueville, Alexis de. *Democracy in America* (New York, Colonial Press, 1899).

Todd, Alpheus. *Parliamentary Government*, S. Walpole ed. 2 vols. (London, Longmans, Green, 1892).

Trevelyan, G. M. *Illustrated History of England* (London, Longmans Green, 1956).

Trial of Alexander Addison (Lancaster, Pa., 1803).

Trial of James Prescott, Probate Judge (Boston, 1821).

"Trial of President Andrew Johnson," *Congressional Globe*, 40th Congress, 2d Session, Supplement (1868).

Tucker, St. George, ed. *Blackstone's Commentaries*. 2 vols. (Philadelphia, Birch & Small, 1803).

Viner, Charles. *General Abridgment of Law and Equity* (London, 1743).

Wade, H. R. W. *Administrative Law*, 2d ed. (London, Oxford University Press, 1967).

Warden, Robert B. *Life of Salmon Portland Chase* (Cincinnati, Wilstach, 1874).

Warren, Charles. *Congress, the Constitution and the Supreme Court* (Boston, Little, Brown, 1925).

———. *History of the American Bar* (Boston, Little, Brown, 1911).

———. *The Making of the Constitution* (Cambridge, Mass., Harvard University Press, 1947).

———. *The Supreme Court in United States History* (Boston, Little, Brown, 1922).

Watson, David. *The Constitution of the United States*. 2 vols. (Chicago, Callaghan, 1910).

Wharton, Francis. *Criminal Law*. 6th ed. (Philadelphia, Kay & Bros., 1868).

———. *State Trials of the United States* (Philadelphia, Carey & Hart, 1849).

Williams, Edwin. *Addresses and Messages of the Presidents of the United States* (New York, E. Walker, 1846).

Willoughby, W. W. *The Constitutional Law of the United States*, 2d ed. (New York, Baker, Voorhis, 1929).

Wilson, James. *Works*, R. G. McCloskey ed., 2 vols. (Cambridge, Mass., Harvard University Press, 1967).

Wilson, Woodrow. *Congressional Government* (Boston, Houghton, Mifflin, 1901).

Wood, Gordon, *The Creation of the American Republic 1776–1787* (Chapel Hill, University of North Carolina Press, 1969).

Wooddeson, Richard. *Laws of England,* 2 vols. (Dublin, E. Lynch, 1792).

Woodward, C. Vann. *Reunion and Reconstruction* (Boston, Little, Brown, 1951).

Zagorin, Perez. *The Court and the Country* (London, Routledge and Kegan Paul; New York, Atheneum, 1969).

ARTICLES

Barraclough, G. "Law and Legislation in Medieval England," 56 *L.Q.R.* 75 (1964).

Berger, Raoul. "Administrative Arbitrariness: A Synthesis," 78 *Yale L. J.* 965 (1969).

———. "Executive Privilege v. Congressional Inquiry," *12 UCLA L. Rev.* 1044, 1288 (1965).

———. "Removal of Judicial Functions from Federal Trade Commission to a Trade Court: A Reply to Mr. Kintner," *59 Mich. L. Rev.* 199 (1960).

———. "Impeachment for 'High Crimes and Misdemeanors,'" 44 *S. Cal. L. Rev.* 395 (1971).

———. "The President, Congress, and the Courts," 83 *Yale L. J.* 1111 (1974).

———. "The Presidential Monopoly of Foreign Relations," 71 *Mich. L. Rev.* 1 (1972).

Bickel, Alexander M. "The Constitutional Tangle," *The New Republic.* Oct. 6, 1973, p. 14.

———. "The Durability of Colegrove v. Green," 72 *Yale L. J.* 39 (1962).

Carpenter, W. S. "Repeal of the Judiciary Act of 1801," 9 *Am. Pol. Sci. Rev.* 519 (1915).

Chrimes, S. B. "Richard II's Questions to the Judges, 1387," 72 *L.Q.R.* 365 (1965).

Clark, Justice Tom C. "Judicial Self-Regulation and Its Potential," 35 *Law & Cont. Prob.* 37 (1970).

Clarke, M. V. "The Origin of Impeachment," in *Oxford Essays in Medieval History* (London, Oxford University Press, 1934).

Cooper, J. P. "Differences between English and Continental Governments in the Early Seventeenth Century," in J. S. Bromley and E. H. Kossman, eds. *Britain and the Netherlands* (London, Oxford University Press, 1960).

Corwin, Edward S. "The Steel Seizure Case: A Judicial Brick Without Straw," 53 *Colum. L. Rev.* 53 (1953).

Curtis, Charles, P. "Review and Majority Rule," in E. Cahn, *Supreme Court and Supreme Law*, 170 (Bloomington, University of Indiana Press, 1954).

Dilliard, Irving. "Samuel Chase," in Friedman, L., and F. Israel, eds. *The Justices of the United States Supreme Court, 1789–1969*, 4 vols. (New York, Chelsea House, 1969), vol. I, p. 185.

Dougherty, J. H. "Inherent Limitations upon Impeachment," 23 *Yale L. J.* 60 (1913).

Downing, Rondal J. "Judicial Ethics and the Political Role of the Courts," 35 *Law & Cont. Prob.* 94 (1970).

Dwight, Theodore. "Trial by Impeachment," 6 *Am. L. Reg.* (N.S.) 257 (1867).

Emerson, Thomas J. "Malapportionment and Judicial Review," 72 *Yale L. J.* 64 (1962).

Feerick, John. "Impeaching Federal Judges: A Study of the Constitutional Provisions," 39 *Fordham L. Rev.* 1 (1970).

Fish, Peter G. "The Circuit Councils: Rusty Hinges of Federal Judicial Administration," 37 *U. Chi. L. Rev.* 203 (1970).

Frankfurter, Felix. "Some Reflections on the Reading of Statutes," 47 *Colum. L. Rev.* 527 (1947).

Frankfurter, Felix, and J. M. Landis. "Power of Congress over Procedure in Criminal Contempts in 'Inferior' Federal Courts: A Study in Separation of Powers," 37 *Harv. L. Rev.* 1010 (1924).

Goebel, Julius, Jr. "Constitutional Law," 38 *Colum. L. Rev.* 555 (1938).

———. "Ex Parte Clio," 54 *Colum. L. Rev.* 450 (1954).

Hamilton, Walton. "The Path of Due Process of Law," in C. Read, ed. *The Constitution Reconsidered*, 167 (New York, Columbia University Press, 1938).

Holdsworth, Sir William S. "Case Law," 50 *L.Q.R.* 180 (1934).

Holloman, John H. "The Judicial Reform Act: History, Analysis and Comment," 35 *Law & Cont. Prob.* 128 (1970).

Humphrey, Alexander. "The Impeachment of Samuel Chase," 33 *Am. L. Rev.* 827 (1899).

Hurst, James Willard. "English Sources of the American Law of Treason," (1945) *Wis. L. Rev.* 315.

———. Treason in the United States, 58 *Harv. L. Rev.* 226 (1944).

Jackson, Justice Robert H. "Back to the Constitution," 25 *A.B.A.J.* 745 (1939).

Jaffe, Louis L. "Standing to Secure Judicial Review: Public Actions," 74 *Harv. L. Rev.* 265 (1961).

Johnson, Herbert. "William Cushing," in L. Friedman and F. Israel, eds., *The Justices of the United States Supreme Court, 1789–1969*, 4 vols. (New York, Chelsea House, 1969), vol. I, p. 57.

Keeffe, Arthur J. "Explorations in the Wonderland of Impeachment," 59 *A.B.A.J.* 885 (1973).

Klein, Milton. "Prelude to Revolution in New York: Jury Trials and Judicial Tenure," 17 *Wm. & Mary Quar.* (Ser. 3) 439 (1960).

Kramer, Robert, and Jerome A. Barron. "The Constitutionality of Removal and Mandatory Procedures for the Federal Judiciary: The Meaning of 'During Good Behavior,'" 35 *Geo. Washington L. Rev.* 455 (1967).

Kurland, Phillip B. "The Constitution and the Tenure of Federal Judges: Some Notes from History," 36 *U. Chi. L. Rev.* 665 (1969).

Lawrence, William. "The Law of Impeachment," 6 *Am. L. Reg.* (N.S.) 641 (1867).

Lillich, R. B. "The Chase Impeachment," 4 *Am. J. Leg. Hist.* 49 (1960).

Lumbard, Judge J. Edward. "The Place of the Federal Councils in the Administration of Courts," 47 *A.B.A.J.* 169 (1961).

McIlwain, Charles H. "The Tenure of English Judges," 7 *Am. Pol. Sci. Rev.* 217 (1913).

McKay, Robert B. "The Judiciary and Non-Judicial Activities," 35 *Law & Cont. Prob.* 3 (1970).

Mayers, Lewis. "Impeachment," *Encyclopedia of the Social Sciences* (New York, Macmillan, 1937).

Moore, James W. "Judicial Trial and Removal of Federal Judges, H. R. 146," 20 *Tex. L. Rev.* 352 (1942).

Nathanson, Nathaniel L. "The Supreme Court as a Unit of National Government: Herein of the Separation of Powers and Political Questions," 6 *J. Pub. Law* 331 (1957).

Otis, Judge Merrill. "A Proposed Tribunal: Is It Constitutional?" 7 *Kan. City L. Rev.* 3 (1938).

Plucknett, Theodore. "Impeachment and Attainder," *Royal Hist. Soc.* (5th Ser. v. 3, 1953) 145.

———. "The Impeachments of 1376," *Royal Hist. Soc.* (5th Ser. v. 1, 1951) 153.

———. "State Trials under Richard II," *Royal Hist. Soc.* (5th Ser. v. 2, 1952) 159.

Potts, C. J. "Impeachment as a Remedy," 12 *St. Louis L. Rev.* 15 (1927).

Rezneck, Samuel. "The Early History of the Parliamentary Declaration of Treason," 42 *Eng. Hist. Rev.* 497 (1927).

Richardson, H. G., and G. O. Sayles. "The Early Statutes," 50 *L.Q.R.* 210, 510 (1934).

———. "The King's Ministers in Parliament," 46 *Eng. Hist. Rev.* 550 (1931).

———. "Parliament and Great Councils in Medieval England," 77 *L.Q.R.* 213 (1961).

Ross, G. W. " 'Good Behavior' of Federal Judges," 12 *U. Kan. City. L. Rev.* 119 (1944).

Russell, Conrad. "The Theory of Treason in the Trial of Strafford," 80 *Eng. Hist. Rev.* 30 (1965).

Shartel, Burke, "Federal Judges: Appointment, Supervision and Removal—Some Possibilities under the Constitution," 28 *Mich. L. Rev.* 870 (1930).

Sindler, Allen P. "Baker v. Carr: How to 'Sear the Conscience of Legislators,' " 72 *Yale L. J.* 23 (1962).

Stephenson, Carl. "The Beginnings of Representative Government in England," in Conyers Read, ed., *The Constitution Reconsidered* (New York, Columbia University Press, 1938), p. 33.

Stolz, Preble. "Disciplining Federal Judges: Is Impeachment Hopeless?" 57 *Calif. L. Rev.* 659 (1969).

Ten Broek, Jacobus. "Partisan Politics and Federal Judgeship Impeachments since 1903," 23 *Minn. L. Rev.* 185 (1939).

Thompson, Frank, and D. H. Pollitt. "Impeachment of Federal Judges: An Historical Overview," 49 *N. Car. L. Rev.* 87 (1970).

Turner, Lynn W. "The Impeachment of John Pickering," 54 *Am. Hist. Rev.* 485 (1949).

Viorst, Milton. "Bill Douglas Has Never Stopped Fighting the Bullies of Yakima," *New York Times,* June 14, 1970, sec. 6 (Magazine) 8.

Warren, Charles. "New Light on the History of the Federal Judiciary Act of 1789," 37 *Harv. L. Rev.* 49 (1923).

Wechsler, Herbert. "Towards Neutral Principles of Constitutional Law," 73 *Harv. L. Rev.* 1 (1959).

Wiggins, J. R. "Lawyers As Judges of History," 75 *Mass. Hist. Soc. Proc.* 84 (1963).

Wofford, John G. "The Blinding Light: The Uses of History in Constitutional Interpretation," 31 *U. Chi. L. Rev.* 502 (1964).

Ziskind, Martha. "Judicial Tenure in the American Constitution: English and American Precedents," *Supreme Court Rev.* 1969, 135.

NOTES

Note, "Exclusiveness of the Impeachment Power under the Constitution," 51 *Harv. L. Rev.* 330 (1937).
Note, "Removal of Federal Judges: New Alternatives to an Old Problem," 13 *UCLA L. Rev.* 1385 (1966).
Note, "Removal of Federal Judges: A Proposed Plan," 31 *Ill. L. Rev.* 631 (1937).

MISCELLANEOUS

Hearings on the Independence of Federal Judges, before the Senate Subcommittee on Separation of Powers (91st Cong. 2d Sess., April–May 1970).
Hearings on Judicial Fitness, before the Senate Subcommittee on Improvements in Judicial Machinery (89th Cong. 2d Sess., February 1966).

GENERAL INDEX

(This index is followed by an Index of Cases)

Good behavior (*continued*)
judicial independence, 156n; insulates from parties, 107
Framers' intention, 136–137; neither Congress nor President can remove for misbehavior, 140, 155–156, 160n, 161n, 181–182; protected by separation of powers, 181; Congress can supplement "judicial power," 140, 181; removal debate and judges, 155–156
Enforcement by courts, 132–135; executive initiation, 138n, 182; proposed judicial machinery, 182–183
Relation to: Address in State constitutions, 159n; forfeitures, 166–167; high crimes and misdemeanors, 97, 129, 166–168, 185; impeachment, 128, 129–130, 154–156, 166, 168–169; insanity-incapacity, 195–200; removal for public good, 197
"In office," 211; outside office, 211–223
See Forfeiture; Incapacity; Insanity; Scire facias
Goodrich, Herbert F.: legal rules and common sense, 324n
Gorky, Maxim, 209n
Grand Inquest: House of Commons, 27
Grant, U. S.: Johnson offered Secretary War, 305
Great offenders, impeachment of: trial by Parliament, 1n, 20n; Framers, 127, 169, 170n, 347–348; petty offenders excluded, 169
Impeachment reserved for great occasions: Clifford, 52, 93n; Somers, 93; Story, 92n, 261; Treby, 93n; Wilson, 93
Great offenses, impeachment for, 93–94, 350
Comments: Holdsworth, 1n; Iredell, 93; Maclaine, 169n; Mason, 90–91, 93, 169n; Story, 93n, 95n
Impeached for less: Archbald, 98; Ritter, 97–98
Grenville, Lord: duty to impeach, 157n; full attendance, 178n
Grey, Chief Justice: protection of judges, 69
Groesbeck, William J.: Johnson counsel, 286
Gurney, Sir Richard: impeachment charges, 72

Habeas corpus, suspension by Lincoln, 120n
Hale, Sir Matthew: authoritative sources, 218; cases originating in Parliament, 18; Parliamentary declaration not conclusive, 18; prejudgment, 241; salvo, 8, 17, 21; Suffolk, 18; Talbot, 17n; weight of cases, 219
Comments: Holdsworth, McIlwain, 17; Stephen, 23
Halford, Sir Richard: impeachment, 74n

Halifax, Lord, 74, 75
Hallam, Henry: appropriations to be spent for specified purpose, 354; attainder voted judicially, 30n; Berkley, 3n; bribery Charles II, 47n; Clarendon, 44n, 45n; Danby, 47n, 48–49; Finch, 3n
On Strafford: accepts St. John re attainder, 38; exactness of Howell account, 32n; proviso in attainder, 40n
Hamilton, Alexander:
Impeachment bridle on Executive, 127, 319n, 343–344; preceding criminal trial, 320, 320–321n, 339n; English model, 177, 179n; exclusivity, 143–144; proposed impeachment be "only" means, 144n; nature of, 100; President suspended until impeachment judged, 320–321n; rules of procedure, looser than at criminal trial, 336; seriousness, 100, 127, 277–278; Senate as tribunal, 84n, 117n, 118–119, 120, 121, 179, 276–277; sits as court, 276; Senators impeachable, 228–229, 231–232
Abuse of trust, 334; good behavior: borrowed from England, 131, 179n; protects against Congress, 160n; incapacity, 193; insanity, 145, 191–193
Binding law, 301; condemns Chase, 238n; Congress can't judge own boundaries, 122n, 304; Congressional exclusion power, 267n; due process of law, 348; punishment of King and President, 325; Senate consent to removal by President, 146n; separation of powers, 303; void law, 300
Judiciary: bulwark, 124–125; fortitude, 118–119; least dangerous, 124; prejudgment, 241, 259, 276–277
Hamlin, Paul A.: State trials, 149n
Hampden, John, the Elder: Strafford, 36; suit to test Ship-Money tax, 33n, 95n; well-loved, 34
Comments: Clarendon, 34n; William Jones, 34n; Trevelyan, 34
Hampden, John, the Younger: Burnet's comment, 53n; condemned on treason charge, 53n; no limit on impeachment, 52–53, 55n; treason outside, *25 E.3*, 52
Hand, Judge Learned: construction, 144
Harlan, Justice John M.: 12-man jury, 213
Harper, Robert G.:
In Blount, 88n; limitations of expulsion, 225; misconduct in office, 208
In Chase: extenuates, 245; indictable crime, 238n; judge's standard of conduct, 245–246; judicial humor, 256; political jury harangues, 237n
Hart, Henry: meaning of "all," 86
Hartley, Thomas: property in office,

INDEX OF CASES

397